LANCASTER COUNTY, SOUTH CAROLINA DEED ABSTRACTS 1787–1811

BY

BRENT H. HOLCOMB, C.A.L.S.

Please Direct All Correspondence and Book Orders to:

Southern Historical Press, Inc.
PO Box 1267
375 West Broad Street
Greenville, SC 29602-1267
or
southernhistoricalpress@gmail.com

----

southernhistoricalpress.com

ISBN #0-89308-213-9

Printed in the United States of America

INTRODUCTION

This volume contains abstracts of the first seven (or now six) deed books of Lancaster County and District. While these deeds were recorded beginning 1787, some of the deeds date from the pre-Revolutionary period. The famous Waxhaw section was in Lancaster County, as well as the town of Camden (until Kershaw County was formed in 1791.) In 1800, all former counties with a few exceptions became districts, and so it was with Lancaster. However, some people were slow to change, and the term county lingered on for a few years in some of the deeds.

These abstracts are quite important, especially since Lancaster County probate records (wills and estates) were destroyed in 1865. Oddly enough, a few wills were recorded in these deed books. Of primary importance are the references to wills and estates within these deed abstracts. What is more surprising is the number of deeds recorded within these volumes which are for land which was in Chesterfield County, which suffered a greater loss of records than did Lancaster. The number of references to York and Chester counties, some showing relationships to persons in Lancaster and others showing former residence in Lancaster make these abstracts some of the most important in South Carolina records.

Of course, in chains of title, there are references to lands granted prior to the formation of Lancaster County--both from North Carolina and South Carolina. The border between the two provinces was not surveyed in this area until 1764. People had been living in the area of Lancaster County since the 1750's or perhaps before, and many had obtained grants from the North Carolina counties of Anson and Mecklenburg, and had recorded deeds, wills and estates in those counties. After 1764, deeds and wills would be recorded in South Carolina records, then at Charleston. In 1781, Camden District was set up as a probate court district, and until 1787, wills and estates will be found there. With these various problems in mind, the following books will be helpful: *Anson County, North Carolina, Deed Abstracts, 1749-1766 Abstracts of Wills & Estates 1749-1795* (Genealogical Publishing Company), *Mecklenburg County, North Carolina, Deed Abstracts 1763-1779* (Southern Historical Press), *Mecklenburg County, North Carolina, Abstracts of Early Wills 1763-1790* (A Press), *North Carolina Land Grants in South Carolina 1741-1773* (A Press), *An Index to the Deeds of the Province and State of South Carolina 1719-1785 and Charleston District 1785-1800* (Southern Historical Press), and *Camden District, S. C. Wills and Administrations 1781-1787* (Southern Historical Press).

Brent H. Holcomb, C. A. L. S.
Columbia, South Carolina
April 7, 1981

BOOK A

N. B. The first 54 pages of this volume are missing

Pp. 55-57: 29 Dec 1786, Joseph Cotes and wife Ann of Lancaster
          Co., to Daniel Kirkland of same, for ₺ 20 sterling,
land on Piney Branch of White Oak Creek, 100 A, adj. Joseph Cotes,
south of the Daniel Kirkland spring branch. Joseph Cotes (Seal),
No wit.

Page 57: I assert that the following is my Stock mark viz Two
         crops and in each ear two Slits. Jas. Houze.

Pp. 58-61: 27 Dec 1786, Joseph Cotes of Camden Dist., to Henry
          Cant of same, planter (lease s5, release ₺), 100
A on White Oak Creek adj. Daniel Kirkland, hele Tatom, Jos.
Misel, part of a grant of 300 A to Joseph Cotes, on White Oak
Creek and Flat Rock Creek adj. Joseph Mezle, John Buk, William
Soctt...Joseph Cotes (Seal), Ann Cotes (X) (Seal), Wit: John
boutin, Henry Keet, Haly Tatum.

Pp. 61-65: 24 July 1786, Robert Hetly of Lancaster Co., planter,
          to Alexander Craighead Carruth of same, planter (lease
s 1, release ₺ 10 sterling)...land granted on bounty to Heatly
2 March 1768, 100 A on waters of Long Cane Creek adj. Township
line of Belfast, land laid out to James Walls...Robert Heatly
(X) (Seal), Wit: Charles Bratton, Jas Carruth, Jas. Bratton,
Jas. Simpson.

Page 66: By Hon. Henry Pendleton, Adanus Burke and John Faucherard
         Grimkie, Esquires, Judges of the Court of Common Pleas
...James Green Hunt late of North Carolina now of South Carolina
is duly qualified to act as a Solicitor and attorney in the courts
of Law and Equity in the said state...7 Dec 1786. Wm. Mason, C.
C.

Pp. 67-69: 27 Dec 1786, Robert Barclay & wife Sarah of Dist. of
          Camden, for ₺ 100 to David Cotes, 50 A in Dist. of
Camden, adj. Alexander McDugal, John Mayerson, James Betty,
land supposed to be laid out to Joshua Palmer...Robert Barclay
(X) (Seal), Wit: John Boutin, Joseph Cotes, Haley Tatum, Henry
Kent.

Pp. 70-73: 16 July 1784, David Horton, planter, of Craven County,
          SC, to Henry Horton, planter of same, for ₺ 200 ster-
ling...200 A in Craven County, N side Wateree River, N side Hanging Rock Creek on both sides of a branch, adj. Hugh Sharers
(Shavers?). Danl Horton (Seal), Wit: Jno Horton, John Taylor,
Harbourt Horton (X).

Pp. 74-77: 14 Jan 1787, Henry Cato and wife Tabitha of Lancaster
          Co., to William Brewer of same, planter, by a grant
10 Nov 1760 to Thomas Wade, 250 A on a branch of Lynches Creek
called Richardson branch in Craven County, adj. Oliver Mchathey,
conveyed by sd. Wade to John Robertson, from Robertson to Zachariah Bell, by Bell to Abraham Peebles, then to Henry Cato, now
for ₺ 35, 200 A...Henry Cato (Seal), Tabitha Cato (X) (Seal),
Wit: Wm. Horton, Wilm. Johnston (X), Glass Caston.

1

Pp. 78-80: 2 Feb 1779, Joseph McCulloch of Craven Co., to Stith
         Fannil of same, for L 500 SC money, 82 A on E side
Cataba on waters of Waxhaw Creek, part of grant to Stephen White
by North Carolina 16 May 1754...Jos. McCulloch, Elinor McCulloh
(CM), Wit: Charles Miller Jr., Thos Drennon, Jno Drennon.

Pp. 80-82: 24 July 1784, Stith Fennel of Camden Dist., to Nathan-
         iel Tomlinson of same, for L 71 sterling...land on E
side Cataba, on waters of Waxhaw Creek, part of grant to Stephen
White 16 May 1754 by N. C....Stith Fennell (LS), Wit: Jno Tomlinson, George Davison, Henry Foster. Ack. before Andw Foster, JP,
24 July 1784.

Pp. 82-84: 2 Sept 1777, Isaac McCullah of Camden Dist., to John
         Tomlinson of same, for L 1 s 12 SC currency...131 A
part of 200 A purchased by McCullah from Stephen White, part of
491 A granted to Stephen White 1754 by N. C., adj. Estate of
Robert Howard decd...Isaac McCullah (A) (LS), Wit: Drury Cook,
Wm. Massey, Jos. McCullah. Prov. by Drury Cook, before John
Drennon, 2 Sept 1777.

Pp. 84-85: 17 Mar 1785, Nathan Tomlinson of Camden Dist., to
         Nathaniel Tomlinson for s5 sterling, 170 A in the
Waxhaw Settlement between the Waxhaw Creek and Twelve Mile Creek.
Nathan Tomlinson (X), Wit: William Wrenn, John Foster, Thomas
Rhodes. Prov. by William Wren, 17 March 1785, before Andw Foster,
J. P.

Pp. 86-87: 22 Nov 1784, Thomas Crawford of Camden Dist., S. C. to
         William Wren of same, for L 150 sterling...land on N
side Waxhaw Creek, originally granted to Joseph Crawford, adj.
Archibald Chrockets (sic) land, including an improvement, adj.
Robert Crawford, 17 A also adj. sd. tract, part of tract granted
to Stephen White, conveyed to White to Isaac McCullah and from
Isaac McCullah to Jos. McCulloch, from sd. Jos. McCulloch to James
Crawford adj. Robert Lockhart, Nathaniel Tomlinsons, I-- Tomlin-
son...Thomas Crawford (LS), Wit: Robert Crawford, Jno Foster,
Jno. Crawford. Prov. by Robert Crawford, before Andw Foster,
J. P., 22 Nov 1784.

Pp. 88-89: 27 July 1784, Thomas Crawford of Camden Dist., to
         Nathaniel Tomlinson of same, for L 7 SC money...23 A
in the Waxhaw Settlement, part of 491 A that fell to the said
Crawford by the death of his Father James Crawford, who purchased
the said tract of 145 A from Stephen White...Thos Crawford (Seal),
Wit: Robert Crawford, John Crawford, William Wier. Prov. by
Robert Crawford, 22 Nov 1784, before Andw Foster, J. P.

April Term 1787

Pp. 89-90: 7 July 1776, William Patton & wife Elizabeth of
         Craven County, SC, St. Mark's Parish, to Nathaniel
Lyon of same, for L 85...170 A in the Waxhaw Settlement, between
the Waxhaw & Twelve Mile Creeks...Wm. Patton (LS), Elizabeth Patton (LS), Wit: Jo. Douglass.

Page 91: Mary Baxly of Anson County, North Carolina for L 100 to
         Henry Richardson, negro man named Bob Elirson(?)...8 Feb
1786. Mary Baxly (X), Wit: James Howard, Labey (Tabey?) Howard,
Sary Wilms. Endorsed to John Adair, 8 Dec 1786. Henry Richason.
Test. John Wade.

Pp. 91-92: Edmund Williams of Washington County, North Carolina,
          appoints Majr. John Adair of South Carolina, Chester
County, attorney, to receive from Capt. Matthew Bass late of
Lancaster Co., one likely negro man Country born under 25 years
old for Ł 120 Va. money...23 Feb 1787. Edmund Williams (Seal),
Wit: John Williams, Wm. Davis, Wm. Moore.

Pp. 93-98: 23 & 24 Jan 1787, Joseph Kershaw of Camden, to Edward
          Neuville of the City of Bristol in the Kingdom of Great
Britain, but now of Charleston, S. C., (lease s 10, release Ł 3465
sterling)...land in or near Camden on the E side Wateree River
on both sides of the mouth of Pine Tree Creek adj. Estate of
Samuel Wily decd and John Payne Deceased, John Chesnut, 800 A
of which some time since belonged to the Copartnership of Messrs.
Kershaw Chesnut & Co. Merchants in Camden, and conveyed by them
to Thomas Jones decd and by him to Joseph Kershaw; also Joseph
Kershaw's square or tract of land 80 A in the center of the extended plan of Camden, adj. Littleton St., DeKalb St., Gordon
Street. J. Kershaw (Seal), Wit: Rich Champion, Jas Atkins,
Joseph Kershaw, Junr.

Page 99: John Duerin of Lancaster County, planter, to wife Ann
         Duren and my son George Durin, exrs...5 March 1787.
John Duerin (Seal), Wit: Jno Caton, Salley Duren, Elenore Catoney.

Charles Barber's Stock mark: a Swallow fork and Slit in each
ear Branch C B.

Page 100: Will of Thomas Gougher of Beaver Creek in Camden District
         ...21 Dec 1786...to my beloved Daughter Jean Roach
and to her children, one shilling sterg, if lawfully demanded;
to the children of my daughter Elizabeth Sims decd., one shilling
sterling if lawfully demanded, as also what I have already delivered to them; to my daughter Agness Kennedy, one shilling sterling
if lawfully demanded; to my daughter Martha Bell widow one shilling sterling; to my daughter Mary McKee widow my lands on Beaver
Creek being 250 A...two daughters Martha Bell and Mary McKee,
Exrs. Thomas Geotche (LS), Wit: Alexand. C. Carruth, James
Carruth.

Pp. 101-104: 9 & 10 April 1783, John Miles of Craven Co., St.
            Mark's Parish, planter, to Thomas Thompson, planter,
(lease s 6, release Ł 400)....100 A on N side Cataba River
adj. an old survey of William Harrison, Wateree River, granted to
William Harrison 20 Oct 1766, which he gave unto Patience Hill,
and conveyed by James Harrison to more fully confirm the same
and also conveyed Thomas Hill to Richard Burge by indenture 20
Jan 1778, and by Richard Burge to John Miles, 4 Nov 1782...John
Miles (LS), Eliz. Miles (X) (LS), Wit: Saml. Dunlap Senr, Thos
Lewis, Saml Dunlap Junr. Elizabeth Miles relinquished dower,
10 Apr 1783, Wit: Saml Dunlap.

Pp. 104-106: 1 & 3 Oct 1785, James Toland of Camden Dist., S. C.,
            planter to Bryan Tolan of same, planter (lease s10,
release Ł 60 sterling)...200 A on the Hanging Rock, adj. Samuel
Mathis, Bryan Tolan, James Toland (LS), Wit: Geo Ross, Charles
Gray (X), William Campbell (X).

Page 107: Arthur Hickland Senior, planter, of Lancaster County,
          to George Hickland, a certain Negro girl about 12 years

old named Sall for one shilling sterling...22 Feb 1787. Arthur
Hickland (X) (Seal), Wit: Midtn. McDonald, Arthur Hickland.

Pp. 107-109: 30 & 31 Jan 1786, Arthur Hicklin Sener of Lancaster
            Co., to George Hicklin of same, for (lease s10,
release s 1 sterling)...100 A on Bare branch on N side Wateree
River, granted 11 Oct 1755 to Christon Liebfriets...Arthur Hicklin (X) (LS), Wit: Wm. Hicklin, Isaih Thompson, Arthur Hicklin.

Pp. 110-111: 3 Feb 1787, Robert Williams in South Carolina, Lan-
            caster Co., to Mary McKee of same, planter, (lease
s 10, release Ł 2 18 7)..50 A on a branch of Beaver Creek on NE
side Wateree adj. Edward Stone, Street Owengs, land formerly
belonging to Thos Gouger, 100 A granted to James Williams, 29 Apr
1772, Rec. in Book SSS, p. 518...Robert Williams (Seal), Wit:
Elir. Alexander, Jo. Coil, Henry Hudson.

Pp. 112-113: 1 Feb 1787, Nicholas Robertson Deputy to Hugh Milling
            Sheriff of Camden Dist., to Benjamin Carter of
Camden, Gentleman...whereas Christopher Williman in the Court of
Common Pleas of the Dist. of Camden did implead Joseph McCay and
John McCay in an action of Debt and in May Term 1785, did obtain
Judgment against the lands, etc. of the sd. John and Joseph McCoy
for Ł 5260 s 14 d 10 sterling, exposed to public sale 24 Jan last
past, two tracts of land, one of which 100 A on the North branches
of Black River in Craven Co., adj. Godfrey B--- land, and the
other tract 100 A on NE side Black River adj. Samuel McCoy...Ni-
cholas Robinson (Seal), Wit: Danl Brown, Geo. Brown, H. Beaumont.

Pp. 114-118: 19 & 20 Mar 1779, William Montgomery and John Mont-
            gomery, both of Bear Creek a fork or prong of Kain
Creek on NE side Cataba River, in Camden Dist., to Isaiah Thompson of Cedar Creek on the NE side Cataba, in same dist., (lease
s5, release Ł 1425)...100 A with a piece of land on which there
is an improvement or clearing, 5 A, both on Beard Creek, part of
200 A granted to Thomas Simpson 10 Nov 1761, Rec. in Book VV page
196, and afterwards sold to William Barr by deeds 13 Feb 1761,
and afterwards to William John & James Montgomery by deeds...
William Montgomery (Seal), John Montgomery (0) (Seal), Wit:
Jas. Bredin, Jas. Montgomery (0), John Carson.

Pp. 118-120: William Gault of Craven Co., SC, Waxhaw Settlement,
            planter, to Thomas Neilson of same co. & state, for
Ł 100...land 96 A on both sides of Camp Creek, E side Cataba River,
in the Waxhaw Settlement, part of tract granted to James Larrimer,
by Mathew Rowan Esqr. pres. of N. C. 17 May 1754, 418 A, which
said tract since the boundary line was run hath fallen into the
State of S. C., whcih sd. tract the sd. James Larrimer sold to
Andrew Pickens, and Andrew Pickens sold to William Davis 268 A,
and Wm. Davis sold to Joseph Barnet, and Joseph Barnet sold to
David Drennon 96 A, and Drennon said to Joseph Gault, and Joseph
Gault sold to William Gault...16 Sept 1779. William Galt (Seal),
Rebekah Galt (X) (Seal), Wit: William Nelson, Robt Gault (C),
Richard Huckaba (X).

Pp. 121-125: 26 Sept 1769, David Adams Junr. to David Adams Senr,
            (lease s5, release Ł 370)...200 A in Craven County on
Bear Creek a branch of Cain's Creek, surveyed 4 May 1762, and
granted 7 May 1762...David Adams Junr (Seal), Ellner Adams (A),
Wit: George Sleger (X), Daniel Price, Sarah Adams (X), David
Day.

Page 125: Matthew Hoods Stock Mark and Brand. Two Slits in each
ear, the middle part cropp'd in each ear Brand 7 H.

Jesse Minton's Stock Mark and Branch. Mark, crop and half crop
in each ear, Brand M.

Pp. 126-130: Blank.

Pp. 131-132:   July-Term 1787
          1 Oct 1784, Robert Barnet of Camden Dist., SC, to
Archibald Cowsart of same, for Ł 36 st., 190 A on both sides of
the Waggon Road which is the State line, between the Waxhaw and
Twelve Mile Creek adj. Dan. Carns, Archd. Cowsart, George McCamy's
land, Pattons land...Robert Barnet (Seal), Wit: Hugh White, Andrew
Barnett, John Foster. Prov. by Hugh White, 1 Oct 1784, before
Jno. McClenahan, J. P.

Page 133: Sheriff & Clerk's Receipt on acct. Shem Thompson.
April 7th 1783, Recd. of Col. William Farrell Ł 3 s 16 d 6 for
selling a Negro wench & boy sold by order of Sale taken by attachment at the suit of the Sd. Farrel from Shem Thompson.
Test: Michl Bairyes(?), Rd. Madison.   Indorsement on the above
receipts. July 14th 1787, We assign over our Right and Title of
the within Negro wench and Child...Ellenor Farrell, Admrx. John
Farrelle.

Pp. 133-134: Elenor Farrell widow and admx. of the Estate of
          William Farrell decd. and of the County of Lancaster
State of S. C. and John Farrell, late of the Kingdom of Ireland,
the Eldest Brother and Heir apparent to him the said decd., for Ł
60 sterling, to Nancy Thompson, one negro or Mulatto wench named
Tamar and her Boy called George, the same as heretofore claimed
as the property of Nancy Thompson, and in possession of John Holzendorf...14 July 1787. Ellenor Farrell (Seal), John Farell (Seal),
Wit: Robt Scott, Rebecca McDonald.

Pp. 135-137: Arthur Hickland Senr of Lancaster Co., for s5 sterl.,
          to John Hickland, one negro woman Nan...5 Mar 1787.
Arthur Hickland (X) (SEAL), Wit: Robt Scott.

26 July 1786, Arthur Hickland Senr. & wife Jane of Lancaster Co.,
          to John Hickland of same, for s5 sterling, 100 A,
part of grant to Andrew McKennie 9 Feb 1755, by James Glen Gov.,
conveyed to James McKown by L & R 1 May 1755, by deed to sd.
Arthur Hickland by William McKown & Margaret McKown heirs of the
said James McKown then deceased 20 Feb 1765, 150 A adj. Widow
Addisons, William Hickland...Arthur Hicklin (X) (Seal), Jane Hicklin (X) (Seal), Wit: Robt Scott, William Johnston, Arthur Hicklin,
William Hicklin. Plat included shwoing bear branch, and adj.
land of Aaron Prescott, Widow Addison, William Hickland, Arthur
Hickland Senr, plat dated 5 Sept 1786, by Jas. Bredin, D. S.

Pp. 138-139: 26 June 1787, Henry Shaver and wife Elizabeth of S.
          C., Camden Dist., Lancaster Co., to Maurice Ronie
of same, for Ł 400 former currency of said state equal to Ł 57
s 2 d 10½ sterl...land in the County aforesaid formerly Craven
County in the State of North Carolina, on Rum Creek, on NE side
Catawba said to be about 33 miles from the Nation, but now found
not to be so much, granted by Wm. Henry Littleont then Gov. of
S. C. to Andrew Shaver (spelled Shiffer in the original grant),
decd father to Henry herein mentioned...Henry Shaver (Seal),

Elizabeth Shaver (S), Wit: Saml Lowrie, Adam Carnahan.

Page 140: on or about August 1770, I David Clanton did see Thomas
        Goutcher Brother to Mary McKee Widow make sign seal
deliver and execute Titles Deeds commonly called Lease and Release
to and for 100 A surveyed for the said Thomas Goutcher Junr on the
Saltketchers being at the time the Head Rights allowed to a sin-
gle Man, unto Martha Goutcher alias Beel sister to said Thomas
Goutcher Junr, and the said David Clanton was a subscribing wit-
ness, also John Findlay then of Beaver Creek in South Carolina
subscribe his name as a wit and Mary Goutcher alias McKee widow
and David Clanton remembers to see Martha Goutcher alias Bell
widow give the said Thomas Goutcher some money...18th July 1787.

Mary McKee (X)
David Clanton.

Rush Hudson of Camden Dist., for Ł 150 to John Marshel of same...
a mulatto Boy named Anthony. 16 Aug 1785. Rush Hudson (R) (Seal),
Wit: James Towland, John Ingram, Theuben Roberts (X).

Pp. 141-143: 14 Apr 1787, John Montgomery and wife Martha of Lan-
        caster Co., to James Montgomery, for Ł 5...land on
Cain Creek, 100 A, surveyed at first to Alexander Nisbet 12 Nov
1770, granted to John Montgomery, 24 Dec 1772...John Montgomery
(Seal), Martha Montgomery (Ɖ) (Seal), Wit: James Johnston, William
Montgomery, Alexander Montgomery. Release gives adj. land owners:
Thomas Campbell, Alexander Nisbet, Joseph Walker

Pp. 144-145: 11 Jan 1785, William Davies of Lincoln Co., North
        Carolina, to Rev. Robert Findly of Camden Dist., S.
C., 30 A granted to William Daveis 1767, 28 Aug, adj. Robert
Findly. W. Davies (Seal), Wit" Henry Foster, James Davis, Alexr.
Carns. Prov. by Henry Foster, Andw Foster, J. P.

Pp. 145-147: 28 July 1784, William Barnet of Camden Dist., to Rev.
        Robert Gindley of same, for Ł 107 s 2 d 10 SC money
...150 A part of grant to Samuel Dunlap, 23 Feb 1754, conveyed
to William Barnet, 7 Jan 1765 on E side Trading Road, adj. William Davies, at a black oak which is the line tree between the
North and South States...William Barnet (X) (LS), Wit: Saml Dunlap, Henry Foster, William Barnet Junr. Attested to by Andw
Foster, J. P.

Pp. 147-148: William Montgomery of Craven Co., S. C., Yeoman, to
        Thomas Wells of same, Camden Dist., BlackSmith, for
one gray gelding...11 A in the Waxhaw Settlement, part of land
granted to John Linn by Matthew Rowan, Pres. of N. C., but since
the boundary line hat been run, it fallen into the South 17 Ma-
1754, for 302 A conveyed by L & R 10 Jan 1757, to Hugh Montgymery,
part of which said tract of land the said Hugh Montgomery in his
last will & testament did bequeath to sd. William Montgomery...
22 Oct 1785. William Montgomery (Seal), Wit: Robt Montgomery,
James Nisbet, James Taylor.

Pp. 149-150: 1778, Joseph Walker and Mary Walker his wife of
        Camden Dist., to Hugh Montgomery, by grant 3 Dec 1778
for Ł 1500 SC money...land on Cane Creek adj. James Walker,
Alexander Nisbet, 100 A...Joseph Walker, Mary Walker (M), Wit:
James Montgomery, John Montgomery, dated 12 Feb 1779 at end of
deed.

Pp. 150-151: 28 May 1787, John Daughurty & wife Judah of Richland
Co., to John Lowrie of Lancaster Co. (lease s5, release Ł 100 sterling)...200 A in Lancaster Co., on N side Wateree
River adj. Nathaniel Hill, John Brown, James Moore...John Dough-
arty ( ) (Seal), Judah Dougherty (Seal), Wit: Robert Lee, William Brown, William Hornsby (X).

Pp. 152-155: 4 Apr 1775, Thomas Charlton Esqr. of Camden, to
John Pownall of Craven Co., for Ł 200 SC currency...
150 A on waters of Rocky Creek on N side Wateree, adj. Ely
Kershaw, granted to Thomas Charlton 15 Apr 1775...Thos Charlton
(Seal), Wit: William Mays, George Pownall. Prov. by William
Mays, 6 Apr 1775, before Thos Sumter.

Pp. 156-157: 1778, Henry Coffee & wife Mary of Camden Dist., to
Thomas Wells of same, by grant 30 Sept 1774, to
Henry Coffee now for Ł 125...100 A on waters of Camp Creek adj.
Henry Coffee, Hugh Montgomery...Henry Coffey (Seal), Mary Coffee
(M) (Seal), Wit: James Johnston, John Gillespie, John Strain. Prov.
by James Johnston, 15 Aug 1779, before James Simpson, a Magistrate.

Pp. 158-160: 19 Apr 1787, John Caston Junr. of Lancaster Co.,
planter, (lease s10, release Ł 100 sterling) to
Glass Caston...land on head branches of Little Lynches Creek,
465 A and on Rocky River Road, granted 5 Dec 1785, John Caston
Jnr. (Seal), Wit: Joseph Caston, Francis Harris (FH).

20 Apr 1787, John Caston Junr to Glass Caston, negro Joe, cattle,
hogs, etc., for Ł 200 sterling. John Caston, Wit: Wm McDonald,
Saml Caston.

Pp. 160-161: Articles of Agreement made between Jesse Minton of
St. Mark's Parish, Craven Co., and Elizabeth Minton
wife of said Jesse Minton, 5 Oct 1785, first that the said Jesse
Minton & wife Elizabeth his present Wife did firmly agree before
their marriage but did not enter into writing but now...the said
Elizabeth was the widow of John ShewMake of St. Davids Parish,
Craven County, S. C....negroes, horses, 700 A, etc...Elizabeth
Minton (E) (Seal), Wit: William Haslam, Ann Marsh (X).
State of South Carolina, Chesterfield County, prov. by Elizabeth
Minton before Charles Evans, J. P., 24 May 1786.

Page 162: Blank.

October Term 1787

Pp. 163-164: 2 Aug 1787, John Galbraith of Camden Dist., Gentle-
man, and Messeurs Graaf Scibles Brasselman & Co. of
City of Charleston, Merchants, for Ł 155 s 15 d 5 sterling...
half lot, which Galbraith purchased from John Chesnut & Joseph
Kershaw Exrs. of L. W. & T. of Ely Kershaw decd...mortgage...J.
Galbraith (Seal), Wit: Daniel Brown, John Hossendorf, B. Perkins.

Pp. 166-169: 19 Apr 1786, John Milhous citizen of Lancaster Co.,
to Richard Champion citizen of the same, for Ł 250
333 A adj. Arthur Cunningham, David Cotes, Richard Champion, granted byJoshua Palmer, 6 Dec 1768, rec. in Book CCC p. 461, sold
by Joshua Palmer & wife Jane 19 Oct 1769 to Thomas Vaughan, and
also from them 1 Oct 1769 to Isaac Vaughan...and by the said
Isaac Vaughan and Mary Vaughan widow and heiress of said Thomas
to James Bettie 2 Sept 1772, and by Bettie to sd. John Milhous,

24 Jan 1776...John Milhous (Seal), Abigail Milhous (Seal), Wit:
John Adamson, Wm. Clark, Richard Lloyd Champion. Prov. by John
Adamson, 17 June 1786, before I. Alexander, J. P. 14 Apr 1787
prov. by Richard Lloyd Champion, before Isaac Alexander, J. P.

Pp. 170-173: 7 Apr 1786, Joseph Kershaw citizen of Lancaster Co.,
to Richard Champion citizne of same, for (lease s10,
release Ł 100 sterling)...land between Grany's Quarter Creek and
Rocky Branch, 200 A, granted 5 Aug 1769 to James Fellows, Rec.
Book DDD p. 343, the other grant to John Mallan 19 Nov 1772, Rec.
Book NNN p. 39(?) adj. Riddle, John Milhouse...Joseph Kershaw
(Seal), Wit: Aaron Loocock, Jas. Kershaw, John Kershaw. Prov.
4 May 1787, by Aaron Loocock, before John McCall, J. P. for
Charleston District.

Page 174: 3 Sept 1785, Rush Hudson of Craven Co., to Rueben Roberts of same, for Ł 100...land on waters of Beaver Creek,
formerly a tract of 100 A with deed bearing date Jany 12 1768, 50
A of said tract adj. Hudson...Rush Hudson (R) (Seal), Wit: James
Carruth, Alexr. Cragd. Carruth.

Page 175: 2 Jan 1787, Glass Caston & wife Elizabeth of Lancaster
Co., to William Marlow Junr. of same, by grant 2 Apr
1762 for 100 A granted to Ephraim Clark on Camp Creek, sold to
James Coil, thence by L & R to Glass Caston 8 Dec 1763...Glass
Caston (Seal), Elizabeth Caston (Seal), Wit: Joseph Caston, George
Hicklin, Henry Kink (King).

Pp. 176-177: 18 July 1787, William Taylor of Lancaster Co., to
James Taylor of same, by grant 8 July 1774, to Isaac
Taylor 350 A on W side Catabaw River in St. Mark's Parish, con-
veyed to George Sleager and by Sleager conveyed 15 Aug 1778 to
Jacob Taylor father of the above William Taylor, being the eldest
son of sd. Jacob Taylor who died intestate, now for Ł 300; conveyed
to Sleager by Isaac Taylor 21 ___ 1775, 215 A exclusive of 20 A
conveyed by George Sleager to John Fleming, conveyed to Jacob
Taylor...William Taylor (Seal), Wit: Thomas Blair, John Blair,
Jacob Taylor.

Pp. 177-179: 10 Jan 1786, Nicholas Robertson (Robinson) and wife
Frances of Craven Co., Dist of Camden, planter, to
Daniel Horton of same, planter for Ł 43 s 10 sterling...land on
Beaver Dam Creek on S side of Great Lynches Creek, 100 A all sides
vacant...Nicholas Robinson (Seal), Frances Robinson (X) (Seal),
Wit: George Taffe, Elizabeth Robenson (X).

Pp. 179-180: 17 Oct 1786, Peter Boyer of North Carolina, Granville
County, to William Baily of Lancaster Co., SC, plan-
ter (lease s1, release Ł 50 sterling)...land in Craven Co., on
E side Wateree River on cedar Creek & the road leading from Rocky
Mount to the Hanging Rock, all sides vacant, where the said Wil-
laim Baily now liveth, grant to Thomas Brannan, and sold by
Brannan to James Mcollough, then to Peter Boyer; 14 Sept 1771
Rec. In Sec. Office Book III p.339...Peter Boyer (Seal), Wit: Jos
Coile, John Stephens, Richard Perry (X).

Page 181: Terrel Anders son Thomas Anders and Francis Anders doth
put himself apprentice to John Creighton inhabitant of
Beaver Creek Camden Dist, for 10 years and 5 months...12 Nov 1784
Fenel(?) Anders (X) Francis Anders (X-her mark), John Creigton,
Wit: Thos Creighton.

Pp. 181-182: William Hood of   planter and Allen Hood   planter,
              for   land in County of Anson, North Carolina,
tract granted to William Hood by Matthew Rowan Pres. of N. C., 25
Feb 1754, 137 A...14 Apr 1778. Will Hood (S), Sarah Hood (X), Wit:
William Galt, Henry Coffy, Jas. Craig. Prov. by Wm Gault, 20
Dec 1778, before James Simpson, magistrate in Camden Dist.

Pp. 183-184: S. C., Craven Co., Roger Smith of Co. aforesd., to
              James & John Craig Jeomen of same, for Ł 762 s 10
...150 A on both sides Camp Creek on E side Catabaw River in the
Waxaw Settlement, granted to James Larremore, by Matthew Rowan,
17 May 1754, 418 A since the boundry line was run hath fallen into
S. C. and said James Larrimore sold to Andrew Pickens, then to
William Davis 150 A, then to Roger Smith...2 Dec 1778. Roger
smith (S), Elizabeth Smith (S), Wit: William Nelson, Samuel McKee,
John Craig.

Page 184: 21 Feb 1787, Zachariah Bell of Camden Dist., binds son
          Thomas Bell apprentice to Robert Dunlap to learn the
occupation of planter, until Thomas Bell come to the age of 21
years...Zachariah Bell (S), Wit: William Dunlap, James Ferguson.
6 years old Novr 30 1786.

Pp. 185-187: 20 July 1775, Joseph Kershaw of Camden, SC., Merchant,
              to William Tomlinson of Craven Co., Parish of St.
Mark, lots in Camden 155, 156, 157, 158, 159, 160, 161 (plat included). Joseph Kershaw (Seal), Wit: Thomas Jones, Richd Wadeson,
John Wyly. Plat by John Belton, D. S. 12 July 1775. Prov. by
richard Wadeson, before William Welch, Camden, April 26th 1783.

Pp. 187-188: 15 Apr 1780, Joseph McCullah and wife Eleanor of
              Camden Dist., to John Tomlinson of same, for Ł 2000
...20 A on N side Waxaw Creek granted to Stephen White by Mathew
rowan 24 Sept 1754, conveyed to Isaac McCullah, sold then to Joseph McCullah, by deed 23 Oct 1778, adj. John Tomlinson, Stith
Fennel; also 80 A part of 100 A granted to Robert Montomgery by Gov.
Montague, 4 Dec 1772, sold to Joseph McCullah 25 Oct 1773 adj.
sd. McCullah, Stith Fennel, Robert Lockhart, Robert Crawford, Jos.
White, Robert Howards estate...Joseph McCullah (L), Eleanor Mccullah (E) (L), Wit: John Tonlimson, William Rives, Elizabeth Maffet
(3). Prov. by John tomlinson Junr, 19 Apr 1780 before John
Drennon, J. P.

Pp. 188-190: 25 Oct 1786, James Love of S. C. planter, to James
              Nichol planter of same, (lease s10, release Ł 600)
...James Love & wife Margaret of Lancaster Co., 300 A granted by
Gov. Bull 30 Sept 1774, to Robert Love father of sd. James Love,
and sd. James Love being heir at Law to the estate of sd. Robert
Love decd, land adj. Hanging Rock Creek a branch of Lynches Creek,
Alexander Ingrem, ... James Love (Seal), Margret Love (Seal),
Wit: James Ingrem, Jordan Ashley, Wm. Ingrem.

Page 191: 30 Sept 1782, John Bird of Craven Co., planter, to
          Thomas Frizle of same, planter, for Ł 500...150 A on
Flat Creek, part of 400 A conveyed to by a deed from James Bratin
adj. William Bratton...John Bird (X), (Seal), Hannah Bird (X)
(Seal), Wit: Sampson Hough, Gale Grizle. Prov. by Gale Frisel, 4
May 1784, before Fredk. Kimball, J. P.

Page 192: 24 March 1787, John Gayton of Lancaster Co., & wife

9

Catherine to Elizabeth Collins of same, for Ⱡ 150 sterling...land
on the great branch running on both sides White Oak Creek to
James McCulloch's line (beling part of a tract belonging to
Reason Nelson), 200 A...John Gayden, Catharine Gayden (O), Wit:
Ed Collins, Willie Collins, George Gayden. 16 July 1788, prov.
by George Gayden, before John Lowry, J. P.

Pp. 192-194: 18 Feb 1779, Robert Ramsey & Margaret Ramsey to Wil-
laim Nisbet, Camden Dist., S. C. for Ⱡ 350 SC cur-
rency, land on S side Cane Creek, 140 A, granted to said Robert
Ramsey, 1752 by Gov. Gabriel Johnston in N. C., it then being
Anson County, North Carolina but now in S. C....Robert Ramsey
(Seal), Margaret Ramsey (O), Wit: John Nisbel, Wm. Moore, James
Ramsey. 13 Aug 1782, prov. by John Nisbet, beforew Andrew Baskin,
J. P. for Camden Dist.

Page 194: William Deason of Lancaster Co., for Ⱡ 80 sterling to
Frederick Kimball...19 head of cattle, 4 feather beds
and furniture, one white mare and colt, one sorrel mare, 7 head
of sheef, 2 dishes, 3 basins, 12 plates of pewter, 25 head of
hogs...14 July 1788. William Deason (Seal), Wit: William Williams,
Thomas Grizzle (O). Prov. by William Williams, 14 July 1788,
before John Marshel, J. P.

January Term 1788

Page 195: 29 Dec 1787, Samuel Caston of Lancaster Co., planter,
to Guy Wallace of Franklin County, North Carolina, car
penter, for Ⱡ 40...640 A on a branch of Little Lynches Creek, adj.
Robert Gaston, Glass Caston, Joseph Caston, granted to Samuel
Caston 1786, 6 Feb...Saml Caston (Seal), Wit: Glass Caston,
William Caston, Joseph Waggoner.

Page 196: 15 Jan 1788, John Love of Lancaster Co., planter, to
Henry Cato, of same, for Ⱡ 5 sterling...250 A on little
Lynches Creek granted to Thomas Cooper 10 Apr 1776, conveyed to
Thomas Larimore, 18 June 1776, by Larimore to James Ezell, 6 Feb
1779, from Ezell to John Love 20 Feb 1779...John Love (Seal),
Jane Love (X) (Seal), Wit: Glass Caston, Saml Caston, John Aye-
wood.

Page 197: 1 March 1780, James Toland of Craven Co., Camden Dist.,
to James Brinkly of same, for Ⱡ 3000...100 A on Little
Lynches Creek, all sides vacant...James Towland (Seal), Fea Towland (Seal), Wit: John Allen, John Taylor.

Pp. 198-199: 5 Dec 1787, Eli Brinkley of Lancaster Co., to Wil-
laim Brewer of same, for Ⱡ 20 sterling...100 A, 50
A on South branch of Lynches Creek adj. John Robinsons land, to
a certain line made by Abraham Peebles, part of 250 A granted to
sd. Abraham Peebles, 1 June 1767, conveyed by Abraham Peebles
to James Brinkley decd, the other 50 A granted to George Cole
and said Cole conveyed 350 A to Zachariah Bell, and Bell to John
Robinson Senr, and conveyed to James Brinkley decd. 50 A...Eli
Brinkley (Seal), Wit: John Marshel, John Middleton, James Marshel.

Pp. 199-200: 26 Apr 1785, John Swann of York Co., SC to Henry Cato
of Lancaster Co., for Ⱡ 32...150 A on Lynches Creek
waters of Peedee, when surveyed in Craven Co., vacant on all sides
granted to Robert Swann, 4 Nov 1762...John Swann (Seal), Wit:
Glass Cason, Wm. Brewer, Saml Caston.

Pp. 200-201: 15 Oct 1787, Henry Cato and wife Tabitha of Lancas-
ter Co., planter, to John Love of same, planter, for
Ł 50...land on S branch of Lynches Creek, waters of Peedee River,
Henry Cato Wit: Glass Caston, Saml Caston, John Arwood.

Pp. 201-202: 1 Feb 1787, Hugh Daverson of Lancaster Co., to James
Massey of same, by certain indentures, recorded in
North and South Carolina, tract of 250 A was George Daversons Senr
and is now Hugh Daversons his Eldest son which fell to him by the
Death of said George Daverson Senr his father, on S side Waxhaw
Creek between Joseph White, William McKee, John Kelsey...except
20 A that belong to a grant of William McKees of an older date...
Hugh Daverson (I) Wit: Wm Doby, Henry Massey, George Massey.

Pp. 202-204: 25 Feb 1788, 2 Nov 1767, Solomon Willy of Craven Co.,
to William Moore of same, (lease s10, release Ł100)
by grant 2 Apr 1762 to Solomon Willy (Wyly), 100 A near Lynches
Creek adj. John Crawford, Plat rec. in Auditor Generals Office
Book F No. 6, page 99...Solomon Willy (S), Wit: William Lankford,
John Twitty. Prov. by John Twitty, 5 Nov 1767, before Thomas
Wade, J. P.

Pp. 205-207: 6 Nov 1775, William Moore of St. Mark's Parish, SC,
to Jesse Minton of same, Craven Co., SC, for Ł 200,
100 A on which said Moore liveth on N fork Lynches Creek, granted
2 Apr 1762, by Gov. Littleton, adj. JOhn Crawford...William Moore
(M) (Seal), Elizabeth Moore (EC) (Seal), Wit: Shadrach Vining,
Benjamin Outlaw (B), Ann Vining (X). Prov. by Shadrach Vining, before John Gaston, 15 Nov 1775.

Pp. 207-209: 5 Nov 1762, John Crawford of Anson County, to William
Moore of Craven Co., SC, for Ł 500...550 A in parish
of St. Mark on N prong of Lynches Creek adj. Solomon Homes, Thomas
Watts...grant rec. Book WW page 28...John Crawford (Seal), Wit:
Solomon Willy, John Twitty. Prov. 5 Nov 1767, by Solomon Willy,
before Thomas Wade, J. P.

Pp. 209-210: 26 Apr 1770, Josiah Cantey of Craven Co., planter,
to Philip Rayford of same (lease s10, release Ł 500)
350 A on S side of North Lynches Creek, ST. Marks Parish, Craven
Co., part of 550 A survey for John Crawford, adj. John Hewet,
Solomon Homes...Josiah Cantey (Seal), Wit: Tho Wescoat, William
Cantey; granted 7 May 1762; Prov. by Thomas Wescoat, before James
Simpson, 23 Nov 1770.

Pp. 211-213: 22 March 1777, Philip Rayford of Johnston Co., N. C.,
planter, (lease s10, release Ł 850...same land in
above deed)... to Jesse Minton of Craven Co., S. C....Philip
Rayford (Seal), Wit; Charles Evans, William Pool (W). Ack. before
Charles Evans, J. P. for Cheraw District, 22 March 1777.

Pp. 213-214: S. C. Lancaster Co., by an order of the Court of
Lancaster Co., begun and holden at the Hanging Rock
on Tuesday the 16 Oct last past directed to Richard Champion, to
bind out apprentices the children of Solomon Staples late of Pedee
Planter deceased by Lucy his wife, who had greatly neglected the
same by living a disorderly life...Winny Staples of 11 years of
age; Jonathan Staples of 9 years, Solomon Staples of 7 years,
and Kerenhappuch of 5 years or therabouts, apprentices with
Richard Champion...1 Nov 1787. All children signed by mark, Wit:
John Lloyd Champion.

Page 215: 16 March 1787, Samuel Lamb and wife Hannah of Union
          Co., SC, to Adam Carnaham of Lancaster Co., for Ł 25
sterling...grant to Samuel Lamb 4 Oct 1768 in Craven Co., Camden
Dist., 100 A...Samuel Lamb (X) (Seal), Hannah Lamb (X), Wit:
William McKenny, Samuel Wood (X), Lot Wood.

Page 216: Will of Elizabeth Cook late resident at Camden being
          weak and low of Body...to my son John Cook, a negro
fellow Darby; to my son William Cook, all my stock of Cattle and
Hogs; to my daughter Elizabeth Rugely, a negro wench Phillis,
a feather Bed and furniture, and wearing apparel...also the rent
of my plantation and the hire of negro fellow and remaining part
of my household Furniture and plantation tools to be equally divided between John Cook and William Cook, 5 July 1787. Elizabeth
cook (Seal), Wit: Isaac Williams, Caty Sanders. (Octr. Term 1787)

Pp. 216-218: James Guthrie of Lancaster Co., planter, to Richard
             Wright of same, for Ł 80...land in the Waxhaw Settle-
ment, 194 A part of a tract granted to William Guthrie, 4 May
1771, and by his L. W. & T. did give to his son James Guthrie...2
Oct 1787. James Guthrie (Seal), Jane Guthrie (Seal), Wit: Thomas
Wells, Robert Walker, Robt Guthrie. Prov. by Thomas Wells &
Robert Guthrie, before John Craig, J. P., 14 Apr 1788.

Page 218: 14 Feb 1788, John Cheshire of Linkon Co., South Carolina,
          Beaufort District, to William Stephens of Lancaster Co.,
100 A on Rocky Creek adj. Thomas Brannum, William Maddocks, Rocky
Mount Road...John Cheshire (Ŧ), Wit: Bailey Fleming, Wm. Walter,
John Guren(?).

Page 219: Field Woodroof of Camden, planter, for love and affection
          to daughter Katharine Woodroff and for s 10...five
negroes (named) 7 Apr 1788. F. Woodroof (LS), Wit: Jas Atkins.
Prov. 14 Apr 1788, by Jas. Atkins, before I. Alexander, J. P.

Pp. 219-222: 20 Dec 1785, Charles Pence cupper of Lancaster Co.,
             to Henry Peebles of Lancaster, planter, (lease 10,
release Ł 100)...land granted 22 Jan 1759, to Robert Harper,
300 A, which the Pence did sell 50 A on Great Lynches Creek,
a branch called Flatt Creek...adj. Catran Bridger, Jonas Griffen
...Carl Bentz (signed in German) (Seal), Wit: James Bridges,
Edward Reynolds, David King. Prov. by James Bridges, 9 Feb 1786,
before John Marshel, J. P.

Page 222:   28 Feb 1788, Joseph Kirkland of Fairfield Co., plan-
             ter, to Sherrod Sims of Lancaster Co., for Ł 60
sterling...land on Beaver Creek, Lancaster Co., 250 A adj. Simon
Shy...Jo: Kirkland (Seal), Wit: Thomas Ballard, Ellot Sims, Joseph
Kirkland Junr.

Page 223: Mary Rush of Lancaster Co., to John Moseman of same,
          planter, for Ł 100 old South currency... 66 A on a
small branch of Lynches Creek called Otter, part of 200 A belonged
to Frederick Rush at his deceased for which he left his will beloved wife by Will the third part of 200 A...___ Aug 1787. Mary
Rush (Seal), Wit: Peter Rape, Daniel Hunter. ‾15 Apr 1788, Prov.
by both wit. before John Craig, J. P.

Pp. 224-226: 23 & 24 Dec 1787, John Robinson of State of Georgia,
             to Alexander Kerns of Lancaster Co., Farmer, (lease

s 10, release Ł 500 old currency)...land granted 24 Sept 1754, to
John White, 300 A on the Cataba River adj. Benjn. Harper, conveyed
to Robert McCorkle, and by him to John Robinson who died and his
heir William Robinson conveyed it to John Robinson Junr., and con-
veyed now to Alexander Carns, adj. line of Joseph White...John
Robinson (Seal), Wit: Benj. Harper (O), Jas. Hall (H), Willm.
Harper. Prov. 15 Apr 1788 by Benjn Harper & William Harper, before
John Craig, J. P. Plat included.

Pp. 226-228: 23 Dec 1787, John Robinson of State of Georgia, to
Benjamin Harper of Lancaster Co., SC (lease 10, re-
leaseŁ 1000 former currency of this state)...200 A on Cataba River
adj. William White, Mr. Carns, F. McClenahans, part of land granted
to John White and conveyed to Robert McCorkle, by him to John
robinson who died and his heir William Robinson conveyed the same
to John Robinson Junr....John Robinson (Seal), Wit: Will.m Harper
Alexdr. Carns, James Hall(H). 13 Apr 1788, prov. by William
Harper, before John Craig, J. P.

Pp. 229-231: 10 Dec 1787, Matthew Hood of Cedar Creek, Lancaster
Co., to Charles Barber of Beaver Creek, co. afsd.,
for Ł 4...100 A, the one half of a tract of 200 A granted to sd.
Matthew Hood, Rec. in the Secretary's Office, Book TTTT Fol. 212,
and in the Locating office Book B, Fol. 456...adj. John Chesnut,
Barber, Noles Giles...Matthew Hood (Seal), Mary Hood (M) Wit:
Elir. Alexander, Jos. Coile, James Gaston. Prov. by James Gaston
before Robt Dunlap, J. P. 16 Apr 1788.

Pp. 231-232: Rebecca Johnston for good will and affection to my
children all my goods, wares, plates, etc; to my
eldest son Samuel Johnston, my dower in all lands left me by my
last husband Wm. Johnston, also one road mare called Janus branded
WJ on the off shoulder...to my son Jonathan Johnston one dark bay
mare, 5 years old, and 1/3 of hogs, etc; to my son James Johnston
one Sorrel mare and colt, 1/3 of stock; to my daughter Hannah
Johnston, one brown mare and her colt; to my daughter Mary Johnston
one year old cot; to my daughter Jane Johnston, cow named Rumbey,
and one heifer...15 Apr 1788. Mary Johnston (X) (LS), Wit: John
Gaston, John Baker (X), Elir. Alexander. Ack. in court before
Robert Dunlap, 15 Apr 1788.

Page 232: John Hudson Senr of Beaver Creek, Lancaster Co., to
Henry Hudson of same, all my goods, chattels, Household
Stuff, etc....30 Apr 1788. John Hudson (Seal), Wit: William Nutt,
Ed. Stonestreet Owings, Joseph Coile.

Pp. 233-235: 30 Jan 1780, James Russell of Beaver Creek, Camden
Dist., SC, to Henry Hudson of Beaver Creek, (lease
s5, release Ł 230)...land on NE side Wateree River, adj. John
Hudson, David Russel, Lewis Clark, granted 13 May 1768, Rec. Book
DDD...James Russell (Seal), Elizabeth Russell (X) (Seal), Wit:
George Devren, Benj. Johnston, William McCorkle.

Pp. 235-237: 22 Oct 1773, Drury Harrington of St. Mark's Parish,
Craven Co., planter, to Henry Hudson for (lease s5,
release Ł 100)...land granted 31 Oct 1769, to Drury Harrington, on
Beaver Creek adj. John Hudson, James Russel, Adam Thompson...
Drury Harrington (D), Elizabeth Harrington (Seal), Wit: John
Peter Hudson, Rush Hudson (R), Wm. McCorkle.

Pp. 237-239: 8 Sept 1775, Drury Harrington of St. Mark's Parish,
            Craven Co., planter, to John Hudson, for Ł 100...
66 A granted to Drury Harrington adj. John Hudson, James Russell,
David Russell, Lewis Clark, William Russell, granted 8 July 1774
...Drury Harrington (D) (Seal), Wit: John Taylor, Benj. Smith.

Pp. 239-241: 8 Sept 1775, Drury Arrington of Craven Co., SC, to
            John Hudson of same, land granted to Drury Arrington,
adj. Andrew Knox, Adam Thompson, Drury Harrington, William Russell
granted 8 July 1774...Drury Harrington (D) (Seal), Wit; John
Taylor, Benjn. Smith.

Between April & July Court 1788

Page 242: Patrick Glaze of Lancaster Co., to sons William and
            Middleton Glaze (excepting the property which the
present wife of Patrick Glaze was possessed with when said Patrick
Glaze married her)...all lands, tenements, stocks, etc.
13 Aug 1787. Patrick Glaze (Seal), Wit: Robt Scott, Wm. McDonald.

Pp. 242-245: 2 Aug 1787, John Graham of Lancaster Co., planter, to
            George Miller (lease s5, release Ł 42 s 17 d 1)...
300 A on the Great Road from Camden to the Waxaw Settlement and
on a branch of Flat Rock Creek adj. Luke Petty, Ford, John Graham,
granted to 3 Apr 1786...John Graham (LS), Winifred Graham (X)
Wit: Thos Creighton, Cornelius Quimlens, John Lake.
Prov. by Thomas Creighton, before John Lowry, J.P. 15 Apr 1788.

Page 246: Robert Ramsey of State of South Carolina for Ł 20 sterl.,
            all horses, cows and calves, plantation implements, etc.
20 May 1788. Robt Ramsey (Seal), Wit: Danl Fleming, Benjn Nisbet.
Prov. by Benjamin Nisbet, 12 July 1788, before John Craig.

Pp. 247-248: S. C. Lancaster County: 10 July 1788, James Craig
            Esqr. Sheriff of Lancaster Co., to Benjamin Cudworth
of same...whereas James Steedman in the Court held for sd. county
did implead David Adams Junr in a plea of Debt...for Ł 108 s 16
d 4...exposed to public sale 16 July 1787, 200 A on Bear Creek
a branch of Cane Creek, for Ł 80 sterling...Jas Craig (Shff(Seal),
Wit; Nathan Barr, John Simpson, Elir. Alexander.

Pp. 248-249: 23 Sept 1781, Benjamin Coward his agent attorney to
            Widow Williams her heirs, etc. the right of 100 A
granted to Ann Thompson on a branch of Beaver Creek, adj. Walter
Sopshire...Benjamin Coward, Milly Coward (X), Wit: John Creighton,
John McClure. Prov. by John Creighton, 15 July 1788, before
Robert Dunlap, J.P.

Page 249: 25 Oct 1781, Widow Williams to John McClure...100 A
            granted to Ann Thompson (same as above)...Widow Williams
(X), Wit: John Creighton, Thomas Creighton. Prov. by John Creighton, 15 July 1788, before Robert Dunlap, J.P.

Pp. 250-252: 9 Apr 1774, John Gray in St. Mark's Parish, Camden
            Dist., Craven Co., Schoolmaster, to James McManus,
of same (lease s10, release Ł 1000...John Gray and wife Mary...
200 A on the middle branch of Little Lynches Creek, waters of
Peedee, adj. John Vizant, granted 16 Jan 1761, granted to Revd.
Henry Ledbetter, conveyed by him and wife Edy to John Gray 23
July 1762...John Gray (Seal), Mary Gray (Seal), Wit: Thos McManus,
Wm. Boyd. Prov. by Wm. Boyd, 15 July 1788, before John Marshel.

Pp. 253-254: John White Junr of Lancaster Co., to John Craig Junr
of same, planter, for ₺ 103 sterling...land on N
side Cataba River, on both sides Cain Creek, granted to Robert
Ramsay, by Matthew Rowan, pres. of N. C., but since the boundary
line hath been run it hath fallen into the South State, 23 Feb
1754, conveyed to George Whit 28 Jan 1765, and at the decease
of said George White, came into the possession of the said John
White Junr he being George White's eldest Legmatick (sic) son...
John White (Seal), Margret White (X) (Seal), Wit: Wm. Nelson, Jas
Craig.   Deed dated 25 Sept 1787

Pp. 254-255: S. C. Lancaster Co.: 10 July 1788, James Craig Esqr.
Sheriff of Lancaster Co., to Richard Wright of same...
whereas James Dunlap in the Court of said county, did implead
George Greerson in an action, July term 1787, did obtain judgment
to levy ₺ 0 s 8 sterling...250 A on a branch of Cane Creek, waters
of Cataba Waxaw Settlement, adj. Thomas Walker, William Guthrey,
Robert Ramsey, Robert Dunlap...Jas Craig H. S. (Seal), Wit: Jno
Simpson, Nathan Barr.

Pp. 255-258: 1 Sept 1788, William Wood of Camden Dist., Lancaster
Co., to Devall Fonderburgh, (lease s10, release ₺ 53)
by grant 2 Oct 1786, 200 A on waters of Great Lynches Creek...Wm
Wood (Seal), Wit; Joseph Fonderburk, Gustavus Rape (X).   Prov.
by Gustavus Rape 1 Sept 1788, before John Craig, J. P.

Page 258: Jacob Evans of Camden Dist., planter, for love and good
will to John Mccoy son to Joseph McCoy of said place,
100 A in Craven County, on the head of Black River about two
miles from the head of Bell's Branch, granted 11 Aug 1774, and
granted to sd. Jacob Evans, and memorial entered 12 Jan 1775...
Jacob Evans (Seal), Wit: William Evans, Joseph McCoy.   Prov. by
Joseph McCoy, 29 Dec 1787, before I. Alexander, J. P.

Page 259: 20 Feb 1772, Hugh Summerville of Craven Co., to George
Summerville, by granted 19 Sept 1770, to sd. Hugh, 100
A on Beaver Creek, now for ₺ 50...Hugh Summerville, Wit: Wm.
Haddin, Isaiah Thompson, James Thompson.

Pp. 260-261: 1788, Robert Ramsey Senr in Lancaster Co., to James
Ramsey of same, for and in consideration of his the
said Robert Ramsey proper and due Maintenace during his life time...
land on N side Cain Creek, whereon said Robert Ramsey & James
Ramsey now lives, adj. James Dunlap now Arons, the said Robert
Ramsey sold to Robert Dunlap, granted to Robert Ramsey by Gov.
Johnston 6 Apr 1752, 400 A...2 May (1788). Robert Ramsey (Seal),
Wit; John Ramsey, Andw McCain, Robt McCain.   Ack. 3 May 1788,
before John Craig, J. P.

Page 261: Benjamin Burnet of Lancaster Co., for ₺ 150 sterling to
Frederick Kimball, negroes Dick & Tom, one brown bay mare
and colt, one small bay mare, one sorrel Filly, two cows, etc...1
June 1788. B. Burnett (Seal), Wit: John Taylor, JosephKimbell.
Prov. by John Taylor, 21 June 1788, before John Marshel, J. P.

The remaining pages in this volume are fragmentary, but abstracts
follow as best as can be read.

Page 262: 14 Jan 1790, Robert Rowan to Edward Collins, for ₺ 80
sterling...land on Beaver Creek granted -- May 1768...

Page 263: end of a deed signed by Henry Rugely and Elizabeth
Rugeley, Wit: William Kirkland, John McMillan.

Page 264-5(?): 13 Jan 1780, Henry Rugeley and wife Elizabeth of
                Fairfield Co., to John Dixon of Lancaster Co.,
by grant __ March 1762, to William Stewart, 300 A, and sd. Stuart
at the time of his decease did give to John Stuart Mary Stuart and
Charles Stuart...land adj. Ann Glading.

Page 265(?): __ Jan 1780(?), Jacob Evans of Camden Dist., to John
                McCay son of Joseph McCay, 100 A granted 11 Aug 1774
...Jacob Evans (Seal), Wit: James Marshel, Jas. Atkins. 19 July
190, prov. by Jas. Atkins, before __ Kershaw, J. P.

Page 267: 21 Aug 1793, Gen. Thomas Sumter of Claremont Co., to
                Daniel Hunter Junr. of Lancaster Co., for s5 sterling,
320 A conveyed to Daniel Hunter, certified by Samuel Kelly 28
June 1793...Thomas Sumter Junr for Thomas Sumter (Seal), Wit/ Saml
tynes, Martin Smith.

END OF BOOK A

Pp. 1-2: Glass Caston of Camden Dist., planter, by Bond, do bind
myself to John Chesnut Esquire of Camden, for the penal
sum of Ł 250 sterling...condition to deliver negroes Tom, about
27 years of age, Phillis about 24 years old, Rachel about 13 years
old, Phebe about 4 years old, with about 40 head of cattle, blacksmith tools, etc., 7 May 1788. Glass Caston (Seal), Wit: Zach
Cantey, Andrew Baskin. Prov. by Zachariah Cantey, 7 May 1788,
I. Alexander, J. P.

Page 2: Francis Boykin of Camden Dist., for Ł 250 sterling to
John Chesnut, negro Harriot about 20 years old, and her
child Nancy, Sabina and her child Neptune, Ben about 25 years
old, and Augusta about 35 years old (male)...7 Sept 1785. Francis
Boykin (Seal), Wit: William Brown, Zach. Cantey. Prov. by Zach
Cantey, 10 May 1788 before J. Alexander, J. P.

Page 3: 4 July 1788, Joseph Kershaw of Village of Camden, to
Nathaniel Alexander of Dist. of Camden, for Ł 100 sterling
...10 A nearly adj. the town lotts to the Northeast of the extended plan of Camden Town, with plan annexed (surveyed and certified by John Belton). Joseph Kershaw (Seal), Wit: Fielding
Woodroff, Willism Whitaker. (Plat included). Prov. by Fielding
Woodroff, 5 July 1788, before J. Alexander, J. P.

Pp. 4-5:4 August 1788, Mary Ingram of Lancaster County, to William Jones of same, for (lease s5, release Ł 24 sterling)
50 A on Hanging Rock Creek, part of 100 A granted to sd. Mary
Ingram 3 Apr 1786, adj. James Rowland, Col. Marshel...Mary Ingram
(M) (Seal), Wit: Fredk. Kimball, John Marshel, Elir. Alexander.
prov. by Frederick Kimball, 5 Aug 1788, before John Marshel, J.P.

Pp. 5-6: 6 May 1786, Joseph Kershaw of Camden, to Aaron Loocock
of Charleston, Merchant, for Ł 700 sterling...lots in
Camden Village #92,81, on Broad Street...Joseph Kershaw (Seal),
Wit: Arch Brown, James Cook, John Craven. Prov. 16 June 1788,
by James Cook, before Rich. Champion, J. P.

Page 6: 6 May 1786, Joseph Kershaw to Aaron Loocock, for Ł 989
sterling, lots in Camden on which the House stands called
the Brew House fronting on Meeting Street on the back on Wateree
Street, on East Broad St. and West on Church St., #115, & L30...
(same sign. and wit. as preceding). Prov. by James Cook, before
Rich. Champion, JP 17 June 1788.

Page 7: 9 May 1786, Joseph Kershaw of Camden, to William Ancrum
of Charleston, for Ł 1020 sterling...lots in Camden,
66, 67, 70, 71, and parts of 65, 68, 69, 72. (plat drawn in
book)...Joseph Kershaw (Seal), Wit: Aaron Locock, John Chesnut,
Jno Craven. Prov. by Aaron Locock, before John Troup, JP for
Charleston District.

Pp. 8-9: 6 May 1786, John Chesnut of Camden, Merchant, and Joseph
Kershaw, William Kershaw, and the said Chesnut Executors
of the Last Will and Testament of Ely Kershaw Deceased, to Aaron
Loocock of Charleston, Merchant...whereas the land herein after
mentioned was intended to be sold in the life time and at the time
of the decease of the said Ely Kershaw, by the will of sd. Ely
Kershaw dated 1 August 1780, did order that his real estate be
sold...now for Ł 200 sterling, lots in Camden #90, 109 on Market
St....Joseph Kershaw (LS), John Chesnut (Seal), Wit: Arch. Brown,

James Cook, Jno Craven. Prov. by 17 June 1788 by James Cook, before Rich. Champion, J. P.

Pp. 9-10: 5 Oct 178_, Joseph Kershaw the younger of Camden, Student in Physic, to William Ancrum of Charleston, for Ł100...240 A in the Dist. of Camden on W side Wateree River, by grant 2 Oct 1786, Sec. in Secretary's Office Book MMMM p. 853... Jo Kershaw (Seal), Wit: Jas. Brown, John Kershaw, Jo. Brevard. PRov. 11 Oct 1787, by Joseph Brevard, before John McCall, J. P.

Pp. 10-12: S. C. Lancaster County, 10 Sept 1788, Benjamin Deason of Flat Creek, Lancaster County, planter, to Francis Bettis and Benjamin Hale of same Creek and County, planters, whereas the said Bettis and Hale became bound with the said Deason in a Bond 13 Feb 1786, for Ł 190, payable to Thomas Frizzle & Frederick Kimball, for the payment of Ł 99 s 4 d 1 part of the purchase of a Negroe Wench named Hagar and her child bought at the sale of the Effects of Neil Johnston Decd., and that sd. Bettis and Hale have been informed that an attachment has been served upon said Negroes upon a pretence that the said Benjamin Deason was about to abscond and leave the State and that the common Process of Law could not be served upon him, and whereas the said Benjamin Deason was not about to abscond or leave the State and the said attachment cannot be served...Negroes are now in the custody of Benjamin Hale constable...Francis Bettis, Benjn Hale (L), Benjamin Deason (O) (LS), Wit: John Massey, Michael Miller (M). Prov. by Michal Miller, 28 Oct 1788 before John Marshel, J. P.

Pp. 12-3:25 March 1788, Samuel Mathis of Camden, Merchant, to James Atkins Esquire of Camden (lease s5, release Ł130 sterling)...lots 235 & 236, on Church St...Saml Mathis (Seal), Wit: John Harker, John Lang. Prov. 20 Oct 1788, by John Lang, before James Kershaw, Esq, J. P.

Page 14: (July Term 1788 Acknowledged), 15 Oct 1787, William Reynolds and Nancy his wife of Lancaster Co., to Jane Gary of same, for s5 ster. money...50 A on SW side of a branch of Beaver Creek, adj. Jacob Everhart, William Nut, John Nixon... William Reynolds ( ) (Seal), Nancy Reynolds (X) (Seal), Wit: Thomas Gardiner, John Nixon, Jean Gardner, Jno Boutin.

Page 15: 4 Dec 1788, John O Daniel of Lancaster Co., to William O Daniel, for Ł 15 sterling...141 A on White Oak Creek adj. John Goodwin, Michal McIlwrath, William O Daniel, Henry Dungworth...John O Daniel (Seal), Wit: David Ballard (X), Thomas Gardner, David Daniel. Prov. by Thos Gardner, 8 Dec 1788, before John Lowry, J.P.

Pp. 15-16: Elizabeth Clark of Camden, Widow...whereas I the said Elizabeth Clark by Bond stand bound to Zachariah Cantey of Camden, Merchant, for the payment of Ł 250 sterling, for my undivided third part of the land, etc. whereof my late Husband William Wyly died possessed of, and to which I am Intitled by virtue of the last will and Testament of the said William Wyly... Elizabeth Clark (LS), Wit: Benjamin Carter, James Atkins. Prov. 18 Oct 1788, by James Atkins, before Richard Champion, J. P.

Pp. 17-19: 23 June 1788, Fielding Woodroof of Camden, planter, to Joachim Gottfried Schutt of same, merchant (lease s5, release Ł 271 s 17 d 6), lots in Camden, #27 & 28 lately belonging to John King on Market Street, adj. to lots of sd. Woodroof, John Wallis...F. Woodroof. Wit: Abraham Gottlob Schutt, James Atkins. Prov. 25 June 1788 by James Atkins, before James Kershaw, J. P.

Page 20: 1 Aug 1788, Thomas Creighton of Lancaster Co., planter, to John Creighton of same, planter, for Ł 30...100 A, part of 200 A granted to James Williams and the said 100 A by him conveyed to Thomas Creighton (now Deceased) and the said Thomas Creighton being heir at law to Thomas Creighton, the said 100 A on Beaver Creek adj. James Miller, James Douglass...Thos Creighton (LS), Wit: John McClure, Jenny Creighton (X). Prov 23 Oct 1788 by John McClure, before John Lowry, J.P.

Pp. 21-22: 6 June 1788, John King of Swift Creek in Claremont County (Eldest son and heir at law of John King late of Camden, Butcher deceased) and wife Alice to John Wallis of Camden, Carpenter, for Ł 108 s 15 sterling...lot # 27 in Camden... John King (Seal), Alice King (X) (Seal), Wit: Henry Rugeley, James Atkins. Prov 25 June 1788 by James Atkins, before James Kershaw, J. P.

Pp. 22-24: 21 & 22 July 1788, Claude Jean Baptise LeDroit DeBussy (late of the Common Wealth of Pennsylvania but now of Camden, Esquire) and wife Magdalen Chabert, to Mordecai Sion and Samuel Levi of Camden, Merchants (lease s5, release Ł 120 ster.) ...lot on Broad St in CAmden, #2, adj. to Court House. Jn Le Droitt deBussy (Seal), Madelaine debussy (Seal), Wit: Joseph DaCosta, James Atkins. Prov. 18 Oct 1788 by James Atkins, before Rich Champion, J. P. N. B. The within mentioned Lott was purchased by Mr. Debussy of Mr. Isaac DaCosta as appears by L & R 14 & 15 July 1785 recorded in the public Register's Office in Charleston Book Y No. 5, page 125 to 129.

Pp. 24-25: 18 Nov 1770, James Brownlow by David Martin his Agent and attorney, to Adam Thompson in Craven County, for Ł 117...100 A granted to James Brownlow as Bounty Land by Gov. Montague, on both sides of Beaver Creek, E side Cataba River in Craven County adj. Tarvis, James Miller...David Martin (Seal), Wit: James Kilpatrick (J), James Kerr. Prov. 23 Oct 1770 by James Kilpatrick before John Newman Oglethorpe, J. P. for Craven County.

Pp. 25-26: Adam Thompson farmer living on Beaver Creek, Camden Dist., Craven County, S. C., for Ł 500 to Thomas Creighton, 100 A on both sides of Beaver Creek adj. Farres, James Miller...18 April 1778. Adam Thompson (Seal), Wit: John Creighton, James Russel. Camden District, prov. by James Russell before Tho: Chartten, April 24th (year not given)

Page 26: 18 Apr 1778, Adam Thompson quit claim to Thomas Creighton, for 100 A on Beaver Creek adj. Farriors, James Miller. Adam Thompson (Seal), Wit: John Creighton, James Russell. Prov. by James Russel before Tho: Charlton, April 24th 1778.

Pp. 26-27: 30 & 31 Jan 1786, George Ganter of Craven County, Camden Dist., to Francis Bell of same, planter (lease s 10, release Ł 20 sterl.)...by grant 19 Aug 1768 to George Ganter, 100 A in Craven County on S side Grany's Quarter Creek on both sides of Rocky Mount Road adj. Daniel Mathis, John Dixon, Richard

Champion (whereon said Francis Bell now lives), grant rec. in Book CCC page 375...George Ganter (Seal), Sarah Ganter (Seal), Wit: Joseph Bulkley, Michal Ganter. Prov. by Michael Ganter, before I. Alexander, J. P.

Page 28: 23 Jan 1786, William Parker of Camden Dist., to Francis Bell of Grany's Quarter in Dist. aforesaid, for ₤ 50 sterling...150 A on Grany's Quarter Creek on S side, granted to Daniel Mathis 1767, and by him conveyed to Abel Thomas, and by divers other conveyances became the property of William Parker... William Parker (Seal), Francis Bell (Seal), Wit: Jo. Brevard, James Rochell. Receipt wit. by James Cook, Bailey. Fleming. Prov. by James Cook 8 Aug 1788, before I. Alexander, J. P.

Feby 3, 1789. William Sprunt's Stock mark. A crop and hole in the right Ear and Crop and Slit in the Left Ear.

Page 29: 6 May 1788, Abraham Livingston of Lancaster Co., to John Linn Senr. of same, for ₤ 35 s 15 sterling...one tract of land in State of Georgia Wilks County on Beaver Dam Creek commonly known by the name of Knoxes Settlement 500 A, part of tract run out for said Livingston by William McRee Dept. Surv., signed by Gov.Mathis Nov. 14th 1787, Rec. Book OOO Fo. 604 ...being the just sum contained in a note of hand given to sd. John Linn from Abraham Livingston and Bruce Livingston Senr. 28 March 1785. Abraham Livingston (Seal), Wit: Robt Thompson, William Barnet. Prov. by William Barnet 17 May 1788, before John Craig, J. P.

Pp. 29-30: S. C. Lancaster County, 1 May 1788, Drury Harrington of Lancaster County, carpenter, to Richard Champion Esq. for ₤ 42...120 A, part of 150 A granted to Daniel Matthews 1 June 1787, Rec. Book BBB p. 62, adj. John Dobbins, David Jordan, John Riddle, Grany's Quarter Creek, sold by L & R 2 & 3 Dec 1763 from Daniel Mathews to Abel Thomas of Craven Co., planter, and by Abel Thomas and wife Mary 23 & 24 Aug 1774, to John Milhouse of Colleton County Millwright, and from him 4 & 5 Sept 1782, to John Holzendorf of Camden Dist., planter, and from Holzendorf & wife Elizabeth 15 July 1784, to William Parker of Camden, Merchant, conveyed 3 & 4 May 1784 to Drury Harrington...Drury Harrington (H) (Seal), Wit: Drury Thompson, Wm. Maxwell, Richard Lloyd Champion. Prov. 13 Sept 178_, by Richard Lloyd Chamipon, before I. Alexander, J. P.

Page 31: James Craig Esqr. Sheriff of Lancaster County, to Middleton McDonald...whereas Richard and Sarah Featherston did implead George Wade admr. of William Featherston Decd. in action for not performing certain promises, and in Oct. Term 1786 did obtain Judgement...for ₤ 82 s 7...did expose to sale on 9 Dec 1786, 100 A on E side Cataba River adj. George Wade, land granted to Christopher Morgan, adj. William Ford, first granted to Thomas Fannon, conveyed to John Foard, then to Richard Featherston, according to law fell...Middleton McDonald being the highest bidder...17 Apr 1787. James Craig (Seal), Wit: Samuel Dunlap, Saml Caston.

Ack. in Court Oct. Court 1788. Mary Bull of Lancaster Co., for natural affection to Rebeckah Johnston my daughter one cow named Suck and her increase amounting to eight head; only one Cow named Lady to my granddaughter Hannah Black; also to Rebecca paltes, pots, etc., one large Bible...28 July 1788. Mary Bull (1), Wit:

John Williams, Samuel Johnston (*), Hannah Johnston (D).

Page 32: 3 Feb 1787, William Walters of Lancaster County, to John
        Baker of same, planter (lease sl, release Ł 30 s 14 st.)
150 A granted to sd. Wm Walters 2 Nov 1785...Wm Walters (LS),
Wit: John Adamson, Francis Wolf, John Fleming.

Page 33: 11 Dec 1787, David Drennon of Winton County, SC, to
        Matthew Jones of Lancaster Co., for Ł 40 sterling, land
on waters of Whiteoak Creek, 100 A adj. Henry Dungworth...
David Drennon (Ɔ), Wit: Joseph Cotes, James Hester, Mathew
Worter. Prov. by Joseph Cotes, before John Lowry, 13 Sept 1788.

Pp. 33-34: 15 Dec 1787, Matthew Jones of Lancaster, to Thomas
        Gardiner of same, for Ł 40 sterling...land on waters
of White Oak Creek, 100 A, adj. Henry Dunnworth. Matt. Jones (X)
(Seal), Wit: Thos Duren, James Adams, Saml McRee. Prov. 10 Dec
1788, by Thos Duren, before Jno. Lowry, J. P.

Page 34: On 15 Jan 1790, we or either of us promise to pay to
Doctor Isaac Alexander Ł 60 sterling for value received, 19
Jan 1789. Joseph Coates, Daniel Kirkland, Test. Wm. Cook.
Tobacco Pork or Indigo delivered in Camden will be received in
Camden at Market price in payment of the within note Pr. I.
Alexander.

On or before the 15th of Jan 1791 we or either of us promise to
pay to Doctor Isaac Alexander Ł 60 sterling...19 Jan 1789. (same
sign. & wit.)

Pp. 34-35: Camden Dist., Lewis Cabasse minor with the approbation
        of his aunt Magdalene DeBussy and Guardian, acting
for her husband LaDiot DeBussy apprentice himself to John Wallace
of Camden carpenter and House joiner to learn his art...he shall
do not damage to his said Master, nor contract matrimony within
the said term, at cards, dice or any other unlawful game he shall
not play whereby his said Master may have damage...20 Aug 1787.
Ls Cabassy (LS), LeDroit Debussy (LS), John Wallis (LS), Wit:
I. Alexander, JP.

Pp. 35-36: 15 July 1788, William Deason and wife Jane to Frederick
        Kimball of Camden Dist., for Ł 50 sterling...tract
granted to Mary Gibson and transferred to Thomas Wade by L & R
14 May 1760, from Wade to John Brotton, from him to Gronomau Zin
then to John Baker, from Baker to Thomas Childera, then to Benjamin Deason, from Deason to Conrod Aron and from Conrod Aron to
his son William Aron, and from said Aron to William Deason, on
Flat Creek granted under Gov. Littleton...Wilm. Deason, Jane Deason (X). Wit: Thos Frizzle, Samuel Turner, Wm. Williams. Prov.
by Thomas Frizzle, before John Lowry, 17 July 1788.

Page 37: Isaac Alexander Physician to Margaret Smith, agreement
        on their intended marriage...to the said Margaret Smith
(being now in her actual possession and expectancy as a residuary
Legatee of William Brisbane her late deceased Father and as one
of the Legatees of Hannah Brisbane her late deceased sister)...
one moiety or half that estate as if a full settlement had already
been made by Adam Fowler Brisbane Exrs. of afsd., William Brisbane...10 Dec 1788. I. Alexander (Seal), Margt. Smith (Seal),
Wit: William Lang, Sarah Lang.

Page 38: "Reid & Woodroof should have been in page 31" otherwise
blank.

Page 39: Holzendorf to Washington 4th April 1789
remainder blank.

Page 40: Blank.

Page 41: Fielding Woodroof of Camden, planter, by three bonds
dated 4 May 1784, bound to John Adamson of Camden, planter, for Ł 200 each...for negroes (named)...25 Oct 1788. F. Woodroof (LS), Wit: James English, James Atkins. Prov. by James
Atkins, before James Kershaw, JP, 25 Oct 1788.

Pp. 42-43: 21 May 1788, William Bagnall of Camden, for Ł 64 s 7
d 6 to William Lang, lot #223 in Camden...William
Bagnell (X), Wit: Henry Rugeley, John Lang. Prov. by John Lang,
30 June 178_, before I. Alexander.

Pp. 43-44: 16 Nov 1784, Wilson Hunt, John Ross and Martha Ross
alias Burnet of the Countys of Rowan and Mecklinburgh
North Carolina, to John Blair of Camden Dist., S. C., for Ł 200
NC specie...land on Cain Creek including the plantation whereon
John Blair now lives, being half of the land granted to Thomas
McElhany for 300 A by NC grant and afterwards conveyed to Charles
Burnet a new Right thereof was obtained in S. C. and remains on
Records, the heirs of said Burnett was Agness and Martha Burnet...
Willson Hunt (Seal), John Ross (Seal), Martha Ross (R) (Seal),
Wit: John Patterson, Andw Martin, William Blair. Prov. 19 Jan
1789 by Wm Blair, before Josh Lee(?) J. L. C.

Pp. 44-45: 16 Nov 1784, Willson Hunt of Rowan Co., and John Ross
& Martha Ross alias Burnet of Mecklinburgh County,
NC, to William Blair of Camden Dist, for Ł 200 NC specie...land
on Cain Creek including the place where William Blair now lives,
150 A granted to Thos McElhany...Wilson Hunt (Seal), John Ross
(Seal), Martha Ross (R) (Seal), Wit: John Patterson, Andrew
Martin, John Blair. Prov. by John Blair, 19 Jan 1789. before
Josh. Lee, J. L. C.

Pp. 45-46: Joseph Kershaw of Camden for natural love & affection
to son James Kershaw of Camden, Esquire, negroes (named)
and one silver spoon...10 Jan 1789. Joseph Kershaw (LS), Wit:
James Atkins, James Pierson. given by Joseph Kershaw to Robert
Henry, as attorney for James Kershaw.

Page 46: Joseph Kershaw of Camden, for natural love & affection
to son John Kershaw of Camden, negroes (named) and one
silver Tea spoon...10 Jan 1789. Jas Kershaw (LS), Wit: James
Atkins, James Pierson. Delivered to Róbert Henry as attorney.

Pp. 46-47: Joseph Kershaw of Camden to son Joseph Kershaw, negroes
(named) and one silver spoon, 10 Jan 1789. Joseph
Kershaw (LS), Wit: James Atkins, James Pierson. Delivered to
Robert Henry, attorney.

Page 47: Joseph Kershaw to son George Kershaw, negroes (named) and
one silver tea spoon...10 Jan 1789. Wit: James Atkins,
James Pierson. Delivered to Robert Henry, attorney.

Pp. 47-48: Joseph Kershaw to son Samuel Kershaw, negroes (named)
and one silver tea spoon. Wit: James Atkins, James
Pierson. Delivered to Robert Henry, attorney. dated 10 Jan 1789,

Page 48: Joseph Kershaw to daughter Mary Kershaw, negroes (named)
and one silver tea spoon. 10 Jan 1789. Same wit, etc.

Pp. 48-49: Joseph Kershaw, to daughter Sarah Kershaw, negroes
(named) and one silver teaspoon, 10 Jan 1789, Same
wit., etc.

Page 49: Joseph Kershaw, to daughter Rebecca Kershaw, negroes
(named), and one silver tea spoon. 10 Jan 1789. Same
wit., etc.

Page 50: 3 June 1786, Joseph Kershaw of Camden, to James Kershaw
his son, lots in Camden #950, 951, 952, 953, 954, 955,
956, 957, 958...Joseph Kershaw (Seal), Wit: John Chesnut, John
Adamson, Robert Brownfield.

Page 51: 23 Feb 1789, Joseph Kershaw of Camden to James Kershaw
Esq., elderst son and Heir apparent of said Joseph,
lots in Camden #33, 34, 35...Wit: Jo Kershaw Junr, James Atkins.
Plat included.

Pp. 52-53: Fielding Woodroff of Camden, planter, stands indebted
to Joseph Kershaw of same, Esquire, for Ł 300 with
an arrear of interest from Nov. last past, do sell negroes (named)
31 Dec 1788. F. Woodroff. Wit: S. Atkins. Prov. by James Atkins,
8 May 1789.

Pp. 53-54: Henry Rugeley of Camden District, Gentleman, whereas
he stands indebted to Zachariah Cantey, merchant for Ł
358 s 11 d 10 sterling...for better procuring, mortgage of
negroes (named)...20 Apr 1789, Heny. Rugeley (Seal), Wit: Edwd
Mortimer, William Brown. Prov. by William Brown, 25 May 1789,
before James Kershaw, J. P.

Pp. 54-55: 2 Jan 1789, Joseph Kershaw of Camden, Esqr., to William Ancrum of Charleston, by several bonds dated 2
May 1785; now this indenture for Ł 19, 743 14/4...the upper
mill tract 3000 A, adj. Joseph Kershaw and the town lotts...Jo-
seph Kershaw (Seal), Wit: Jo Brevard, John Kershaw. Prov. by
Joseph Brevard, before John J. Pringle, J. P. Charleston District
Registers Office, Recorded in Book B, No. 6, page 176. 2 Feb
1789.

Page 56: 7 Feb 1789, Joseph Kershaw of Camden, to William Ancrum
of Charleston, for Ł 75 sterling...100 A on Sanders Creek
Camden Dist., originally granted to John Kennedy, 2 Apr 1762
and by John Kennedy and wife Elizabeth conveyed to William Scrugg,
and by said William Scurgg and wife Mary conveyed to Joseph Kershaw, also another tract on E side Wateree River originally granted to Hugh Brennan, by Gov. Thomas Boon, and by Hugh Brannon and
wife Eleanor conveyed to Joseph Kershaw...Joseph Kershaw (Seal),
Wit: Jo Brevard, Isaac Ross Junr., John Craven. Prov. 11 Feb
1789, by John Craven, before James Kershaw, J. P.

Page 57: James Cook of Camden, by my bond dated 1 Feb 1788, bound
to John Julius Pringe of Charleston, for Ł 360 sterling

negroes (named) James Cook, Wit: Jo Brevard, Wm Mayrank. prov.
by Joseph Brevard, before Richd. Champion, J. P. 2 May 1789.
Instrument dated 17-March 1789,

Pp. 57-58: 2 May 1788, Joseph Kershaw of Camden, Esquire, to Jo-
       seph Brevard, for Ł 65 sterling...lots in Camden on
Fair St. and King Street, #639 & 640...Joseph Kershaw (Seal),
Wit: John Craven, Philip Platt. Prov. by Jno Craven before James
Kershaw, J. P. 20 May 1788.

Pp. 58-59: 17 Jan 1789, John Blair and wife Jane of Camden Dist.,
       farmer, to Thomas Blair, farmer, of same...whereas in
and by two conveyances from John Arnold Pender to James Blair
decd. (father of the above John and Thomas) of 2 tracts of land
on E side Cataba, one 75 A granted to John Arnold Pender & Henry
White and by said Arnold on 10 Aug 1778, conveyed to James
Blair who dying intestate the said land fell by descent unto his
heir at law the above John Blair; the other tract of 49 A granted
to William Taylor, and conveyed by him to Jacob Taylor, and then
to John Arnold Pender, and by Pender 10 Aug 1778 to James Blair
...John Blair (Seal), Janet Blair (Seal), Wit: Mat McClure,
Wm. Blair, Wilm. Harper. Prov. by William Blair, before Joseph
Lee, Esqr. Justice of the Court of Lancaster, 17 Jan 1789.

Page 59: 29 Oct 1790, George Evans of Lancaster county, planter,
       to Samuel Jones of same, planter, for Ł 80 sterling...
whereas the said George Evans stands indebted to sd. Samuel Jones
for Ł 80 upon a bond given by the said Samuel Jones and Mr. Robert
Jones to the State for the appearance of the aforenamed George
Evans at a county court to be holden at Mr. John Ingram's near
Hanging Rock the third Tuesday in January next...George Evans,
Wit: Francis Bettis, Benj. Hale Junr. Prov. by Benjamin Hale, Jr.,
19 July 1791. John Simpson, J. L. C.

Page 60: Arthur Hicklan Senr of Lancaster Co., to my son John
       Hicklin of same, the residue of my former tract including
all the former imporvements viz. Houses, buildings, orchards,
clear'd land &C whereon I the said Arthur Hicklin now live...11
July 1787, Arthur Hicklin (ₕₕ), Wit: Robt Scott, William Hicklin
Arthur Hicklin Junr. Prov. by Arthur Hicklin Junr., before Robert
Dunlap, 3 June 1790.

       State of S. C., Lancaster County, Jeremiah Joiner of Lan-
caster Co., for Ł 56 s 3 d 4 sterling to Charles Barber...negroe
wench Phillis about 40 years of age...9 Dec 1788. Jeremiah Joiner
(J) (Seal), Wit: Elir. Alexander, Margaret Alexander.

Page 61: James Cook of Camden, boudn to James Kershaw Esqr. of
       same, for Ł 1000 sterling in gold or Silver Specie, at
the rate of s4 d 8 to the Dollar, or Ł 1 s 1 to the guinea...dated
6 Feb 1789, for payment of Ł 500, on or before 26 March next.
James Cook (Seal), Wit: James Kerr. Mortgage of negroes (named)
6 Feb 1789, impowers John Julius Pringle as attorney to confess
judgt.

       James Cook for Ł 330 sterling, to Joseph Kershaw, sale
of negroes (named), 9 Apr 1789. James Cook (LS), Wit: Frederick
Briggs.

Page 62: James Cook of Camden, carpenter, appoint James Kershaw
       Esqr. attorney ...24 March 1789, Wit: Robert Henry,

James English.

Page 62: 12 July 1788, David Jones of Craven Co., SC, to David
          Gardiner of Lancaster Co., for Ł 30 sterling...land on
waters of White Oak and Beaver Creek, adj. Jacob Everhart, granted
15 Mar 1787...David Jones (Seal), Wit: N. Patterson, Reuben Collins,
Thos Gardiner. Prov. by Thos Gardniner, 13 Jan 1789, before
John Lowry, J. P.

Page 63: Joseph Kershaw of Camden, by four Bonds bearing date 2
          May 1785, to William Ancrum of Charleston for Ł 19,843
s 13 d 4...mortgage of negroes (named)...2 Jan 1789. Joseph Kershaw (S), Wit: Jo Brevard, John Kershaw. Prov. by Jo Brevard
before J. J. Pringle, 31 Jan 1789.

Page 64: 18 Mar 1789, John Hutchins of Camden, House Carpenter,
          to Aaron Locock of Charleston, Marchant, by bond in
the penal sum of Ł 911 s 16 sterling ...mortgage of lots in
Camden. John R. Hutchins, Wit: George Logan, Will Clarkson.
Prov. by Wm Clarkson, 30 March 1789 before Peter Freneau, J. P.
Charleston District. Rec. Charleston Book A, No. 6, p. 444.

Page 65: 6 Feb 1789, Robert and Mary Williams to John Creighton
          all of Lancaster Co., for Ł 50 sterling...100 A on
branch of Beaver Creek...Robert Williams, Mary Williams (+).
Wit: Thos Creighton, Jas. Miller Junr. Prov. 22 July 1789, by
Thomas Creighton, before Robert Dunlap, J. P.

Pp. 65-66: 26 Aug 1777, John Fail planter of Johnston Co., N. C.
          to William Fail of Craven Co., St. Davids Parish,
S. C., planter, for Ł 5...land on S side Great Lynches Creek
adj. the ford called the Flat Rock ford, 150 A, part of 400 A
granted to Thomas Faile Senr by Wm Bull gov of S. C., 15 March
1771, and the said Thomas Faile Senr being Decd the said John
Faile his son being the true heri at law...John Faile (Seal),
Wit: Benjn. Marlin, Richmond Terrell. S. C. Camden Dist., prov.
by Richmond Terrel, 28 May 1784, before Fredk. Kimball, J. P.

Page 66: 26 May 1789, George Sanders Senr & wife Agness of Lan-
          caster Co., to George Sanders Junr of same, for Ł 50
...150 A granted to Oliver Mahaffy on Granny's Quarter Creek,
adj. George Ross, Thomas Maples...George Sanders (+), Agnes
Sanders (+), Wit: David Sanders (X), Sarah Sanders, John Ashley.

Page 67: 29 Sept 1788, Arthur Ingram of Lancaster Co., to Francis
          Grham of same, for Ł 35...100 A on a branch of Beaver
Creek adj. James Miller...Arthur Ingram (Seal), Wit: John Taylor,
John Hood. Ack. in open court

          18 Dec 1783, Charles Gent of Craven Co., planter, to
Arthur Cunningham...by grant 16   1754 to Charles Ghent 143 A
on N side Wateree, for 100 guineas...Charles Gent (Seal), Wit:
Israel Moore, Richard Moore, James Cunningham. Prov. 22 Oct
1788 before Richard Champion, by James Cunningham.

Page 68: 13 Feb 1789, William Woods in Camden Dist., Lancaster
          Co., to Henry Ployler of same, (lease sl0, release Ł
28 sterling)...100 A on waters of Lynches Creek, granted to sd.
William Woods, 1 Oct 1787...William Woods (Seal), Wit: William
Graham, Paul Plyler. Prov. by Paul Plyler before John Craig,
J. P.

Page 69: 15 July 1789, Richard Drakeford of Lancaster Co., to
John Drakeford of same, for Ł 10 sterling...200 A on E
side Flat Rock Creek, which belonged to my Father except 45 A
adj. Dunlap, Alexander Burnside, David Hunter, Robert Barclay,
Jacob Hickman, ...Richard Drakeford (LS), Wit: John Boutin,
William Daniel, William Scot.

15 July 1789, George Sanders Senr & wife Agness of Lancaster Co.,
planter, to John Ashley, planter, for Ł 50...200 A granted to sd.
George Sanders Senr. on Lick Branch, Rec. in Book HHH p. 287,
adj. James Chesnut, Jacob Hickman...George Sanders (+), Agness
Sanders (+), Wit: John Cook, Israel Moore & Sarah Sanders.

Page 70: Elizabeth Guthrie & William Guthrie of Lancaster Co.,
spinster & Cordwainer, to William Spruntz of same, planter...229 A on N side Cane Creek in the Waxaw Settlement, granted
to William Guthrie 26 July 1774 by Gov. Bull, which by his L. W.
& T. did devise to his well beloved wife Elizabeth and son Wm.
guthrie...25 July 1788. Elizabeth Guthrie (Φ) (Seal), Wm. Guthrie (Seal), Wit: John Craig, Robert Guthrie, John Hood (X).
Certified by John Craig, J. P., 7 Jan 1789.

Entered June 24th 1790. Edward Rogers's Stock Mark & Brand A
Smoothe crop in the Left ear, And figure seven in the Right,
Bran E R

Entered June 24th 1790 Hekekiah(sic) Loves Stock mark Crop &
Slit in the Right ear, and Left ear Whole

Page 71: 9 May 1778, John Chesnut of Camden, merchant, to James
Perry of Camden Dist., planter, for (lease s10, release
Ł 1000) 250 A in Craven County on N side Wateree River adj.
Wateree River, granted 15 May 1751, Rec. in Book NN folio 24,
granted to Benjamine Duke, and by Benjamin Duke & wife Mary sold
to Robert Humphreys, and sold by Nehemiah Joiner Junr to sd.
Chesnut...John Chesnut (Seal), Wit: Wm. Kirkland, Wm. Harrison,
Sion Cotes. Prov. by William Kirkland 22 Apr 1789.

Page 72: 15 Sept 1791, Jannet Miller otherwise now Jannet Knox
of Chester Co., Widow, to John Love of Lancaster Co.,
planter, for Ł 50...land on the South branch of Little Lynches
Creek waters of Peedee...Jannet Knox (X) (Seal), Wit: John Gaston,
Samuel Love, William Gaston. Prov. by Samuel Love, 26 Oct
1791, before John Simpson, J. L. C.

Pp. 72-73: 15 Dec 1791, Barbary Kinsey of York Co., Widow, to
John Love of Lancaster Co., for Ł 40...land on S
branch of Lynches Creek waters of Pedee, 150 A...Barbara Kenzie
(X) (Seal), Wit: James L. Gaston, James Love, William Love.
Prov. by William Love in Chester Co., before William Gaston, J.
C. C.

Page 73: S. C. Camden Dist., Benjamin Blackburn to son John
Blackburn a plantation on both sides Great Lynches Creek
at the mouth of Tuckahowe, tract granted to John Armstrong,
conveyed to David Griffith, then to Petter Aaron (I believe),
and from said Peter Aaron (I believe the conveyance being almost
obliterated) to Benjamin Blackburn, all my tight and title in
bond for said land, for caows, etc. (marks given)...18 July 1778
Benj Blackburn (B) (Seal), Wit: Banun Martin Lewis Faile & William Faile. Prov. by Lewis Faile before Andrew Baskin, 23 July

BOOK B

1778.

Page 74: Blank.

Page 75: 16 Apr 1788, John Wallis of Camden, carpenter, and wife
          Isabelle to Solomon Wolf of same, merchant, for Ł 370
...lots in Camden...John Wallis (Seal), Isabella Wallis (Seal),
Wit: James Atkins, Ezra Alexander. Prov. 17 Apr 1789, by James
Atkins, Ezra Alexander, before James Kershaw, J. P.

Pp. 75-76: 17 Apr 1789, Solomon Wolf of Camden, merchant & wife
            Rachel, for Ł 300 to John Wallis of same, carpenter,
two lots in Camden...Solomon Wolf (Seal), Rachel Woolf (Seal),
(same wit as preceding). Prov. 20 Apr 1789, by James Atkins,
before James Kershaw, J. P.

Page 76: Solomon Wolf of Camden, merchant to John Wallis of
          same, Carpenter for Ł 620...bond to pay Ł 310...
Solomon Woolf (Seal), Wit: James Atkins. Prov. 20 Apr 1789.

Pp. 77-78: 23 July 1788, Mordecia Lion of Camden, and wife Sarah,
            to Claude Jean Baptist Le Droit De Bussy of same,
for Ł 100 sterling...lots in Camden...bond with Samuel Levi...
M. Lion (Seal), Samuel Levi (Seal), sarah Levi (Seal), Wit:
Joseph DaCosta, James Atkins. Prov. by James Atkins, before
James Kershaw, J. P., 20 Apr 1788.

Page 78: Isaac Alexander of Camden, binds his brother Ezra
          Alexander an apprentice to John Wallis of Camden, car-
penter...for four years...1 Jan 1787. Wit: James Nesbit, Mary
Conaan, I. Alexander J. P.

6 Aug 1791, John Crawford of S. C., to George Wrenn of Lancaster
Co., for Ł 100 sterling...land on N side Waxhaw Creek adj.
Robert Ivey, Moses White, Robert Lockhart, William Wrenn...John
Crawford (Seal), Wit: Benjn. Perry, Bridges Pair (X), Thos Chad-
wick (X). Prov. by Bridges Pair, 2 Feb 1792, before Hugh White,
J. L. C.

Page 79: S. C.,Lancaster Co., John Craig planter to Jacob Ploy-
          ler, of same, for Ł 15 sterling...land on a branch of
Lynches Creek waters of Peedee River, granted to sd. Craig 14
Aug 1774...25 March 1789. John Craig (LS), Mary Craig (M) (LS),
Wit: James Craig, Henry Ployler.

Page 80: 17 Apr 1787, Nathaniel Pace of Camden Dist., to William
          Bailey, of same, for Ł 10...100 A on Cedar Creek Cataw-
ba River...Nathaniel Pace (Seal), Micajah Crenshaw, James Crenshaw. Prov. by Nathaniel Pace, 22 Apr 1789, beofre Robert Dunlap, J. P.

Pp. 80-81: 13 Jan 1789, William Harper, of Camden Dist., Lancas-
            ter Co., to Jacob Karn of same, for (lease s10, re-
leaseŁ 30)... 100 A on a branch of Wild Cat Creek, granted to
sd. Harper 13 May 1768...William Harper (R), Wit: John Bibbe,
Nathaniel Bibbe. Prov. 17 Jan 1789 by John Bibbe, before John
Craig, J. P.

Pp. 81-82: 24 Sept 1791, John Tomlinson & wife Rebekah to Moses
            Heath, for Ł 100 st., 130 A in the Waxhaw Settlement

27

it being part of a tract belonging to the Est. of Robert
Howard deceased, adj. Robert Crawfords line...part of tract granted to Stephen White in the year 1754 by Matthew Rowan, Gov.
of N. C...John Tomlinson, Rebecca Tomlinson (X), Wit: Isaac
Anderson, Thomas Ware, John Russell.

Pp. 82-83: 29 Oct 1788, Devall Fonderburgh of Lancaster Co., planter, by grant 12 Feb 1772, to sd. Fonderburk, 150 A
on two branches of Lynches Creek called Otter, now this moiety,
75 A to Daniel Hunter of same county, for Ł 50...(signed in
German), Wit: Wm. Adams (&), John Lotzinger, John Bibbe. Prov.
10 March 1789, by William Adams, before John Craig, J. P.

Pp. 84-85: 14 July 1773, Benjamin Maddox of St. Marks Parish,
Craven County, SC, Yeoman, and Rose his wife, to
Samuel Dunlap, for Ł 100...200 A on Cane Creek and Kemp on the
North side, of the waxhaws... granted 1 Feb 1753, granted by
Gov. Glenn...Benjamin Madox (B), Rose Maddox (Seal), Wit: Henry
Foster, William Morris, William Ramsey. Prov. by William Morris,
before James Patton, J. P., 15 July 1773.

Pp. 85-86: 27 Nov 1773, Samuel Dunlap Senr & wife Mary of Camden
Dist., to Robert Dunlap of same, by grant 13 Feb
1773 on Cane Creek and Camp Creek...Samuel Dunlap, Mary Dunlap
(X), Wit: Geo Dunlap, Thomas Dunlap, Sarah Ramsey (⍉). Prov. by
Thomas Dunlap, 8 Sept 1791, before Jos. Lee, J. P.

Page 86: 5 Aug 1790, William Denman (Joiner) of Lancaster Co.,
to John Blackburn, Hatter, of Chesterfield Co., land in
Lancaster Co., on the springs and drains of Tuckohoe waters of
Main Lynches Creek, 150 A granted to sd. William Denman 7 Aug
1786, Rec. Book LLLL, p. 586...William Denman (Seal), Sarah Denman (X) (Seal), Wit: John Smith, John Scarborough. Prov. by John
Scarborough, before Benjamin Hale, 12 Feb 1791.

Page 87: 16 May 1791, Jacob Baker to Peter Rape, the said Baker
living in Lancaster Co., SC, the said Rape living in
Mecklinburg Co., NC, for Ł 20, 100 A on S side Pole Cat Creek
branch of big Lynches creek, part of 226 A granted to sd. Jacob
Baker 1787...Jacob Baker (Seal), Wit: William Nisbett, Jacob
Shoffner. Prof. by Jacob Shofner, 14 Dec 1791, before John
Craig, J. P.

Pp. 87-88: 7 Dec 1789, John Johnston of Lancaster Co., to Jacob
Shofner of same, for Ł 20...land on head waters of
Great Lynches Creek granted to John Johnston, 11 Aug 1774...John
Johnston (X), Wit: Benjamin Harper, Robert McCorkle. 1 Feb 1792,
prov. by BenjaminHarper, before John Craig, J. P.

Page 88: 26 Mar 1790, Finney McClenahan agent and attorney for
William Brown, to Benjamin Harper of Lancaster Co., for
Ł 120...two tracts on twelve mile creek on E side Catawba River,
adj. Robt McCorkle, Samuel Burnett, 265 A and 150 A granted to
Andrew Nut conveyed 27 July 1758 to William Brown, the other
part 115 A part of grant to William Alexander and by him conveyed
22 July 1758 to sd. William Brown...Finney McClenahan (Seal),
Wit: William Brooket, Jno McClenahan, Wm. Harper.   2 March 1792,
prov. by Wm. Harper, before Isaac Donnom, J. P.

Pp. 88-89: 19 Dec 1782, Henry Peebles of St. Marks parish, planter, to Edward Cannington of same, for (lease s10,

release L300)...150 A on both sides Flat Creek in Craven Co.,
adj. Matthias Ardias, granted to John Wisener...Matthias Archer
(??)...Henry Peebles (Seal), Mary Peebles (X) (Seal), Wit: Richn.
Terrell, Thomas Rolan (X). Prov. by Richmon Terrell, 10 July 1783,
before William Welch, J. P. for Camden Dist.

Pp. 90-91: 1 Dec 1788, Henry Hunter Sheriff od Dist. of Camden,
        to John Kershaw (the younger)...Ely Kershaw late of
said State deceased was seized of three lots in the Town of Camden,
and at the time of his demise in the hands of Joseph Kershaw &
John Chesnut, Exrs. of the last will and testament of sd. Ely
...William Ancrum did recover against Joseph Kershaw and John
Chesnut in the year 178- at Charleston...H. Hunter Shff C. D.
(Seal), Wit: Zack Cantey, William Brown, Jno Craven. Prov. by
John Craven, 6 July 1789, before James Kershaw, J. P.

Pp. 91-92: 1 Jan 1787, Joseph Kershaw of Camden in the Dist. of
        Camden, to John Kershaw of Camden also, for L 55...
5 A in the Eastern extremiry of the said village, lot #7...
Wit: B. Carter, Jo Brevard, Saml Doby.   6 July 1789, prov. by
Jos. Brevard, before James Kershaw, J. P.

Page 92: 1 May 1789, Joseph Kershaw of Camden, to John Kershaw
        of same, for L 100...lot #1 in Camden. Wit: Benj.
Carter, Jo Brevard, James Kershaw.   Prov. 6 July 1789, by Jo.
Brevard, by James Kershaw, J. P.

Page 93: Plat showing streets of Camden and land laid out to
        Jas. Brown Senr, John Kershaw, Dr. Charlton, James Ker-
shaw.

Pp. 93-94: 29 Nov 1787, Joseph Kershaw & John Chesnut Surviving
        Exrs. of Ely Kershaw Decd., to John Kershaw the Elder
of Camden, for L80...two lots in the town or Village of Chatham...
Wit: William Brown, John Kershaw, Jno Craven. Prov. by John
Kershaw Junr, 6 July 1789, before James Kershaw, J. P.

Pp. 94-95: 29 Nov 1787, Joseph Kershaw & John Chesnut, Exrs. of
        Ely Kershaw,Decd.,to Joseph Brevard of Camden, Gent.,
two lots in Chatham...Wit: Wm. Brown, John Kershaw, Jno Craven.
Prov. by Jno Craven, 6 July 1789, before James Kershaw, J. P.

Pp. 95-96: 27 July 1787, Joseph Kershaw of Camden, to John Ker-
        shaw of same, for L 300...lots in Camden, 644, 645,
646...Wit: James Kershaw, Joseph Brevard, Joseph Kershaw Jr.
Prov. by Jo Brevard, 6 July 1789.

Pp. 96-97: 14 Sept 1787, George Brown of Fairfield Co., miller,
        to Samuel Mathis, James Pierson & Samuel Midwood, by
the style & Title of Mathis Pierson & Co., mortgage for two lots
in Camden...George Brown (Seal), Wit: Robert Henry, H. Beaumont.
Prov. by Robert Henry 4 July 1785, before I. Alexander, J. P.

Page 97: 16 Aug 1787, William Lang of Camden Dist., and wife
        Sarah, to Natl. Cairy of same...two lots in Camden, 444
& 445...William Lang (Seal), Sarah Lang, Wit: John Adamson, John
Hatfield. Prov. by John Adamson, 22 Aug 1789, before I. Alexander.

Page 98: 29 Dec 1774, Joseph Kershaw of Camden, merchant, to
        Nathaniel Cary of same, merchant, for ₺ 300...lots in
Camden, 304, 305, 306, 307, 308...Wit: Dolling Jones, George
Reynolds, James Cayrey. Prov. 29 Dec 1774, by Dolling Jones
before Thomas Charlton, Esqr.

Pp. 98-99: 27 July 1789, Minor Winn of the Village of Winnsborough,
        Esq., to Nathaniel Cary, for ₺ 40...land granted 5
March 1787, adj. Mr. Kershaw, John Adamson, Mrs. Reid, 300 A...
M. Winn (LS), Wit: John Reed, Jno Craven, John Malone. Prov. by
John Craven, before Isaac Alexander, J.P., 27 July 1789.

Pp. 99-101: 11 Oct 1764, Walter Rowe of Parish of St. Mark, SC,
        to John Cook of same (lease s 10, release ₺ 125)...
100 A on S side Grany's Quarter Creek on Peedee Road, vacant
on all sides, granted 10 Nov 1761...Walter Rowe (M), Wit: Danl
Dwight, Joseph Kershaw. Craven County: proven by Joseph Kershaw
before John Newman Oglethorp, J. P., 7 Feb 1766.

Pp. 101-103: 13 Oct 1777, Creed Childres of Craven Co., carpen-
        ter, to Nathaniel Cary, of same, merchant, (lease
s 10, release ₺ 200)...250 A on east branches of Grany's Quarter
Creek, adj. John Cook Junr, William Barnet, George Sanders,
granted to Creed Childers 13 March 1772...Creed Childers (LS),
Wit: Jeremiah Simmons, James Bittie, Wm. Murrell. Prov. by
William Murrell, 18 Oct 1777, before Jno. Newman Oglethorp, J. P.

Pp. 103-105: 6 Oct 1777, Jno Cook of St. Marks Parish, SC, plan-
        ter & wife Elizabeth, to Natl. Cary of same, (lease
s 20 , release ₺ 1000)...land granted 10 Nov 1761 to Walter
Rowe on Grany's Quarter Creek, Craven county on Peedee Road,
conveyed to John Cook 11 & 12 Oct 1764...John Cook (LS), Eliz.
Cook (LS), Wit: Josias Whtea, William Cook, Francis Carter.
Prov. by Francis Carter, before John Newman Oglethorp, J. P., 7
Oct 1777.

Pp. 105-106: William Ford by bond dated 29 Oct 1784 bound to
        Joseph Kershaw of Camden, merchant, for ₺ 125 for
payment of ₺ 62 s 10, before 21 Nov 1785...mortgage of 114
A on Haigs branch of Rocky Creek purchased by me of Henry Hales
& wife Sarah, also adj. tract purchased of James Winn Esqr., 36
A, also stock of cattle, etc, 18 Sept 1789. Wm Ford Junr. (LS),
Wit John Craven, James Atkins. Provn in Camden Dist., by John
Craven before James Kershaw, J. P., 18 Sept 1789.

Page 106: 22 Sept 1789, Joseph Kershaw of Camden, for ₺ 200 to
        Joseph Kershaw Junr. Surgeon...lots in Camden, Wit:
George W. Kershaw, John Craven. Prov. by John Craven before
James Kershaw, 22 Sept 1789.

Page 107: 1 May 1789, Joseph Kershaw of Camden, to James Kershaw,
        for ₺ 200...tract on both sides Pinetree creek, 201 A
adj. Joseph Kershaw, Dr. Charlton, and lots adj. the extended
part of the Town of Camden...(plat included), Wit: Benj. Carter,
Jo Brevard, John Kershaw. Prov. 15 Aug 1789, before Arthur
Brown Ross, J. P. by John Kershaw.

Page 108: James Munford & Lucy Kennon Munford...James Munford by
        bond dated 21 May 1787 bound to William Lang of Camden
planter, mortgage of negroes (17, named)...2 Nov 1789. Wit: John
Lang. Prov. by John Long, before I. Alexander, J. P. 27 Nov 1789.

BOOK B

Pp. 108-109: 1 March 1786, Thomas Burns of Camden, Silver Smith,
         to John Adamson of Camden, planter, for Ł 20...
lots in Camden...Thomas Burns (Seal), Wit: Francis Woolf, Isaih
Bush, Samuel Denkins. Prov. 15 Oct 1789, by I. Bush, before
James Kershaw, J. P.

Page 109: Samuel Breid of Camden, Taylor, bound to David Bush &
         Company of Camden, Storekeepers, for Ł 140..29 Dec 1789
bond for payment of Ł 70...Samuel Breid (LS), Wit: Joachim G.
Schultz, I. Bush.

Page 110: Samuel Breid of Camden, Taylor, by bond 29 Dec 1789 to
         David Bush & Co...two negroes Fish & Tenah...(same
wit. as before.)

Pp. 111-112: Samuel Montgomery of Ninety Six District, planter,
         to William Montgomery of Camden Dist., for Ł 51 s
8 sterling...land in Camden Dist., Waxhaw settlement, 82½ A,
part of grant to John Linn, 17 May 1754, of 302 A, conveyed by
L & R 10 Jan 1757 to Hugh Montgomery, and in his last will &
testament did give to Saml Montgomery...29 Oct 1787. Saml Montgomery (LS), Wit: John Montgomery, John Johnston, James Johnston.
Prov. 4 Feb 1790 before Robert Dunlap, by John Montgomery.

Pp. 112-114: 6 May 1789, Samuel Tines of Lancaster County, Cam-
         den Dist., SC, to Peter Wikoff of Philadelphia,
Pa., merchant and Isaac Wikoff of County of Monmouth, New Jersey
(lease s5, release Ł 352 6/8)...750 A on south prong of Lynches
Creek waters of Pedee, granted to Peter Wikoff and Isaac Wikoff
under the hands and seals of John Belton of S. C. & wife Mary 27
Apr 1777, rec. in public registers office Book V No. 4, pp. 260-
262...Saml Tynes (LS), Wit: John Chesnut, Duncan McRa. Prov.
8 May 1790 before John Marshel, J. P. by John Chesnut.

Page 114: Andrew Baskin's Stock Mark, Swallow fork & under Keel
(or Fish-hook) in each ear Brand on the Horses AB and on Cattle
A only. April 5th 1790.

April 5th 1790. Mary Marshel's Stock Mark & Brand, Mark A crop
& under Keel (or Fish hook) in the Right eat & a figure of three
in the left Branch 27.

Pp. 115-123: 24 Feb 1790, Joseph Kershaw of the Village of Camden,
         to William Ancrum, Edward Darrell, James Fisher,
Robert Henry & James Kershaw, five of the Creditors and Trustees
of the said Joseph Kershaw(lease s5, release Ł 20,000)...lots
in Camden, and tracts known as Morgan Browns mills, now Richmond
mills, also 1000 A on Little Lynches Creek adj. Augustine Preston,
200 A in Ninety Six District on a branch of Stephens's Creek,
adj. Moses Kirkland, Ogdell Cockroff; 200 A in Ninety Six Dist.,
on waters of Warriors Creek adj. Thomas Buckles, Henry Linder,
Drury Smith; 200 A in Ninety Six Dist., on Rayburns Creek, adj.
James Williman, Charles Broadway, William Eleson, Richard Hill,
200 A in Colleton County on waters of Cuffy Town creek adj. James
Harvis, Field Pardues, Samuel Anderson,Daniel Sullivan; 200 A
in Grenville Co., on a branch of Stephens Creek adj. Joel Crawford, also lands on Saluda River above the mouth of Reedy River
near Ninety Six, surveyed 1768; tract in Craven County on SW side
Wateree River on a branch of Thorn Creek; 250 A on Fishing Creek
adj. Laurence Gallaher, William Nettles; 100 A on Wateree Creek
at the time of survey known as McGourts mine, 200 A on Loves Creek

31

formerly the property of Matthew Floyd adj. Pauls land, granted
by Gov. Tryon to Andrew Campbell 26 Sept 1760; 100 A on a brach
of Lynches Creek originally granted to Sarah Bell; 200 A in the
fork between Broad & Saluda Rivers on Indian Creek a branch of
Enoree River; 200 A called Canteys mill tract on Swift Creek;
250 A adj. Humphrey Barnet on Wateree River, 65 A at the fork
White oak on a branch of Wateree River, 135 A between Sanders
and Grany's Quarter Creek, 100 A on Steels survey on a branch
of Lynches Creek, 100 A on Twenty five Mille Creek called Well's
place, 415 A in St. John's Parish Charleston District, on Biggin
swamp, which said Joseph Kershaw purchased from Thomas Hill...
also negroes (named)...Wit: William Robertson, Robert Turnbull.
S. C. Charleston Dist., prov. by William Robinson, before Daniel
Smith, J. P. 27 Feb 1790.

Pp. 123-128: 24 & 25 March 1790, Samuel Mathis of Camden Dist.,
            Esqr., and Edward Darrell, Robert Henry and James
Kershaw, three of the Creditors and Trustees of sd. Samuel Mathis
...1/4 of tract of 640 A on SW side Lynches Creek adj. John Reid,
Robert Carter, James Alexander; 1/4 part of 428 A on the dividing
line between Camden and Georgetown Districts, granted to Robert
Brownfield; 1/4 tract of 640 A on S side Lynches Creek adj.
Richard Gee, granted to James Alexander, 1/4 of 640 A adj. Robert
Brownfield; 1/4 640 A adj. last mentioned tract; 1/4 of tract of
640 A granted to Peter Bremar; 1/4 of 350 A adj. to the District
line granted to Peter Bremar; 1/4 of 5740 A adj. District line,
granted to Isaac Alexander, Robert Brownfield, Samuel Mathias and
John Smith; also 1/4 of 100 A granted to Samuel Chandler; 1/4
of land granted to Joseph Hall Ramsey; 1/4 of 1000 A granted to
Joseph Hall Ramsey; 1/4 of 600 A granted to Joseph Hall Ramsey;
1/4 of 200 A granted to Daniel Miers, adj. Thomas Lehre; 1/4 of
150 A granted to Mr. Nettles; 1/4 of 640 A granted to Samuel
Mathis; 100 A on Bellons Road granted to George Duren; 640 A
granted to John Milbanks; 640 A on Gum Swamp adj. Joseph Brevard,
granted to John Millbank; land adj. to William Nettles, granted
to George Patterson; 640 A on English's Road, granted to John
Thompson; 1273 A on Broad Branch waters of Black River adj. Thomas Timothy's land, adj. Addison Scarborough, James Wood, Samuel
Mathis; 1280 A on Turkey Creek adj. Andrew Shirrar, John Cook,
Samuel Mathis; Saml Mathis (LS), Wit: Joseph Kershaw.

Page 128: 26 March 1788, William Lang of Camden Esqr. & wife
            Sarah and Dinah Wyly widow, to James Atkins of Camden,
for ₺ 84 sterling...lots in Camden...William Lang (LS), Sarah
Lang (LS), Dinah Wyly(LS), Wit: John Harker, Jno Lang. Prov.
18 Jan 1790 before James Kershaw, J. P., by John Lang.

Pp. 129-130: 2 July 1789, William Lang of Camden & wife Sarah
            to Joseph Kershaw, Adam Fowler Brisbane, Isaac Alex-
ander, William Tate, John Adamson, John Kershaw, John Chesnut and
James Atkins (who with the said William Lang are the Standing
Committee nominated elected and chosen by a Society in Camden
aforesaid called the Camden Orphan Society Incorporated by an
Act of General Assembly...27 Feb 1788)...lots in Camden Wit:
Sarah Atkins, William Adamson. Prov.19 Apr 1790 by S. Atkins,
before James Kershaw, J. P.

Pp. 130-131: 9 Aug 1787, Claude Jean Baptiste le David DeBussy of
            Philadelphia, Pa., Gentleman, and Magdalain Chabert
his wife, to John Reid of Twon of Camden, County of Lancaster,
Inn Keeper, for ₺ 100 lawful money...lots in Camden...Ledroit

DeBussy (LS), Madelane de bussy (LS), Wit: Daniel Brown, F. Wood-roof, John Cason. Prov. by F. Woodroof, 6 March 1790.

Pp. 131-132: 29 Sept 1789, Joseph Kershaw of Camden, to James
            Atkins of Camden, for ₺ 32 sterling...32 A being
near Camden aforesaid, Lands belonging to Doctor Isaac Alexander
(on which he has a Brick yard), adj. Abraham Boltonan,   Tomlinson...Joseph Kershaw (LS), Wit: James Kershaw, John Craven. Prov.
by John Craven before James Kershaw, J. P., 30 Sept 1789.
(Plat included).

Page 133:   March 1780, Isaac Taylor and wife Rachel to Jacob
            Taylor...for ₺ 10,000...land adj. Culps mill creek, 100
A...Isaac Taylor (T), Rachel Taylor (R), Wit: John Barnett,
David Adams, John Davis. Prov. by John Davis before Samuel
Dunlap. 21 March 1790. (Plat included)

Page 134: Robert Lee of Camden Dist., planter, by bond dated same
            as these present, for the payment of ₺ 257...to Doug-
las Starke, John Blanton & Willis Whitaker...mortgage of negroes
(Names and ages given)...2 Dec 1789. Robert Lee (LS), Wit: Zach
Cantey. Prov. by Zach Cantey, 7 Apr 1790, before James Kershaw,
J. P.

Pp. 134-135: Thomas Ballard of Camden Dist., planter, by bond
            bearing same day, for payment of ₺ 125...to
Douglas Starke, John Blanton ,Willis Whitaker...mortgage of
negroes (names and ages given)...2 Dec 1789. Thomas Ballard (LS),
Wit: Zach Cantey. Prov. by Cantey 7 Apr 1790, before James
Kershaw,J. P.

Pp. 135-136: John Adamson of Camden Dist., planter, by bond of
            same date, to Douglas Starke, John Blanton, Willis
Whitaker...mortgage of negroes (names and ages given)...2 Dec
1789. Wit: Duncan McRa, Zach. Cantey. Prov. by Cantey, 7 Apr
1790, before James Kershaw, J. P.

Pp. 136-137: Reuben Starke of Camden Dist., planter...to Douglas
            Starke, John Blanton, Willis Whitaker...mortgage of
negro Gunny about 35 years of age...2 Sept 1789, Reuben Starke
Junr. (LS), Wit: Zach Cantey, William Brown. Prov. by Cantey
before James Kershaw, 7 Apr 1790.

Pp. 137-138: Arthur Cunningham of Camden Dist., to Douglas Starke,
            John Blanton, Willis Whitaker, mortgage of negroes
(names and ages given)...5 Dec 1789. Wit: William Brown. Prov.
by Brown 7 Apr 1790, before James Kershaw, J. P.

Page 138: Middleton McDonald of Camden Dist., to Douglas Starke,
            John Blanton, Willis Whitaker...mortgage of negroes
(names and ages given)...2 Sept 1789. Wit: William Brown, Zach.
Cantey. Prov. by Cantey, 7 Apr 1790 before James Kershaw, J. P.

Page 139: Benjamine Perry of Camden Dist.,planter, to Douglas
            Starke, John Blanton Willis Whitaker...mortgage of
negroes (names and ages given)...2 Dec 1789. Benjamin Perry (LS),
Wit: Duncan McRa, William Brown. Prov. by William Bornw, 7 Apr
1790, before James Kershaw.

Page 140: 8 June 1787, Joseph Kershaw of Camden, to William

Lang & Dinah Wyly Senior of Camden, for Ł sterling...20 A on
Pinetree Creek adj. William Lang, John Payne...Joseph Kershaw
(LS), Wit: William Whitaker, John Craven, Philip Platt. Prov.
by John Craven 2 March 1790, before I. Alexander, J.P. (plat
included)....

Page 141: 1 Sept 1788, Henry Hunter Esqr. Sheriff of Camden Dist.,
          to John Reid of Camden, Inn Keeper, 400 A commonly
called Edward McCays land on or near Lynches Creek...the said
Edward McCay being indebted to John Holzendorf of same, for Ł 107
s 6 d 6 sterling and recovered in court of Common pleas...Henry
Hunter S. C. (LS), Wit: F. Woodroof, Nicholas Robinson. Prov.
by Fielding Woodroof, 6 March 1790, before I. Alexander, J P.

Pp. 142-143: 1 May 1789, John Holzendorf of Camden & wife Eliza-
             beth, to Henry Rugely of Fairfield County, for Ł 550
...lots in Camden, and tract on NE side Wateree River adj. William
Lang, Isabella Reid widow, Joseph Kershaw, 150 A...J. Holzendorf
(LS), Elizabeth Holzendorf (LS, Wit: James Pierson, James Atkins.
Prov. 11 Aug 1789, by James Atkins, before James Kershaw, J. P.

Page 143: Richard Dawkins of Dist. of Camden doth bind his daugh-
          ter Ferraby Dawkins minor, an apprentice unto John
Reid and Sarah Reid of the Town of Camden, for 5 years, to expire
9 Sept 1781...9 Sept 1786. Richard Dawkins (LS), Ferraby Dawkins
(X) (LS), John Reid (LS), Sarah Reid (LS), Wit: I. Alexander, JP.

Pp. 144-145: 5 & 6 Aug 1765, William Shepherd of Craven County,
             planter, and wife Jemimah, to Robert Garner of same,
planter (lease s5, releas Ł 200)...150 A granted to sd. Shepherd
7 May 1762 on Faulkenborough's branch...William Sheperd (W),
Jemimah Sheperd (X), Wit: Benjamin Deason (X), Benjamin Enlow
(B). Prov. by Benjamin Enlow, 12 July 1766, before Jno. N. Oglethorpe.

Page 146: 2 Aug 1772, William Shepherd of Craven Co., planter,
          to Robert Garner of same, for s 5...land granted to
Shepherd 24 Nov 1764...William Shepherd (W) (Seal), Jemimah
Shepherd (I) (Seal), Wit: William Clark, John Knight (X).

Pp. 146-147: John Howard of Cataba River, Camden Dist., miller,
             bound to William Clark of Singletons Creek, for Ł
10,000...whereas I John Howard am now resolved to travel to the
southward or elsewhere, and am possessed of 100 A on NE side
Cataba adj. Col. Kershaw, granted to sd. John Howard...John
Howard (X), Wit: James Bredin, Mary Bredin (X), John Breden.
Prov. by James Bredin, 6 May 1788, before Saml Dunlap, J. P.

Page 147: 20 Feb 1785, William Clark of Camden Dist., to George
          Hays, weaver of same dist., land conveyed to sd. Clark
by John Howard...William Clark (W) (LS), Mary Clark (X) (LS),
Wit: John Veason, Henry Hust. Prov. by John Bideon, 21 Feb 1785,
before John Lowry, J. P.

Page 148: 18 Feb 1790, Samuel Mathis of Camden, to William Craig,
          of Beaver Creek, for Ł 150 sterling...land known as
Down's place on Hanging Rock Creek, 2096 A in two surveys granted
to William Downs, and 640 A granted to Fielding Woodroff, 200 A
granted to William Hextly; grant to Thomas Archer 640 A... Saml
Mathis (LS), Wit: John Graham, John Taylor.

Page 149: 21 Apr 1790, Andrew Nutt of Lancaster Co., planter, to
Samuel Nutt of same, for Ł 10...½ of 300 A granted to
Thomas Harrington, 25 Jany 1771, on E side Wateree River, con-
veyed to sd. Andrew Nutt by L & R 18 Nov 1771...Andrew Nutt (LS),
Wit: Elir. Alexander, William Taylor.

Page 150: 30 Sept 1789, Elizabeth McClenahan of York Co., SC, to
Hugh White of Lancaster Co., by grant 31 March 1755, by
Matthew Rowan, Govr. of N. C., 200 A in Craven County (in the
province of South Carolina since the boundary line was run) on
N side Cataba River adj. John Linns land (formerly Joseph Whites)
Henry White, Waxhaw Creek, made over from Samuel Young to Hugh
Robinson by deed 10 March 1762, to Robert McClenahen by deed 15
Apr 1764, and by the last will and testament of the said Robert
McClenahan dated 4 Feb 1767 to Elizabeth McClenahan Relict of the
said Robert, now for Ł 25 to Hugh Shite...Elizabeth McClenahan
(C), Wit: John McClenahan, Isaac Dunnam, John Simpson.

April Court 1790

Pp. 150-151: 2 Nov 1789, William Haggins of Mecklenburgh County,
NC, to William Porter of Lancaster Co., SC, for Ł
50 SC money...140 A in Lancaster County, on both sides of the
Mill Stone branch on the East of Cataba adj. John Haggans line,
granted to James Miller by patent 10 Apr 1765, Rec. in the Se-
cretarys Office Liber No. 10 * page 335...Wm Hagains (LS), Wit:
John Crocket, Hugh White, Jo Douglas.

Pp. 151-152: 6 Sept 1786, Robert Corckett of York Co., SC, to
John Arnold Pender of Lancaster Co., for Ł 120
sterling...land on S side Waxhaw creek, adj. Joseph White, 50 A
granted to sd. Robert Crocket 5 Dec 1785...Robert Crocket (LS),
Wit: Hugh White, Abraham Livingston, Andw. Linn.

Page 152: 22 Feb 1785, Frame Woods of St. Mark's Parish, Camden
Dist., to Edmund Hull of same, (lease s 10, release
Ł 250....land granted 13 July 1770, to Joseph Woods, 250 A,
paid by John Baker....Frame Woods (LS), Wit: William Boyd, John
Baker (X).

Pp. 153-155: 22 Feb 1790, John Adamson of Camden, planter, to
John Lewis Keall Holzendorf of same (lease s5, release Ł 43 s 10)...lots in Camden...John Adamson (LS), Elizabeth
Adamson (LS), Wit: Margaret Adamson, James Atkins. 1 July 1790,
prov. by James Atkins, before James Kershaw, J. P.

Pp. 155-158: 8 May 1790, John Chesnut of Camden, Esq., to Samuel
Boykin & Zachariah Cantey, of Dist. of Camden,
for and in consideration of the natural love and affection that
the sd. John Chesnut hath for his daughter Mary McRa wife of
Duncan McRa of Camden and for s 5...lots in Camden and negroes
(names and ages given) John Chesnut (LS), Wit: Robert Dow,
Daniel Peak, Wm. Tate. Prov. by William Tate, 10 May 1790,
before John Marshel, J.P.

Page 159: Thomas Charlton of Camden, Doctor, by bond to Zachariah
Cantey, for Ł 765 s 10 sterling, mortgage of negroes
and cattle...16 July 1790. Tho: Charlton (LS), Wit: William
Brown, Ely Kershaw.

Page 159: January 28th 1791. Abraham Hagler's Stock mark.
Crop and Slit in the Right ear and Swallow Fork and
half Moon in the left ear.

Pp. 160-161: 17 Dec 1789, David Fonderburk of Lancaster Co., to
John Fonderburk of same (lease s5, release s 10)
land granted6 Aug 1787, 162 A, 81 A, adj. John Stroud, on Lyn-
ches Creek...David Fonderburk (F) (LS), Wit: Devalt Fonderburk,
Henry Fonderburk. Prov. by Devalt Fonderburk (D), before Ben
Haile, J. P., 22 March 1790.

Page 162: 18 June 1790, Col. John Marshel of Lancaster Co., to
Benjamin Haile of same, for ₺ 60...2869 A on waters
of Lynces Creek, adj. Robert Delaps, David Fonderburk, Isaac
Fonderburk, Thomas Knight, Francis Bettis, Benjamin Hale, William
Berry, Henry Massey, Lewis Faile, John Massey, John Cartledge,
great Lynches Creek, Michael Miller, Joseph Taylor, George Miller,
John Falkenberrys, John Marshel, granted 31 Dec 1788...John
Marshel (LS), Wit: Elir. Alexander, John Scott, John Simpson.

Page 163: 8 March 1790, Benjamin Cudworth of State of S. C.,
planter, to John Splatt Cripps of Charleston, Merchant,
for one shilling sterling...tract in the Waxhaw, on which the
said Benjamin Cudworth now resides, 350 A old measure in Lancaster (formerly Craven) County adj. James Simpson, Hannah Lindsay,
William Carson, Thomas Simpson, also tract on Bear Creek a branch
of Cane Creek 200 A bounded at the time of survey in Nov. 1756,
on all sides by vacant land, also 640 A in Ninety Six Dist., on
the branches of Twenty three mile creek, waters of Savannah,
adj. Capt. John Hunter, 1784, Henry Hunter...Benjamin Cudworth
(LS), Wit: Thos Gadiden, John F. Schmeds. S. C. Charleston Dist.,
prov. by John Frederick Schmids, 17 Aug 1790, before Jas Bentham,
J. P.

September 25th 1790. James Tribbles stock mark, Smoothe Crop in
the right ear, and under Keel (bit or halfpenny) in the left.

Pp. 164-165: Release for land in deed on page 163, Benjamin Cudworth to John Splatt Cripps...by bond dated 1783,
...Benjamin Cudworth and wife Catharine....

Page 166: William Campbel & Elizabeth Campbel late wife to John
Upinger, appoint Samuel Tines our lawful attorney...
William Campble (M) (LS), Elizabeth Campble (X) (LS), Wit: Arche-
laus Watkins. Prov. by Archelaus Watkins, 27 Aug 1790, John
Marshel, J. P.

Martin Trentham Junior of Lancaster Co., appoint Samuel Tines
attorney...7 Sept 1790. Martin Trentham (LS), Wit: Archelaus
Watkins. Prov. before Andrew Baskin, J. P., 7 Sept 1790.

Page 167: William Terry of Lancaster Co., appoint Samuel **Tines**
attorney...24 Aug 1790. to receive all that part of my Estate
left to me by my father Stephen Terry late of Virginia....
Wit: Archelaus Watkins.
Similar power of attorney to recieve what is due from estate of
his mother (not named) in Virginia. 24 Aug 1790.

Arthur Ingram's Stock mark. A Hole in the Right and the figure
7 or half crop the under side in the left ear.

Page 168: William Terry of Lancaster Co., for ₺ 60 sterling, to
Samuel Tines, sells his part of his father's estate....

Page 169: 10 Feb 1790, Jean Stanley to Adam Fowler Brisbane,
        Gentl., for Ł 35 sterling...lots in Camden...Jean
Stanley (X) (LS), Wit: Zach Cantey, John Reid, James Peirson.
Prov. by John Reid, 2 Aug 1790, before James Kershaw, J. P.

Pp. 170-171: 27 Aug 1786, Joseph Kershaw and John Chesnut, sur-
        viving executors of Ely Kershaw, Decd., to Adam Fow-
ler Brisbane, for Ł 60...lots in Camden...Wit: Joseph Brevard,
William Lang. Prov. 10 June 1790, by Jos. Brevard, before I.
Alexander, J. P.

Pp. 171-172: 2 March 1790, Joseph Kershaw, John Chesnut, William
        Ancrum & Aaron Loocock in S. C., Esq., to Adam
Fowler Brisbane of Camden, for Ł 60...lots in Camden...
wit: Joseph Brevard, William Lang. Prov. by Joseph Brevard, 16
June 1790, before I. Alexander, J. P.

Page 172: S. C., Camden Dist.: Elizabeth Jones of Lancaster Co.,
        by and with the consent and approbation of the worship-
ful Justices of the Court for Lancaster Co., puts herself apprentice to John Reid of Camden, Innkeeper, and wife Sarah, for 8
years...11 July 1788. Elizabeth Jones (B) (LS), John Reid (LS),
Sarah Reid (LS), Wit: J. Alexander, J. P.

Page 173: 20 Dec 1791, Adam Fowler Brisbane of Camden Dist.,
        planter, to Jesse Roper of North Carolina, for s 5...
264 A in Camden Dist., on E side Cataba River and N side Waxhaw
Creek, and formerly occupied by Drury Cook, adj. Robert Crawford,
also 28 A adj. the sd. tract being the place whereon the house
formerly the dwelling of Drury Cook now stands...Adam F. Brisbane
(Seal), Wit: William Watson, Cathbert Coleman. Prov. by Watson
19 May 1792, before Isc. Donnom, J. P.

    24 May 1792, Jesse Roper of Lancaster Co., to George Wrenn,
for Ł 50...part of a grant to sd. Jesse Roper by Adam F. Brisbane
in Dec. 1791, near Hery Ivey...Jesse Roper (Seal), Wit: William
Wren, James Roper.

Page 174: Daniel Brown of Camden, by bond to Daniel Jennings &
        John Wodrop and Josiah Smith, Daniel Desaussure and
Edward Darrell of Charleston in the penal sum of Ł 149 s 8 d 4
...mortgage of negroes. 7 Dec 1790. Daniel Browne (LS), Wit:
Joseph brevard. Prov. 14 Dec 1790 before John Kershaw, J. P.

Page 175: John Marshel of Camden Dist., planter, bound to Samuel
        Boykin in the penal sum of Ł 264 s 10 to be paid 16
April next...mortgage of negroes...14 Apr 1790. Wit: Edward
Rutledge. Prov. 10 Jan 1791, before I. Alexander, y. P.

Page 176: State of S. C., Chesterfield County, John Stroud of
        Co., aforesaid, to Jacob Sheffner of Lancaster Co.,
Miller, for Ł 20...100 A on both sides Big Lynches Creek in both
the counties stated above, adj. John Fonderburk, Peter Crons(?),
Jacob Baker, David Fonderburk, Deall Fonderburk...1 Jan 1791.
John Stroud (X), Wit: John Bibbe, Leonard Kegle (X). Prov. 3
Jan 1791, by John Bibbe, before John Craig, J. P.

Pp. 177-9:1 Jan 178_, Robert Crawford of Camden Dist., to Adam
        Fowler Brisbane of same, for (lease s 10, release Ł
200)...land on N side Waxhaw Creek, formerly occupied by Drury
Cook, 264 A & 28 A...Wit: Jas Brown, James Shaw, Leah Ervin(X).

BOOK B

Prov. by James Brown, 9 Dec 1790, before James Kershaw, J. P.

Pp. 179-181: 21 Feb 1788, William Lang of Camden to James Wilson,
           late of London, but now of Charleston, for Ł 4000
...one moiety of a Plantation on Camden Ferry Road, on Wateree
River, adj. tract formerly belonging to Edward Maloy but now to
sd. Wm Lang, Joseph Kershaw, also 1/2 tract on Wateree River
adj. Joseph Kershaw, William Lang, and lots in Camden, also 1/2
tract adj. John Payne....Wit: John Rhodes. S. C. Charleston
Dist. Prov. by John Rhodes, 26 Feb 1788, before P. Horry, J. P.
Rec. in Charleston Register's Office, Book Y No. 5, page 328, 26
Feb 1788. Peter Horry, Register.

Pp. 181-182: William Lang of Camden, Craven County, bound by bond
           1 March 1785, in the penal sum of Ł 9020...mortgage
of negroes and cattle...Wit: John Rhodes. Prov. in Charleston
Dist., by John Rhodes, before Peter Freneau, J. P., 12 March
1788.

Pp. 182-184: 14 Feb 1785, Dinah Wyly widow and relict of Samuel
           Wyly Gent. of Camden, Decd., William Wyly and Sarah
the wife of William Lang, two surviving children of the sd.
Samuel Wyly decd, and William Lang of Camden, Esq., to Joseph
Bulkley of Dist. of Camden, for (lease s10, release Ł 1)...by
the will of said Samuel Wyly and of the Will of Robert Wyly decd.
one of the sons of the said Samuel as well as by the Death of
John & Samuel Wyly two other sons of sd. Samuel Wyly...two tracts
of land near Camden...Wit: Joseph Kershaw, Joseph Bulkley.
Prov. by Henry Beaumont, 22 Feb 1785, before John Galbraith,
J. P. for Camden Dist.

Pp. 185-186: Plats for above lands

Pp. 187-188: 16 Feb 1785, Joseph Bulkley of Dist. of Camden,
           Gent., to Dinah Wyly & William Lang, both of Camden,
(Lease s 10, release Ł 1)...lots in Camden- Wit: Joseph Kershaw,
H. Beaumont. (plat included) Prov. by H. Beaumont, before John
Galbraith, J. P. 22 Feb 1785.

Pp. 189-193: 16 Feb 1785, William Wyly of Dist. of Camden, plan-
           ter, to Dinah Wyly, William Lang and wife Sarah of
same (lease s5, release Ł   )...103 town lots in Camden, also
400 A in Craven County on Beavern Creek, N side Wateree, adj.
William Johnstons, Edward Simms, James Kennedy & Francis Hodges,
Walter Shropshire, John Bell, Ephraim Clanton, John Hillard,
John Finlay; 300 A on south prong of Lynches Creek in Craven Co.,
adj. John Belton; 200 A in Fredericksburg Township, adj. Wateree
River, George Sanders, Robert Stewards; 100 A on little Lynches
Creek adj. John Marshel...Wit: Joseph Kershaw, H. Beaumont.
Prov. by H. Beaumont, before John Galbriath, J. P., 22 Feb 1785.

Pp. 193-194: 16 Nov 1790, William Lang to John Bold, merchant,
           all that undivided moiety of a plantation of 300 A
granted to James McCormack, adj. Camden Ferry Road, Edward Maloy,
Joseph Kershaw, also 1/2 of 150 A in Camden Dist., granted to
McCormack, adj. Dinah Wily Senr; also 20 A adj. McCormack,
Maloy, John Payne, Joseph Kershaw, also lots in Camden...also 50
A granted to Payne, sold by him to William Scott, and 100 A gran-
ted to James Wilson, adj. land granted to William Barefoot...
Wit: Zach Cantey.

BOOK B

Pp. 194-196: 14 Nov 1790, William Lang of Camden, and wife Sarah,
to John Bold of Charleston, for s 5 sterling, and
also for the purpose of paying unto James Wilson a Debt due by
sd. William Lang...300 A in Camden Dist., granted to James Mc-
Cormack, adj. Camden Ferry Road, Wateree River, Edward Maloy,
Joseph Kershaw, also ½ of plantation of 150 A granted to Edward
Maloy, adj. land granted to Patrick McCormack, Dinah Wyly Senr,
Joseph Kershaw, William Lang; ½ of 20 A granted to Patrick McCormack, adj. Edward Maloy, John Payne, Pinetree Creek, also lots
in Camden, 150 a granted to Samuel Belton, adj. William Payne,
granted to Payne and sold to William Scott, 100 A granted to James
Wilson. Wit: Zach Cantey.

Pp. 197-200: 20 Oct 1790, Claude Jean Baptiste Le Droit DeBussy
of Camden to Angus Bethune of Charleston, merchant,
(lease s5, release £ 422 s 10 d 5)...100 A on Flat Rock, Craven
Co., adj. Martin Fifer, also lots in Camden...Jno Le Droit de
Bussy (LS), Madelaine DeBussy (LS), Wit: John J. Pringle, Robert
Douglass. Prov. by John Julius Pringle, before Richard Champion,
J. P.

Page 200: (January Court 1791) Will of William Dodson on the
waters of Cedar Creek in Lancaster County, Camden
District, I order the payment of all my just debts and calling
to mind that there were other children charged to me (before I
had this wife) whose mothers behaviour and misconduct induces me
to die in the following just sentiment that they William Dodson
Junr. may have and demand one shilling sterling of my Estate Real
and personal and no more, and the like sum to Thomas Dodson and
every other child of their mother that goes or is called by my
name. these my children Samuel Dodson, Ann Dodson, Charles Dodson and Elizabeth Dodson my children by my present loving and af-
fectionate dutiful wife Nancy Dodson otherwise Ren be raised and
schooled of my Estate real & personal...James House and William
Marlow Junr Exrs...17 Dec 1790.   his
                                   William F Dodson
Wit: James Bredin   mark
     Thomas House
     Nancy Hewbart (n)

Page 201: 22 May 1790, William Nealens of the State of Georgia,
planter, to James Sowel of Lancaster Co., SC, for £
25 ...100 A on both sides Lynches Creek, granted to sd. William
Nealens, 5 May 1773...William Neallns (Seal), Wit: Sarah Jones
(X), Lyda Jones (X), James Toland. Prov. 11 Oct 1790 by James
Toland, before Andrew Baskin, J. P.

(The under written alludes to a Mortgage Recorded in this Book
 Page 139)   Recd. 21st of December 1793 of Mr. Benjamin Perry
£ 259 18.6 in full for Principal & Interest due upon the within
bond.   McRa Cantey & Co.

Pp. 202-204: 13 Dec 1785, Jacob Wietner and wife Barbara of St.
Mark's Parish, SC, Craven Co., to Jerom Miller of
Anson Co., N. C., for £ 125 sterling...200 A on both sides of
Great Lynches Cr-ek granted to Jacob Wietner 5 Oct 1763...Jacob
Weidner (LS), Barbra Weidner (X) (LS), Wit: John Weaver, John
Brown, Isaac Weidner. March 3, 1790, prov. by John Weaver before
Benjamine Hale.

BOOK B

Page 204: Evrard House of Claremont County, SC, for ₺ 105 st.,
to John Flecther of Lancaster Co., two negroes Feby and
Jevey...2 April 1789. Evd. House (LS), Wit:James Cowser, Joseph
Singleton.

Page 205: Francis Graham of Lancaster Co., SC, for 12,000 weight
of Tobacco to John Fletcher, one negro wench, Peggy
and child Tom...9 Apr 1791. Francis Graham (LS), Wit: John Graham, John Robinson (X).

Pp. 205-206: Daniel Wade of Lancaster Co., by bond dated 11 Dec
1790 to Daniel Jennings, John Woddrop, Josiah Smith,
Daniel Desaussure and Edward Darell, in the penal sum of ₺ 324
s 9 d 4...mortgage of negroes...Danl Wade (LS), Wit: Duncan McRa,
Zach Cantey.

Pp. 206-208: 14 Nov 1790, Patrick Glaze and wife Nancy of the
Catawba River, (lease s 1, release ₺ 10)...95 A on
NE side Catawba River, grant rec. in Book KKKK, page 451...
Patrick Glaze (LS), Nanny Glaze (X) (LS), Wit: Nathaniel Pender-
grass, Joel Carliles (X). Prov. by Nathaniel Pendergrass, before
Jesse Tilman, J. P. 22 March 1792.

Page 208: Receipt from Madelaine le droit Debussy for mortgage
pd. by Mordecai Lion & Samuel Levy, for lot # 2 in
Camden. I. Alexander, J. P., 24 June 1791. The above receipt
upon a Mortgage recorded in this book Page 77.

For ₺ 20 sterling Margret Donnom to Isaac Dunnam one negro boy
Tom...24 June 1791. Prov. by David Patton, before Samuel C.
Dunlap, J. P.

Margret Donnom for ₺ 20 sterling to Isaac Donnom, negro woman
Bellar...24 June 1791. Same wit.

Margaret Donnom for ₺ 20 sterling to Isaac Donnom a negro woman
Wuna, 24 June 1791. Same wit.

Page 209: Four deeds from Margaret Donnom to Isaac Donnom, 24
June 1791 for negroes Dick, Bess, Will, Sharlotte, all same wit.

Page 210: Margaret Donnom of Lancaster Co., for ₺ 110 to Hugh
White Esqr. of same, negro woman Mary about 23 years
old and child John about 3 years old...30 May 1791.
Margret Donnom (Seal), Wit: Jno Simpson, Andrew Herron.

Pp. 210-211: 21 Feb 1792, James Adams of State of Georgia, plan-
ter, to Nathan Barr of Lancaster Co., SC, Inn Keeper,
for ₺ 100 sterling...two parcels or tracts of land in the Waxhaw
Settlement on Gills Creek originally granted to Richard Cowsard
24 Sept 1754, for 302 A and conveyed to George White, and by
George White and wife Isabella 18 Jan 1762, a part, 100 A, to
James Adams; also 100 A granted to William Baird 8 July 1774,
conveyed to James Adams by L & R 9 & 10 Feb 1779 adj. David Adams,
James Montgomery, Richard Cowsard...Jas. Adams (Seal), Wit:
Robt Dunlap, J. L. C, James Crawford, Elir. Alexander. (plats
included). Bond to Nathan Barr from James Adams, to insure dower
of Mary Adams, wife of James Adams.

Page 212: South Carolina, Lancaster. Samuel Dunlap of said
county, appeared before Robert Dunlap, J. P. and swore

40

that he saw Samuel Thompson a lawful Surveyor run the upper line
of Henry Foster's plantation which struck the River at a black
gum about 86 rods above the upper end of his
5 Oct 1786, before Robert Dunlap, J. P.

17 Dec 1788, William Johnston of Lancaster Co., to John Stover,
of same, for 4,000 weight of inspected Tobacco...
100 A on Beaver Creek whereon the said John Stover now lives...
William Johnston (Seal), Jean Johnston (Seal), Wit: Thomas Bradford, Samuel Bradford (B). Sworn 24 Sept 1791, Thomas Ballard,
J. P.

Page 213: 26 March 1768, David Drennon of South Carolina Craven
County, Farmer, to John Fleming of same, for Ł 10 ster.,
150 A on waters of Cane Creek a branch of Wateree River in the
Waxhaw in Craven County...David Drennon, Wit: Robert Mctyre,
Alexander McMillan, Par. Cheque. S. C. Chester County, prov. by
Robert Mctyre, before John Pratt, J. P. 17 Aug 1793.

Pp. 213-214: 8 Oct 1778, Benjamin Cook of Craven Co., SC, plan-
ter, to William Tilman, Blacksmith of same, for
(Lease s10, release Ł 300)...land granted to John Douglass, 200 A
on both sides Camp Creek, in Parish of St. Mark's, adj. survey of
Abraham Summerford, granted 9 Jan 1755, transferred to William
Mitchel by deed 8 March 1755...Benj. Cook (LS), Wit: John Shew-
bart, Jessee Tilman. Prov. by Jesse Tilman 17 Nov 1778, before
James Simpson, Magistrate.

Pp. 215-216: 7 Oct 1773, Benjamin Cook of St. Marks Parish,
Craven County, SC, planter, to William Tilman of
same, planter, (lease s10, release Ł 200)...land granted 5 Aug
1766, to Abraham Summerford, 150 A, adj. John Douglass...Benj.
Cook (Seal), Wit: John Shewbart, Jesse Tilman. Prov. 7 Nov
1778, before James Simpson, by Jesse Tilman.

Pp. 216-217: 27 June 1782, James House & wife Milley of S. C. to
Jesse Tilman (lease s5, release Ł666 s 13 d 4)...
166 A part of grant to Thomas Singleton 8 Nov 1769, on Camp
Creek adj. James Denton, Jesse Tilman, James Howe...James Houze
Milley Howze (X), Wit: John Shewbart, Robt Lee. Prov. Craven
County, 25 July 1782, by Robert Lee, before Charles Pickett.

Pp. 217-218: 27 Aug 1782, George Plat Junr & wife Sukey of S. C.
to Jesse Tilman of same (lease s5, release Ł 100)
100 A in Craven Co., on N side Cataba adj. Rawle Cornelius,
Thomas Glaze, granted to George Plat Junr 13 Feb 1775...George
Plat (Seal), Susy Plat (X) (Seal), Wit: William Tilman, Charles
King (X). Prov. by William Tilman, 18 Feb 1792, before Robert
Dunlap, J. L. C.

Pp. 218-219: 15 May 1778, William Bishop, planter of S. C., to
James House for (lease s5, release Ł 200)...500 A
on Camp Creek adj. George Plat, John Douglas, Abraham Summerford,
on Catawba River, granted to Thomas Singleton 8 Nov 1769...
William Bishop (Seal), Elizabeth Bishop (Seal), Wit: Wil hanks,
Wm. Thomas, Robert Lee. Craven Co., 25 July 1782, prov. by
Robert Lee, before Charles Pickett, J. P.

Page 220: S. C. Lancaster Co., David Usher & wife Margaret planter to Daniel Hunter of same, Black smith, for Ł 50...
100 A granted 13 May 1766 to John Usher, the above said David

Usher now being heir to said land on the creek of Wild Cat...
7 Jan 1792. David Ushart (O) (Seal), Margaret Ushart (V) (Seal),
Wit: James Craig, John Craig, J. P., John Craig. Prov. by James
Craig, 7 Jan 1792, before John Craign, J. P.

Samuel Boykin for regard to Nathaniel Pace, two tracts of land
250 A on N side Catawba River on Camp Creek known by the name of
Cornelius land...11 Feb 1786. Samuel Boykin (Seal), Wit:
William Boykin, John Yarborough, William Nettles (X). Prov. by
John Yarborough, 17 Nov 1792, before John McKenny, J. P.

Pp. 221-222: 9 Feb 1779, William Baird of Camden Dist., to James
          Adams of same (lease s 10, release Ł 5)...100 A in
Craven Co., on Gills Creek in the Waxsaws Settlement, adj. David
Adams, James Montgomery, Richard Cowsert, granted 8 July 1774...
William Baird (Seal), Wit: Robert Baird, Rebeca Baird, Mary
Baird. Jean Baird, wife of William Beard, relinquished dower
10 Feb 1779. Prov. 15 Apr 1779 before John Gaston by Mary
Baird.

Page 223: Bailey Fleming of Lancaster Co., for natural affection
          to my son in law Solomon Mackey of same, Horses, cows,
sheep, hogs, one feather bed, household furniture...10 Jan 1792.
Bailey Fleming (Seal), Wit: Benedict Best, Fredk. Weaver (X),
William Rogers. Prov. by Benedict Best, before Jesse Tilman, J.
P., 11 Feb 1792.

John Fleming of Lancaster Co., to Solomon Mackey, that tract of
land that he is now living on, adj. Mr. David, on a branch of
Rockey Creek, thence up said branch to a Drain that leads to
William Rogers spring branch, 260 A...10 Feb 1792. John Fleming
(Seal), Wit: Jonathan McKay, Benedict Best, Abner Dunavent.
Prov. before Jesse Tilman, 11 Feb 1792.

Page 224: 26 Jan 1792, Bailey Fleming of Lancaster Co., to John
          Baker, for Ł 31 s 17 sterling...tract whereon the sd.
Baker lives, 371 A on Dry Creek, granted by Gov. Moultrie....
Bailey Fleming (Seal), Wit: William Rogers, John David(d), John
Fleming. Prov. by John Fleming, before Jesse Tilman, J. P. 11
Feb 1792.

Bailey Fleming of Lancaster Co., for natural affection to my son
John Fleming, tract where sd. John now lives on S side Dry branch
part of grant to Joseph Lee 150 A, 1772...26 Jan 1792. Bailey
Fleming (Seal), Wit: William Rogers John David (D), John Baker.
Prov. by John Baker, 11 Feb 1792, before Jesse Tilman, J. P.

Pp. 224-225: George White of Lancaster Co., whereas Henry White
          Senr did by his last Will and Testament did demise
(sic) unto his son Henry White Junr, 227 A on E side Cataba about
a mile above the Waxhaw Creek of which codicil or will not proving
valid and good in law and the said George White by Heirship being
entitled to the possession of said plantation, now, the said
George for and in consideration of the great respect he has for
the will of his Father and natural affection for his brother,
surrendered the said land...16 July 1791. George White (Seal),
Wit: John Simpson, Andrew Linn, Hugh White. Plat included by
John McClenahan, 9 Nov 1790.

Page 225: Mary Ann McCulloch of South Carolina, Late from Ireland,
          bound to Abraham Wright of Craven Co., SC, weaver, for

Ł 200 SC money, dated 4 Feb 1773...Mary Ann McCullock (O), Wit:
John Pickens, John Walker, William Young. Prov. 7 July 1792,
by John Walker, before John Craig, J. P. Signed over to John
Boyd, 2 Feb 1776, Wit: William Baird, Robert Baird. Signed over
to Robert Ramsey Junr, 17 Jan 1778, Wit: Robt Ramsey Senr, James
Ramsey (J). Signed over to Robrt Ramsey Senr, 4 June 1791, Wit:
Hance McEune, John Gillispie, John Ramsey, Signed over to John
Ramsey, 14 June 1792, Wit: Andw Boyd, James Ramsey.

Page 226: Camden Dist., Lancaster Co.: agreement between William
                 Stubs and Eleanor Farrell before marriage, if the said
Eleanor Farrell has any surviving child or children by the sd.
Stubs, her the said Eleanor Farrel her negroes that she is en-
titled to by her own property at this time with their increes
is to decend on his own child or children, if she has no living
child or children her Negroes return back into her one (sic)
Blod Relation again....17 Sept 1789. William Stubbs (X), Wit:
Midn. McDonald, Jesse Tilman. Prov. by Jesse Tillman, before
Jos. Lee, J. P. 8 Sept 1792.

Pp. 226-227: James Houze in consideration of the natural love &
                  affection to my beloved sons Henry Houze, Clabon
Houze, and Isaac Houze, part of my plantation 334 A on the Ca-
tawba River adj. Jesse and Isaac Tilmans land, Camp Creek...
Milla my wife, my other two sons Littleon and Anderson House,
238 A on N side Catawba, also my daughters Penelope Parr, Patty
Houze & Jenny Houze, 6 negroes (named)...8 Nov 1792. James Houze
(Seal), Wit: John Videon, Thomas Howse. Prov. by Thomas Houze,
9 Nov 1792, before Jesse Tilman.

Page 227: 26 Sept 1792, James Avent and wife Jane of Lancaster
                 Co., SC, to Jesse Roper, for Ł 10 sterling...10½ A adj.
Robert Crawford, on the waggon Road being the state line...
James Avent (LS), Gean Avent (X) (LS), Wit: Daniel Carnes, George
Wren, James Roper.

Page 227: Andrew Jackson of the County of Davidson and District
                 of Mers in the Territory of the U. S. A. south of the
River Ohio, appointed James Crawford of Lancaster Co., my true
and lawful attorney, to convey unto Shared Gray by L & R 200 A
in Mecklinburg Co., NC, on the waters of twelve mile Creek...28
Nov 1792. Andrew Jackson. Wit: Abrm. Boyd. Prov. by Abraham
Boyd, 26 Dec 1792, before Jno Simpson, J. L. C. C.

Page 228: Mary Arnold Bender of Lancaster Co., for Ł 58 sterling
                 to James Smith of York Co., one negro woman Slave
Venus near 60 years od age, cattle, sheep, hogs, furniture, etc.
3 May 1792. Mary Arnold Bender (X), Wit: John Simpson, John Mc-
Clenahan. Prov. by John McClenahan, before Hugh White, J. L. C.,
3 May 1792.

Pp. 228-229: Charles Cliffton & James Cliffton of Lancaster Co.,
                  bound to William Barnett and Eliezar Alexander for
Ł 56...7 May 1792, whereas on the 5th inst., William Barnett
Sheriff of Lancaster County did expose to sale property late of
James Denton decd., by virtue of a Fieri facias in favor of the
admrs. of William Farrell Decd., which Charles Cliffton bidd off
at Ł 28 s 7 he being the highest bidder, and the sd. William Barnett also had a writ of fieri facias in favor of John Winn (which
is the property of the said Alexander) against the admrs. of

William Farrell aforesd...a Judgment obtained by Genl. Thomas
Sumter against the admrs. of William Farrell....Charles Cliffton
(Seal), James Cliffton (Seal), Wit: C. Mothershead, Joseph Moore.
Mortgage of Negroes (named), Prov. May 14, 1792, by C. Mothers-
head.

Page 229: John Crocket's mark and brand entered May 7th 1794.
Brand I C on the near buttock: (Mark) a Swallow Fork in each ear

Page 230: 24 Feb 1779, Robert Lee of St. Mark's Parish, SC, to
            John Pendergrass of same, planter, (lease s 10, release
Ł 570)...75 A on Cedar Creek in Craven Co., on Wateree River,
granted recorded in Book YY, folio 535. Robert Lee (Seal), Wit:
William Tilman Senr, William Tilman Junr (X).

Page 231: S. C. Lancaster Co.: John Dunlap planter, appoint my
            Brother Thomas Dunlap, farmer, my attorney, to receive
from John May late of Charleston (who purchased the plantation
from me whereon I now live) merchant, Ł 30 due 2 June 1792...
20 Sept 1792. John Dunlap (Seal), Wit: Eliezar Alexander, Robert
Montgomery. Prove by Eliezar Alexander, before Robt Dunlap,
J. L. C., 7 Jan 1793.

Page 232: Andrew Linn of Craven Co., SC, bound to John Johnston
            in the penal sum of Ł 4000, 13 Feb 1779, to make title
to 130 A, half tract patten'd by Andrew Linn decd, adj. James
Patton, William Linn...Andrew Linn (LS), Wit: Benja. Lowrey, Sarah
Lowrey. James Haggins and Martha Haggins prov. handwriting of
Andrew Linn 18 Feb 1793. before John Simpson, J. L. C. C.

James Cozes of Lancaster Co., to Martin Smith of same, for Ł 50,
one Bay horse and Bay mare, cattle, furtniure, and crop, 29 Aug
1793. James Cuffy(?). Wit: John Belk Senr, Lorn(?) Miller [German
signature]

James Ferguson of Lancaster Co., planter, for love, good will &
affection to my loving sons Richard Hunley and Absalom Hunley of
same, negroes (named)...31 July 1792. James Farguson (Seal), Wit:
James Ferguson, Lydia Bridges. Prov. by James Ferguson, Junr.,
1 Aug 1792, before Ben Haile.

Page 233: 20 May 1791, Jerom Miller & wife Rachel of Chesterfield
            Co., to James McDonald of Lancaster Co., for Ł 200...
land in both the counteys of Lancaster and Chesterfield, on both
sides big Lynches Creek, on Hills Creek, conveyed to said Jerome
Miller by Jacob Witener, granted to sd. Witener 5 Oct 1763...
Jerom Miller (Seal), Rachel Miller (X) (Seal), Wit: James McDonald
Junr., Samuel Witner (X). Prov. by Samuel Witener, 16 March 1792,
before Benjn. Hale, J. P.

Pp. 233-234: William Hamilton of Camden Dist., bound to John In-
            grem of same, in the penal sum of Ł 119 s 15 d 8...
mortgage of horses, cattle, and plantation tools 24 Feb 1791.
William Hamilton (0), Wit: A. Alexander.

Page 235: Benjamin Clifton of Lancaster Co., to Charles Clifton,
            negro Dinah and child Antony a boy, for Ł 60, by last
of Nov next in Tobacco or other property suitable to answer the
discharge of the Executions now against the said Estate that the
said Clifton is concerned to settle...28 July 1791. Benjn. Clifton
(Seal), Wit: John Morton, Abner Dunavents, Thomas Addison.

Pp. 235-236: 22 Nov 1791, James Winn of Fairfield Co., to Jacob
          Shoffnerr of Lancaster Co. (lease s5, release Ƚ
15)...73 A in Dist. of Camden, on waters of Great Lynches Creek,
granted 5 March 1787...J. Winn (LS), Wit: Elir. Alexander, Geo.
Brown. Prov. by Eliezar Alexander, 15 Dec 1791, before Robt.
Montgomery, J. P.

Pp. 236-237: 9 Nov 1782, George White of Camden Dist., Sadler,
          to James Blair of same, yeoman, by grant 4 July
1760, to John Arnold Pender and Henry White 150 A on E side
Cataba, and conveyed to them by lease 5 Feb 1774, now for Ƚ 626
75 A, conveyed to sd. George White from John Kennedy, and 55 A
adj. John Foster, in the whole 130 A, parts of different tracts
...George White (LS), Mary White (LS), Wit: Alexd. Maxfield,
John Blair, Wm. Steel. Prov. by John Blair, 30 May 1786, before Joseph Lee, J.P.

Page 237: 8 July 1790, John Blair and wife Jane of Lancaster Co.,
          to James Blair, farmer, of same, by conveyance 9 Nov
1782, George White and Mary to James Blair deceased, father of
the above James and James (sic, for John?)...John Blair (LS),
Janet Blair (LS), Wit: Wm. Ferrell, Thomas Blair, John Cantzon.
Prov. by John Cantzon, before Joseph Lee, Esqr., 3 July 1790.

Pp. 237-238: 6 Feb 1793, John Caston & wife Milla of Lancaster
          Co., to Charles Knowland of same, for Ƚ 100 sterling,
232½ A on a branch of Little Lynches Creek, part of 465 A,
first laid out for John Caston and then conveyed to Glass Caston,
then conveyed by Glass Caston to sd. John Caston, 5 Dec 1785...
John Caston, Milla Caston (X) (LS), Wit: William Ward, Samuel
Caston, Budd Knowland (X).

Page 238: 6 Feb 1792, Mark Stevens of Lancaster Co., to William
          Stevens of same, 50 A on E side Wateree on both sides
Rockey Creek, part of 300 A granted to William Madocks, 6 Oct
1767, conveyed to Richard Perry by William Madocks by L & R
dated 22 Nov 1786, sold by Richard Perry to Mark Stevens 28 Feb
1791...Mark Stevens (LS), Wit: William Rogers, John David (D),
Jas. Coile.

Page 239: Nathan Tomlinson and wife of Craven Co., Camden Dist.,
          to Lucas Tomlinson of State of Virginia and County of
Greenville (sic), 6 Nov 1786, for Ƚ 100...70 A in Craven Co.,
SC, granted to Stephen White 27 Sept 1754, conveyed to Joseph
McCulloch, 23 Oct 1778, adj. John Timlinson, Stith Fennel, also
80 A, part of 100 A granted to Robert Montgomery 2 Dec 1772,
conveyed to Joseph (sic) 25 Oct 1773, and by sd. McCullcoh granted to John Tomlinson, and conveyed to Nathan Tomlinson, 20 Jan
1783, adj. Stith Fennell, Robert Lockhart, Robert Crawford, Joseph White, Robert Howards estate...Nathan Tomlinson (LS), Rebecca Tomlinson (LS), Wit: W. Goodin, Susannah Tomlinson (X), Feriby
Tomlinson. Prov. by Susanna Tomlinson, 7 Nov 1792, before Isaac
Donnom, J. P.

Pp. 239-240: 7 Nov 1791, John Gillispie and wife Margaret of
          Mecklinburg Co., NC, to John Craig of SC, for two
guineas, 100 A on Camp Creek waters of Catawba adjj. John Craig,
...John Gillispie, Margaret Craig (O), Wit: Thomas Walker,
William Craig, Patrick Develin (W). Prov. by Patrick Develin,
before Isaac Donno, J. P. 19 Feb 1793.

Page 240: 27 Nov 1792, John Drennon of York Co., SC, to John
          Shepherd of Lancaster, for Ƚ 28 sterling, 200 A on

both sides Twelve Mile Creek (The Indian Claim only excepted)
adj. William Porter...Jno Drennan (Seal), Wit: Samuel Bigger,
Henry Foster, John Bigger (I), Prov. by Henry Foster, Junr.,
before Andw Foster, J. P. 16 Feb 1793.

Pp. 240-241: James and Archibald Hood of Lancaster Co., to John
             Hodd, planter, for Ł 60...100 A on Camp Creek waters
of Cane Creek in Craven Co. (now Lancaster), granted to George
Douglas 4 June 1759, transferred by L & R by George Douglas
and wife Mary to William Hood 24 July 1762, which the sd. William Hood by his last Will and Testament did give to James
and Archibald Hood, dated 7 Apr 1783...18 Feb 1793. James Hood
(Seal), Mary Hood (X) (Seal), Archibal Hood (Seal), Catharine
Hood (X).

Pp. 241-242: 28 Feb 1767, John Hudson of Craven Co., Laborer,
              to Moses Dickey of St. Mark's Parish, SC, Wheel-
Wright, by grant 27 Aug 1764, to John Hudson, 100 A above Cane
Creek near the Wateree River adj. Matthew Wilson, now for Ł 88
John Hudson (Seal), Ann Hudson (Seal), Wit: F. Imer, Benjamin
Maddox (B). Prov. by Frederick Imer and Benjamin Maddox, 26
Feb 1767, before John Cantzon.

Pp242-243: 7 May 1790, Moses Dickey of Lancaster Co., Farmer,
           John McDow, farmer, land granted to John Hudson,
27 Aug 1764, and conveyed to Moses Dickey WheelWright, who dying
intestate said land fell by descent to his son Moses Dickey, now
for Ł 37...Moses Dickey (Seal), Wit: Thomas McDow, John Davis,
William Harper. Prov. 8 May 1790, by Thomas McDow, before Jos.
Lee, J. L. C.

Pp. 243-244: 26 Feb 1793, John McDow of Lancaster Co., farmer,
             to Robert McDow, of same, land granted 27 Aug 1764
to John Hudson....John McDow (Seal), Wit: William Harper, Wm.
McDow, Wm. Crawford. Prov. by William McDow who swore that he
saw his Father John McDow, sign and seal the within deed...26
Feb 1793, before Joseph Lee, J. P.

Pp. 244-245: 22 Apr 1777, John Wisenor of Craven Co., planter,
             to Martin Wisenor of same, planter, for s 10...100
A, part of 300 A which has been the property of Jacob Wisenor
decd on a branch of Great Lynches Creek known as Flat Creek, adj.
Henry Wisenor, in the last will and testament of Jacob Wisenor,
he bequeathed 100 A to his son Martin Wisenor and intitled to
him by his oldest Brother John Wisenor and Ruth his wife, granted
8 May 1758...John Wisnor (Seal), Ruth Wisnor (X) (Seal), Wit:
Edward Cannington (X), John Cannington (X), Clemon Gardner (C).
Prov. by John Kennington, before William Welch, J. P., 6 Apr 1782.

Pp. 246-247: 9 March 1786, Joseph Ferguson & wife Catharine of
             Lancaster Co., planter, to John Baker of same, plan-
ter for Ł 100...part of 300 A which has been the property of
Jacob Wisener decd, adj. John Wisenor, Henry Wisener...Joseph
Ferguson (Seal), Caty Ferguson (Seal), Wit: Richmond Terrell,
Gale Frizzle (G). Prov. 16 Aug 1788, by Richmond Terrell, before
Andrew Baskin, J. P.

Page 247: Frederick Weaver of Lancaster Co., for natural affec-
          tion to son Rolley Weaver of same, three feather beds
and furniture, 5 head of cattle, one bay horse and one Filley
mare...22 Apr 1793. Frederick Weaver (F) (Seal), Wit: William
Isom (X), P. Burford, John Weaver. Prov. by William Isom of Dry
Creek, 30 Apr 1793, before Josh. Lee, J. P.

Page 248: Richard Wood of Lancaster Co., for Ł 140 to Benjamin
          Perry, four negroes (named) 25 Jan. (no year).
Richard Wood, Wit: John Caulkins. Prov. in Fairfield Co., by
Mr. John Caulkins, 17 June 1793, before G. W. Yongue, J. P.

Pp. 248-249: 14 Aug 1784, John Williams Silver Smith to William
          Ward, Wheel Wright, for s5...land on waters of Lit-
tle Lynches Creek, 150 A adj. sd. Williams, Barnet Johnston,
William Laughlin, Wylie, granted to Daniel Williams 23 Jan 1773
and said Williams is the proper heir at law...John Williams
(Seal), Wit: James Blackman, Edwd Williams, Abraham Estridge(X).
S. C. Camden Dist., prov. by James Blackman, before Fredk.
Kimball, J. P. 4 Feb 1785.

Pp. 249-250: 13 Apr 1789, John Williams of Lancaster Co., to
          William Ward of same Wheel Wright, for Ł 50, land
now the property of John Williams, being part of both tracts
one of which is known by the name of the old survey 250 A, granted to Daniel Williams 6 March 1759...John Williams (Seal), Wit:
James Blackman, John Hill (I), Aquilla Hill (1). Prov. 11 Feb
1792 before John Craig, J. P., by James Blackman.

Page 250: 23 Apr 1791, Isom Shierling of Lancaster Co., to Wil-
          liam Ward, part of tract which the said John Williams
deceased by virtue of a grand under Gov. Littleton, 19 Sept
1758, for Ł 20 which said Isom Shurlen bought at the vendue
of John Williams decd on little Lynches Creek...Isom Shirling
(Seal), Sarah Shierling (X) (Seal), Wit: James Blackman, Obadiah
Williams, William Adams. Prov. 11 Feb 1792, by James Blackmon,
before John Craig.

Page 251: 18 July 1793, James, Robert, John & Hugh Montgomery,
          and John Kirk and their wives, planters, of Lancaster
Co., to Jonathan Mackey of same, sadlar, for Ł 30 sterling, 200
A grn. 2 Oct 1767, granted to Thomas Campbell and transferred
to Hugh Montgomery and bequeathed by said Hugh Montgomery unto
the above names James Robert John & Hugh and John Kirk....
(wives did not sign). Wit: Wm. Barkley, David Crenshaw, James
Taylor. Recept wt. by John Kneely (-).

Pp. 251-252: 15 Apr 1793, Isom Shurlen and wife Sarah of Lancas-
          ter to John Caster of same, land bought at the
vendue of John Williams deceased bested in fee simple in the
lifetime of Daniel Williams deceased, granted 19 Sept 1758
adj. Isom Shirlen, William Ward....Isom Shurliens (Seal), Sarah
Shierling (Seal), Wit: William Ward, William Archcraft (X),
Elizabeth Ward (X).

Pp. 252-253: 9 Apr 1791, Jesse Hays and William Ward Exrs. of
          the last will and testament of John Williams decd.,
of Lancaster Co., to Isom Shierling, whereas the lands herein
after mentioned and intended to be hereby bargained & sold were
in the lifetime and at the time of the death of Daniel Williams
(Father of the said John Williams deceased) vested in fee simple
to Daniel Williams deceased, by grant 19 Sept 1758, and the sd.
John Williams being the eldest son and heir at law...by his last
will and testament dated 14 Jan 1791 did direct that all his
estate be sold and divided into six shares in the manner following one share to his brother Edward Williams, one share to his
sister Eleanor Williams, one share to his sister Phebe Williams,
and the remaining three shares to his son Obadiah Williams, now

for Ł 54...250 A...Jesse Hays (Seal), William Ward (Seal), Wit:
Jacob Gray, James Blackman, John Marshel. Prov. by James Blackman, 11 Feb 1792, by John Craig, J. P.

Pp. 253-254: 1 Apr 1792, George Vickory of Lancaster Co., to
            William Harper Senr of same, by grant 17 Feb 1767
to John Belk Senr, 250 A on Bear creek a branch of Cane Creek,
and sd. John Belk Senr did transfer to William Montgomery, 125
A, and sd. William Montgomery did sell to Joseph Gell Mothershead
100 A and the sd. Mothershade to William Harper Senr, now
for Ł 70...George Vickory (O) (LS), Wit: John Kirk, James Wilson,
Joseph Graves. Prov. by James Wilson, 9 May 1793, before John
Craig, J. P.

Pp. 254-255: 1 June 1792, John Dunlap and wife Elizabeth of
            Lancaster Co., to John May of same, merchant, land
granted 11 Feb 1762, to William Gamble, 150 A, and sd. Gamble
did grant to Samuel McClellan, and sd. McClellan and wife Jane
to John Dunlap, 150 A on E side Wateree on Cane Creek, now for
Ł 85...John Dunlap (Seal), Elisabeth Dunlap (Seal), Wit: Elir.
Alexander, John Marshal. Prov. by Eliezar Alexander, before
Jo. Lee, J. P. 21 July 1792.

Pp. 255-256: S. C. Lancaster County: Daniel Ushart & wife Marga-
            ret to David Ushart of same, for Ł 13 sterling, land
on W side Cataba River on Little Fishing Creek in Craven Co.,
SC, 100 A granted to Alexander Camble, 13 May 1768, and by sd.
Campbell for Ł 13 to Daniel Usher 23 Sept 1784...27 Dec 1792.
Daniel Usher (Seal), Margaret Usher (O), Wit: John Craig, J. P.,
William Craig, John Hall (+). Prov. 27 Dec 1792 by John Craig.
Prov. by Abraham Adams, 1 Jan 1794, before John Craig, J. P.
S. C. Lancaster County, David Usher personally appeared...sworn
that a certain deed of 100 A on the waters of Cane creek, adj.
Hugh Montgomerys line was made over to David Usher Junr by George
Campble and that the above mentioned deed was lost, 1 Jan 1794.
David Usher (O), John Craig, J. P.

Page 256: 7 Nov 1793, John Fleming of SC, Richland Co., to
          William Woods of Lancaster Co., for Ł 60 sterling, 150
A granted to Philip Walker 16 Jan 1765 in the Waxhaw Settlement,
vacant on all sides. John Fleming (Seal), Wit: Harrison Hunt,
Anne M Fleming, Ninen Montgomery (X). Prov. by Ninen Montgomery
Junr, 24 Dec 1793, before Robt. Montgomery, J. P.

Page 257: 13 May 1793, Robert Crawford and wife Jane of Lancaster
          Co., to Robert Hancock of same, for Ł 140 sterling,
376 A granted to Samuel Burnet, 200 A, part of sd. grant, adj.
Moses White, Joseph White...Robert Crawford (Seal), Jean Crawford
(Seal), Wit: William Crawford, William Wrenn.

Charles Miller Senr of York Co., for love, good will & affection
to my daughter Pricilla Miller, two tracts on waters of twelve
mile Creek in two separate surveys in Lancaster Co., , 109 A;
send adj. land granted to Robert McKlehenny and is now in possession of William Porter, conveyed from Francis Bassett to Charles Miller Senr, 162 A (only the Catawba Indian claim excepted)
...5 Jan 1793. Charles Miller (Seal), Wit: Lewis Kirk, Jesse
Miller, Robert Ivey (X).

Pp. 257-258: 7 Jan 1793, Priscilla Miller of York Co., to James
            Clifton of Lancaster Co., for Ł 100...land on waters
of twelve mile creek, two separate surveys...Priscilla Miller

BOOK B

Lewis Kirk, Jesse Miller, Rober Ivery (X), wit.

Page 258: 27 July 1792, Nathaniel Tomlinson, sells to Isaac Anderson, both of Lancaster Co., 170 A between the Waxhaw Creek and Twelve Mile Creek, being the plantation Edward
Ivey now lives on...Nathaniel Tomlinson (X), Wit: Geo. Anderson,
John Anderson,Arthur Collier.

Pp. 258-259: John Craig Junr of Lancaster Co., planter, to James
Craig of same, for ₤ 23...75 A on both sides Camp
Creek, in the Waxhaw Settlement, part of 418 A granted to James
Larimore, by Matthew Rowan, Gov. of N. C., 17 May 1754, sold to
Andrew Pickens, then to William Davis, then to Roger Smith, then
to James and John Craig, then John Craig sold to James Craig his
half...John Craig (Seal), Mary Craig (O) (Seal), Wit: John Gillispie, Robert White. Prov. by Robert White, planter, 20 Dec
1793, before Robert Montgomery, J. P.

Page 259: S. C., Lancaster Co.: 8 March 1794, William Isom, yeo-
man, to Abraham Deason, for ₤ 30...William Isom & wife
Margaret, 1200 A...William Isom (X), Margaret Isom (X), Wit:
Benjamin Deason, Little John Belk, Samuel Deason (X). Prov. by
Samuel Deason, before James McDonald, J. P., 14 March 1794.

Page 260: 28 Jan 1794, Daniel Clark of Lancaster Co., planter,
to William Isom of same, planter, for ₤ 25...200 A
on Wild waters of Great Lynches Creek...Daniel Clark (Seal),
Caty Clark (X) (Seal), Wit: Benjamin Deason, Elijah Clark (X),
John Chester ( ). Prov. by Elijah Clark, 14 March 1794, before
James Mcdonald, J. P.

Pp. 260-261: 13 Aug 1793, John Shepherd, planter, of Lancaster
Co., to Titus Laney of same, for ₤ 7 s 17 d 1,
139 A, part of grant to James Larrymore by Gov. Arthur Dobbs of
N. C., but now in the South State, which land the sd. Larrimore
gave William Davis a power of attorney, and sold to Hugh Coffee,
and the said Hugh Coffee deceased made over said land to his
son John Coffee, and said Coffee sold sd. land to Henry Coffee
and him to James Haggins, and Haggins to Thomas Wells, and Wells
to John Shepherd, adj. John Hood, Grace Taylor...John Shepherd
(J) (Seal), Wit: Danl Clark Junr., John Laney. Prov. by John
Laney (X), before James McDonald, J. P. 14 March 1794.

Page 261: Ack in open Court 19 Feb 1794. 22 Feb 1790, John
Simpson, Shff of Lancaster Co., to Middleton McDonald,
whereas James Denton deceased was at the time of his death pos-
sssed of a plantation of 300 A on E side Catawba granted to George
Platt, adn sd. James Denton was at his death indebted to Col.
William Farrell...by a writ of fieri facias, 28 July 1789, now
for ₤ 97...Wit: Robert Dunlap, Hugh White.

Page 262: William Barnet late of N. C., to Joseph Douglass of
Lancaster Co., two feather beds with furniture, two
fauling axes, a Broad ax and hand ditto, etc., 14 Aug 1793.
Wm Barnett (LS), Wit: Thos Barnett, Thomas Douglass, David Morrow.
Prov. by David Morrow, 17 Feb 1794, before Jesse Tilman, J. P.

William Barnet late of N. C. for ₤ 34 s 10 to Joseph Duglass,
sale of horses, (Same wit.) Prov. 17 Feb 1794, by David Morrow.

Page 262: 25 March 1794, James Ferguson Senr of Lancaster Co.,
to James Ferguson Junr of same, for Ł 10 sterling...
200 A on head branches of Turkey Creek, granted to Joseph Ferguson...James Ferguson (Seal), Wit: Wm. Denman, Joseph Haile,
Wam Baker (X). Ack before Ben Haile, J. P. 9 March 1794.

Page 263: S. C., Lancaster Co.: William Scarborough of Lancaster
Co., to John Scarborough, for Ł 35 sterling...horse 16
years old 13½ hands high, branded S, bay mare 14 years old 13½
hands high, branded S, and other cattle, swine, furniture, etc.
21 Sept 1793. William Scaborough. Wit: Thomas Kirkley, George
Kirkley. Ack. before Ben Haile, J. P., 20 Sept 1793.

8 March 1794, William Isom, yeoman, to Abraham Deason, for Ł 30
sterling...land on waters of Wild Cat...William Isom (X) (Seal),
Margaret Isom (X) (Seal), Wit: Benjamin Deason, Littleton Belk,
Samuel Deason (X). Prov. by Samuel Deason, before James McDonald,
J. P. 14 March 1794.

Page 264: William Graham of Lancaster Co., by note of hand dated
1 Nov 1792, for Ł 86 sterling, 150 A where I now live
on Turkey Quarter Creek, also cattle, sheep, hogs, furniture,
etc...30 Nov 1793. Wm. Graham (Seal), Robert Ker, John May, William Barr. Prov. by Robert Kerr, 14 Dec 1793, before Jos. Lee,
J. P.

Robertson Carpenter of Kershaw Co., SC bound in penal sum of Ł
100 sterling to John Graves, planter, of Lancaster Co., for title
to half of tract on both sides of a branch of Bear Creek, known
as dry branch, 293 A, part of which sd. Graves now lives on...
7 Nov 1793. Robert Robinson (Seal), Wit: John Hagins, John Petti-
grew. Prov. by John Hagins, 31 Dec 1793, before Jos. Lee, J. P.

Page 265: 21 Aug 1793, General Thomas Sumter of Claremont County,
SC, to Gale Frizzle of Lancaster Co., for s 10 sterling,
200 A on Buffaloe Creek...Thos Sumter Junr for T Sumter (Seal),
Wit: Samuel Tynes, Saml Kelly. Ack. in Lancaster Co., 21 Aug
1793, before Ben. Haile, J. P.

26 Feb 1794, Littleton Raines, of Lancaster Co., to James Doug-
lass, for Ł 12 sterling, land on Rum Creek and run for Andrew
Shaver, ½ of 150 A...Littleton Raines(X) (Seal), Wit: Henry
Shaver, Francis Mothershed, Benjn. Maddox (B). Prov. before
Joseph Lee, J. P., by Benjamin Maddox, 22 Aug 1794.

Page 266: 14 March 1794, Thomas Smith of North Carolina, planter,
to Matthew Kirk of S. C., Lancaster Co., planter, by
a granted dated 12 Sept 1768, to sd. Thomas Smith 350 A on E side
Little Lynches creek on both sides Grogey branch, vacant on all
sides, now for Ł 20...Thomas Smith (X) (Seal), Wit: James Wilson,
Samuel Smith. Prov. 2 Aug 1794, before John Craig, J. P., by
James Wilson.

Waxhaw May 12th 1794, recd. of James Cowser Ł 90 sterling for 3
negro boys Harrison, Bob and Thompson, which negroes said Cowser
is to return to Mr. John May on his the said May paying the Ł 90
sterling in gold or silver before 1 Nov this ensuing...John May,
Wit: Robert Ker. Prov. by Robert Ker, 5 July 1794, before Robert Dunlap, J. L. C.

Page 267: Wade Hampton, of Camden Dist., by virtue of a Writ of
Fieri Facias from the Court of Common Pleas to levy of
goods and chattles, etc. of William Sims Senior and Thomas Murphey
Ł 350 sterling which Powel Hopton and Company, otherwise called
Samuel Brailsford and Company lately recovered against sd. Sims
and Murphey...sold negroes to George Hays for Ł 40 s 10...13 May
1784. Wade Hampton Sheff C. D. (Seal), Wit: Geo Barnes.

John Ingrem of Lancaster Co., have sold negro Boy Dick to George
Hays, 3 June 1794. Wit: Sarah Ingrem. S. C. Lancaster County:
Prov. before Stewart Dickey J. P. for Georgetown Dist., by Sarah
Ingrem, 3 June 1794.

William Steel planter on waters of Cedar Creek in Lancaster Co.,
to Samuel Dunlap Esqr. Senr and William Johnston planters in sd.
county, all estate real and personal excepting one mare known as
Bess, for value received...10 Dec 1792. William Steel (LS), Wit:
Saml Lewers, W. Morrison, Robert Bell. Prov. by W. Morrison,
before Saml C Dunlap, J. P. 28 Jan 1793.

Benjamin Cudworth of Lancaster Co., SC, bound to James Craig,
Sheriff, for Ł 400 sterling, 10 July 1788, to indemnify the sd.
James Craigg for Sheriffs deed to sd. Benjamin Cudworth, for
200 A the property of David Adams Junr, on Bair Creek a branch of
Cane Creek survey to Thomas Wright 7 Nov 1756...Benjamin Ducworth
for James Steedman (Seal), Wit: Nathan Barr, Jno Simpson...July
1794.

Page 268: Frederick Kimball of Lancaster Co., bound to James Craig
Junr for Ł 100 sterling 22 Dec 1788, from 3 Aug 1786
indemnify sd. Craig for sheriffs deed to above Frederick Kimball,
100 A on both sides of Cedar Creek adj. William Johnston, Adam
Thompson, Widow Summerville, originally granted to Isaiah Thompson,
by him sold to William Maze. Fredk. Kimball (Seal), Wit: John
Craig, William Craig. Provd. in Court July 1794.

Page 269: 7 Sept 1793, Charles Miller & wife Margaret of S. C.,
Lancaster Co., to Guy Wallace, for Ł 50 sterling, land
on N side of muddy branch, adj. Nathan Tomlinson...Charles Miller
(Seal), Margaret Miller (LS), Wit: George Wren, William Miller.

18 Nov 1794, Jacob Shofner of Lancaster Co., to Michal Costly of
Anson Co., N. C., for 60 Silver Dollars...1173 A in
several tracts all joining together...Jacob Shofner (Seal), Wit:
James Holliman, John Wiles. Prov. by James Holliman, before
James McDonald, 29 Nov 1794.

Page 270: William Massey of Lancaster Co., for love, good will and
affection, to James Massey my eldest son of same co.,
130 A on S side Waxhaw Creek...5 Nov 1790. William Massey (Seal),
Wit: Henry Massey, Daniel McDonald, William Massey Junr.

26 March 1793, Edward Narramore of Camden Dist., to Jacob McDonald, of Chesterfield County, SC, for Ł 50 sterling, 100 A adj.
Wideners line, E side Big Lynches Creek, within a few steps of
Stokes Amonds Mill seat so called to the lower line of 250 A
patent Thomas McManum decd being the patentee, including all the
improvements on the E side of Big Lynches Creek and also in the
fork between said creek and Wild cat...Edward Narramore (E), Wit:
John Weaver, David Meyers. Prov. by John Weaver, before James
McDonald, 27 March 1793.

7 Jan 1793, Priscilla Miller of York County, to James Clifton of
        Lancaster Co., for Ł 100 sterling...land on waters of
Twelve Mile Creek in two separate surveys, in Lancaster co., one
granted for the use of Robert McElhany and now is in the possession of William Porter; the other 190 A, excepting only the Catawba Indians claim on the N side of the twelve mile creek...Priscil-
la Miller (Seal), Wit: Lewis Kirk, Robert Ivey (X), Jesse Miller.

Page 271: Charles Miller Senr of York Co., for love, good will &
          affection to daughter Priscilla Miller of same county,
land on twelve Mile Creek in two separate surveys...109 A on Mill-
stone branch; grant to Robert McIlhany now in possession of William Porter, conveyed from Francis Basset to Charles Miller Sr.,
162 A on both sides twelve mile creek (except Catawba Indians
claim)...5 Jan 1793. Charles Miller (Seal), Wit: Lewis Kirk,
Robert Ivey (X), Jesse Miller.

17 Nov 1792, James Adams of Green County, Georgia, to William Al-
len, of Lancaster Co., by grant 1774, rec. in Auditor Genls. of-
fice 25 March 1775, to James Adams as was then St. Marks Parish,
SC, 100 A on E side Cane Creek, adj. James Gamble, John White, for
Ł 20 sterling...James Adams (Seal), Wit: John Barkley (O), John
B. Davis. Prov. by John Barkley Senr, before Robt Dunlap, J. L.
C, 12 May 1793.

Pp. 271-272: William Steel planter on the waters of Cedar Creek
             Lancaster Co., to Samuel Dunlap Esqr. Senr. and Wil-
liam Johnson, planters, all estate real and personal, except
one mare Bess, 10 Dec 1793. Wit: Saml Lewers, W. Morrison, Volet
Bell.   Before Saml C. Dunlap, Wm. Morrison.

Page 272: 13 Jan 1795, Jonathan Mackey and Margaret Morris his
          mother of Chester County, SC to Thomas Mackey of sd.
State and Lancaster Co., for Ł 40 sterling...later Jonathan McKee
100 A on Camp Creek adj. Henry Clark, granted to John Mackey,
1768, memorial hereof entered in Audr. office Book H N. 8, page
466, 6 July 1768...Jonathan Mackey (X), Margaret Morris (X) (Seal),
Wit: Samuel Telford, Benjamin Morris, Margret Telford. Prov. in
Chester County, by Benjamin Morris Junr. before John McCreary, J.
P., 14 Jan. 1795.

Page 273: Alexander Douglass of Lancaster Co., SC, for Ł 60 ster-
          ling, to John McMaster of same, planter, one sorrel
mare branded with a heart, and other cattle (marks and brands
given), and swine, furniture...17 Nov 1795. Alexander Douglass
(Seal), Wit: James Cowser. Prov. by James Cowser in Kershaw County, 1 Dec 1795, before Thos Creighton, J. P.

Page 274: Mary Ingram to W. Ingram. (remainder of page blank).

Page 275: 20 Dec 1774, Alexander Carnes and wife Rebekah of St.
          Mark's Parish, Craven Co., to Dennis Titus of same, by
grant 2 June 1769 to sd. Alexander Carnes, 117 A in the Waxhaws,
on waters of Catawba River, adj. John Cantzon, Thomas McIlhaney,
Rev. William Richardson, Charles Burnet, now for Ł 207 current
money...N. B. As Thomas McInhany pretends a claim to about 13
acres of the above mentioned tract, the sd. Carnes and wife will
not defend said 13 acres. Alexander Carnes (Seal), Rebekah Carns
(X) (Seal), Wit: Geo Dunlap, Archibald Davies, John McDowel (X).
Prov. Craven County, Camden Dist., 21 Dec 1774 by Archibald Davie,
before James Simpson, J. P.

BOOK B

Pp. 275-276: 15 Sept 1779, Dennis Titus and wife Mary of Camden
Dist., to Samuel Dunlap Junr. of same, by grant 2
June 1769 to Alexander Cairns...(same land in preceding deed), for
₤ 8500...Dennis Titus, Mary Titus (N), Wit: Cornelius Anderson,
Thomas Dunlap, Jno Miller. Prov. in Lancaster Co., by Thomas
Dunlap, before Robert Dunlap, 5 Jan 1791.

Page 276: 27 March 1789, Samuel Dunlap Junr, farmer, and wife
Lidday, of Lancaster Co., to William Farrell, of same
Bricklayer, by grant 2 June 1769 to Alexander Cairns...(same land
as preceding), for ₤ 80 sterling...Samuel Dunlap, Lydda Dunlap
(X), Wit: Abrm Livingston, Robt Thompson, John Davis. Prov. 5
Jan 1791, Abrm Livingston, before Robt Dunlap, J. P.

Page 277: 17 Feb 1767, Benjamin Maddox of Craven Co., SC, Laborer,
to John Cantzon of same, Practitioner of Physic, by
grant dated 30 Nov 1762, to Benjamin Maddox, 100 A on Camp Creek
in the Waxhaw Settlement, adj. Stephen Gamble, Hugh McKrin, sd.
Maddox, for ₤ 180...Benjamin Maddox (B) (Seal), Rosemond Maddox
(Seal), Wit: F. Imer, Moses Dickey. Prov. before John Gaston,
by Frederick Imer, 23 Sept 1767.

Pp. 277-278: 23 Jan 1792, Moses Cantzon and Sarah Harper, Heirs
of State of S. C., Lancaster Co., to Robert Dunlap,
planter of same, by grant 3 Nov 1762, to Benjamin Maddox, 100 A
on Camp Creek, and conveyed 17 Feb 1767, to John Cantzon, now by
Moses Cantzon and Sarah Harper, for ₤ 44 sterling...Moses Cantzon
(Seal), Sarah Harper, Wit: Samuel Findly, William Farrel, Thomas
Dunlap. Prov. by William Ferral, 16 Apr 1793, before Jo Lee, JP.

Page 278: 23 Jan 1792, Moses Cantzon and Sarah Harper, Heirs of
Lancaster Co., SC, to Robert Dunlap of same, by grant
28 Aug 1767 to John Cantzon, 60 A in the County of Lancaster, adj.
land formerly Benjamin Maddox, Charles Burnet...Same sign & wit.
Prov. by William Farrel, 16 Apr 1793, before Joseph Lee, J. P.

Pp. 278-279: 24 Nov 1789, Samuel Graham, late from the Kingdom of
Ireland, planter, & William Caston of Lancaster Co.,
for ₤ 42 sterling, 640 A in Lancaster Co., on each side of the
great road to Charleston on a branch called Turkey Quarter part
of Cane Creek on E side Catawba when surveyed vacant on all sides
granted 5 Dec 1785, rec. Book GGG page.185...William Caston (Seal),
Wit: William Graham, Joseph Caston, Seth Caston. Prov. by William
Graham, 10 March 1790, before Jos. Lee, J. L. C. (Land was conveyed from William Caston to Samuel Graham.)

Page 279: 16 Nov 1791, Edward Sims of Edgefield County, SC, Wheelwright to Alexander C. Carruth of Lancaster Co., planter,
for ₤ 50...land on NE side Catawba River on Beaver Creek, 100 A
granted to Elisabeth Gougher on the bounty 21 Jan 1769, adj. Roger
Pinckney & William Johnston, Jeremiah Joiner, James Kennedy...
Edward Sims (Seal), Jane Sims (X) (Seal), Wit: Robert Henry, William McMans, Crenshaw Duke. Prov. by Crenshaw Duke, 5 July 1793,
before Jesse Tilman, J. P.

12 Feb 1789, Charles Miller of Lancaster Co., to John Hagins, for
₤ 5 sterling...100 A on the waters of Waxhaw creek in Lancaster
Co., adj. James and Allen Hood, William Massey, James Barnet, by
virtue of a bargain and sale made by Charles Miller and wife Margaret to sd. John Hagins...Charles Miller, Margaret Miller (Ɨ),
Wit: Moses White, William Miller. Acknowledg & Recorded.

53

Pp. 279-280: 26 Sept 1792, Jesse Roper & wife Biddy of Lancaster
         Co., to James Avent of same, for Ł 10 sterling, 10½
A on the waggon Road adj. sd. Roper and Avent...Jesse Roper, Bid-
dy Roper (X) (Seal),Wit: Daniel Cairns, George Wrenn, James Roper.
Proved in Court. (no date).

Page 280: 27 July 1792, Nathaniel Tomlinson to Isaac Anderson,
         both of Lancaster Co., 170 A between the Waxhaw Creek
and Twelve Mile Creek, the plantation Edward Ivey now lives on...
(stricken and written "This is entered in Page 258).

21 Aug 1793, Charles Miller and wife Margaret of Lancaster Co.,
To Nathan Tomlinson, for Ł 50 sterling...100 A adj. Robert Craw-
ford, Charles Miller, part of 600 A granted to Griffith Rutherford,
on E side of Twelve Mile Creek...Charles Miller (LS), Margaret
Miller (X) (LS), Wit: Robt Hancock, Guy Wallace, Wm. Miller.
Acknowledged.

Acknowledged Jan. 28th, 1795. 10 Dec 1794, Andrew Boyd and Andrew Foster of Lancaster Co., Executors of the last will and Testament of William Barnett decd., to Adam Heathe of same, for Ł
120 sterling...land on N side Catawba River 162 A on the waggon
road, adj. Andrew Boyd, William Davis, James Cureton...Andw Boyd
Andw Foster, Wit: James Cureton, Jesse Heath, Nancy Heathe (X).

Page 281: 26 Feb 1793, Henry Cato & wife Tabitha, planter, of
         Lancaster Co., to Vinson Cato of same, for Ł 40 ster-
ling...100 A on waters of Little Lynches Creek, part of 250 A
granted to Thomas Cooper, 10 Apr 1771, conveyed from sd. Thomas
Cooper, 18 June 1776, to Thomas Laremore, by Laremore to James
Ezel, 9 Feb 1779; conveyed from sd. Ezell to John Love 20 Feb
1779; by sd. Love to Henry Cato 10 Jan 1788; when first laid out,
adj. to Reuben Peables, John Gray, Jesse Morton...Henry Cato (Seal)
Tabitha Cato (T) (Seal), Wit: Samuel Caston, Charles Robinson,
Needham Cato. Prov. by Charles Robinson, 17 Apr 1794, before B.
Haile, J. P.

Pp. 281-282: 1 Feb 1775, Felix Kennedy & wife Agness of Craven
         Co., SC, to John Davies of same, by release 7 Jan
1775, from John Kennedy by virtue of which the aforesd. Felix
Kennedy and Agness his wife conveyed to John Davies 108 A, a tract
granted to sd. Felix Kennedy, and conveyed to JohnKennedy; for
Ł 55...Felix Kennedy (O), Agness Kennedy (Y), Wit: John Kennedy,
David Carnes.   Prov. by John Kennedy, before John Gaston, J. P.,
8 Oct 1779.

Page 282: 10 Feb 1790, Rush Hudson of Lancaster Co., to Reuben
         Roberts of same, for Ł 30...land on N side Beaver Creek,
a branch of Wateree River 43 A, part of 100 A laid out to John
Caben part of which the sd. Roberts now lives on, adj. land laid
out to Lewis Clark being now the property of James Carruth...
Rush Hudson (X) (Seal), Wit: Alexander C.Carruth, Wm. Hudson,
James Carruth. Prov. by Alexander C Carruth, 28 Jan 1794, before
Wm. Kirkland, J. P.

Pp. 283-284: James Bredin of Lancaster Co., Deputy Surveyor, to
         Jacob Plyler, planter, of same, for Ł 30 sterling...
290 A on branches of Wild Cat Creek adj. James Craig, Widow Rush,
Amos Richie, granted to James Bredin 2 June 1788...Jas Breden
(Seal), Wit: William McBride, John Miller (X). Prov. 28 Jan 1795,
by William McBride, before John Craig, J. P.

BOOK B

Page 284: 16 Aug 1793, John Fleming of Lancaster Co., to Dennis
Cain of same, for Ł 30 sterling, 100 A on waters of Dry
Creek, part of 600 A granted to John Fleming adj. John David, on
a conditional line between John Fleming and Solomon Mackey ...
John Fleming (Seal), Wit: John Baker, George Marler, Jas Coile.

S. C. Lancaster Co., David Usher of co. aforesd., planter, for
love, good will and affection to his son David Usher of same, all
goods and chattels now being in my dwelling house and my land,
300 A where I now live, all my cattle, hogs, house and furniture,
money and debts...16 May 1794. David Usher (O), Wit: William
Galloway, Hugh Montgomery, Ninon Montgomery. Prov. 28 March 1795
by Hugh Montgomery, before John Craig, J. P.

Pp. 284-285: 28 March 1795, John McAterr of Lancaster Co., planter,
to David Usher for Ł 10 sterling...land 380 A granted
to sd. John McTeer, 4 Nov 1793 on Wild Cat Creek and Gills Creek
adj. Robert Kirk, William Galloway, Edmund Hull, William Harper,
Frederick Carnes, James McCammon, Ringing Montgomery...John Mc-
Ateir (O), Wit: John Craig, Elizabeth Craig (O), William Craig.
Prov. 28 March 1795, by Elizabeth Craig, before John Craig, J. P.
28 March 1795.

Page 285: William Massey of Lancaster Co., to Richmond Terrell of
same, for Ł 70 sterling...negro boy Grippa, 31 Oct 1794.
William Massey, Wit: John Kennington (X). Prov. before Thomas
Welsh, by John Kenningston, 27 Feb 1795.

27 Nov 1794, Jesse Roper to Moses Heath both of Lancaster Co., for
Ł 60, land on both sides of the Waggon Road on N side Waxhaw Creek
and mostly in the above named county, the remainder in Mecklinburg
Co., NC, adj. James Avent, John Pair, Widow Cowsart, Robert Ivey,
and sd. Roper it being part of the tract he now lives on, granted
to him by Adam Fowler Brisbane, 1791, 150 A...Jesse Roper (Seal),
Wit: Heny Massey, Rhos Threwer, Arthur Collier. Prov. by
Henry Massey, J. P., 27 March 1795.

Pp. 285-286: (Provd Jan. Court 1795) 6 Jan 1795, James Elliot of
Lancaster Co., to William Tomlinson, for Ł 32 ster,
land on S side 12 mile Creek, 110 A granted by Andrew McCorkle to
Thomas Elliot, 1781, and by sd. Thomas Elliot decd left to said
James Elliott adj. Robert Crocket...James Elliot (Seal), Wit:
Arthur Collier, Andw Linn, Daniel Connell.

Page 286: 9 Oct 1794, Joseph White and Henry Massey of Lancaster
Co., to Thomas Thower of same, for Ł 28 sterling, land
on N side Waxhaw Creek adj. Moses White, Robert Lockhart...Joseph
White (Seal), Henry Massey (Seal), Wit: James Massey, William
Massey. Prov. by James Massey, 1 May 1795, before Isaac Donnom,
J. P.

Pp. 286-287: 17 Sept 1788, Gen. New River Col. Ears and the other
head men of the Catawba Nation in York Co., SC, to
James Greer of Mecklenburg Co., NC, by grant to our Nation of
15 miles Square, lease of 320 A on Climes branch on Steel Creek
road adj. Mr. Miller   Genl New River's mark
Wit: Charles Miller   Col. John Carr's mark
     Thomas Spratt   Major John Browne's mark
     Andw Foster   Peter George his mark
I assign my right of this 99 year lease to John Kelliah and Robert
Vernor, 17 Oct 1790, James Greer (LS), Wit: James West, Agness

Culp (X). Prov. by James West before Andrew Foster, J. P., 25
July 1795.

Page 287: John Shepherd in Lancaster Co., yeoman, to John McMurray
    couper, of same, for Ł 21 sterling,139 A on waters of Camp Creek
adj. John Hood, Grace Taylor, granted from NC to James Larramore,
26 March 1755, by power of attorney to William Davis did sell to
Hugh Coffee decd, which Hugh Coffee made over to his son John, and
John to Henry Coffee, and Henry Coffee to James Haggins and James
Haggins to Thomas Wailes, and by Wailes to sd. John Shepherd...
1 Jan 1795. John Shepherd (J) (Seal), Wit: James Craig, Hugh
Coffey. Prov. 12 Sept 1795, by James Craig, before John Craig,
J. P.

Page 288: 17 March 1795, George Platt & wife Ann of Kershaw Co.,
    yeoman, to James Trantham of same, yeoman, for Ł 75
sterling...100 A in an Island of the Catawba River known as Moun-
tain Island, and also little Island adj. McDonnol, Massey...George
Platt (Seal), Ann Platt (X) (Seal), Wit: David Graham, David
Carwell(X). S. C. Kershaw County: Prov. by David Carwell, 8
Aug 1795, before Francis Boykin, J. P.

15 Nov 1793, John Barkley Senr. of Lancaster Co., to William Barkley of same, for Ł 480 sterling...five parcles of land in all 1000
A on Bear and Gills Creeks, in the Waxhaw Settlement, on part
thereof the sd. John Barkley Sern now lives...Jno Barkley (B) (LS),
Wit: Robt Ker, Saml Graham, William Graham. Prov. by William Gra=
ham, 1 Feb 1794, before Robert Dunlap, J. L. C.

Page 289: Blank.

Page 290: Daniel Finn of Parish of St. Marks, SC, planter, for
    love, good will and affection to Elizabeth Gowen, widow
of John Gowen decd.,of same...14 Nov 1784. Daniel Finn (D), Wit:
Saml Dunlap, J. P., Elizabeth Dunlap. Prov. 28 Nov 1795 before
Saml Dunlap, before Samuel C. Dunlap, J. P.

S. C., 19 Aug 1795, Thomas Sumter Esqr. of Claremont County, to
Titus Lany of Lancaster Co., for Ł 7 10/8 sterling...land on S
side Big Lynchs Creek 113 A, part of 15,000 A granted to sd.
Thomas Sumer Esqr. 2 April 1787...Thos Sumter (LS), Wit: Saml
Tynes, John Horan. Prov. by Samuel Tnes 8 Sept 1795, before
John Welsh, J. P. (Plat included in deed) by Richard Bettis,
D. C.

Page 291: Blank.

Page 292: S. C., 6 Dec 1785, William Jones and wife Rebekah of
    Orangeburgh District, to William Adams of Camden Dist.,
for Ł 55 s 5 sterling...350 A the upper part of sd. tract on Camp
Creek in the Waxhaw Settlement adj. James Boyd, James Wilson...
William Jones (W) (Seal), Rebekah Jones (R) (Seal), Wit: John
Kirk, William Montgomery, John Montgomery.

Page 293: Alexander Douglas to James Douglass, for Ł 49 sterling,
negro wench Kate and her child Doll...13 Nov 1796. Alexander
Douglass. Wit: James Houston, William Barton. Prov. by William
Barton, 13 Nov 1795, before Elir. Alexander.

1795, 3 Dec., Revd. Bryce Miller to William Grimes, both of Lancaster Co., for Ł 200...3000 A on waters of Gills Creek, also 2

plats on waters of Camp Creek 672 A, also 600 A in N. C., 940 A of the Catawba claim on waters of Sugar Creek, 1000 A on waters of Turkey Quarter, adj. James Hall; also 337 A, 200 A on said waters, 200 A on waters of Bever Creek, also 200 A on waters of Bear Creek, adj. James Walker, also 4000 A formerly the property of Joseph Singleton...Bryce Miller (LS), Wit: John Anderson, Thomas Miller. Prov. by John Anderson, 27 Feb 1796, before Wm. Barkley, J. P.

Page 294: 10 July 1790, John McCrory of N. C. to William Montgomery of Lancaster Co., for Ł 3 sterling...100 A in Lancaster Co., between Camp and Gills Creeks, branches of Wateree River in the Waxhaw Settlement adj. Richard and John Cowsart, Thomas McCrory, John Gillispie...John McCrory (LS), Wit: Archd. Cowsart, Mary Cowsart, John Cowsart. Prov. by Archibald Cowsart, before _____, 11 Oct 1790.

Joseph Montgomery of Georgia, Hancock Co., (Hatter), for Ł 50 to William Montgomery of Lancaster Co., planter, 82 A on both sides camp Creek in the waxhaw settlement, adj. Alexander Montgomery, part of 302 A granted to John Linn by Gov. of NC, 17 May 1754, conveyed to Hugh Montgomery by lease 10 Jan 1755, and bequeathed to sd. Joseph Montgomery...22 Jan 1796. Joseph Montgomery (LS), Wit: John B. Davies, Saml Dunlap. Prov. by both wit. before Nathan Barr, J. P., 29 Jan 1796.

Pp. 294-295: 25 Apr 1794, Minor Winn of Fairfield Co., Esqr., to Ann Ingrem of Lancaster Co., widow and Extx of L. W. & T. of Alexander Ingrem decd., whereas the sd. Minor Winn in the lifetime of sd. Alexander Ingrem had promised for a consideration to make titles to sd. Alexander Ingrem of 440 A on head branches of Hanging Rock Creek adj. Elleby, Thomas Wade, James Gaston, and the sd. Alexander Ingrem by his L. W. & T. dated 2 Nov 1791 did authorize his Extx Ann Ingrem to make payment and receive titles and that the same with all his other lands should be equally divided among his children (except 115 A which he willed to his wife and mother during their lives)... M. Winn (LS), Wit: Midn. McDonald. E. Alexander. Prov. by Eliazer Alexander before John Simpson, J. L. C., 13 Aug 1796.

Pp. 295-296: James Young and wife Jean of Mecklinburgh Co., NC, & Robert Young of York Co., SC, for Ł 46 s 13 d 4 sterling, land on both sides of a branch than runs into cane creek, 112 A in the Waxhaw Settlement, part of grant to Robert McCorkle by NC 5 July 1753, 224 A, by the last will and testament of sd. RobertMcCorkle made by deed to Thomas Moore, 57 A of sd. tract, and Thomas Moor sold to Thomas Ambros, and by sd. Ambrose to Philip Walker, and by Philip Walker to Joseph Barnet, the remainder by sd. Thomas Moore to Joseph Barnet, and the exrs. of the L. W. & T. of Joseph Barnet, viz John Walker and Matthew Patton sold to William Young, 1/2 of sd. tract, the sd. William Young sold to John Stephenson, the remainder viz 112 A the sd. James and Robert Young are the true owners of sd., land, and for sd. consideration to James Hughey...30 Dec 1795. James Young (LS), Robert Young (LS), Jean Young (X) (LS), Wit: Tunis Shaffer, Ezekiel Black, Thos Walker. Prov. 21 Jan 1796, by Thomas Walker, before John Craig, J. P.

Pp. 296-298: 3 Apr 1777, John Wisnor of Craven Co., planter, and wife Ruth, to Jacob Wisnor of same, planter, by a grant 8 May 1758 to Jacob Wisnor decd., 300 A on a branch of Great Lynches Creek called Flat Creek and sd. Jacob Wisenor at his

death bequeathed unto his son Jacob Wisenor 100 A to be leased &
released by his son John Wisnor to Jacob Wisnor, adj. John Canning-
ton, Charles Spencer, now for Ł 10...John Wisnor (LS), Ruth Wisnor
(H) (LS), Wit: Edward Cannington (X), John Cannington (X), Clemen
Guardner (X). Prov. by John Kennington, before Benjamin Haile, J.
O., 1 Dec 1789.

Pp. 298-299: 19 March 1788, Jacob Wisenor of Lancaster Co., to
          William Denman, for Ł 71 s 8 d 4...land on a branch
of Great Lynches Creek,called Flat Creek adj. John Baker, John
Cannington, Catey Bridges, granted to sd. Jacob Wisenor, and
bequeathed to his son Jacob Wisenor...Jacob Wisnor (LS), Wit: William Bridges, Ferguson Hale (X), Daniel Shehorn. Prov. by William
Bridges, 21 Dec 1789, before B. Hale, J. P.

Page 299: 17 June 1788, Jacob Patton of Lancaster Co., Blacksmith,
          to Thomas Blair, by grant 1 May 1786 58 A on N side Ca-
tawba River on S side Waxhaw Creek adj. sd. river and creek,
for Ł 25...Jacob Patton (Seal), Wit: Daniel Harper, Sarah Harper,
Wm. Simpson. Prov. by William Simpson, 9 Sept 1794, before Robert
Dunlap, J. L. C.

Pp. 299-300: 3 Apr 1794, Thomas Blair, farmer, of Lancaster Co.,
          for Ł 8 to John Latta, 58 A on N side Catawba
granted to Jacob Patton...Thos Blair (Seal), Wit: John Davis,
John Foster, Margaret Blair. Prov. by John Davis, 9 Sept 1794,
before Robert Dunlap, J. P.

Page 300: 23 Dec 1793, Charles Knowland of Lancaster Co., to John
          Caston for Ł 100 sterling...233 A part of grant to John
Caston, 5 Dec 1785, 465 A, then part of sd. tract conveyed from
John Caston to Charles Nowland adj. Indian branch, William Wylie,
William Tate...Charles Knowland (X) (Seal), Wit: James Blackman,
Philip Ward. Prov. by James Blackman, Thomas Welch, J. P., 28
Feb 1795.

Pp. 300-301: 23 July 1795, John Caston and wife Milla of Lancaster
          Co., to William Ward, for Ł 100 sterling...land
granted to John Caston 5 Dec 1785, 465 A...John Caston Junr (Seal),
Millea Caston (X) (Seal), Wit: Saml Caston, William Caston, Seth
Caston. Prov. by Saml Caston, before James Ingrem, J. P., 23
July 1795.

Page 301: Henry Cato and wife Tabitah of Lancaster co., for Ł 5
          to William Horton of same, 150 A on Little Lynches Creek
the uppermost part of grant to Thomas Cooper 10 Apr 1776, adj.
William Blackman, John Blackman, conveyed from sd. Cooper to
Thomas Larramore 18 June 1776, conveyed from sd. Larramare to
James Ezell 6 Feb 1779, conveyed from Ezell to John Love 20 Feb
1779, from Love to Henry Cato 15 Jan 1788, now to William Horton,
26 Jan 1796. Henry Cato (Seal), Tabitha Cato (X) (Seal), Wit:
James Deason, Henry Horton (X), Sterling Horton. Prov. 26 Jan
1796 by James Deason, before Thomas Welsh, J. P.

Page 302: S. C. Lancaster Co., 21 Sept 1795, Henry Peebles, plan-
          ter, of Georgia, to Richmond Terrell, planter of Lancas-
ter Co., 200 A granted to Henry Peebles, granted 1786, on S side
flat Creek adj. Edward Cannington...H. Peebles (Seal), Wit: William Terrell, Edward Kannington, Jesse Peebles. Prov. by Edward
Cannington, 10 March 1796, before Benjn. Haile, J. P.

Page 302: 4 Oct 1771, Peter Arrant of St. Davids Parish, Craven
Co., to Thomas Faile Senr of same, for Ł 350...116 A,
part of tract surveyed to Capt. James McManus 466 A at the mouth
of Neelands branch, Lynches Creek, German signature(Seal), Wit:
Conrod Arrant, John Cartledge. Prov. by Conrod Arrant, 4 Oct
1771, before Thomas Wade.

Page 303: 20 May 1774, Thomas Faile planter in St. Davids Parish,
to Lewis Faile of St. Marks Parish, for Ł 350...land
granted by letters patent in N. C. to James McManus late of St.
Davids Parish decd, and conveyed by Thomas McManus heir of James
McManus to Peter Arrant, by deed 20 May 1771, conveyed by Peter
Arrant to Thomas Faile, 116 A...Thos Faile (LS), Wit: Benjn.
Martin, Wm. Narramore (X), William Faile. Prov. 23 May 1774, by
William Nattamore, before Tho: Charlton.

Pp. 303-304: 8 July 1795, Francis Bettis of Lancaster Co., to
Abraham Hagler of same, for Ł 50...208 A in Chester-
field Co., on the Reedy fork a prong of Fork Creek, adj. sd.
Bettis, John Blackburn, 5000 A granted to sd. Bettis 1 March 1790
Francis Bettis (LS), Wit: John Ferguson, Leonard Kegle(X), Richard
Bettis. Prov. by Leonard Kegle, 10 Sept 1795, before John Welsh,
J. P.

Page 304: 9 March 1795, Jacob Shofner & wife Elizabeth of Lancaster Co., to David Funderburk of same, for Ł 87 s 12...
land in Lancaster and Chesterfield County on both sides Great Lynches Creek 100 A adj. Peter Arrans, Devault Funderburks, John
Funderburk, Gustavus Rape, David Funderburk, where he now lives,
Jacob Shofner (Seal), Elizabeth Shofner (Seal), Prov. 10 Apr
1795, before John Craig, J. P.

Page 304: 20 May 1771, Thomas McManus of St. David's Parish, SC,
planter, to Peter Arrand of same, for Ł 350 SC currency,
116 A, part of tract surveyed for Capt. James McManus 466 A at
the mouth of Nealands branch, Lynches Creek...Thomas McManus
(Seal), Wit: Peter Beller, John Mulcaster. Prov. by Peter Beller,
3 Oct 1771, before Thomas Wade, J. P.

Page 305: 4 Oct 1792, Benjamin Hale of Lancaster Co., to William
Covey, land on head of Wisenors branch adj. Denmans lo-
wer corner, John Fermor...Benjn Hale (Seal), Wit: Benjn Hale Junr,
Hugh Blakeney. Prov. by Benjamin Hale Junr, before Benj Hale, J.
P., 16 March 1793.

10 Apr 1795, Benjamin Harper of Lancaster Co., to John Bibbe of same,
for Ł 130 Va. money...land on both sides Wild cat a branch of
Great Lynches Creek...Benjamin Harper (P) (Seal), Wit: Elir Alexander, Jas. Holliman. Prov. by Elir Alexander, before John Craig,
J. P., 10 Apr 1795

Page 306: 13 Dec 1794, Hugh McManus of Chesterfield Co., to Joseph
Hough of State of Ga., county of Washington, for Ł 200
...land where James McDonald now lives part of a tract surveyed by
Jacob Wisenor containing 200 A included in a 500 A tract laid out
for James McManus decd. lying on both sides Great Lynches Creek...
Hugh McManus, Wit: John Hough, J. Holliman. Prov. by John Hough,
before James McDonald.

Page 306: 13 Dec 1794, James McDonald of Lancaster Co., planter
to Joseph Hough of Washington Co., Ga., for £ 5...land
adj. John Welsh, Genl Sumpter, McManus, part of 15,000 A survey
of Genl. Sumter...James McDonald (Seal), Wit: John Hough, Hugh
McManus, J. Holliman. Prov. by John Hough, 11 Feb 1796, before
John Welsh, J. P.

Peter Andrews of Lancaster co., planter, to Samuel Caston, one
filley branded C, one sorrel yearling colt, seven head of black
cattle, two feather beds & furniture, for £ 10 s 7 sterling...19
June 1795. Peter Andrews (Seal), Wit: John Caston, Hugh Manor (X).
Prov. by John Caston Junr., before James Ingrem, J. P., 27 July
1795.

Pp. 306-307: S. C., Lancaster Co., 16 July 1795, Charles Mackey
Senr. and his wife of co. afsd., to John Best, of
same, for £ 40 sterling...300 A with the present crop and plantation tools, adj. John Caston Senr, Knowles Giles, which land Charles Mackey purchased of Glass Caston, part of two surveys granted to Knowles Giles and Charles Mackey...Charles Mackey (C)
Wit: Wm. T. Linton, Jacob Vickory, Mark Robinson. Prov. by Wm.
Thomas Linton, 21 July 1795, before James Ingrem, J. P.

Page 307: Charles Mackey of Lancaster Co., for £ 10 to John Best,
3 feather beds and furniture, parcel of pewter, one
weaving loom, etc., 21 head of geese, one chest and table...16
July 1795. Same sign. & wit.

Charles Mackey to John Best for £ 17 sterling, hogs, etc...16
July 1795. Same sign and wit.

Page 308: 18 Sept 1792, Mary Magdalen Free and Jacob Free Exx. &
Exor. of the Estate of Jacob Rree decd. both of Orange-
burgh District, SC, to Amos Hough of Anson Co., NC, for £ 20...
land in the county of Chesterfield, on a branch of Big Lynches
Creek granted 19 March 1773, 100 A...Mary Magdalen Free (111)
(Seal), Jacob Free (Seal), Wit: John Hough, James McDonald, Abra-
ham Hough (X). S. C. Chesterfield Co.: Prov. by John Hough before
Richard Bettis, J. P., 12 Aug. 1794.

2 Dec 1795, Joseph Haile of Lancaster co., planter, to Amos Hough
of same, for £ 85...land on Flat Creek, 100 A, part of 200 A
granted to Mary Gibson, transferred by L & R to Thomas Wade 14
May 1760, and by Wade to John Bratton, by Bratton to Coonrod
Aaron (Arrant), by sd. Coonrod Aaron to his son William Aaron,
from sd. William Aaron to William Deason, by sd. Deason to sd.
Joseph Haile...Joseph Haile (Seal), Elizabeth Hale (X) (Seal),
Wit: William Denman, Wm. Ferguson, Edwd Narramore. Prov. by Wm.
Ferguson, before John Welsh, 10 March 1796.

12 Feb 1793, Peter Arrant of State of Georgia, planter, to Amos
Hough of Anson Co., NC, farmer, for £60 sterling...100 A on Flat
Creek, part of 200 A granted to John Bratton by Lease and Release
...Peter Arrant (Seal), Wit: James McDonald, John Hough, John
Baker (X). Prov. by John Hough, before James McDonald, J. P.,
28 Dec 1794.

13 Dec 1794, James McDonald Esqr. & wife Sarah of Lancaster Co.,
to Joseph Hough of Washington Co., Ga., planter, for £ 200 ster.,
land on both sides Great Lynches Creek in Chesterfield Co., Hills
Creek...whereon sd. James McDonald now lives, purchased from Jerry

BOOK B

Miller, granted to Jacob Weidner 5 Oct 1763...James McDonald
(Seal), Sarah McDonald (Seal), Wit: John Hough, James Holliman,
Hugh McManus. Prov. by John Hough, before Jno Welsh, 11 Feb 1796.

Pp. 308-309: 21 Dec 1791, John Voile of   District, SC, to
          Bennet Highfield of Lancaster co., planter, by grant
12 Oct 1770 to Frederick Rush, 100 A on waters of great Lynches
Creek, conveyed to Abraham Rush...John Voile (V) (Seal), Wit:
Jacob Shoffner, Susanna Hunter (X). Prov. by Jacob Shoffner, 29
Aug 1794, before John Craig, J. P.

Page 309: 20 Nov 1795, Abraham Deason of Lancaster co., planter,
          to William Meyers of Chesterfield Co., planter, for Ŀ
20 sterling, land in Lancaster co., on S side Wild Cat Creek...
Abraham Deason (Seal), Wit: James Holliman, Nicholas Welsh (X).
Prov. by James Holliman, 9 Dec 1795, before John Welsh, J. P.

S. C. Lancaster Co.: 3 Sept 1795, Genl Thomas Sumter to Robert
Garner, planter, for Ŀ 40 currency...300 A part of grant to
Thomas Sumter 2 Apr 1787 on Faulkenberrys Mill creek, a branch
of Flat Creek adj. Francis Bettis, Thomas Sumter Junr, John
Gardner...Thos Sumter (Seal), Wit: John Sumter, John Gardner.
Prov. by John Garner, before B. Haile, 21 Jan 1797

Page 310: 17 Apr 1797, James Bredin & wife Mary near the mouth
          of Cedar Creek on the Catawba River in Lancaster Co.,
to George Hayes of the Catawba River, same co., for Ŀ 32 s 10 ster.,
100 A on the springs and drains of Cedar Creek, Tyres branch, adj.
Hayes, part of grant to James Bredin 5 Dec 1785...James Bredin
Mary Bredin (X). Wit: James Douglas, George Parkerson, Robert
Douglass. Prov. 17 Apr 1797, by Geo Parkerson, before Jesse
Tilman, JP (Plat included)

Page 311: 30 Jan 1797, Robert Crawford of Lancaster Co., to James
          Crawford Junr of same, for $800...250 A on Moses Heath's
line, Robert Crawford...deed made to Robert Crawford by Andrew
Pickens...Robt Crawford (Seal), Jane Crawford (O) (Seal), Wit:
John Cowser, Robert Crawford, John Crawford. Ack. by Major
Robert Crawford, before Samuel C. Dunlap, J. P., 29 March 1797.

1 Sept 1785, Genl. New River Col. Ears and Major Brown of the
Catawba Nation, on behalf of the head men and young warriors of
their nation, to William Potts of Mecklenburg Co., NC, for Ŀ 44
NC money...land on Six mile creek, adj. John Kings fishing road...
Wit: Andrew Foster, Charles Miller, Thomas Sprott, Nath. Irwin.
Prov'd in Court on a Trial. Potts vs Keilah and Vernor.

Page 312: Samuel Mathis of Camden attorney at law for Ŀ 40 pd.
          by Thomas Mabry of Lancaster Co., planter, land granted
to Catharine Powel or Powers 100 A, said to contain 115 A by resurvey on the head of Dry Creek adj. Bailey Fleming...18 Oct 1796
Samuel Mathis (Seal), Wit: Hugh Fairfield, Thomas H Miller. Prov.
by T. H. Miller, 18 Oct 1796, before Is. Dubose, J. K. C.

Pp. 312-313: 5 Dec 1795, David Ushart of Lancaster Co., planter,
          to James McTier of same, for Ŀ 60 st., 100 A granted
to Mary Campble 2 Oct 1767 in Waxhaw Settlement in Lancaster Co.,
adj. Joseph Barnet, Robert McDaniel, Joseph Walker, Alexander Nisbet, Joseph Greer...David Ushart (O) Wit: Thomas Hart, James
Craig. Prov. 25 Apr 1796, by Thomas Hart before John Craig,
J. P.

Page 313: James Strain of the Waxhaws, SC, Lancaster Co., bound
        to Joseph Strain of same, for ₺ 100 to be pd. 1 Nov 1790,
to make titles to 116 A part of the old tract of land he bought
of John Adams...Wit: James Haggins, Saml Haggins. Prov. by
Samuel Hagins, 27 June 1797, before Elir Alexander, C. L. C.

Pp. 313-314: 5 Dec 1795, Thomas Warr & wife Agness of Lancaster
        Co., to Thomas Lant Hall and William Dowdy of same,
for ₺ 50 s 1 sterling...land on waters of twelve mile creek, 132
A...Thomas Ware (X) (Seal), Agness Ware (X) (Seal), Wit: Wike
Ivey, Robert Ivey, Richard Woodroof.Prov. by Wike Ivey and Robert
Ivey, before Henry Massey, J. P., 4 June 1796.

Pp. 314-315: 6 Sept 1794, Joseph Caston of Lancaster Co., to
        William Nutt Junr. of Kershaw Co., for ₺ 100 sterling,
land granted to Joseph Caston, 640 A, 6 Feb 1786, on the waggon
road from Camden to Rockey River adj. Enoch Anderson...Joseph
Caston (Seal), Wit: Walter Carruth, John Nixon Senr, William
Nixon. Prov. by Walter Carruth, 5 May 1796, before Thos Ballard,
J. P.

Page 315: S. C. Kershaw Co., I have this day given to my daughter
        Elizabeth and their heirs of her body, one likely young
negro boy named London...4 May 1796. William Nutt (Seal), Wit:
Walter Carruth, Wm. R. Carruth. Prov. in Kershaw Co., by Walter
Carruth, 5 May 1796, before Thos Ballard.

Thomas Sumter of Clarement Co., to Stephen Cordle, 280 A in Lancaster Co., comprehending the Mill Quarry of Rocks near the
meeting house adj. Gale Frizzle, on Buffaloe creek a branch of
Lynches Creek, part of 5000 A granted to Thomas Sumter 2 Apr
1787...Thos Sumter (Seal), Wit: Richard Haynsworth, John Freeman.
Prov. by John Freeman, 15 March 1797 before Benj. Haile.

Pp. 315-316: 10 March 1797, John Freeman to Abraham Deason of
        Lancaster Co., for ₺ 12...100 A part of 5000 A gran-
ted to Thomas Sumter 2 Apr 1787, adj. James Ferguson, Mr. Hailes,
John Kannington...John Freeman (⊕), Wit: Richmond Terrel, John
Farrow (X). Prov. by John Farrow, before Benjamin Haile, 15 Mar
1797.

Page 316: Gibbes Lam of Lancaster Co., to John Murfey, one negro
        woman Jenny, three head of horses, cattle, sheep, corn,
household furniture ...1 Aug 1796. Gibbes Lam (X) (Seal), Wit:
Robert McKain, William Nutt. Prov. by both wit. before William
Ward, J. P. 5 Dec 1796.

Page 317: Blank.

Page 318: Thomas Wells, blacksmith, and wife Jean of Lancaster
        Co., to Berry King of Kershaw Co., for $209, 139 A,
part of grant to James Larramore by Arthur Dobbs Gov. of N. C.,
then in Anson County Camp Creek a branch of Catawba River, now in
Lancaster Co., granted 26 March 1755, conveyed by Larramore by
power attorney to Hugh Coffey, then falling to John Coffey, by
said John Coffey to Henry Coffey, then to James Hagins, then to
Thomas Wells, adj. John Hood, Grace Taylor...Thomas Wells (Seal),
JAne Wells (O) (Seal), Wit: Letel j. Belk, John Coffey. Prov.
10 Sept 1796 by John Coffey. Deed dated 31 May 1796.

Page 318: 28 Dec 1797, William Steel and wife Martha of Cedar
          Creek, Lancaster Co., to Nathaniel Pendergrass of Cedar
Creek, for Ⱡ 10 sterling...100 A on a drain of Cedar Creek and
both sides of a Road from Camden to Wades Ferry adj. George King,
Carlisle, William Dodson....William Steel (Seal), Martha Steel
(X) (Seal), Wit: Jas Bredin, John Pendergrass. Prov. by John
Pendergrass, 20 Jan 1798, before Jesse Tilman, J. P.

Page 319: 2 Feb 1795, Bailey Fleming of Lancaster Co., to William
          Bailey of same, for Ⱡ 30 sterling....100 A, part of 654
A granted to sd. Bailey Fleming 5 March 1792 on Rocky Creek adj.
Benedict Best....Bailey Felming (Seal), Wit: Benedict Best, John
Baker, Solomon Mackey (X). Prov. by Benedict Best, 26 Apr 1795,
before Robt Bratney, J. P.

Pp.319-320: 5 & 6 Jan 1783, Patrick Glaze of the Catawba River
            in Camden Dist., planter, & wife Ann, to Aaron Pres-
cot of same, blacksmith, (lease s5, release Ⱡ 500)...land on
bear branch, 150 A adj. Daniel McDonald, Andrew McKinney, Glass
Caston...Patrick Glaze (Seal), Ann Glaze (X) (Seal), Wit: Arthur
Hicklin, John J. Hicklin, James Bredin. Prov. by James Bredin,
before George Wade, J. P. 10 Dec. 1789.

Page 320: 17 July 1792, Jesse Hays and William Ward, Exrs. of the
          L. W. & T. of John Williams decd, to Phebe Williams of
Lancaster Co., whereas the lands herein after mentioned & intended
to be hereby conveyed granted to Daniel Williams and at his death
became vested in John Williams eldest son& heir at law of sd.
Daniel Williams, by John Williams' will dated 14 Jan 1791 did
order that his whole estate be sold at 12 months credit and be
divided in six shares to be given to his son Obadiah Williams, one
to brtoher Obadiah Williams, one to his sister Eleanor Williams,
one to his sister Phebe Williams...sd. Phebe Williams was highest
bidder...land on little lynhces creek including the house & improvement wherein the sd. Daniel Williams & John Williams decd. used to
live, 100 A & adj. 50 A...Jesse Hays (Seal), William Ward (Seal)
Wit: Elir Alexander, John Love. Prov. by Eliezar Alexander, before
James Ingrem, J. P., 2 Apr 1796.

Pp. 320-321: 20 Feb 1796, Phebe Williams to John Love...for Ⱡ 60
             sterling, 100 A granted to Daniel Williams (land in
preceding deed), granted 25 Apr 1765...Phebe Williams (X) (LS),
Wit: Levy Strickland, Henry Love, Enoch Anderson. Prov. by John
Love, before James Ingrem, 6 March 1797.

Page 321: 20 Feb 1796, Phebe Williams of Lancaster Co., to John
          Love, for Ⱡ 30 sterling, 50 A granted to Daniel Williams
...Phebe Williams (X) (Same wit as above). Prov. 6 March 1797.

Page 322: 27 Feb 1797, William Ingrem of Lancaster Co., to John
          Love of same, for Ⱡ 20...150 A part of 591 A granted
to William Ingrem Captain, by William Moultrie, Gov. of S. C....
William Ingrem (LS), Wit: Samuel Hilton, Willm Blewer, Keziah Hays
(X). Prov. by Samuel Helton, before Jas Ingrem, J. P.

27 Feb 1797, Samuel Hammond of Kershaw Co., to John Love of Lancas-
ter Co., for Ⱡ 30 sterling...300 A on E. of JOhn Loves, adj. Jordan
Ashley, William Brewer, William Caot...Saml Hammon (X), Wit: Danl
Monaghon, James Haise (X), Keziah Haise (X). Prov. by Keziah
Haze, before James Ingrem, 6 March 1797.

Pp. 322-323: 2 Feb 1793, William Doby & wife Mary of Lancaster Co.,
     to John Brown, Minister of the Gospel, of same, land
granted 31 Aug 1753 by Gov. Matthew Rowan of N. C., to William
Moore, on both sides Cane Creek, 514 A, in the Waxhaw Settlement
conveyed by deed to John Lockhart, and by said Lockhart in 1778
to John Doby of Lancaster Co., at his deceased by will to above
mentioned to William Doby, now for Ł 150...Wm. Doby (LS),Mary
doby (LS), Wit: Moses Stephenson, John Stephenson, Robert Kirkpatrick. Prov. by Moses Stevenson, 2 Feby 1793, before Jos. Lee,
J. P.

Page 324: Blank.

Page 325: Daniel Shehorn planter of Lancaster Co., to Frederic
     Kern, for $10...land on a branch of Wild Cat a branch
of Lynches Creek adj. Gen Sumter, Jacob Ployler, Paul Ployler,
150 A granted to sd. Shehonr, 4 Nov 1793...Daniel Shehorn & wife
Hannah, 11 March 1796. Danl Shehonr (Seal), Wit: Jacob Pluiler,
Henry Cay.

John Gambles Stock mark entered 27 Aug 1799. A smoothe crop off
each ear with a slit in the right formerly held by his father William but now resigned in his son John's favor.

20 Dec 1797, James Holliman of Lancaster Co., to Fredk. Kern of
same, for 30 silver dollars, land on head branches of Wild Cat
Creek, part of 15,000 A granted to Thomas Sumter 2 Apr 1787, adj.
Jacob Shafner, John Bibbey, Rush, Danl Hunter, 60 A...James
Holliman (Seal), Wit: Thos Pulley,John Welsh. Prov. by John
Welsh, J. P.

Page 326: 4 Oct 1792, Benjn. Hale of Lancaster Co., to John Farmer,
     for Ł 5...land at the head of a drain that runs through
the Flat Rock, adj. Denman...Ben. Haile (Seal), Wit: Benjamin
Haile, Junr. Hugh Blakeney. Prov. by Benjn Haile Junr, 16 March
1793, before Benjn Haile, J. P.

31 Jan 1798, John Welsh Esqr. of Lancaster Co., to John Farmer,
for Ł 5 sterling....land on Flat Creek between the double branches
and the Jumping Gully, part of land that John Welsh purchased of
Genl Sumter, adj. Mrs. Cowhorn...Wit: Charles McManus, Robert
Welsh (X). Prov. by Charles McManus, 5 March 1798, before
John Welsh.

Page 327: 3 Sept 1793, Benjn Haile of Lancaster Co., to Thomas
     Farmer of same, for Ł 50...land on fork of Flat and big
Lynches creek adj. Isaac Fortenberry, Widow Gin, George Taylor,
Michael Miller, Francis Bettis...Benjn Haile (Seal), Wit: Benjamin
Haile Junr.,Molley Night (X). Ack. 6 Sept 1793 before James
McDonald, J. P.

Pp. 327-328: 1 March 1790, James Crawford Senr of St. Marks Parish,
     Craven Co., to James Crawford Junr his son of same,
land granted to Thomas McIlhany 600 A, 3 Apr 1752, conveyed by
him to Charles Burnet, half whereof was conveyed to James Gamble,
by deed 20 March 1758...100 A on SW side Reedy Creek...James
Crawford (Seal), Wit: Robert Crawford, William Crawford. Prov.
2 Apr 1781 by Robert Crawford, before John Drennon.

Pp. 328-329: James Crawford of Lancaster Co., planter, to John

McMurray of same, cooper, for Ł 145 sterling...land in the Waxhaw
Settlement, 150 A, part of tract granted to Thomas McIlhany, 3
Apr 1752, made over to Charles Burnett, 300 to James Gamble, 20
March 1748, conveyed by Gamble to James Crawford 12 Dec 1772, 150
A by sd. James Crawford Senr to James Crawford Junr 1 March 1780
....James Crawford and Christiana his wife...14 Oct 1796. James
Crawford (Seal), Christiana Crawford (CC) (Seal), Wit: James
Craig, William Simpson. Prov. by James Craig, before E. Alexander,
9 May 1797.

Page 329: 12 Sept 1796, Robert Bratney of Lancaster Co., to Thomas
        Chawthon of same, for Ł 140 sterling....250 A on NE
side Catawba River on both sides Rockey Creek, granted 5 May 1773,
conveyed to sd. Robert Bratney by Hugh Summerville 5 Oct 1784
(the sd. Somerville having purchased from Thomas McIlhany, 1 & 2
Aug 1774) also 75 A surveyed for Charles Bratney 4 March 1786, adj.
land formerly the property of William Maddox...Robert Bratney
(Seal), Henrietta Bratney (X) (Seal), Wit: Joseph Coil, William
Bailey, Richard Perry (X). Prov. by Joseph Coil, before Henry
Massey, J. P. 27 Jan 1797.

Pp. 329-330: State of S. C., St. Lukes Parish: George White of
        Georgia, McIntosh County, for Ł 100 sterling, to
Moses White, 212 A in S. C. adj. Joseph White, Samuel Dunlap,
Benjamin Harper, Robert Hancock, Susanna Tomlinson, Catharine
Howard...9 Jan 1797. George White (Seal), Wit: El Hipp, John
Crawford, Henry White. S. C. Beauford District: Prov. by Henry
White, before Geo Hipp J. P., 9 Jan 1797.

Page 330: 2 May 1787, William Hagins of N. C. Mecklinburg Co., to
        Thomas Drennon of York Co., SC, for Ł 20 sterling...33 A
on S side Telve Mile Creek in Lancaster Co., to the road leading
from the place where Joseph Douglass formerly lived to John Drennons....William Hagan (Seal), Wit: Jo Douglass, Robert Crocket,
Jno Drennon. Prov. by Robert Crocket, before Henry Massey, 12
Sept 1795.

18 Oct 1791, Thomas Drennon, of York Co., to John Brown of Chester
Co., for Ł 20 sterling...33 A on S side 12 Mile Creek adj. Widow
Elliot, John Drennon, Thomas Drennons spring branch....Thomas
Drennan (Seal), Wit: John Tomlinson, Thomas Ware, Jesse Roysdon.
Prov. by John Tomlinson, before Henry Massey, 12 Sept 1795.

Page 331: 17 Feb 1797, John Foster of Lancaster Co., to Nathaniel
        Sturdevant of same, for Ł 50 sterling...100 A in the
Waxhaw Settlement, part of land granted to John Hood, conveyed
to John Foster....John Foster (Seal), Wit: Moses Stephenson,
Robert Kirkpatrick, John Stevenson. Prov. by Moses Stephenson,
10 Feby 1798, before Elir. Alexander, J. P.

Page 332: 18 Aug 1796, John Findley and wife Elizabeth of Chester
        Co., to Francis McTier of N. C., Mecklenburg Co., for
Ł 25...land on waters of Cain Creek, part of 300 A granted to Jacob
Hart, March 1768 adj. John McTier, N. C. line....John Findley
(Seal), Elizabeth Findley (X) (Seal), Wit: James McATier, William
Stevens. Prov. 15 Feb 1797, by James McTier, before John Craig.

16 July 1793, John Coffey of Lancaster Co., to Hugh Coffey, for
Ł 10...150 A granted to James Walker 22 Sept 1769 in the Waxhaw
Settlement adj. James Walker, George Walker...John Coffey (LS),
Susanna Coffey (O) (LS), Wit: Hercules Huey, James McAteer. Prov.

BOOK B

25 Apr 1796, before John Craig, by James McAteer.

Page 332: Thomas Dunlop of Lancaster Co., for Ł 65 sterling, to
          Revd. James W. Stephenson of Williamsburgh Co., negro
woman Rose and child Banny...21 Sept 1795. Thos Dunlap (Seal),
Wit: Moses Stevenson, Robt Dunlap, J. L. C.

Pp. 332-333: 27 Jan 1796, William Johnston of Lancaster Co., to
             Robert Williams of same, for Ł 50 sterling...land on
Rockey Creek a branch of Cedar Creek, 100 A granted to William
Johnston, adj. Arthur Hicklins fence, William Curry, Mark Stevens
...William Johnston (Seal), Wit: Charles Stewbart (X), William
Wallace, Samuel Johnson. Prov. by Charles Shewbart, before Robert
Bratney, J. P., 27 Feb 1796

Page 333: 23 Jan 1796, Richard Perry of Lancaster Co., to Robert
          Williams, for Ł 25 sterling...64 A on waters of Rockey
Creek adj. William Johnstons old survey, adj. Richard Perry, William Curry (deed not completed)

Page 334: 6 Nov 1797, Alexander Carnes of Montgomery Co., Tenn.,
          to Benjamin Harper (all after date stricken), Thomas
Lant Hall, William Dowdy and Rebecca Dowdy of Lancaster Co.,
to Alexander Carnes of State of N. C., for Ł 50 s 10...land on
the mill stone branch, waters of 12 mile creek...132 A...Thos Lt.
Hall, William Dowdy, Rebecca Dowdy (X). Wit: Wike Ivey, James
Sprayberry (X), John Carnes. Prov. by Wike Ivey, before Samuel
C. Dunlap, J. P. 21 Apr 1798.

Robert Barkley of Fairfield Co., for Ł 29 s 13 d 4 to William
Marion of Chester Co., 586 A granted to sd. Barkley on Turkey
Quarter Creek in Camden Dist....5 Jan 1798. Robert Barkley (Seal),
Wit: Margery Turner, John Turner, Molly Peggy Turner. Ack. by
Barkley 4 Jan 1799, before Jno Simpson, J. L. C.

Page 335: 18 June 1798, Owen Reed of Cedar Creek, Camden Dist.,
          to Charles Barber of Beaver Creek, Camden Dist., for Ł
20...land in Lancaster Co., on Cedar Creek, 100 A, part of 200 A
granted to Matthew Hood, from him to sd. Barber, then to Owen
Reed adj. Matthew Hood, Mr. Chesnut, Charles Barber, Nathaniel
Barber....Owen Reed (X) Wit: John Joynor, Delilah Reed (X). Ack.
by Owen Reed, 5 Oct 1799, before _____. Also wit by Middleton
Joiner.

6 Feb 1796, William Davis of N. C., Mecklinburgh Co., to Adam
Heath of Lancaster Co., 62 A part of grant to Juditha Reyserion
by title 22 Sept 1767...Wm. Davies (Seal), Wit: Joseph Baker,
Jesse Heath, James Cureton.

Page 335: 3 July 1796, William Davis of N. C., Mecklinburgh Co.,
          to James Cureton of Lancaster Co., 31 A, granted to
David 1767....William Davies (Seal), Wit: Henry Massey, Robert
Lackey, William Cureton. Prov. 27 July 1796.

Page 336: 3 Sept 1796, Abdon Alexander, Sheriff of Lancaster Co.,
          to Daniel Clark, farmer, whereas John Williams decd. of
Lancaster in his lifetime was possessed of a plantation of 800 A
on waters of little Lynches creek and was indebted to Daniel
Clarke for Ł 9 d 10 sterling...action against William Ward and
Jesse Hays, Exrs. of John Williams...Abdon Alexander (LS), Wit:
Elir Alexander, James Clack. Prov. by Eliezar Alexander 24 Feb

1797, before John Simpson, J. L. C.

Page 336: 10 March 1795, Sarah Bottoms of Lancaster Co., to Thomas
          Pulley of same, for Ŀ 45...100 A on Rum Creek on NE side
Catawba adj. Benjamin Maddox, granted by Gov. Moultrie to sd.
Sarah Bottoms....Sarah Bottoms (O) Wit: Francis Mothershead, Jas
Douglass, William Mothershead. Prov. by William Mothershead, 1
July 1796, before Jesse Tilman, J. P.

Page 337: 10 March 1797, John Freeman to John Farrow, planter,
          25 A part of 5000 A granted to Thomas Sumter 2 Apr
1787 adj. Richmon Terrell...John Freeman (LS), Wit; Richmond Terrell, Edmund Deason (X. Prov. by Abraham Deason, before Ben.
Haile, 15 March 1797.

15 March 1797, Richmond Terrell to Tully Biggs of Lancaster Co.,
for Ŀ 70...100 A granted to sd. Terrell 10 Aug 1796 on waters of
Lick Creek a branch of Flat Creek adj. Kennington, Edward Cannington...Richmond Terrell Wit: Richard Hunley, Ferguson Haile. Prov.
by Richard Hunley, before Benjamin Haile, J. P., 15 March 1797.

15 March 1797, Richmond Terrell to Tully Biggs, 150 A part of
400 A granted to sd. Richmond Terrell, cert. 10 Aug 1796 on
waters of Lick Creek...Same wit. and prov.

Page 338: 22 Apr 1780, Joseph McMean & wife Jane of St. Marks
          Parish, Craven Co., to Alexander Galloway of same, by
grant dated 22 July 1778, to James Wood, 100 A adj. William Moore,
Thomas Wright, Henry Hays, John Grier, now for Ŀ 150...Joseph
McMean (Seal), Jane McMean (8) Wit: JAmes Wood, Margaret Wood,
William Christmas (X).

Pp. 338-339: 2 Jan 1795, Alexander Galloway of York Co., SC, to
          Robert Kirkpatrick of Lancaster Co., for Ŀ 50 ster-
ling...land on E side Catawba, 100 A, in the waxhaw Settlement,
water of Cane Creek surveyed 26 July 1769, for Joseph Moore,
granted 2 Feb 1771, to James Wood, by Wood & wife to Joseph
McMean 2 Feb 1771, and by McMeen to Galloway 22 July 1778, adj.
William Moore, Thos Wright, Henry Hays, John Greer....Alexander
Galloway (LS), Wit: Elir Alexander, Saml Lewers, Andw Foster.
Prov. by Elir. Alexander, before Andw Foster, J. P. 2 Jan 1795.

Page 339: 15 Nov 1790, Isolm Shirling and his wife of Lancaster
          Co., Sarah, for Ŀ 40 to William Blackman...250 A gran-
ted to sd. Blackman 5 March 1787 adj. William Clark, Elisha Nettles, John Love, conveyed by sd. William Blackman and wife Peggy
to Isolm Shurling...Isom Shirling (Seal), Sarah Shirling (X) (Seal),
Wit: John Williams, Thomas Small (X), Christopher Small (X). Prov.
15 Nov 1790.

Page 340: 26 Feb 1793, Elizabeth Leger and Eliza Love Hutchinson,
          to James Blackman, for Ŀ 40 sterling...250 A in Craven
Co., on N branch of South Lynches Creek granted to Peter Leger
(by whom it was devised to sd. Elizabeth Leger and Elizabeth Love
Hutchinson) adj. John Swaney, Daniel Williams, Barnard Johnston,
Benjamin Stogner....Elizabeth M. Leger (Seal), Eliza Love Hutchin-
son(Seal), Wit; Mary Taggart, Sarah Haig.

James Douglass for $250 to Adam Carnaghan, our negro slave Flora
...26 Apr 1799. James Douglas (Seal), Wit: George Wade. Prov.
by George Wade that James Douglas of Anson Co., NC did deliver the

BOOK B

within instrument to Adam Carnahan, of Lancaster Co., 29 July
1799, before Elir. Alexander J. P. Also deed from James Douglass
to Adan Carnahan, negro boy Julius....

Pp. 340-341: Robert Montgomery of Lancaster Co., planter, for
$500 to David Montgomery and Ninien Montgomery of
Lancaster Co., planters, 110 A on waters of Camp Creek, in the
Waxhaw Settlement, adj. John Gideon Sempkins, David Strain, sd.
tract granted to John Hood by Gov. of N. C., 25 Feb 1754, sold by
Hugh Montgomery Senr to sd. Robert Montomgery Senior...20 Oct
1796. Robert Montgomery Senr (Seal), Wiţ ,John Montgomery Junr,
Nenen Montgomery. Prov. by John Montgomery Junr, 20 Oct 1796.

Pp. 341-342: 13 Feb 1793, John Hagins and wife Margaret of Macklinburg Co., NC, to William Massey of Lancaster Co.,
for Ł 50 sterling...100 A on waters of Waxhaw Creek adj. James
and Allen Hood, James Barnett, William Massey...John Hagins (Seal),
Margret Hagins (/) (Seal), Wit: Roger Gibson, James Massey, Nathaniel Tomlinson (+), Prov. by James Massey, before Henry Massey,
J. P., 25 Apr 1795.

Pp. 342-343: 27 July 1795, John Mothershed & wife Lucy of Lancaster Co., to George Curry of same, for Ł 10...land
adj. Wm. Gibson, in the upper fork of George Curreys pring branch,
granted to Arthur Cunningham 13 May 1768....John Jett Mothershead
(LS), Lucy Mothershead (LS), Wit: William Currey, Adam Carnaghan,
John Carnanghan (X). Prov. by William Currey, 9 March 1798,
before Jesse Tilman. J. P.

Pp. 343-344: Whereas John Barkley decd in his life time was seized
of 300 A adj. John Simpson, on which the Court House
of Lancaster stands, Nathaniel Cowsarts land; also a tract 200 A
adj. Estate of Peter Edwards decd, John Barkley and Graves old
place, which tracts were not mentioned in the last will and testament of John Barkley...1 Feb 1799. Wm Allen (Seal), Robert Barkley (Seal), Wm. Couser (Seal), John Barkley (Seal), Hugh Montgomery (Seal), William Montgomery (Seal), Wit: Nathan Barr Senior,
John Couser Jur., Robert McIlwain. Prov. by Nathan Barr, Esq.
27 Apr 1799, before Elir. Alexander, J. P.

Page 344: 28 Nov 1796, Alexander Carnes of Montgomery Co., Tenn.,
to Benjamin Harper of L. C. & State of S. C. for Ł 50...
land on ye main Catawba River adj. Ben Harper, Wil Harper, Benjn &
Wm Harper, 100 A where the sd. B. Harper now lives...Alexander
Carnes (Seal), Wit: William Carnes, Saml Dunlap, John Carnes.
Prov. by William Carnes, 18 Feb 1797, before Samuel Dunlap, J. P.

Pp. 345-346: 25 Sept 1790, Adam Baird of Lancaster Co., to Isom
Pully of same, for Ł 45 sterling...250 A on N side
Catawba River on S side Cane Creek on Rum Creek adj. George Bot-
toms, Andrew Shaver, granted 15 Nov 1774, rec. Book M. N. B.(?)
paged 470...Adam Baird (Seal), Wit: John White, Simon Baird,
JohnBaird. Prov. by John White, 28 July 1797, before Danl Wade,
J. L. C.

END OF VOLUME.

N. B.   This book was made from two older books, and therefore have
        two sets of page numbers.   Because of duplication of num-
bers on the older pages, the "new" set of numbers is being used
here.   About 17 or 18 pages were missing at the time this books
were combined.   A list of these deeds compiled from the index
will appear at the end of these abstracts.

Page 1: (end of deed)...Joseph Fludd(X), Wit: Samuel Mathis, James
        Cook Junr, Alexander Goodall, Joseph Brevard.   Prov. by
Samuel Mathis before I. Alexander, J. P., 8 July 1789.

Pp. 1-3: 7 Nov 1786, Joseph Fludd of Camden, Ship builder, to
        Joseph Brevard, yeoman, by grant 640 A near Lynches
Creek, on S side of the same...(may be release to preceding in-
strument)...Joseph Brevard (Seal), Joseph Fludd (X) (Seal), Wit:
Samuel Mathis, James Cook Junr., Alexander Goodall.   Prov. by
Samuel Mathis, 18 July 1789.

Pp. 3-4: 7 Oct 1788, George Johnson and wife Sarah of Lancaster
        Co., to Benjamin Croxton, for ℔ 20 sterling...50 A
conveyed from John Chesher 14 & 15 Sept ____...George Johnston
Sarah Johnston (O), Wit: William Johnston, Lewis Croxton, Samuel
Caston.   Ack. 21 July 1789.

Pp. 4-8: 21 & 22 Jan 1785, Micheal Ganter of Camden Dist., to
        Joseph Thomson of same, (lease s 10, release ℔ 78 s 11
d 5)...land on N side Wateree River, waters of grannys quarter Cr.
adj. lands granted to Thomas Kemp; 100 A granted to sd. Michael
Ganter, 13 Apr 1769, two parcles granted to Thomas Kemp 23 Oct 176-
conveyed by Kemp to sd. Michael Ganter 11 Aug 1779...Michael
Ganter (Seal), Wit: Jno Milhouse, J. Galbraeth, Samuel Belton.
Prov. 20 __ 1788, by Samuel Belton, before Richard Champion, J. P.

Pp. 8-11: 3 Nov 1789, William Montgomery of Lancaster, S. C.,
        and wife Margaret, planter, to William Harper, planter,
by grant 17 Feb 1767 to John Belk Senr, 250 A on Bear Creek, a
branch of Cane Creek, and sd. John Belk Senr did transfer to sd.
Montgomery,1/2 of said plantation...William Montgomery (Seal),
Margert Montgomery (Seal), Wit: Charles Orr, John Walker.   Prov.
by John Walker, before John Craig, J. P.

Pp. 11-12: Last will and testament of Patrick Laton of Dist. of
        Camden...to Elisabeth my wife the plantation where we
now live; to grandson Feady, grandson Patrick, 100 A adj. to it,
and 150 A where he now lives.... if grandson Feady dies, his land
to fall to William Feady; likewise grandson Patrick, his land to
go to his uncle Patrick if he dies without an heir lawfully begot-
ten; N. B. the branch on the north of the dwelling house is to
davide the land betwixt Feady and William...18 Oct 1785.   widow
to be sole executrix. Patrick Laton (O) (Seal), Wit: Thomas Mickle,
Jean Mickle.   Prov. by Thomas Mickle before Andrew Baskins, 7 Oct
1786. (The recording of the will here is difficult to explain.
It should have been recorded in Camden.)

Pp. 12-15: 7 Dec 1789, Abraham Rush of Orangeburgh District, to
        John Viles Snr. of Lancaster Co., for(s 10, lease & re-
lease)...100 A on a branch of great Lynches Creek granted 12 Oct
1770...Abraham Rush (A) (Seal), Wit: Peter Sutrigs, John Letsinger.
Prov. 16 Dec 1789 by Peter Sturges before John Craig, J. P.

Pp. 15-17: 28 July 1775, Jennet Patterson in St. Marks Parish, Craven Co., SC, to James Hall of Co. aforesd., by grant 31 Aug 1770 to Je-net Patterson, 100 A on E side Cataba on waters of Cane Creek adj. David Leard...Jennet Patterson (O) (Seal), Wit: William Graham, Benjamin Prefect (C), Ann Simpson. S. C. Camden Dist., 13 Jan 1776, prov. by William Graham, before James Simpson.

Pp. 17-19: 9 Feb 1789, John Creighton of Lancaster Co., to John McLure of same, for Ł 25 sterling...100 A on head of Beaver Creek which sd. John Creighton purchased from Robert Williams...John Creighton (Seal), Nancy Creighton (X) (Seal), Wit: Thomas Creighton, William Peach (⌒). Ack. by Creighton, before Samuel Dunlap, J. P.

Article of Agreement 20 Jan 1790 between John Creighton and John McClure, concerning that land which John Creighton purchased from Robert Williams 100 A...dated 13 Jan 1790, Wit: Thomas Creighton, Jenny Creighton (X).

Page 19: 17 Apr 1787, Nathaniel Pace of Dist. of Camden, to William Bayley of same, for Ł 6...100 A in Camden District, Ceder Creek...Nathaniel Pace (Seal), Wit: Micajah Crenshaw, James Crenshaw. Sworn to 22 Apr 1789, before Robert Dunlap, J. P.

Pp. 20-22: 21 July 1789, James Kerr Gentleman to Archibald Kerr of Camden, planter, (lease s 10, release Ł 10)...land between Boonesborough and Bellfast Township, 350 A adj. Hugh Duff...James Kerr (Seal), Wit: Thomas Winstanley, Tobias Bowles. Prov. by Thomas Winstanley, 14 Jan 1790, before James Nickolson, J. P.

Pp. 23-24: S. C. Camden District, William Starke & Benjamin Perry have finished a mill upon Cataba River which is supposed to be situated upon a tract formerly surveyed by William Harrison but now belongeth to me Thomas Thomson...Thomas Thomson Blacksmith, sold mill and mill seat with 5 acres to sd. Starke & Perry...14 May 1785. Thomas Thomson (Seal), Wit: Thomas Govin, Moses Duke (X), Daniel Sain (2). Ack. in Court.

Page 24: April the 22 1789. State of South Carolina, Lancaster County. This day Ann Jones appeared in open Court and maketh oath on the holy Evangelists of Almight God that according to the best of her memory and recolection that in the year 1776 in the Month of March She saw John Cornelius and Charity Joiner joined together in the band of wedlock and that the rights of Matrimon (sic) were performed by the Revd. Thomas Stinger (Stringer?) according to the from of the Church of England as directed by the Liturgy & that Roger Cornelius son of John Cornelius & Charity Cornelius sworn in open Court was born more than ten months after said marriage this 22d day of April 1789. Elir Alexander. Ann Jones

Pp. 24-25: Kenneth MacCallum of Camden Dist., planter, for love, good will and affection to my griend Benjamin MacCay, stock (brands given)...5 Dec 1783. Kenneth McCallum, Wit: John McCoy, William Newman, William Brown. Prov. by John McCay, 12 Fev 1785, before Thomas Hall, J. P.

70

Pp. 25-27: 28 Jan 1789, James Hall & wife Sarah of Lancaster Co.,
        SC, to James Yancey, Esqr., Attorney at law, for Ł 50
land on a branch of Bear Creek, a prong of Cane Creek, NE side
Cataba adj. Benjamin Cudworth, John McElhenny, David Adams, John
Carson, James Hall, granted to James Hall 7 May 1787...James Hall
(Seal), Sarah Hall (S), Wit: William Montgomery, James Hall Junr,
William Hay.

Pp. 27-29: 28 Jan 1789, James Hall and wife Sarah to James Yancey,
        for Ł 50...100 A in County of Lancaster (formerly
Craven) on waters of Cain Creek, granted to Jennet Patterson, 21
Aug 1770, conveyed to James Hall 28 July 1775...(same sign. & wit)

Page 29: Benjamin Ladd Senr. of Lancaster Co., to Benjamin Ladd
        Junr. the plantation whereon he now lives, 100 A, on Lick
Branch...16 Feb 1786. Benjamin Ladd (Seal), Wit: Richard Terrell,
Stephen R. Eady.

Pp. 29-30: John Reed of Camden, Vintner, at the request of F.
        Woodroof of Camden, planter, by bond to John Chesnut
& William Lang of Camden, in the penal sum of Ł 520 s 8 d 2...
mortgage of Negroes. (not dated)

Pp. 30-32: S. C. Lancaster County: 29 Feb 1789, John Baker & wife
        Frances of Lancaster Co., to John David of same, for
Ł 40 sterling...150 A on a branch of dry Creek on N side Catabaw
River, granted by Gov. Bull unto Watters, and by said Watters to
sd. John Baker and Francis his wife a Memorandum whereof may be
seen in the surveyors Generals office dated Nov. 2 1786, and
certified 11 Feb 1771 Glascock Deputy Surveyor...John Baker (Seal),
Francis Baker (+) (Seal), Wit: Bailey Fleming, Joseph Coile, William Rogers. Prov. by Joseph Coile, 21 Mar 17--, before Samuel
Dunlap, J. P.

Pp. 32-34: 18 Jan 1789, Andrew Foster of York Co., SC to Thomas
        Lackey of Lancaster Co., for Ł 120, 150 A granted to
sd. Andrew Foster 2 Aug 1768, adj. Joseph White, Stephen White, on
Waxaw Creek...Andrew Foster (Seal), Wit: Robert Ivy, Robert
Cearnes, William Harper. Prov. by Robert Ivy 22 Feb 1790, before
Hugh White, J. P.

Pp. 35-37: 3 Oct 1789, Thomas Lackey of Mecklinburgh Co., N. C.,
        to Henry Massey of Lancaster Co., SC for Ł 120...150 A
a tract granted to Andrew Foster 2 Aug 1768, adj. Joseph White,
Stephen White, on Waxaw Creek... Thomas Lackey (Seal), Wit:
Jeremiah Cureton, William Cureton, James Massey. Prov. by James
Massey, before Hugh White, J. P. 22 Feb 1790.

Pp. 37-39: 29 June 1789, The Revd. Robert Finley of Lancaster Co.,
        to James Cureton of Mecklinburgh Co., NC, for Ł 150...
150 A, part of grant to Samuel Dunlap, 23 Feb 175-, conveyed to
William Barnett, 7 Jan 1765, and then to Rev. Robert Findley, 28
July 1784, on NE side Catabaw River, adj. William Davis, also part
of grant to William Davis 28 __ 1767, 30 A, conveyed to Revd. Robt
Finley, 11 Jan 1785...Robert Finley (Seal), Rebecca Finley (Seal),
Wit: James Massey, Jeremiah Cureton, William Cureton. Prov. by
James Massey, before Hugh White, J. P., 22 Feb 1790.

Pp. 39-40: 10 Jan 1790, Arthur Giles & Henry Hudson both of Lan-
          caster Co., for Ł 100 pd. by sd. Henry Hudson to sd.
Arthur Giles, land on branches of Shinglestons Creek, part of a
survey of Robert Hoods, 470 A, granted 1789 adj. James Russel,
Mr. Kell...Arthur Giles (Seal), Wit: John Taylor, Thomas Duren.

Pp. 40-43: 10 Feb 1774, Griffith Rutherford of Roan Co., N. C.
          to Charles Miller Junr of Craven Co., SC, for Ł 30...
land on S side Twelve Mile Creek adj. John Haggins, Samuel Bar-
nets, William Brown...Griffith Rutherford (Seal), Wit: Charles
Miller Senr, Henry Rutherford, James Lindsey (X).Prov. 13 Feb
1775, by Charles Miller Senr, before James Patton, J. P. in Craven Co., SC

Pp. 43-45: 23 Dec 1789, Richard Ross and wife Ann of Lancaster
          Co., to Thomas Stephenson sadler of same, by grant
dated 11 Feb 1762, to Mary Moore, 150 A on N fork Cane Creek,
lying below a tract of land granted to David Strain now in the
possession of Moses Stephenson, now for Ł 80...Richard Ross
(Seal), Ann Ross (A) (Seal), Wit: John Crocket, Moses Stephenson,
Robert Montgomery. Prov. by Moses Stephenson, before Robert Dunlap, J. P. 23 Dec 1789.

Pp. 45-46: __ June 1785, Joseph Greer of Wateree River near the
          mouth of White Oak in Camden District, to John Fegan
of Sullivan County, North Carolina [now Tennessee--BHH], 150 A,
half of 300 A formerly the property of Edward Howard, granted to
sd. Howard 25 June 1751...Joseph Greer (Seal), Nancey Greer (X)
(Seal), Wit: Charles Barber, John Hood, William Twadell. Prov. by
Charles Barber, 9 March 1790, before Samuel Dunlap, J. P.

Pp. 46-48: 18 Dec 1787, Henry Massey of Lancaster Co., to Benjamin
          Hail, for Ł 19 sterling...land granted to Henry Massey
3 Apr 1785, rec. in Grant Book JJJJ p. 313, 640 A...Henry Massey
(Seal), Wit: Benjamin Hail Junr, John Ferguson, Francis Bettis.
Prov. by Benjamin Hail Junr, 24 Jan 1789, before John Marshel, J.
P.

Pp. 48-49: 27 July 1789, Jonas Griffin of State of Georgia, to
          Ferguson Haile of Lancaster Co., for Ł 100 sterling...
land on Flat Creek, 150 A part of 300 A conveyed from Robert
Harper, to John Sill, and from John Sill to Jonas Griffin...
Jonas Griffin (Seal), Wit: James Ferguson, Benjamin Hail, George
Palmer. Prov. by James Ferguson, before Benjamin Hail, J. P., 22
March 1790.

Pp. 49-52: 19 Oct 1786, Charles Pence, Cooper, to Benjamin Haile
          Senr. & Catharine his wife, of Camden Dist., St. Marks
Parish, Lancaster Co., for s 10...land part of 300 A surveyed for
Robert Harper Jr(?), granted 1756, by Gov. Lyttleton on N prong
of Lynches Creek, memorial entered 21 Sept 1759, conveyed to
Nathaniel Shepherd, and then to Charles Pence, adj. Benjamin Hail
where the said Charles Pence lived last whilst kept house in this
state whereon the said place Andrew Faulkenberry now lives on....
Charles Pence (Carl Bentz--signed in German), Wit: Daniel Monaghan,
Elijah Phillips(1), Richard Knight (+)

Pp. 52-54: 11 Feb 1775, John Martan Strofer of Craven Co., and
          wife Sarah, to Benjamin Hail of same, planter, 75 A in
St. Marks Parish, Craven Co., on both sides Flat Creek, adj. Robert
Harper, Andrew Jones, surveyed 5 Oct 1758 for John Baker...

BOOK C & E

John Martain Strofer (MJ) (Seal), Sarah Strofer (S) (Seal), Wit:
Jonas Griffin, P. P. Clerk. Prov. by Jonas Griffin, before
William Welch, 30 Jan 1779.

Pp. 54-55: John Stroud of Chesterfield County, for Ł 15 to Ben-
          jamin Haile (bond), land granted to me, 18 Jan 1765...
9 March 1790. John Stroud (S) (Seal), Wit: Peter Sturgis, James
Blakeny, Elizabeth Funderburk. Prov. by James Blakeny, before
Benjamin Haile, J. P., 3 Apr. 1790.

Pp. 55-56: 7 Apr 1780, Nickolas Robinson of Craven Co., to Tho-
          mas Shurley of St. Marks Parish, for Ł 5...200 A on
S side North Lynches Creek, granted 8 July 1774...Nickolas
Robinson (Seal), Wit: James Marshel, Daniel Monaghan. Prov. by
James Marshel, 20 April 1790, before Andrew Baskins, J. P.

Pp. 57-9:5 May 1789, Jesse Minton of Lancaster Co., Camden Dist.,
          planter, for s 10, to James Sowel, 1000 A on Big and
Little Lynches Creek, adj. James Bredin...Jesse Minton (Seal),
Elizabeth Minton (E) (Seal), Wit: Benjamin Watts, Thomas Watts
(T). Release gives grant date 4 Feb 1788. Prov. by Thomas
Watts, 23 March 1790, before Andrew Baskin, J. P.

Pp. 59-60: 15 June 1785, Joseph Greer of the Wateree in Camden
          Dist., to John Fegan of Sullivan Co., N. C., for Ł 800
...½ of 300 A on Wateree River, granted to Edward Howard 25 June
1751...Wit: Charles Barber, John Hodd, William Twadle. (this
is the release for the deed on pp. 45-46). Prov. by Charles
Barber 9 March 1790, before Saml Dunlap, J. P.

Page 61: William Starke & Thomas Starke bound to Andrew Armstrong,
         John Thomson, and Moses Duke, Exrs. of the estate of
John Duke decd, for Ł 254 sterling, 23 Feb 1790....Wit: William
Sorsby, Saml Dunlap.

Pp. 62-63: 8 & 9 May 1790, Nathaniel Pace of Claremont Co., SC,
          to Thomas Morton of Lancaster Co., (lease sl, release
Ł 40)...640 A on drains of Crooked creek a prong of Kemps creek
in Lancaster Co., adj. James Rodgers, William McGarrah, Alexander Douglass...Natl Pace (Seal), Mildred Pace (Seal), Wit: Richard Buckelew, William Hicklin, William Gibson. Prov. by William
Gibson, 26 Nov 1791, before Jesse Tilman, J. P.

Page 64: 21 Aug 1793, Gen. Thomas Sumpter of Claremont Co., to
         Daniel Hunter Jun. of Lancaster Co., for Ł 10 sterling,
150 A surveyed by Samuel Kelly 28 June 1793....Thomas Sumpter Jr.
for Thomas Sumpter (Seal), Wit: Saml Tynes, Martin Smith. (plat
included)

Pp. 65-66: 4 Apr 1789, John Hood Junr. & wife Elizabeth in Lan-
          caster Co., to Archabald Hood of same for Ł 50 ster.,
land on Persimon branch of Ceder Creek on E side Cataba, on the
waggon road from Ceder Creek to Beaver Creek, land granted 5
June 1786...John Hood (Seal), Elizabeth Hood (+) (Seal), Wit:
Bennedict Best, James Hood, John Hood Senr.

Pp. 66-68: 4 May 1789, Mason Daviss of Lancaster Co., Camden
          Dist., planter to Jesse Minton of same planter...
(lease & release) 200 A on the great Road near Lynches Creek...
Mason Davis (M), Wit: William Haslam, Hannah Brooks (.). Prov.
by William Haslem, before Charles Evans, a J. P. for Chesterfield.

73

BOOK C & E

Pp. 68-69: 30 Sept 1788, William Kerr of York Co., SC to Thomas
        Duren of Lancaster Co., for Ł 25 sterling, 100 A in
Lancaster Co., on w branch of Beaver Creek, adj. Mr. Hodges,
land granted to James Kennedy and vacant land...Wm. Kerr (Seal),
Wit: William Steel, Reuben Collins, Martha Steel (Ŧ). Prov. by
Reuben Collins 10 Apr 1789, before John Lowrie, J. P.

Pp. 69-70: 18 Jan 1791, John Creighton of Lancaster Co., planter,
        to Andrew Graham, for Ł 75 sterling...land in main
branch of Beaver Creek, part of 200 A laid out for James Williams
adj. Frances Graham, James Douglas...Widow Creighton (*), John
Creighton, Nancey Creighton, Wit: John Graham, Thos Creighton.

Page 70: 19 Aug 1790, Samuel Tines of Lancaster Co., to James
        Cowser of same, for Ł 100...negro Hearsey and her two
children, Judy and Parish...Saml Tines (Seal), Wit: Andrew Baskin, J. P. James Robinson.

Pp. 70-71: 25 Aug 1790, George McCamy of N. C., County of Mecklin-
        burgh, to Elizabeth Crawford of Lancaster Co., niece
of sd. George McCamy, for natural love and affection and s 5 ster.,
negroe Girl Venus about 7 years old...George McCamy (O) (Seal),
Wit: John Stephenson, James Crawford. Prov. by John Stephenson
in Lancaster Co., before Robert Dunlap, J. P., 11 Sept 1790.

Pp. 71-72: 6 Nov 1790, Mathew Jones to Jame Gunn, for Ł 100...
        part of a survey of Eleanor Adams, also 60 A, part of
survey of John Goodwin, on N side of the cane brake branch, also
part of survey of Joseph Cotes, adj. Meagles line...Mathew Jones
(+) (Seal), Sarah Jones (+) (Seal), Wit: William Connell, Zachariah Hester, James Hester. Prov. by James Hester, before Ben
Hail, J. P., 18 Jan 1791.

Pp. 72-73: 16 July 1789, James Duren of Lancaster Co., to Reuben
        Collens, land, 300 A, adj. James Marlow, James Kil-
patrick, Jean Tompson, Alexander, Henry Tompson...James Duren
(Seal), Wit: Thomas Gardner, Jean Gardner, Elizabeth Colley (X).
Prov. 19 Jan 1791, Thomas Gardner, before John Marshel, J. P.

Pp. 73-74: 3 Nov 1789, James McGawley and wife Jean, for Ł 30
        sterling, 100 A on waters of White Oak Creek adj.
Henry Dunsworth...James McGawly (Seal), Jane McGawley (+) (Seal),
Wit: Thos Gardner, John Colle, Travass Nixson. Prov. by Thos
Gardner, 19 Jan 1791, before John Marshel.

Pp. 74-76: 6 July 1790, Richard Middleton of Camden Dist., to
        William Middleton of same, planter (lease & release)
3 tracts (1) 100 A on SW side Lynches Creek near below Jumping
Gully, granted to William Lankford, 23 Aug 1765 (2) land on SW
side Lynches Creek granted to John Wade 1 Feb 1763 (3) 70 A
part of tract granted to Thomas Watts 13 July 1770...Richard
Middleton (Seal), Wit: George Evans, Josiah Canty. Prov. in Kershaw County, by George Evans, before John Marshel, J. P. 6 Jan
1791.

Pp. 76-79: 29 Jan 1789, Peter Wikoff of Philadelphia, Pa., mer-
        chant, Isaac Wikoff of Manmouth Co., New Jersey and wf
Martha, to Samuel Tines, of S. C., 750 A on S prong of Lynches
Creek the waters of Pee Dee in Craven Co, granted to sd. Peter
Wikoff and Isaac Wikoff under the hands and seals of John Belton
of S. C. and wife Mary 27 Apr 1777...lease & release...Peter

Wikoff (Seal), Isaac Wikoff (Seal), Martha Wikoff (Seal), Wit:
John Covenhoven, Cornl. Covenhoven, John J. Holmes.   Prov.
4 Feb 1789, by grantors before John Chetwood, Esqrs., one of the
Judges of the Supreme Court of Judicature for the State of N.J.
Also prov. in Charleston District, by Mathew Strong who swore
that he and John Bridge were wit., 14 Apr 1789.

Page 80: 22 May 1790, Hezekiah Love of Lancaster Co., to Edward
          Rogers, for L 100 sterling...land granted 31 Oct 1769,
on Flat Rock Creek in Lancaster Co., at the time of survey on all
sides by vacant land but now adj. Joseph Williams, which he sold
to Isabella Reid, Edward Rogers, Samuel Smiths, Thomas Mickes...
Hezekiah Love (Seal), Ann Love (Seal), Wit: William Cook, Mary
McNiel, Margaret Thompson.

Page 81: Blank.

Page 82: 12 March 1792, William Patton & James Patton & Elizabeth
          Patton & Mary Patton of York Co., SC, to Robert Ivey of
Lancaster Co., SC...180½ A adj. sd. Ivey...William Patton (Seal)
James Patton (Seal), Elizabeth Patton (+) (Seal), Mary Patton (S)
(Seal), Wit: George Wren, Wike Ivey.

Pp. 82-83: 31 Dec 1790, Robert Montgomery & wife Margaret of
          Lancaster Co., to Thomas Cauthorn of Mecklenburg Co.,
NC, for L 30, 127 A in the Waxhaw Settlement, on both sides of
Cane Creek....Robt Montgomery (Seal), Margaret Montgomery (M)
(Seal), Wit: Henry Massey, James Hagins, William Draffon.

Pp. 83-84: 17 July 1792, James Simpson of Ceder Creek, Lancaster
          Co., to James Sprunt of same, planter, for L 25 ster.,
200 A on N side Catabaw River on Ceder Creek, originally granted
to Frederick Touchstone, 14 Sept 1771(?), conveyed to sd. James
Simpson by John McCain by deed 28 July 1782, on E side Touchstone's
branch...James Simpson (Seal), Wit: William Bailey, Thomas Cauthon, Jos. Coile.

Page 84: Camden District, Sept. 8, 1781: G. Wade have sold to
          Elizabeth Henderson of sd. District, negro Rose and
young girl child Mary, for L 6000 provential currency of S. C...
G. Wade (Seal), Wit: Christopher Morgan (C), Alexr Crafford.
Prov. in Lancaster County, by Alexander Crafford, 12 Apr 1791,
before Josh. Lee, J. P.

Pp. 84-85: 1 Nov 1790, John White of York Co., SC, to John Ander-
          son, for L 100 sterling...land adj. Robert Karnes,
Charles Miller, William Porter...John White (Seal), Wit: James
Alexr Watson, Charles Miller, Andrew Foster. Prov. by James
Alexander Watson, 19 May 1792, before Is. Dunnom, J. P.

Pp. 85-86: 15 Aug 1791, Timothy Anderson & wife Elizabeth, of
          Lancaster Co., to Sarah Harper of Chester Co., for L
160 sterling, 200 A in the Waxhaw Settlement, part of 400 A granted to Samuel McLeveny, then of Anson County and by a north patent, adj. Jacob Taylor...Timothy Anderson (Seal), Elizabeth Anderson (1) (Seal). Prov. by Moses Cantzon, 3 Feb 1792, before Josh. Lee,
J. P.

Pp. 86-87: ___ 1777, Thomas Niel & wife Agnes of Camden Dist.,
          to John McMurry of same, by grant 7 May 1754, under
the hand of Matthew Rowan, Gov. of N. C., to John Arnold Pender
400 A on Camp Creek, then in Anson County, N. C., sold to Robert

Gault, by sd. Gault to Jno Cain, and sd. Cain to James Boyd, &
Boyd to Wm. Adams, and sd. Adams to Thomas Niel, now for Ⱡ 176,
100 A....16 Aug 1777. Thomas Niel (Seal), Agness Niel (Seal),
Wit: Jas Boyd, John Adams, William Adams.

Pp. 87-88: 3 Oct 1792, James Hood of Lancaster Co., to John Hood
            Senr. of same, for Ⱡ 100 sterling, 100 A on a branch
of Ceder Creek, granted to Jordan Ashley 27 Aug 1764, by John
Wade Deputy Surveyor, and recorded in Gen. Surveyors office 26
Feb 1788...James Hood (Seal), Wit: Jos Coile, Absolom Clark,
Archibald Owings. Prov. by Joseph Coile, before Robt Montgomery,
J. P., 8 Oct 1792.

Pp. 88-89: 10 Apr 1792, Jesse Tilman & wife Rebecca of Camden
            Dist., to Barnet Johnson, for Ⱡ 30 sterling...300 A
part of 500 A granted to Jesse Tilman, by Gov. Moultrie...Jesse
Tilman (Seal), Rebecca Tilman (Seal), Wit; James Henderson, Is.
Mc. Tilman. Prov. by I. Mc. Tilman, 8 Apr 1793, before Jesse
Tilman, J. P.

Pp. 89-90: S. C. Camden Dist., John Coffee of Craven County,
            planter, to Hugh Coffee of same, 100 A in ye Waxhaw
Settlement, Craven Co., adj. Geo Douglass, William Davis, granted
to John Coffey, 12 Apr 1768...__ March 1784, John Coffey, Susannah Coffey (Seal), Wit: Alexander Montgomery, Hugh Coffey Junr.

Pp. 90-91: Robert Gault of State of South Carolina of Pacolet,
            planter, for Ⱡ 2 s 10 sterling to Thomas Cowsart, 100
A on Camp Creek waters of Catabaw in the Waxhaw Settlement, first
granted to John Cold, by Gov. William Bull, 31 Aug 1774, sold to
Robert Gault...5 Nov 1783. Robert Gault (R) (Seal), Isabella
Gault (G), Wit: William Nelson, Thos Nelson, William Gault. Prov.
by William Nelson in Lancaster Co., 17 July 1793, before Robert
Dunlap, J.P.

Pp. 91-92: 20 Jan 1793, John Stephens of Lancaster Co., to
            Frederick Joiner (Joyner), land granted to Joseph Lee
Esqr. 250 A on Dry Creek, and sd. Joseph Lee sold 100 A to John
Stephens, by deed 1789, now for Ⱡ 50 sterling...John Stephens
(LS), Wit: Jos Coile, Wm Rogers (m), Archibald Hood.

Page 92: Prov. in Court July 1793. William Mothershead of S. C.
            Lancaster County, to Sarah Bottoms, one negroe woman
named Seal, only ½ of the increase of the sd. negroe excepted
to the heirs of William Mothershead...30 Apr 1793. William Mothershead (Seal), Wit: Andw McIlwain, Margret McIlwain.

Pp. 92-93: 6 June 1792, Andrew Countryman of York Co., SC, for
            Ⱡ 43 sterling, to Samuel Love of Lancaster Co., land
on South branch of Lynches Creek, waters of Pee Dee River, 150 A
...Andrew Countryman (Seal), Wit: John Love, James Gaston, John
Countryman.

Page 93: Abraham Sasportas of Charleston, Merchant, for Ⱡ 45
            sterling, to Benjamin Hale of Lancaster Co., negro girl
Patience about 14 years old...1 Apr 1791. Abm. Sasportas (Seal),
Wit: Samuel DaCosta, John Massey. Prov. by John Massey, 10 Feb
1794, before B. Haile, J. P.

Page 94: John Ingram of Kershaw County, for Ł 108 s 15 sterling,
          to Henry Horton, negro man Cosom about 26 years old...
12 Feb 1794. John Ingram (Seal), Wit: None.

Pp. 94-95: 19 Sept 1793, Wm. Brewer of Lancaster Co., planter,
          to Willm. Horton, for Ł 10 sterling, land granted to
sd. Brewer 2 Apr 1787, adj. Wm Johnson, Henry Cotes(?)...Wm
Brewer (Seal), Wit: Saml Caston, Wm. Ellis. Prov. 17 Feb 1794,
by Samuel Caston, before John Craig, J. P.

Pp. 95-96: 9 Oct 1793, Joseph Singleton of Gills Creek, a prong
          of Cane Creek, Yeoman, to Jacob Kerns of Wild Cat
Creek, for Ł 20...390 A on Wild Cat Creek a prong of Big Lynches
Creek, adj. Jacob Kernes, John Bibbys, Gen. Sumpter, part of 2000
A granted to sd. Joseph Singleton 6 May 17--, by Gov. Moultrie
Joseph Singleton (Seal), Wit: Deval Funderburk (A), Daniel Shehane.
Prov. by Daniel Shehane, before James McDonald, J. P. 21 Oct
1793.

Pp. 96-97: 27 Jan 1797, Abdon Alexander esquire, Sheriff of Lan-
          caster Co., to William Sprung of same, farmer, whereas
Thomas Thomson was seize of 100 A on NE side Catawba adj. William
Harrison, land originally granted to Wm. Harrison, and sd. Thomas
Thompson being indebted to Richard Wright of Lancaster Co., for
Ł 19 s 6 d 7 sterling, and in court Jly term 1793 did recover...
by a writ of Fi fa tested by Eliezar Alexander, clerk of Lancaster
Co., ...the sd. Abdon Alexander then lawful deputy of William
Barnett Esq. and now sheriff....A. Alexander (Seal), wit: James
Huey, Wm. Nisbet, Thos Barkley. Ack. in Court 27 Jan 1797.

Pp. 97-98: 8 Apr 1797, Abdon Alexander Sheriff of Lancaster Co.,
          to William Sprunt, farmer, whereas Enoch Deason of
Lancaster Co., was seize of 125 A on Little Lynches Creek adj.
William Denman, Samuel Caston, James Blackman, Sterling Cato,
Joseph Bowies, Needham Cato; sd. Enoch Deason was indebted to
Moses Sarsedas, for Ł 13 s 10 d 10 sterling, in court Jan.
term 1796, did recover...Wit: Elir Alexander, Nathan Barr, John
Montgomery. Prov. by Eliezar Alexander, 27 Apr 1797.

Page 99: 27 Jan 1795, Elisha Shite, of Lancaster co., planter, to
          John Freeman, for Ł 14 sterling...part of 825 A granted
to Elisha White 1790, adj. William Narramore, Edward Kannington,
John Wright...75 A...Elisha White (E) (Seal), Wit: Richmond
Terrell, James Butler, William Denman. Prov. by Richmond Terrell,
14 March 1795, before Thomas Welsh, J. P.

Pp. 99-100: 22 Dec 1795, John Freeman of S. C. Lancaster Co., to
          Edward Narramore of same, for Ł 8 sterling...75 A,
part of 825 A (same land as in preceding deed)...John Freeman
(LS), Wit: Richmond Terrell, Thomas Henry (X), Wm. Narramore.
Prov. by Richmond Terrell, 22 Dec 1795, before Thos Welsh, J. P.

Page 100: Edward Narramore, of Lancaster Co., for Ł 5(?) to Wil-
          liam Narramore, of same, 75 A on Flat Creek, adj.
William Cannington, William Narramore, Edward Cannington, William
Narramore, Elisha White...5 Feb 1798. Edwd Narramore, Wit: Richmond Terrell, William Terrell, Benj. Ladd (B). Prov.21 March
1798, by Richmond Terrell, before Thomas Welsh, J. P.

Pp. 100-101: 27 Apr 1794, Richmond Terrell of Lancaster Co., planter, to Stephen Caudle of same, Blacksmith, for Ł 5...part of 400 A granted to Richmond Terrell 1788, 50 A adj. James Gracey, Randal McDonald...Richmond Terrell (LS), Catharine Terrell (LS), Wit: Danl Monaghon, John Freeman, Eleanor Freeman (X). Prov. by John Freeman, 14 March 1795, before Thomas Welsh, J. P.

Page 101: 17 Nov 1795, Stephen Caudle of Lancaster Co., planter, to William Narramore of same, for Ł 7...400 A granted to Richmond Terrell, 1788, part of sd. grant, 50 A...Stephen Caudle (S), Wit: Richmond Terrell, James Butler, Catharine Terrell (X). Prov. by Richmond Terrell, before B. Haile, 10 March 1796.

Pp. 102-3:22 Aug 1784, Henry Peebles & wife Mary to William Narramore, both of Camden Dist., land granted to Henry Peebles, 20 Jan 1773, on Flat Creek, a branch called Lick Creek, adj. Benjamin Ladd, Joshua Hickman, Samuel McKenny...Henry Peebles (LS), Mary Peebles (X) (LS), Wit: Fredk. Kimball, Richmond Terrell, Benjamin Ladd. Prov. by Richmond Terrell, 14 July 1785, before Frederick Kimball, J. P.

Page 103: William Narramore, of Lancaster Co., planter, for love good will & affection to my griend Grace Terrell, one brown mare 9 years old, six head of cattle, etc. 28 Aug 1798. William Narramore (X), Wit: Jesse Mallet, Benjamin Ladd (B). Prov. by Benjamin Ladd, 28 Aug 1798, before Thomas Welsh, J. P.

Page 104: 25 Aug 1795, James Butler of Lancaster Co., planter, to Avret Yerby of Mecklinburgh Co., N. C., for Ł 60... 150 A, part of 400 A conveyed by James Bratton, adj. Wm. Bratton ...James Butler (X), Gracey Butler (X), Wit: William Denman, Amos Hough. Prov. by Amos Hough, 18 Dec 1795, before John Welsh, J. P.

Pp. 104-105: 8 Dec 1796, Gen. Thomas Sumter to Robert Welsh of Lancaster Co., for Ł 100 sterling, 1000 A on W side Big Lynches Creek, surveyed of 15,000 A 2 Apr 1787...Thos Sumter (LS), Wit: William White, John Sumter. Prov. by William White, 11 March 1797, before Thomas Welsh, J. P.

Pp. 105-106: 11 Dec 1797, Robert Welsh of Lancaster Co., to James Holliman of same, for Ł 40 sterling...land in the fork of Wild Cat Creek and part of Lynches Creek (same land in preceding deed) 1000 A...Robt Welsh (X) (LS), wit: John Welsh, Nicolas Welsh. Prov. by John Welsh, J. P.

Page 106: Archibald Davie of Chester Co., SC, to my daughter Mary Crocket of Lancaster Co., land on the Waggon Road adj. Elijah Crocket, John Blair...5 July 1797. Archibald Davie (Seal), Wit: W. R. Davie, Wm. Taylor, Wm. Simpson. Prov. in Lancaster Co., by William Simpson 8 Oct 1798, before Elir. Alexander, J. P.

Page 107: Blank

Page 108: 28 Dec 1793, Charles Adams and wife of Mecklinburg Co., NC to John Welsh of Lancaster Co., for Ł 64 ster., land on Wild Cat Creek, 200 A adj. James McDonald, plat dated 26 Nov 1757, William Islar being the patentee....Charles Adams (Seal), Wit: Thos Neil, Edward Costillo. Prov. by Edward Costillo 5 Nov 1796, before John Welsh, J. P.

BOOK C & E

Pp. 108-109: 18 March 1799, Frederick Cern of Lancaster Co., to
            Daniel Shehorn...land on Wild Cat Creek part of
375 A surveyed for Frederick Cern, 1788...Frederick Kern (Seal),
Wit: Jacob Kern, John Bibbe. Prov. by Jacob Kern, before John
Craig, 29 March 1799, before John Craig, J. P.

Page 109: 8 Dec 1795, John Lany of Lancaster Co., to George
            Laney, for Ł 7 sterling...87½ A, ½ of tract granted to
sd. John Laney, 2 Dec 1793 on Lynches Creek...John Laney (X)
(Seal), Wit: Michael Oats, David Baker (X). Prov. by David Baker,
before John Welsh, J. P. 2 Jan 1797.

Pp. 109-110: 9 Oct 1795, Bennet Highfield of Lancaster Co., plan-
            ter, to Henry Shute for Ł 70 sterling, 100 A on both
sides a branch of Great Lynches Creek called Silver run, patented
by Frederic Rush, 12 Oct 1773...Bennet Highfield (Seal), Wit:
James Holliman, William McBride, Philip Ward. Prov. by William
McBride, before Nathan Barr, J. P., 26 March 1796.

Page 110: 3 Oct 1796, Martin Smith of Lancaster Co., to Jacob
            Plyler, of same, for Ł 25 sterling, land on waters of
Lynches Creek adj. Sumter, Mossman, James Bredon, Jacob Plyler,
granted 4 Aug 1794...Martin Smith (Seal), Wit: John Welsh, Coonrod Plyler (X). Prov. by John Welsh, 3 Oct 1796.

Pp. 110-111: 14 Jan 1799, James Holliman of Lancaster Co., to
            Leonard Rush of same, for $20...60 A, part of 15,000
A granted to Thomas Sumter, 2 Apr 1787...James Holliman (Seal),
Wit: Abraham Rush (X), Jacob Rush. Prov. by Abraham Rush, 23
Feb 1799, before R. Hunley, J. P.

Page 111: Benjamin Ladd Senior of Lancaster Co., for Ł 12 to
            Benjamin Ladd Junior...200 A on waters of Lick Creek,
adj. Isaac Mallet...25 Feb 1799. Benja. Ladd (Seal), Wit: Tully
Biggs, Richmond Terrell. Prov. 27 March 1799, by Tully Biggs,
before Richd Hunley.

Pp. 111-112: 10 March 1797, James McManus of State of Georgia, to
            John Welsh of Lancaster Co., for Ł 50...100 A on
a branch of Big Lynches Creek called Wild Cat adj. tract surveyed
for Lany, granted to Titus Lany, surveyed 16 Feb 1763...James
McManus (X) (Seal), Wit: Charles McManus, James Belk. Prov. 21
March 1798, by Charles McManus, before Thomas Welsh, J. P.

Page 112: 28 Jan 1797, Gen. Thomas Sumter of S. C. to Robert
            Welsh of Lancaster Co., for Ł 35 sterling...part of
15,000 A granted 2 Apr 1787. Thos Sumter (LS), Wit: Jacob Shoffner, Natl. Forseberry. Prov. by Jacob Shofner, before Jesse
Nettles, J. P., 15 June 1797.

Pp. 112-113: 25 Feb 1797, Henry Kee of Lancaster Co., to Gustavus
            Rape of same, for Ł 28 sterling...land in the county
of Chesterfield 114 A on NW side Great Lynches Creek...Henry
Kee (X) (Seal), wit: J. Holliman, Jno Welsh. Prov. in Chesterfield County, by John Welsh, 1 Apr 1797, before James Blakeney,
J. P.

Page 113: 1 March 1797, Robert Wlesh of Lancaster Co., to George
            Laney, for Ł 10 sterling....land whereon the sd. George
now lives, 175 A, part of 305 A granted to Titus Lany 7 May 1787,
obtained by sd. Welsh by purchase of and from Gen. Sumter of an

79

elder patent, adj. George Lany, Titus Lany...Robt Welsh (X) (Seal),
Wit: John Welsh, James Holliman. Prov. by James Holliman, 11 Mr
1797 before Jno Welsh, J. P.

Page 114: 6 Oct 1795, Samuel Whitener of Lancaster Co., being
the lawful heir at law of Isaac Whitener, to John Lany
for ₤ 60...land on both sides of Great Lynches Creek part in the
county of Chesterfield and part in Lancaster, 100 A on E side
of said Creek...Saml Widener (S) (Seal), Wit: Daniel Clark,
George Laney, Elijah Clark. Prov. by George Laney, 2 Jan 1797,
before Jno Welsh, J. P.

Page 115: Blank.

Pp. 116-117: 29 Jan 1790, William Patton & wife Elizabeth & Jas
Patton & wife Mary and Elizabeth Patton their Mother
all of York Co., SC to John Brown of Lancaster Co., for ₤ 20....
land on waters of Twelve Mile Creek called the Mill Stone branch
198 A...William Patton (Seal), Elizabeth Patton (X) (Seal), James
Patton (Seal), Mary Patton (+) (Seal), Elizabeth Patton (--).
Wit: Jas Massey, Jas. Canmore. Prov. by James Massey, before
Hugh White, J. P., 22 Feb 1790.

Pp. 117-118: 30 Jan 1790, John Brown & wife Elizabeth of Lancas-
ter Co., to Wake Ivy of same, for ₤ 49 sterling...
land on mill stone branch waters of Twelve Mile Creek, 156½ A...
John Brown (Seal), Elizabeth Brown (+) (Seal), Wit: Wm. Sharp,
Robert Ivey, Thomas Ware. Prov. by William Sharp, before Hugh
White, 22 Feb 1790.

Page 118: 4 March 1790, John Tomlinson & wife Rebecca of Lancaster Co., to Thomas Ware of same, for ₤ 20 sterling...
land on Mill Stone branch of Twelve Creek (sic) 90 A...John
Tomlinson (Seal), Rebecca Tomlinson (Seal), Wit: Wm. Sharp,
Wike Ivey. Prov. by William Sharp, before Hugh White, 15 Apr
1790.

Page 119: 30 Jan 1790, John Brown & wife Elizabeth of Lancaster
Co., to Thomas Ware of same, for ₤ 10...land on waters
of Twelve Mile Creek called the Mill Stone branch, 42 A...John
Brown (Seal), Elizabeth Brown (+) (Seal), Wit ,Arcld. Cousart,
Wike Ivey, Wm. Sharp. Prov. by William Shpar, 15 Apr 1790,
before Hugh White, J. P.

Pp. 119-120: 3 March 1790, William Denman of Lancaster Co., planter, to Richard Knight of same, for ₤ 20...100 A
granted to sd. William Denman on Tuckahoa branch of Lynches Creek
...William Denman (Seal), Wit: B. Haile.

Pp. 120-121: 31 Oct 1789, Haley Tatum of S. C. Lancaster Co., to
Joseph Cotes of same, land on piney branch waters of
Whiteoak formerly surveyed for Eleanor Adamson, 40 A...Haley
Tatum (LS), Wit: John Boutin, Mathew Jones (+), Harwill Coates.

Page 121: 14 Nov 1789, Haley Tatum of Lancaster Co., Marthew
Jones, for ₤ 100 sterling...120 A on waters of White
Oak Creek part of 2 tracts, one granted to John Woodwin, the
other to Joseph Coates...Haley Tatum, Wit: Joseph Coates, Harwill
Coates, William Scott.

Pp. 121-122: George Perry sold to Alexdr. Archer, my two negroes
& tract of land on which I now reside one Simon the
other Jemimah, 3 Apr 1790...mortgage for debt...George Perry
Wit: Claud Ingram, Alexander C Carruth. Prov. by Alexander C.
Carruth, before Samuel Dunlap, J. P., 18 Jan 1791

Page 122: 6 Dec 1788, James Brownlow & John Brownlow to Thomas
Ballard, for L 80 sterling...350 A on waters of Beaver
Creek adj. David Russel, sd. Ballard, McMahon, John Brown...James
Brownlow (Seal), John Brownlow (X) (Seal), Wit: John Boutin,
John Brown (B), Frances Graham.

Pp. 122-123: 19 Apr 1790, Thomas Ballard of Lancaster Co., to
John Graham of same, for L 20...203½ A part of a
tract originally surveyed for Thos Ballard on waters of Beaver
Creek adj. George Miller, Charles Barber, sd. Graham, John Lake,
David Russell....Thos Ballard (Seal), Wit: J. Boutin, A Fleming
(O), Peter Thomson

Pp. 123-124: 23 Nov 1790, Charels Barber & wife Margret of Lancaster Co., to Ashbourn Sims of same, for L 2500
of Camden Inspected Tobacco...land granted 1 June 1789, 100 A
on Pissimon (sic) branch, adj. Kirkland, Robt McElwain, Josias
Cantey, William Walker...Charles Barber (Seal), Margaret Barber
(+), Wit: William Sims, James Sims, Elisabeth Barber. Prov. by
William Sims, before Samuel Dunlap, J. P., 18 Jan 1791

Page 124: S. C., Lancaster County: John Simpson Sheriff of Lan-
caster Co., by virtue of an order from the County
Court of Lancaster to sell a plantation adj. George Underwood,
Lynches Creek, land granted to James Brigs; the property of
William Tommerlin, and a certain suit which Daniel Brown hath
lately recovered...now for L 13 sold to George Evans...19 Oct
1790. John Simpson (Seal), Wit: Elir Alexander, Daniel Brown,
Saml Lowrie.

Page 125: James Love of Chester Co., bound to the Decenting (sic)
Presbyterian Society of the Hanging Rock to the trustees to be
hereafter appointed who have asociated tnemselves together with
others by the name of Decenting Presbyterian Society for Reli-
gious Purposes and having divine service performed (at a place
on the waters of Hanging Rock Creek in late Lancaster County and
State of South-Carolina aforesaid known by the name of James Loves
old place whereon stands a Meeting house)...19 Aug 1790, to make
titles...Jas Love (Seal), Wit: James Gaston, Glass Caston, John
Love.

Pp. 126-127: Richard Middleton, John Middleton, Josiah Middleton
and William Middleton, agreement....in a brotherly
manner, whereas since the death of our father that the land
belonging to said Estate devolve as Right of Inheritance by heirship to our Eldest brother Richard Middleton as above mentioned
and since the death of our father a certain evil disposed Benjamin Burnit aided by a Frederick Kimbell hath imposed on our Brother to mortgage said land for L 250 sterling...division of property,7 Jul 1790. Wit: George Evans, Josiah Canty. Kershaw
County: Prov. by George Evans before John Marshel, J. P., 6 Jan
1791.

Pp. 127-128: 27 Feb 1789, James Nickle of Lancaster Co., Miller,

to Thomas Gaston of same, Waggon maker, for ₤ 30...100 A part of
a tract originally granted to Robert Love by Gov. Bull 30 Sept
1774, 300 A on the Hanging Rock Creek adj. Alexander Ingram,
Robert Love, and on 25 Oct 1786 and 29 June 1787 was by L & R
conveyed by James Love (son and heir of Robert Love) & wife Margaret to sd. James Nickle...James Nickle (N) (Seal), Thomas Gaston (Seal), Wit: Elir. Alexander, Margaret Alexander, James Purdy.

Page 129: 27 Nov 1792, James Douglass of Lancaster Co., to Isom
Pulley, for ₤ 12 sterling...land adj. Sarah Bottom,
Benjamin Maddox, Isom Pulley, near the course of a Path called
Bairds Path, 60 A...James Douglass (Seal), Wit: Benjn Maddox
Junr, Benjn Maddox, Sen.

Page 130: 22 June 1794, Sarah Harper of Lancaster Co., Widow,
to Moses Cantzon of same, for ₤ 160 sterling...land on
E side Catawba River in the Waxhaw Settlemtn part of 400 A granted by George II by a N. C. Grant to Samuel McLanvey, conveyed
& alienated to Hamilton Ross and by sd. Ross to Cornelius Anderson
...Sarah Harper (Seal), Wit: John Cantzon, Allen Anderson, Richard Graves. Prov. by John Cantzon, 10 Nov 1794, before Josh. Lee.

Page 131: S. C. Lancaster County: William Tate heir to the deceased
William Tate of Lancaster Co., for ₤ 40 to Joseph Haile,
100 A on a ridge between the heads of two branches of Lynches
Creek one called Flat creek the other Williams's Creek, granted
to Nathaniel Shepherd by Gov. Bull 24 Nov 1764...27 Jan 1797.
William Tate (Seal), Wit: Edward Narramore, Jos Coile. Prov.
by Joseph Coile, before William Ward, J. P., 27 Jan 1797.

Pp. 131-132: 10 Feb 1797, Gen. Thomas Sumter to John Freeman,
for ₤ 34...340 A, part of 15,000 A granted to sd.
Sumter, 2 Apr 1787, adj. John Cannington, Benjamin Haile...Thos
Sumter (Seal), Richard Haynsworth, Stephen Cordle (S). Prov.
by Stephen Caudle, before Benjamin Haile, J. P. 15 March 1797.

Pp. 132-133: 20 May 1775, Joshua Bradley and wife Jenny of
Georgia to Isaac Wiedner of Craven County, S. C.,
by grant 7 June 1774 to Joshua Bradley, 100 A on both sides of
Great Lynches Creek...Joshua Bradley (Seal), Jane Bradley (I)
(Seal), Wit; David Thweat, Daniel Coleman. Prov. by David
Thweat, before Leroy Hammond, J. P.

Pp. 133-134: 22 Sept 1795, Henry Peebles, planter, of the State
of Georgia, to William Terrel, planter, of Lancaster Co., SC, for ₤ 40...150 A granted to Joshua Hickman, 7 Feb
1758, on both sides Lick Creek a branch of Flat Creek, 150 A...
H. Peebles (Seal), Wit: Jesse Peebles, John Baker, Jacobus
Leaird, Durantea Vites. Prov. by John Baker before B. Haile,
J. P., 10 March 1796.

Pp. 134-135: 9 Jan 1792, Henry Cato to Lancaster co., planter,
to Edmund Deason of same, planter, for ₤ 14 s 5...
part of two surveyed 50 A from a grant to Lewis Peebles, 19 Mar
1773, the remainder being part of grant to Thomas Wade 20 Dec
1758...Henry Cato (X) (Seal), Tabitha Cato (X) (Seal), Wit:
Tarry Jones, Samuel Helton (Hilton), Starling Cato. Prov. by
Samuel Hilton, 9 Apr 1794, before B. Haile, J. P.

Page 135: 21 Dec 1795, William Smith of Lancaster Co., to John
        Hood of same, for Ł 70 sterling...150 A on E side Ca-
tawba River, on waters of Rocky Creek, part of 300 A granted to
William Maddox...Wm. Smith (Seal), Tabitha Smith (Seal), Wit:
Da Crenshaw, Ely Clark. Prov. before Robert Bratney, J. P., by
Ely Clark, 1 Sept 1796.

Page 136: 28 March 1795, Thomas Clendenon and wife Margaret of
        York County, to William Cureton of Lancaster Co., for
Ł 7 sterling...35 A (excepting a part of said tract which is
within the lines of an older tract which was granted to William
Guttrie) granted to Margaret Barnett, 1 Jan 1787....28 March
1795. Thos Cleninen (Seal), Margaret Clendinen (Seal), Wit: Jeremiah Cureton, Wm. Hasslet Clendenen. Prov. by Jeremiah Cureton
before Henry Massey, J. P. 6 June 1795.

Pp. 137-146: Blank.

(N. B. With page 147 commences what was apparently the original
book E, and begins with page 3 of this older book. The first
deed is fragmentary)

Pp. 147-148: for Ł 50 sterling currency of S. C. pd by William
        Caston, 200 A in Lancaster Co., on branches of
Turkey Quarter Creek on the great road surveyed for sd. Glass
Caston, granted 6 Feb 1786...Glass Caston (Seal), Elizabeth
Caston (O) (Seal), Wit: Saml Caston, Joseph Caston, Seth
Caston. Prov. in Court 27 July 1798.

Pp. 148-149: Middleton McDonald of Lancaster Co., for Ł 5 ster.,
        to William Marlow, Thomas Houze, George Hickling,
Gedeon Glase, and John Graham Trustees for Camp Creek Meeting
house be it for the use of the Methodist Episcopal Church in
County and State aforesaid, a certain tract for the use of
the Methodist Episcopal Church with the meeting House, part of
a tract granted to Major Minor Winn and conveyed to sd. M. Mc-
Donald, 3 June 1797, on N side Lakes line...10 July 1798. Middleton McDonald (Seal), Wit: Richard Buckelew, Middleton McDonald
Junr., Jas Douthit. Prov. by Middleton McDonald Junior, 27 Oct
1798, before Danl Wade, J. L. C.

Pp. 149-150: 7 May 1798, Robert Hancock and Sarah Hancock of
        Lancaster Co., to Mark Meacham of same, for Ł 37
ster., land in Lancaster Co., 53 A adj. John Tomlinson...Robert
Hancock (Seal), Sarah Hancock (Seal), Wit: John Tomlinson, Jesse
Roper Jur., Henry Harper. Prov. by John Tomlinson, 11 March
1799, before Samuel C. Dunlap, J. P.

Pp. 150-152: 22 Aug 1795, Thomas Blair & wife Jane of Lancaster
        Co., to James Taylor of Chester Co., for Ł 100...
land on E side Catawba River, part of 2 tracts one originally
granted to John Arnold Pender and Henry White 150 A and 75 A of
sd. tract was conveyed to James Blair and it fell to John Blair
by birth & by John Blair to Thomas Blair the other 49 A part of
a grant to William Taylor and by William Taylor, to Jacob Taylor,
by Jacot Taylor to John Arneld Pender and by sd. Arneld to James
Blair which fell to John Blair as the former & then it was conveyed by John Blair to Thomas Blair...Thomas Blair (Seal), Jane
Blair (X) (Seal), Wit: Patrick Graves, Wm. Taylor, Sarah Taylor.
Prov. in Chester County by Patrick Graves, before James Crawford,
J. P., 2 Sept 1795.

Pp. 152-154: 1 May 1778, Henry Pearson of MacklenBurgh Co., N.
C., and wife Jean to Richard Pearson of same, for
Ł 110...land in St. Marks Parish, Craven Co., SC on N side
Catawba River part of 599 A granted to John Barnett 23 Feb 1754,
conveyed to Revrd. Robert Miller by deed 27 March 1757, by sd.
Miller to James Barnett by deed 23 Feb 1758, and by him conveyed
to sd. Pearson by deed 5 Jan 1775....Henry Pearson (Seal), Jean
Pearson (M) (Seal), Wit: Isaac Starrett, Hez. Alexander. Prov.
in Mecklenburg County, October term 1779, by Hezekiah Alexander,
before Sam Martin, C. M. C.
    (for the deeds from John Barnett to Robert Miller and from
    Robert Miller to James Barnett, see my Anson County, N. C.
    Deed Abstracts--BHH)

Pp. 154-156: 1 Oct 1778, Richard Pearson of Mecklenburg Co.,
N. C., to Hugh Rogers of St. Marks Parish, Craven
Co., SC, by granted 3 Feb 1754 by N. C. to John Barnett of Anson
County, 599 A on N side Catawba River, conveyed by sd. Barnett
to Reverd. Robert Miller minister of the Waxhaws by an indenture
27 March 1757, and by sd. Robt Miller 23 Feb 1758 to James
Barnett by sd. James Barnett to Henry Pearson 5 Jan 1775, 174½ A
and by sd. Henry Pearson to Richard Pearson 1 May 1778; for
Ł 1950 SC currency...Richard Pearson (Seal), Wit: Jas Nickelson,
Edward Erwin, John Johnston. Prov. in Mecklenburg Co., Oct. term
1779, by John Johnston, before Sam Martin, C. M. C.

Pp. 156-158: 15 Oct 1785, Samson Gray of Macklinburg Co., N. C.,
to John Crockett of Craven Co., S. C., for Ł 100
sterling, 100 A in Craven County, SC originally patant to Henry
Boykin on both sides Little Linches Creek surveyed by Thos Waid
6 Oct 1753 all sides vacant, granted in Book 11 page 316, con-
veyed by Henry Boykin to Abraham Peoples 18 Aug 1759, then to
John Blakeney 11 July 1765, to Nicholas Welsh, 1 Nov 1771, to
Lewis Pepls (sic) 17 Jan 1774, than to Sharad Gray 22 Jan 1782,
then to Samson Gray 9 Oct 1785...Samson Gray (Seal), Wit: Jacob
Gray, Jacob Gray Senr (Ɨ), William Crockett. Prov. by William
Crockett in Lancaster Co., 8 Aug 1791, before Robt Dunlap, J.
L. C.

Pp. 158-159: 22 Sept 1795, Wm. Allen of Lancaster Co., SC to
John Crockett for Ł 20 sterling, 100 A granted to
James Adams, 25 March 1775, adj. Jas Gamble, Robt Dunlap, John
White, John Crockett on Cane Creek, which land James Adams sold
to William Allin 17 Nov 1792, and now to John Crockett...Will
Allin (Seal), Wit: Jno B Barkley, Andrew Corckett. Prov. by
Andrew Crockett, 28 May 1799, before Robt Dunlap, J. L. C.

Pp. 159-161: 4 Oct 1787, John Thompson & wife Martha of Lancas-
ter Co., to Thomas Dunlap, planter, for Ł 120 ster.,
land on NE side Catawba River one Cane Creek...John Thomson (Seal),
Martha Thomson (P) (Seal), Wit: Robt Dunlap, Henry Foster, James
Delany. Prov. by Robert Dunlap, 2 Sept 1796, before Elir.
Alexander, C. L. Ct.

Pp. 162;179-80:4 Oct 1787, John Thompson planter & wife Martha
to Thomas Dunlap, planter, by grant dated 16 May
1754 by Matthew Rowan, Gov. of N. C. to Benjamin Thompson, 163
A adj. Samuel Dunlap, for Ł 175 sterling...John Thomson (Seal),
Martha Thomson (O) (Seal), Wit: Robt Dunlap, Henry Foster, James
Delany. Prov. by Robt Dunlap, before Elir. Alexander 2 Sept
1796.

BOOK C & E

N. B. Pages 163-178 of this volume contain a court docket for
1815-1816 and are not transcribed here. They were probably
bound within this book by mistake.

Pp. 180-181: S. C., Lancaster County: Owen Reed, planter, to
Frederick Joyner planter, for $30...mortgage of
land 17 Sept 1799, 100 A...17 Sept 1799. Owen Reed (R) (Seal),
Wit: Middleton Joyner, Delilah Reed (X), John Joyner (E).

Page 181: S. C.: Micajah Hughes of Lancaster Co., to Phillimon
Starke of same, for penal sum of Ł 400 sterling, bound
10 Dec 1795 to make title to 180 A on E side Waterree River...
Micajah Hughs (Seal), Wit: Samuel Starke, Elizabeth Pickett.
Prov. by Saml Starke, 9 Apr 1796, before Jesse Tillman, J. P.

Page 182: S. C., Camden Dist.: Thomas Watts of Kershaw County,
for s 5, to Reubin Starke of Lancaster & Kershaw Co.,
(sic!) 250 A, part of tract laid out for Thomas Watts 1 Feb 1768
adj. Francis Kirkland...22 Feb 1796. Thos Watts (Seal), Wit:
Nicholas Peay, Austin Peay, Elijah Ivey. Prov. by Austin Peay in
Fairfield County, 11 Apr 1796, before Chas. Pickett,J. P.

Pp. 183-184: S. C., Camden District, Lancaster County: 17 Nov
1795, William Stark of Fairfield Co., planter, to
Reubin Starke of co. aforesaid, planter, for Ł 60 sterling...
land on N side Catawba River adj. an old survey of William
Harrison, granted to William Harrison 20 Oct 1766, which he gave
unto Patent Hill & conveyed by James Harrison, and also conveyed
to Thomas Hill to Richard Burge, by indenture 17 Nov 1795, and
sd. Burge to John Miles 4 Nov 1782, originally granted to William
Harrison by Gov. Montague 20 Oct 1766...Wm. Starke (Seal), Wit:
Gray Briggs, Elizabeth Pickett, Saml Starke. Prov. by Samuel
Starke, before Jesse Tillman, J. P., 9 Apr 1796.

Pp. 184-185: Thomas Watts of Kershaw Co., bound for s 5 to Austin
Peay of Lancaster Co., 200 A laid out for Thomas
Watts 1 Feb 1768...23 Feb 1796. Thomas Watts (Seal), Wit: Nicho-
las Peay, Reubin Starke, Saml Starke. Prov. by Reubin Starke, 11
Apr 1796, before Chas Pickett, J. P. in Fairfield County.

Pp. 185-186: S. C. Lancaster County: John Craton for Ł 15 to
James McClure, 100 A part of a survey to John
Craton on a branch of Little Lynches Creek...surveyed 25 July 1795
recorded in Grant Book P No. 5, page 374...29 Sept 1798. Jno
Creighton (Seal), Wit: John McClure, Abraham Keanlick. Prov.
by James McClure, before Jas. Ingrem, J. P., 30 Nov 1798.

Pp. 186-188: S. C. Lancaster County: 13 Dec 1787, Arthur Massey
and wife Elizabeth, planter, to Solomon Owens of
same, for Ł 150 Sterling...150 A, part of 200 A on both sides
branch of Lynches Creek called Bufelow, granted to John Boatright
31 Oct 1769, Rec. in Book D D D page 485, memorial entered Book
K No. 910, page 13, 8 Dec 1769...Arter Massey (Seal), Elizabeth
Massey (X) (Seal), Wit: Richard Holley, Danl Monaghan, John
Owens (X). Prov. by John Owens (X), before Andrew Baskin, J. P.

Pp. 188-189: 7 Sept 1786, Nathaniel Pace of wife Mildred of Swift
Creek, in Claremount County, Camden District, to
Richard Buckelow of Camp Creek in Lancaster Co., for Ł 25 ster.,
200 A on the drains of Crooked a prong of Camp Creek in Lancaster
Co., adj. Wm. Marlow...Nathl. Pace (Seal), Mildred Pace (Seal),

85

Wit: Micajah Crenshaw, Wm. Garrah (X). Prov. by Micajah Crenshaw, 19 Dec 1797, before Jesse Tillman, J. P.

Page 190: Solomon Smith of Lancaster Co., for Ł 17 sterling to William McDonald Junr. of Chester Co., horses, cattle, household furniture...28 July 1797. Solomon Smith, Wit: Jno May. Prov. by John May in Lancaster Co., 31 July 1797.

Pp. 190-193: 15 Feb 1794, Samuel Graham of Lancaster Co., planter, to John Scott, of same, by grant dated 5 Dec 1785, 640 A in the Dist. of Camden on east side of the Great Road to Charleston on a branch of Turkey Quarter waters of Cane Creek, granted to Wm Caston, and by sd. Cason conveyed to Samuel Graham...Saml Graham (LS), Wit: Jno Kirk, William Harper (a), Prov. by John Kirk, before William Barkley, 8 Feb 1796.

Page 193: Michael Patton for natural love and affection to my cousin Hugh White and family, horses, cow and calf, my bed and furniture, etc. 7 March 1795. Michael Patton (8) (Seal), Wit: Jno Simpson. Rec. 17 June 1795.

Pp. 193-194: Matthew Hood of Lancaster Co., for Ł 55 to Mark Robinson, cattle and sheep, hoggs...10 Jan 1795. Matthew Hood (Seal), Wit: Charles McKey (C). Prov. by Charles McKey, 6 March 1795, before Jas. Ingrem, J. P.

Pp. 195-196: S. C. Lancaster Co: 10 Sept 1795, William Johnston acting attorney for George Johnston of State of Kentuckey, to Matthew Hood of Lancaster Co., for Ł 40...100 A... William Johnston (Seal), Wit: William McCorkle, John Batchellor (X), Robert Hood. Prov. by John Batchelor, 1 Apr 1796, before Elir. Alexander, J. L. C.

Pp. 196-198: S. C. Lancaster District, 10 Sept 1795, William Johnston of State of Kentuckey acting attorney for George Johnston of sd. state of Kentuckey, to Matthew Hood of Lancaster Co., for Ł 30 sterling...land on waters of Bare Creek 260 A, adj. Thos Miller, Walker, James Douglass, granted to sd. George Johnston 3 June 1793...William Johnson (Seal), Wit: William McCorkle, John Batchelor (X), Robert Hood. Prov. by John Batchelor, 1 Apr 1796, before Elir. Alexander.

Pp. 198-199: 10 Sept 1795, William Johnson of State of Kentuckey atty for George Johnston to Matthew Hood, 95 A on Bare Creek. Same sign, wit., and proving date.

Pp. 199-201: 22 Feb 1794, James Hood of S. C., Lancaster Co., to Samuel McElhany of sd. county, for Ł 25 sterling, 50 A, part of 450 A surveyed for sd. James Hood and granted 4 Sept 1786...James Hood (Seal), Wit: Ely Clark, Archibald Hood. J. Coile. Lancaster County: Prov. by Joseph Coile, 9 March 1796, before Robert Bratney, J. P.

Pp. 201-202: Benjamin Vaughan of Lancaster Co., for Ł 80 sterling, for Ł 80 to Matthew Hood, negro Joe about five feet ten inches high and 25 years old....9 Jany 1795. Benjamin Vaughan (Seal), Wit: Mark Robinson, Rolley Weaver. Prov. by Mark Robinson, 11 Apr 1795, before Jas. Ingrem, J. P.

Pp. 202-203: 11 July 1795, Charles Barber of Kershaw County,

to George Marlow of Lancaster Co., for Ł 20 sterling, part of
480 A granted to Charles Barber 1787, also 50 A part of 95 A
granted to Charles Barber 1792, and 128 A part of grant of 1795
A granted 6 Aug 1787, adj. Arthur Ingram, Fedk Joyner...Charles
Barber (Seal), Wit: Jos Coile, Saml Nutt, Patience Coile (X).
Prov. by Samuel Nutt, 29 July 1795, before Jas. Ingram, J. P.

Pp. 203-205: 24 Feb 1784, Robt Craighed of North Carolina, Mack-
lenburgh County, to Samuel Dunlap, of S. C., Craven
Co., by granted 23 Feb 1754 by N. C. to John Barnett of Anson
County, conveyed to Rvd. Robt. Miller, than to James Barnett,
then to Henry Pearson, then to Richard Pearson, and by Richd
Pearson to Hugh Rodgers, 1 Oct 1778, and by sd. Hugh Rodgers
conveyed to Thomas B. Craighead, 24 Sept 1779, and by sd. Thos
B. Craighead to Robt Craighead 28 Oct 1783, now for Ł 101...
Robt Craighead (Seal), Wit: Robert Dunlap, Alexr Crafford, Alexr
C. Carruth. Prov. by Robt Dunlap, Esqr., 24 Aug 1798, before
Elir. Alexander, J. P.

Pp. 206-207: 9 Feb 1799, William Eastridge, of S. C., Lancaster
Co., to Jonathan Johnston of same, for Ł 50 sterling,
land, 160 A surveyed to Jesse Mesho 7 Dec 1794 on waters of
Little Linches Creek adj. Enoch Anderson, John Williams, Joseph
Caston...William Estridge (*) (Seal), Wit: Britn. Fuller, William
Ward, Joseph Johnston, dated 9 Jan 1799 at end of deed. Prov.
by William Ward, before R. Hunley, J. P., 14 March 1799.

Pp. 207-208: Peter Twitty for Ł 100 sterling to Winn Twittey,
a negroe man Charles 25 years old...25 Jan 1799.
Peter Twitty (Seal), Wit: Samuel Hammond (X), James Clack   Ack
in open Court Jan. 29 1799.

Pp. 208-210: 28 Jan 1799, Abraham Joseph Eastridge of Lancaster
Co., to Jesse Masho of same, planter, for Ł 10 ster.,
25 A on Little Linches Creek part of 200 A granted to William
Johnston 3 July 1772, and sd. William Johnston conveyed to
Edward Williams part of sd. tract supposed to be 50 A and sd.
Edward Williams conveyed to sd. 50 a unto Abraham Joseph and
William Eastridge, adj. William Ward, Joseph Johnston....Abraham
Eastridge (L), Joseph Eastridge (X), Mary Eastridge (/), Wit:
John Mesho, William Chambers. Prov. 4 Feb 1799, by William
Chambers, before R. Hunley, J. P.

Pp. 210-211: 17 Sept 1792, Isaac Smith of York County, to William
Hammet of Lancaster Co., for Ł 30 sterling, land on
S side Waxhaw Creek, 57 A with a mill on it...Isaac Smith (Seal),
Wit: John McClenahan, William Taylor, Andrew Linn. Prov. by
William Taylor, 18 Sept 1792, before Isc. Donnom, J. P.

Pp. 212-213: 24 Apr 1798, Minor Winn of Fairfield County, to
Nathan Barr of Lancaster Co., for Ł 17 s 10, 150
A granted to Minor Winn 5 March 1787, surveyed for John White
6 Feb 1786...M. Winn (Seal), Wit: William Massey, Jno Simpson.
Prov. by John Simpson, Esqr., 13 May 1799, before Elir. Alexan-
der, J. P.

Pp. 213-214: Mary Rowel of Lancaster Co., for love, good will &
affection to George McGarrah my son in law husband
to my daughter Mary Rowell of county aforesd., negro girl Patience
12 years old, Mary Rowell (/) (Seal), Wit: Isaac Stewart, William
Rowel, John Masy. Prov. by William Rowel 29 Dec 1797.

BOOK C & E

Pp. 214-215: 25 July 1797, Ashbourn Sims of Lancaster Co., to
     William Dukes of same, for Ł 20 curreny money and
500 lbs. of tobacco, land on W side of Road leading from Camden
to F. Joyners. Not signed in book. Wit: Saml Hammond, James
Cauthorn (X), Billey Holland.

Page 215: whereas a law suit has subsisted between John Latta
     plaintiff and Ann Thompson and James Thompson Defendants
concerning the rights of the plantation on which she now dwells...
rights of dower, 15 May 1787. Ann Thomson (A), Wit: George White,
Hugh Whiteside. Prov. by Hugh Whiteside, in Chester County,
before John McCreary, J. P., 4 May 1795.

Pp. 216-217: 20 July 1793, William Barnett sheriff of Lancaster
     Co., to William Blair, planter, whereas James Yancey
decd was in his lifetime possessed of two tracts, of 300 A, and
sd. James Yancey was indebted to William Blair a certain sum...
action in the County Court of Lancaster against Abigail Yancey as
Executrix...by writ of fieri facias, 23 Feb 1793, for Ł 15 ster.
...William Barnett (Seal), Wit: David Crenshaw, Hugh Wells.

Page 218: Blank.

Page 219: State of Alabama, Perry County: John Welsh Snr of
     co. & state aforesd. appoint Michael Miller of Chester-
field District, my attorney, to sur for parcel of land purchased
from Genl. Thomas Sumter...2 June 1834. John Welsh Snr (LS),
Wit: K. Clarke, Duncan Clarke. Prov. by Duncan Clarke in Chesterfield District, 11 July 1834, before W. J. Hanna, Q. U.

Pp. 220-221: Mary Barber, Hiram Allen and Dianna Allen his wife,
     all of Lancaster Dist., for $1000 to Burrel Beckham
of same, 304 A in Kershaw District, on waters of Beaver Creek
adj. William Brewer, William Ingram, John Cunningham, Mrs. Ingrem,
land originally surveyed for Charles Barber & Mary Ingrem, the
whole of Charles Barbers grant of 250 A surveyed 20 July 1784
and a prt of Mary Ingrems grant for 400 A sur. 5 Jan 1785...4
Jan 1834. Mary Barber (X) (LS), H. Allen (LS), Dianna Allen
(Seal), Wit: J. P. Thompson, Will G. Cox. Prov. by W. G.
Cox, before J. P. Thomspon, J. P. 1 Jan. 1834. Dianna Allen
relinquished dower 9 Apr 1824.

Pp. 222-223: Francis K. Brummitt of Lancaster Dist., for $1000
     to John McKenzie of same, land in the village and
suburbs of the villageof Lancaster 3 acres near a Gin House,
Dinkins & Robbins corner, Danl Houze, Doctor T. L. Dunlap...5
Apr 1834.   R. K. Brummitt (Seal), Wit: Henry McKenzie, E. F.
Crockett. Prov. by Henry McKenzie, 6 Oct 1834.

Pp. 223-224: John McKenzie of Lancaster Dist., for $2500 to
     Benjamin F. Saddler of same, lot in Village of Lan-
caster, which appears by a plat made by Saml Dunlap 11 Feb 1812,
plat attached to a deed made by Sampson Stewart, Wm. W. Stewart
and others to John McKenzie 19 Aug 1824...29 July 1834. Jno
McKenzie (Seal), Wit: J. H. Witherspoon Jr., C. W. Sims. Prov.
by C. W. Sims, 8 Oct 1834. Mrs. Eliza McKenzie, wife of John,
relinquished dower before Simon Beckham, J. Q., 8 Oct 1834.

Page 225: Plat of Jno Stewarts Land, shows adj. to Jno Foster.
"Copied from Comr of Locations Book 14 Oct 1834."

Page 226: John McKenzie of Lancaster Dist., for $300 to Saml
Robinson of same, land on the Ridge dividing the waters
of Gills & Camp Creek adj. lands of James Adams, Wm Taylor,
John J. Rodgers, Rebecca Dowsart(?), William Taylor Esqr. (now
Darling Belk) and Andrew B. McCain now David Taylors, 242 A...
14 Oct 1834. Jno McKenzie (Seal), Wit: C. W. Sims, John McAtur.
Prov. by C. W. Sims 18 Oct 1834.

Pp. 227-228: J. A. Carter of Lancaster Dist. bound to John John-
ston in the sum of $1000 17 Jan 1831, to make titles
to 766 A known by the name of George Hays old plantation near to
Rocky Creek... A. Carter (Seal), Wit: J. F. G. Mittag, J. M.
Stringfellow. Prov. by J. F. G. Mittag, 18 Oct 1834, before S.
Beckham, Clk.
Assigned by John Johnston to Abner D. Johnston, 14 Sept
1834.
In compliance with the Court of Equity, I assign my right
to Wm Williams Shff to make me titles 8 Oct 1834. Abner D.
Johnston.

Pp. 228-230: S. C., Lancaster District, In chancery. Whereas
John Barnes and James Johnston, Wm McWillie & Howard
& Minor Clinton on 2 Oct 1832 did exhibit their bill of complaint
against Abner D. Johnston...land to be sold by Comr of said Court
...sold to John Barnes, tract on E side Catawba River adj. Mc-
Cullough, Zadoc Perry, Wm McKenna, Joshua Perry & John Barnes,
766 A...6 Oct 1834. J. H. Witherspoon (Seal), Wit: Zadock Perry,
James Duren.

Pp. 230-231: Alfred J. Williams of Dist. of Lancaster, for $450
to John Truesdell of same, land on waters of Hanging
Rock Creek 98 A adj. sd. John Truesdell, Thos Cauthen, Cynthia
Ussery, William Ingrem decd., being the same that belonged to
Saml Ussery decd...30 Dec 1833. Alfred J. Williams (LS), Wit:
Eli Williams, Wylie Horton, Thos Cauthen. Prov. by Wylie Horton,
11 March 1834, before Thos Twitty, Q. U. Elizabeth Williams,
wife of Alfred J., relinquished dower 11 March 1834.

Pp. 231-233: S. C. Lancaster Dist. Mary Stevens widow, the wife
of Joab Stevens decd, for $205 to Thos M. Belk of
same, 90 A, on Gills Creek, 321 A, granted to William Galloway
Jr., and conveyed to John Porter, then to Nathl Hough, then to
Joab Stevens...14 Oct 1834. Mary Stevens (X) (Seal), Wit: James
Porter, Elias Stevens (X), William Stevens. Prov. by James Porter, 15 Oct 1834, before Robert Nelson, J. Q. Plat included
made 21 Aug 1833 by John Sims, showing the dwelling house.

Pp. 234-235: Henry C. Horton of Lancaster Dist., for $2400 to
John Rutledge and Dianna Rutledge of same, land on
both sides of Lick Creek, 400 A...7 March 1823. Henry C. Horton
(LS), Wit: Thos Cauthen, John Baker. Prov. by Thos Cauthen, 15
Nov 1823, before William R. Horton, J. Q. Elizabeth Horton, wife
of William R., relinquished dower 15 Nov 1823.

Pp. 235-237: S. C. Lancaster Dist.: Clabourn Horton of Dist. of
Lancaster, to John Rutledge, for $2100, land on
waters of Hanging Rock Creek 431 A...23 Jan 1826. Clabourn Horton
(LS), Wit: Jesse Horton, Elvin Horton, Woodford Ussery. Prov.
by Jesse Horton, 13 March 1825, before William Ward, J. Q.
Margaret Horton, wife of Clabourn Horton, relinquished dower 13
March 1826, before William Ward, J. Q.

Pp. 237-238: Joseph Lee ofCamden, for $2000 to Ann B. Crawford,
of the Town of Lancaster, lots in Lancaster, 18, 19,
20, 29, 30, 31 nn Broad St...20 Oct 1834. Joseph Lee (LS), Wit:
A. C. Dunlap, Wm. J. Vaughan. Prov. by Alexr C. Dunlap, 26 Nov
1834, before Simon Beckham, Q. U. S. C. Kershaw Dist,: Catharine
C. Lee, wife of Joseph, relinquished dower, 14 Nov 1834(?) before
Hall T. McGee, J. Q.

Pp. 239-240: John Countryman of Dist. of Lancaster, for $350, to
George W. Dunlap, 100 A whereon the sd. John at
present resides granted to Isabel Carnanghan, adj. Alexander
Wright, Saml Couser, Abram Perry, Hugh Hood...26 June 1834. John
Countryman (LS), Wit: Geo W. Witherspoon, Saml F. Dunlap. Prov.
by George W. Witherspoon (no date). Mary, wife of John Countryman, relinquished dower 25 Nov 1834, before Simon Beckham, U. Q.

Pp. 241-242: By an order from the Court of Com. pleas for Lan-
caster Dist., on a writ of partition in the case of
Sally Funderburk et al vs Uriah Funderburk et al...217 A, on 17
Jan 1833 exposed to public outcry, sold to John Roberson for
$216....Wm Williams Sheriff (Seal), Wit: Jno Adams, Jonas Funder-
burk. Prov. by John Adams, 27 Nov 1834, before Simon Beckham,
Q. U. (Plat included)

Pp. 243-244: James M. Ingrem of Lancaster Co., for $89.75 to Thos
Cauthen of same, land on waters of Hanging Rock
Creek 19 A below Thos Cauthens Mill...17 Feb 1834. James M. Ingrem (LS), Wit: Wylie Horton, Chapman L. Rallings, Micl. T. Horton. Prov. by Micl. T. Horton, 2 Aug 1834, before J. P. Thompson, J. P.

Pp. 244-245: Thomas Hancock of Lancaster Dist., for natural love
& affection, to my three daughters to wit, Elizabeth
Tallent, Mary Hancock and Nancy Hernigan, all of dist. aforesd.,
400 A formerly belonged to Francis Hancock decd., given or
granted to William Walker son of Joel Walker deceased and to me
by sd. Francis decd...3 Oct 1834. Thos Hancock (LS), Wit: Josiah
M. Croxton, Andrew McMurry, James Croxton. Prov. by James Croxton, 10 Nov 1834, before S. Beckham, Q. U.

Pp. 246-247: James T. Stinson of Lancaster Co., for $250, to
William Thrower , land on Waxhaw Creek, 25 A on Stin-
sons Mill Road, adj. Thos Thrower...15 Nov 1831. James T. Stinson
(LS), Wit: J. W. White, Wm. S. Stinson. (Plat included made 12
Nov 1831)

Pp. 248-249: Austin F. Peay of Fairfield District, for $18,670
to Roland Cornelius of Kershaw District, 1260 A,
in the Districts of Kershaw & Lancaster on NE side Wateree River
adj. William Cunningham, Land sold by Stark Perry to Jackey
Perry, Land called the McWillie (?) tract, lands belonging to
the estate of Sion Coats decd, and lands formerly belonged to
Josiah Perry decd being composed of several tracts and parts of
land, one tract granted to Thomas Watts, one granted to Richard
Kirkland, and parts of two others was originally owned or was
in possession of Lamb Perry, Jonathan Barns, Philemon Stark, by
resurvey by Alexander McCaskill D. S. 23 Novr 1834...22 Nov 1834.
A. F. Peay (Seal), Wit: Sterling P. Howel,John E. Peay. Prov. by
Sterling P. Howel, 30 Nov 1834, before E. Sill (GILL?), J. P.
Pp. 250-252: Plat to above, 23 Nov 1826.

N. B. With page 253, the older deeds (1790's) resume. Apparently the deeds were in poor condition, and the first one is
fragmentary.

Page 253: Henry Rugeley and wife Elizabeth to John Dixon....Wit:
William Kirkland, John McMillan. (date missing)

Pp. 253-254: 15 July 1790, James Nickle of Lancaster Co., Miller,
to James Purdy, of same, weaver, for Ł 25 sterling
...100 A on Hanging Rock Creek, part of 300 A granted to Robert
Love, and at deceased fell to his son and heir James Love who
granted to same to James Nickle....James Nickle (M) (Seal), Wit:
Elir. Alexander, Abdon Alexander.

Pp. 254-255: 2 July 1790, James Hood and wife Mourning of Lancaster Co., to Mathew Hood, of same, for Ł 50 sterling
1/2 of 440 A in the district of Camden on both sides Ceder Creek,
on NE side Catabaw on the left hand of the old Rocky Mount road...
James Hood (Seal), Mourning Hood (Seal), Wit: Arthur Hinesee (X),
Jos Coile, Benedict Best.

Pp. 255-256: 19 Apr 1790, John Graham of S. C., Lancaster Co.,
to John Roberson of same, for s 5, 33 A on waters
of Beaver Creek adj. George Mills land, Charles Barber, sd.
Graham...John Graham (Seal), Wit: John Boutin, John Branham, Beer-
shaba Collins (+).

Page 256: 22 Feb 1790, Hugh Milling of Fairfield County, to Kene-
day(?) Bailey, for s 10, 250 A... H. Milling (LS), Wit:
Wm. Durphey, John Elison. Prov. by John Elison, 22 Feb 1790, before Saml Dunlap. J. P.

Page 257: 16 July 1790, William Nutt of Lancaster Co., to James
Carruth of same, for Ł 100 sterling, land on waters of
Beaver Creek, a branch of Wateree River, 190 A, part of 400 A
granted to Lewis Clark 1759...William Nutt (Seal), Wit: Alex C.
Carruth, Walter Carruth, William Nutt.

Pp. 257-258: 16 July 1790, William Nutt, to Walter Carruth, for
s 1 sterling, part of 225 A ...William Nutt (Seal),
Wit: James Carruth, William Nutt, Alex C. Carruth.

Page 258: 20 Aug 1789, Henry Eady of Lancaster Co., planter, to
Mary Dixon of same, for Ł 10 sterling...200 A adj.
Robert Dixon...Henry Eady (H) (Seal), Wit: Robert Dunvill, James
Trentham, Robert Dunvill Junr.

Page 259: 22 Feb 1790, Hugh Milling of Fairfield Co., to Kenaday
Bailey of Lancaster Co., for Ł 50 sterling...250 A on
a branch of Ceder Creek, granted to Hugh Milling, 5 March 1787...
H. Milling (Seal), Wit: Wm. Durphey, John Elison. Prov. by
John Elison, 22 Feb 1790, before Saml Dunlap, J. P.

Page 260: Article of agrement between Benjamin Parnel and Martha
Scott, the sd. Benjamin Parnel for the use of the
plantation and tracts of land formerly belonging to William Scott
decd and whereon Henry Kents (Hents?) now lives durin g the natural life of sd. Martha Scott to enter occupy and enjoy the same,
also a horse bridle, etc. to become Benjamin Parnels property at
her decease...28 Nov 1789. Benja Parnel (⊕) (Seal), Martha Scott
(M) (Seal), Wit: Thos Gardiner, George Gardiner, James Hester.

Pp. 260-263: 20 Sept 1782, Daniel Fuller and wife Angelina of
Craven Co., St. Marks parish, planter, to Benjamin
Hail of same, for one Mexican dollar...150 A on a branch of
Main Lynches Creek, known as Flat Creek, conveyed by Andrew Jones
to Joseph Kershaw, and than to Daniel Fuller, conveyed 2 & 3
Nov 1768, Joneses to Kershaw and from Kershaw to Fuller 26 & 27
Aug 1778...Daniel Fuller (≠) Angelica Fuller (X), Wit: John
Cherry, James Ferguson. Prov. by James Ferguson, before William
Welsh, 10 Nov 1782.

Page 264: 15 Oct 1796, Joseph Douglass of Lancaster Co., to Wil-
liam Brown, of Wils Co., N. C., for Ł 20 NC currency,
66 A granted to John Clark 100 A, part of the tract whereon John
Brown now lives, adj. John Crennons line...Jo Duglass (Seal),
Wit: John Tomlinson, John Brown. Prov. by John Tomlinson, before
HEnry Massey, J. P., 17 Oct 1796.

Pp. 264-265: 1 Jan 1790, Thomas Blackwood of Mecklinburg Co.,
N. C., to George Glenn of Lancaster Co., SC, 106 A
originally granted to William Guthrie, dated 4 May 1771, left to
Robert Guthrie by the Lastt will of sd. William Guthrie, and by
Robert Guthrie conveyed to Thomas Blackwood, 16 Sept 1788...Thomas
Blackwood (Seal), Wit: Goerge Glen, Bruce Livingston, Hannah
Blackwood, Margret Blackwood. S. C. Lancaster Co,: Prov. by
Bruce Livingston, 4 Apr 1792, before Robt Dunlap, J. L. C.

Page 266: 27 Aug 1796, Robert McIlwain of Lancaster Co., to William Vallandingham of same, for Ł 77 sterling, 208 A
adj. John Hood Junr, George Miller, on the head springs & drains
of the Pissimon branch of Cedar Creek, granted to Robert McIlwain
17 May 1787...Robert McIlwain (Seal), Mary McIlwain (Seal), Wit:
John Simpson, John Weaver, Benedict Best.

Pp. 266-267: 29 Nov 1796, William Prewer of Lancaster Co., to
James Cauthorn, for Ł 14 sterling...land on Sherwood
Sims line, Ashburn Sims line, John Holzendorf...William Prewet
(W) (Seal), Wit: Henry Vallandingham, Philip Burford, William
Cauthorn (X). Prov. by William Cauthorn, 31 July 1797, before
Elir. Alexander, J. P.

Pp. 267-268(?) (page numbers confused here): 17 Jan 1797, James
Purdy of Lancaster Co., to Henry Shaver, land on
branches of Bear Creek, granted to William Johnston 5 Apr 1790,
adj. John Neely, Samuel Casky, Glass Caston, sold by execution
as the property of sd. William Johnston by William Barnett Sheriff, 5 Apr 1795, to William Rogers, and by him conveyed to James
Purdy, 28 Apr 1795...James Purdy, Wit: William Nisbet, George
Vickory (X). Prov. by Major William Nisbit, before Elir. Alexander (date missing)

Pp. 268-269: 30 Apr 1795, Benjamin Harper and wife Martha of
Lancaster Co., for ____, 132½ A at the mouth of 12
mile Creek...Benjamin Harper (O) (Seal), Martha Harper (X) (Seal),
Wit: James Johnston, Robert Harper. Prov. by James Johnston, 21
Agu 1795, before __ Donnom, J. P.

Pp. 269-270: __ Sept 1789, William Richardson Davie of Hallafax
Co., N. C., to Elijah Crocket of Lancaster Co., for
Ł 100 sterling...land on Cane Creek adj. Thomas McIlhany, 300 A
granted to William Barnett, confeyed to John Frohock, then to William R. Davie....(Wit. missing) Prov. 28 Oct 1795.

BOOK C & E

Page 270: 4 Feb 1795, Bailey Fleming, for Ł 26 to John King,
        100 A on Cedar Creek, adj. Daniel Fleming(?)...Bailey
Fleming (Seal), Wit; William Owen, John Fleming, Robert Clarke
(X). Prov. by John Fleming, 23 May 1795, before Jas. Ingram,
J. P.

END OF VOLUME

The following list is from the original index at the beginning of
Book C & E. Presumably it was the index to the original volume
E.

93

Pp. 1-5: 21 March 1774, John Graves Senior of Craven County,
Parish of Saint Mark, planter, to John Chesnut and Ely
Kershaw of same county and parish, merchants, for Ł 1200...162 A
on S side Wateree River bounding at the time of the original
grant on sd. river, James Mickie Esqr., and vacant land, granted
to Anthony Wright by Gov. Glen, 7 June 1751, and by sd. Anthony
Wright and wife Mary 1 & 2 Apr 1753 to Edward Kirkland, and by
sd. Kirkland to John Graves 5 & 6 July 1759, also one other tract
100 A on S side Wateree River adj. Est. of James Mickie, Esqr.,
late the property of John Greeves Senior, Robert Belton & William
Starkes, Burnsides, granted to sd. John Graves Sr., by Gov. Bull
5 May 1773...John Greeves, Wit: Thomas Jones, Richard Walteson,
William Boykin. Prov. by Thos Jones, 4 July 1774, before J. N.
Oglethorpe, E. Sqr., J. P. in Craven Co.

Pp. 6-10: 3 Dec 1774, Joseph Kershaw, John Chesnut, Ely Kershaw,
William Ancrum and Aaron Loocock, Merchants, to Thomas
Jones of Camden, Craven Co., St. Marks Parish, yeoman, for Ł 6500
lots in Camden... Wit: William Boykin, John Wyly.

Page 11: Blank.

Pp. 12-18: 4 Dec 1774, Thomas Jones of Camden, yeoman, to Aaron
Loocock, for Ł 6500...lots in Camden. Thomas Jones.
Wit: John Wyly, William Boykin, Richd Wadeson. 5 Dec 1774, prov.
by John Wyly, before Jno Numan Oglethorpe, Esqr.

Pp. 18-24: 2 Sept 1779, Aaron Loocock of Charlestown, S. C.,
merchant, to Ely Kershaw, and John Chesnut of Camden,
S. C., merchants, for Ł 50,000 current money of S. C., 15 lots
in Camden. Aaron Loocock, Wit: Wm. Ancrum, Alexr Walker.

Pp. 25-27: 2 Aug 1785, Burwell Boykin of Camden District, planter,
to John Chesnut of Camden, merchant, for Ł 200...land
in Craven County on Head of Camp Creek, N side Wateree, land
granted 5 June 1771. Burwell Boykin, Wit: John Milhous, John
Craven, Zach Cantey. 7 Jan 1790, prov. by Zach Cantey, before
Joseph Kershaw, J. P.

Pp. 28-31: 11 Apr 1777, Joseph Kershaw, of Camden, in St. Marks
Parish, Craven County, Merchant, to John Chesnut, of
same, for Ł 250...8 lots in Camden, Joseph Kershaw (LS), Wit:
William Rea, John Adamson. Prov. in Lancaster Co., by John Adamson,
17 Jan 1790, before John Kershaw, J. P.

Pp. 32-36: 10 Apr 1777, Joseph Kershaw, John Chesnut, Ely Kershaw,
William Ancrum, and Aaron Loocock, of S. C., merchants,
to Duncan McRa of Camden Dist., Craven Co., for Ł 1989...21
adjoining lotts in Camden...Wit: John Adamson, William Rea.
Prov. by John Adamson in Lancaster Co., 17 Jan 1790, before
John Kershaw, J. P.

Pp. 37-41: 10 Apr 1777, Joseph Kershaw, John Chesnut, Ely Kershaw,
William Ancrum and Aaron Loocock of S. C., merchants,
to Duncan McRa, for Ł 500...9 adjoining lotts in Camden. Same
wit. & proof.

Pp. 41-45: 10 Apr 1777, Joseph Kershaw, John Chesnut, Ely Kershaw,
William Ancrum and Aaron Loocock, to Duncan McRa, for
Ł 4095, 8 adjoining lotts in Camden. Same wit. & proof.

BOOK D

Pp. 46-51: 24 May 1777, Duncan McRa of Camden, Craven Co., St.
Marks Parish, to John Chesnut of same, merchant, for
Ł 3531...46 lotts in Camden...Wit: Thomas Jones, Henry Houseman,
Alexr Irvin. Prov. in Lancaster Co., 8 June 1789, before
Alexander Irvin, before Isaac Alexander, J. P.

Pp. 52-55: 1 May 1788, Henry Hunter, Esqr. Sheriff of the Dist.
of Camden, to John Chesnut of Camden, Esquire, William
Ferrel late of the said state deceased, was seized in his Demsene
as of Fee, of 350 A on Hanging Rock branch, known as the Hanging
Rock plantation, at the time of his demise, in the hands of
Elizabeth Ferrel, Extx. of L. W. & T. of sd. William Ferrel, and
sd. William Ferrel being indebted unto James Hacket...action in
the Court of Common please, in the year 178-, at Camden, for
Ł 76 s 4 d 6...Henry Hunter, Wit: Jo: Brevard, Daniel Brown.
Prov. by Joseph Brevard, 10 Jan 1789, before I. Alexander, J. P.

Pp. 56-59: 20 Dec 1785, Joshua Palmer of Craven Co., Baptist
Preacher, to John Chesnut of Camden, for Ł 200...50 A
in Craven Co., on N side Wateree River, above the Great Falls,
adj. George Jones, William Jones, Wateree River, granted to sd.
Joshua Palmer, by Gov. Bull...Joshua Palmer (Seal), Wit: Peter
Cassity, William Brown, John Craven. Prov. 7 Jan 1790, before
Isaac Alexnader, J. P., by William Brown.

Pp. 60-63: 6 May 1790, John Chesnut of Camden, to Duncan McRa,
and Zachariah Cantey of Dist. of Camden, for natural
love & affection to his daughter Sarah Chesnut, and for s 5...
slaves (named)...John Chesnut (LS), Wit: Robert Dow, Wm. Tate,
Daniel Peak. S. C. Lancaster Co.: 10 May 1790, prov. by William
Tate, before John Marshel, J. P.

Pp. 64-67: 6 May 1790, John Chesnut of Camden, to Duncan McRa
and Zachariah Cantey, for natural love & affection
to daughter Harriet Chesnut, and s 5...negroe slaves (named)...
same wit. & proof.

Pp. 68-71: 6 May 1790, John Chesnut of Camden, for natural love
& affection to his daughter Margaret Rebecca Chesnut &
s 5 to Duncan McRa and Zachariah Cantey...negroes (named), same
wit. and proof.

Pp. 72-75: 13 May 1776, Mary Milhous Extx John Milhous, Henry
Milhous and Abel Thomas Exrs. of the L. W. & T. of
Samuel Milhous deceased of Craven County and Camden Dist., to
John Chesnut of Camden merchant, whereas Samuel Milhous was in
his life time and at his death seized of a certain tract of 300
A on Beaver Dam Creek a branch of Saludy River, granted 19 Aug
1774...Wit: William Boykin, Thomas Cox, Duncan McRa. Prov. in
Camden Dist., 23 Jan 1790, by Duncan McRa, before Isaac Alexander,
J. P.

Pp. 76-79: 16 March 1786, William Tate of Camden, Carpenter, to
John Chesnut Esquire of Camden, merchant, for Ł 81
s 11 d 3...lott # 188 in Camden...William Tate (Seal), Wit: John
Craven, John Holzendorf, Zachariah Cantey. Prov. 7 Jan 1790
by Zach Cantey, before James Kershaw, J. P.

Pp. 80-83: 12 June 1790, John Chesnut of Camden, planter, to
           Duncan McRa of Camden, for Ⱡ 150...lots in Camden...
Wit: Samuel Mathis, Zach Cantey. Prov. by Saml Mathis, 12 June
1790, before James Kershaw.

Pp. 84-86: _____ 1778, Aaron Loocock of Charles Town, merchant,
           to John Chesnut of Camden, Merchant, for Ⱡ 500...
lots in Camden, Wit: William Boykin, Wm. Murrell. Prov. in
Claremont County by Wm. Murrell, 2 Jan 1790, before W. R. Davis,
J. P.

Pp. 87-89: 24 Nov 1774, Matthew Walter of Ninety Six District,
           to John Chesnut of Camden Dist., merchant, for Ⱡ 100
100 A in Craven Co., on both sides Sanders Creek a branch of
Wateree River, granted 27 Sept 1769...Matthew Walters (M) (Seal),
Catharine Walters (X) (Seal), Wit: Israel Pickens, Derrill Hart.
Prov. 25 Nov 1774, by Devill Hart, before Champness Terry, J. P.
in Ninety Six District.

Pp. 90-92: 9 March 1775, Thomas Davis of Parish of St. David,
           County of Craven, to Ely Kershaw of same county &
Parish, for Ⱡ 92 s 10 d 2, 300 A on Thompsons Creek in Craven
Co., adj. George Dobbs, granted 20 Oct 1763, by S. C....Thomas
Davis (X), Wit: Duncan McRa, Jno Billups, Jonathan Davis. Prov.
3 June 1785, by Duncan McRa, before John Chesnut.

Pp. 93-94: 9 Dec 1778, Benjamin Cook of Craven Co., St. Marks
           Parish, Planter, to John Chesnut & Ely Kershaw, of
Camden, for Ⱡ 300...500 A in Tredericksburgh Township, N side
Wateree River adj. Widow Felins, Waters, Majors, Thomas Marshell,
John Chesnut, Widow Smith, Joshua Palmer, granted 1 March 1775
Benjn Cook (Seal), Wit: B. Waters, John Rankens (Ɨ), Frederick
Briggs. Prov. by Frederick Briggs, 9 June 1779, before Wm.
Arther, J. P.

Pp. 94-95: 25 Aug 1778, Aaron Loocock of Charles Town, merchant,
           to Ely Kershaw, of Camden in Craven Co., merchant,
for Ⱡ 1500...two plantations (1) 500 A on E side Wateree River,
granted 10 Jan 1771 unto Sir John Colleton, adj. Mathew Singleton
(2) 250 A on NE side Santee River in Craven Co., on Santee Swamp,
adj. John Deas, part of grant 5 Apr 1765 to John Deas...Aaron
Loocock (Seal), wit: Archl Brown, William Clarkson. Prov. in
Charlestown District, by William Clarkson, 19 Nov 1778.

Pp. 96-97: 15 Aug 1788, Adam Fowler Brisbane to Fielding Woodroof
           of Camden, for Ⱡ 200...lot on Church St. in Camden.
Adam F. Brisbane (Seal), Wit: Robert Henry, Thos Brown. Prov.
by Thos Brown, 10 Oct 1788, before I. Alexander, J. P.

Pp. 97-98: 1 May 1786, Joseph Kershaw of Camden, Esqr., to Field-
           ing Woodroof of same, InnKeeper, for Ⱡ 50...lot #2 in
Camden...Wit: John Craven, William Nettles, Philip Platt. Prov.
1 July 1786, by Philip Platt, before I. Alexander, J. P.

Pp. 98-100: 14 Apr 1788, Fielding Woodroof of Camden, to Isaac
            Alexander, also of Camden, Physician, for Ⱡ 163 s 2
two lots in Camden, Church st., Elizabeth, wife of Fielding Woodroof....F. Woodroof (Seal), Wit: Benjn Carter, John Reid. Prov.
by John Reid, 10 June 1788, before A. B. Ross, J. P.

BOOK D

Pp. 100-101: 10 Apr 1789, Adam Fowler Brisbane of Clermont Co.,
S. C., to Isaac Alexander of Camden, Physician,
for Ł 200...lots in Camden....Adam F. Brisbane (LS), Wit: Joseph
Brevard, Thomas Denkins. Prov. by Thomas Denkins, 15 June 1789,
before A. B. Ross, J. P.

Pp. 102-103: 13 Mar 1787, Adam Fowler Brisbane to Hannah Brisbane
of Camden, for Ł 1000...lots in Camden. Adam F.
Brisbane (LS), Mary Brisbane (LS), Wit: Robert Henry, Thos Brown.
Prov. by Thomas Brown, 13 May 1787, before I. Alexander, J. P.

Pp. 103-104: 12 July 1786, Joseph Kershaw of Camden, to Isaac
Alexander of Camden, for 50 Guineas, land adj. the
town lots of Camden, 10 3/4 A...Wit: Jo Brevard, James Smith,
Adam Swann. Prov. by James Smith, 15 Sept 1786, before A. B.
Ross, J. P. (plat included), by John Belton, D. S., shows adj.
Abraham Belton, Doctor Alexander, Camden line.

Page 105: 1 Jan 1784, Joseph Kershaw of Town of Camden, to Isaac
Alexander, Physician, of same, for Ł 50, lots in Camden.
Wit: John Craven, Joseph Kershaw Junr, James Tate. Prov. 22
Feb 1784, before Jas. Kershaw, J. P. by Jno. Craven.

Page 106: 10 July 1784, Col. Joseph Kershaw of Craven Co., St.
Marks Parish, Merchant, to Isaac Alexander of same,
Physician, lots in Camden. Wit: S. Mathis, Jo Brevard, Hugh Young.
Prov. by Hugh Young, 5 Aug 1784, before J. Galbraith, J. P.

Page 107: 10 Feb 1790, Adam Fowler Brisbane to Jean Stanley, for
Ł 100...lot in Camden, #426...Wit: John Reid, Zach
Cantey, James Pierson. Prov. by John Reid, 1 Feb 1790, before
I. Alexander, J. P.

Page 108: Charles Mackey of Lancaster Co., to John Mackey, my
son, all my goods, chattels, etc, 28 March 1798.
Charles Mackey (C) (Seal), Wit: Jos Coile, Tignal Perry, Sarah
Bests (C). Prov. by Tignal Perry, 5 Apr 1798, before James Ingrem, J. P.

Pp. 108-109: 1 Nov 1795, Thomas Sumter, to Devault Fonderburk,
for Ł 20...land in Lancaster Co., on SW side of Pole
Cat Creek a prong of Great Lynches Creek, 86 A, part of grant of
15,000 A. Wit: Saml Tynes, Adam Gibhart (X). Prov. by Saml
Tynes, 1 Nov 1797, before Thomas Welsh, J. P.

Page 109: 26 Aug 1797, John Welsh Esqr. of Lancaster Co., to
Jethrow Weaver of same, for Ł 50 sterling, 465 A on a
small branch of Wild cat creek, whereon the sd. Weaver now lives
...John Welsh (Seal), Wit: James Holliman, Nathan Weaver (X).
Prov. by James Holliman, 30 Jan 1798, before John Welsh, J. P.

Pp. 109-110: 22 Dec 1791, Michal Barnett exr. of L. W. & T. of
Humphrey Barnett decd, to John Ingrem of Kershaw
County, land granted to Humphrey Barnett 18 Jan 1765, and sd.
Humphrey Barnett by his L. W. & T. dated 26 Dec 1790, directed
that the two tracts be sold by his exrs. Michal Barnet and James
Hester...50 A on Road to Charleston below the Hanging Rock...
Michael Barnet (LS), Wit: Elir Alexander, James Ingrem, James
Miller. Prov. by Eliezar Alexander, 13 Aug 1796, before Jno
Simpson, J. L. C. (plat included)

BOOK D

Pp. 110-111: Eleanor Stubbs (late Eleanor Farrell) of Lancaster
Co., of my own free will & choice, quit claim to
John Ingrem all right to 200 A on the great road between Camden
& Waxhaws settlement on the head springs of Beaver Creek and
waters of Hanging Rock Creek, known as Cole's old place or field,
originally granted to Eleanor Cole, bargained & sold by my lawful
husband William Stubbs to John Ingrem...29 Sept 1791. Ellenor
Stubs (Seal), Wit: Joseph Kimbal, Wade Kimbal, Wm. Hamilton (O)
Prov. by Jno Simpson, J. L. C. 10 Aug 1796.

Page 111: 1 July 1796, Matthew Hood to John Ingrem, for Ŀ 60
sterling, land on a branch of Cedar Creek originally
granted to Jordan Ashley, 26 Feb 1788...Mathew Hood (LS), Wit:
Wm. T. Linton, James Ingrem, Harman Platt. Prov. bef.James
Ingrem, 9 July 1796, by Harmon Platt.

Page 112: 6 July 1796, Mathew Hood to John Ingrem, for Ŀ 100...
two surveys on head waters of Cedar Creek and Hanging
Rock, 200 A, granted to Mathew Hood, 7 May 1787...Wit: Wm. T.
Linton, James Ingrem, Harman Platt. Prov. by Harman Plat, 9
July 1796, before James Ingrem, J. P. Mary Hood, wife of Matthew,
relinquished dower 15 July 1796, before James Ingrem, J. P. Wit:
Wm T. Linton, James Gaston, Katharine Gaston (J). Prov. 10
Aug 1796, by James Gaston.

Page 113: 25 Apr 1797, James Clifton & wife Nancy of Lancaster
Co., to Frances P. Vaughan, for Ŀ 170...land on waters
of Twelve Mile Creek in two separate surveys...James Clifton
(Seal), Nancy Clifton (X), Wit: James Massey, Moses Dickey, Henry
Massey. Prov. by Henry Massey, J. P. 25 Apr 1797.

Mark Eaves of Chester Co., sold to George Hayes, negro Claber...
28 Nov 1797, Mark Eaves, Wit: William Tilman, Isaac Tilman. Prov.
in Lancaster Co., by William Tilman & Isaac Tilman, 28 Nov 1797,
before Jesse Tilman, J. P.

Page 114: 25 Oct 1773, Robert Montgomery of Craven Co., St. Mark's
Parish, to Joseph McCullah of same, for Ŀ 40 S. C.
currency, 100 A adj. Robert Caldwell, in the Waxhaw Settlement...
Robert Montgomery (Seal), Wit: Robert Howard, Robert Lockhart,
William Brown. Prov. 25 Apr 1774, before James Patton, by
Robert Howard.

Pp. 114-115: 17 Nov 1780, John Tomlinson & wife of Camden Dist.,
to David Tomlinson of same, for Ŀ 7500...20 A on N
side Waxhaw Creek, granted to Stephen White, 24 Sept 1754, by
Gov. Rowan of N. C., conveyed to Isaac McCullah, and then to Jo-
seph McCullah 22 Oct 1778, adj. John Thompson, Stith Fennell...
also 80 A part of 100 A granted 4 Dec 1772 to Robert Montgomery,
conveyed to Joseph McCullah 25 Oct 1773, to John Tomlinson 15
Apr 1780 adj. Robert Lockhart, Stith Fennell, Robert Crawford,
Joseph White, Thomas Howards Estate...John Tomlinson (Seal),
Susannah Tomlinson (X) (Seal), Wit: Drury Cook, James Crawford,
John Tomlinson. Prov. by John Tomlinson, 13 Jan 1799, before
Saml C. Dunlap, J. P.

Pp. 115-116: 10 May 1793, Benjamine Haile of Lancaster Co., to
Caty Bridges, for Ŀ 10 sterling, land on N side of
Flat Creek adj. William Denman, Wm. Covey, Henry Massey, James
Ball, the big branch, dividing Ferguson Haile & Caty Bridges, 250
A...Benjn Haile (Seal), Wit: William Bridges, Richard Hunley,

James McVey. Prov. by James McVey, 18 May 1793, before Benjn Haile, J. P.

Pp. 116-117: 20 Feb 1797, Catey Bridges of Lancaster Co., to
            William Danzy of same, for Ł 32 sterling, land on N
side Flat creek adj. William Denman, William Covey, James Ball,
Henry Massey, Ferguson Haile, 250 A...Caty Bridges (C) (Seal),
Wit: Richard Hunley, Ferguson Haile, Phebe Martin (X). Prov. by
Ferguson Hale, 24 Feb 1798, before Thomas Welsh, J. P.

Page 117: Micajah Hughes of Lancaster Co., for Ł 200 to Jeremiah
         Burge of Fairfield County, 150 A on N side Wateree
River...14 ___ 1797. Micajah Hughes (LS), Wit: William Lorsby
(Soesby?), Philimon Starke. Prov. in Fairfield Co., by Philimon
Starke, 14 Nov 1797, before Charels Picket, J. P.

Pp. 117-118: 12 Jan 1799, Arthur Collier and wife Ferreby to Wil-
            liam Tomlinson, each of Lancaster Co., for Ł 200...
land on S side Twelve Mile Creek adj. Robert Carnes, 240 A...
Arthur Collier (Seal), Ferreby Collier (Seal), WitL John Tomlinson, Joseph Baker, Nathaniel Tomlinson, (X). Prov. by John Tomlinson, 14 Jan 1799, before Samuel C. Dunlap, J. P.

Page 118: Richard Carlisle of Lancaster co., for Ł 21, to Nathan-
         iel Pendergrass of same, land on Dry creek a branch of
Rockey Creek of Cedar Creek in Lancaster Co., adj. George King,
William Green...land which by the rights of Primogeniture I fell
Heir to on the death of my Grandfather Richard Carlisle and
Father John Carlisle, originally granted to my Grandfather sd.
Richard Carlisle...Richard Carlisle (LS), Wit: John Pendergrass,
Philip Shewbart. dated 1 Oct 1798. (plat included). Prov. by
Philip Shewbart, before Danl Wade, J. L. C. 9 Oct 1798.

Page 119: 8 Dec 1796, Gen. Thomas Sumter to John Welsh of Lancas-
         ter Co., to Ł 210 sterling, 3500 A...plat by John
Barron D. D. 20 Oct 1793...Wit: Wm. White, Jno Sumter. Prov. by
William White 11 March 1797, before Thomas Welsh, J. P.

Pp. 119-120: William Cato and Susan Cato of Fairfield Co., for Ł
            31 s 14 d 4 to William Ingrem of Lancaster Co.,
planter, 675 A in Camden Dist. on Hanging Rock Creek waters of
Catawba River granted to sd. William Cato 5 Dec 1785...W. Cato
(Seal), Susan Cato (X) (Seal), Wit: George Reddish, Charles
Palmer, Phi. Pearson. Prov. by George Reddish, 29 Oct 1796,
before Benjamin Mayp, J. P. in Fairfield County.

Page 120: 22 March 1797, Capt. William Ingrem of Lancaster Co.,
         to James Ingrem of same, 675 A granted to William Cato,
part of that tract, 100 A...William Ingrem (Seal), Wit: Danl
Monaghon, Arthur Ingrem, Saml Helton. Prov. by Samuel Helton,
22 March 1797, before Jas. Ingrem, J. P.

Pp. 120-121: 30 Oct 1770, Jacob Hart of Craven Co., planter, to
            John Philips of same, weaver, for Ł 100...100 A,
part of 300 A, granted March 1768, to sd. Jacob Hart...Jacob
Hart (LS), Susanna Hart (X) (LS), WitL Arthur McDonald, Robert
Ramsey, William Guthrie. Prov. 16 Sept 1773, by Robert Ramsey,
before James Simpson.

Pp. 121-122: 11 Dec 1794, Daniel Hunter of Lancaster Co., Blacksmith, to Jacob Funderburk of same, for Ł 40...land
on both sides Wild Cat creek, granted to John Usher 13 May 1768.
Daniel Hunter (LS), Wit: Henry Funderburk, Bennett Highfield.
Prov. by Henry Funderburk, 1 Jan 1795, before James McDonald.

Page 122: 28 Feb 1797, Gen. Thomas Sumter to Jacob Funderburk,
for Ł 20 sterling, land on both sides Wild Cat Creek,
part of 15,000 A...Wit: Jacob Shofner, Robert Welsh (X). Prov.
by Robert Welsh, before John Welsh, 24 June 1797.

Pp. 123-5:16 Oct 1773, Robert Patton & Agness Richardson of St.
Marks Parish, Craven Co., SC Exr. & Extx of the L. W.
& T. of the Rev. William Richardson decd., to John Arnold Pender
of same (lease & release), 150 A, part of grant to Thomas McHoney
and conveyed to sd. William Richardson...Robt Patton (LS), Agness
Dunlap (LS), Wit: John Blair, William Blair, John McDowel (O).
Prov. in Lancaster Co., before Robert Dunlap, by John McDowel,
16 Aug 1791.

Pp. 125-127: 16 May 1777, John Arnold Pender of St. Marks Parish,
to George Dunlap, land granted to Thomas McHoney
and conveyed to Rev. William Richardson (same land as preceding
deed)...John Arnold Pender (7) (LS), Mary Pender (C) (LS), Wit:
John Blair, William Blair, John McDowel (O). Prov. by John
McDowel 16 Aug 1791, before Robert Dunlap, J. L. C.

Pp. 127-128: John McDowel of Lancaster Co., Farmer, for Ł 20
sterling, to George Dunlap, 50 A on a branch of
Catawba River adj. Henry Foster, Robert McDow, Thomas McDow,
and sd. George Dunlap, 20 Sept 1796. John McDow (LS), Wit: Jane
Carryl, Thomas McDow, John Cantzon. Mary McDow, wife of John,
relinquished dower 20 Sept 1796, before Josh. Lee, J. P. (Plat
included). Prov. by John Cantzon, 20 Sept 1796, before Josh
Lee, J. P.

Pp. 128-129: John Hood of Lancaster Co., planter, to James Craig,
for Ł 80 sterling, land on both sides Camp Creek,
waters of Cane Creek, waxhaw settlement, land granted to George
Douglass, by Gov. Littleton, 4 June 1759, conveyed by L & R by
George Douglass & wife Mary to William Hood, 24 July 1762, and sd.
William Hood by his L. W. & T. to his beloved sons James and
Archibald Hood, the will of William Hood 7 Apr 1783, which sd.
James & Arch. Hood by deed to John Hood 18 Feb 1793...John Hood
(H) (LS), Elizabeth Hood (X) (LS), Wit: John Craig, William Craig,
Prov. by William Craig Junr, 9 May 1797, before John Craig, J. P.

Pp. 129-130: John Craig Senr of Lancaster Co., Esq., quit claim
to a plantation on both sides Camp Creek...17 July
1794. John Craig (LS), Wit: William Craig, Agness Dickey (X).
Prov. by William Craig Junr, 9 May 1797, before John Craig, J. P.

Page 130: James Craig of Lancaster Co., quit claim to land on
both sides Camp Creek as the Property of John Craig
Senr (where he now lives), 17 July 1794. Jas Craig (LS), Wit:
William Craig, Agness Dickey (X).

Pp. 130-132: 11 June 1762, Eleanor Adamson of Craven Co., planter, to Thomas Simpson Esqr. of same, for (lease s 10, release Ł 20), 150 A on Cane Creek adj. Arnold Pender, Gills Creek, granted 10 Nov 1761 to sd. Eleanor Adamson...Eleanor Adamson (C) Wit: Saml Kelly, John Chesnut. Prov. before Saml Wyly, J. P., by John Chesnut, 9 Nov 1764.

Pp. 133-134: 10 Jan 1765, Jas. Patton & Robert Patton Exrs. of Est. of Thomas Simpson, in compliance to Thomas Simpson Will of Craven Co., St. Marks Parish, planters, to William Simpson, of same (lease s10, release Ł 200)...150 A granted 10 Nov 1761 to Eleanor Adamson...James Patton (Seal), Robt Patton (Seal), Wit: Thos Wiggins, Benjn Maddox (B). Prov. by Benjamin Maddox, before John Gaston, 23 Sept 1767.

Pp. 135-136: 10 June 1765, William Simpson of St. Marks Parish, SC, to John Cantzon, Practitioner of Physic...same land in preceding deeds). Will Simpson (Seal), Wit: Thos Wiggins, Benjn Maddox (B). Prov. by Benjamin Maddox, before John Gaston, 23 Sept 1767.

Pp. 135-137: 11 Feb 1794, Moses Cantzon son of Doctor John Cantzon decd., heir at law of sd. Doctor and of his elder brother William Cantzon both decd, and Sarah Harper widow of the same place & Relict of the sd. Doctor John Cantzon decd., to Eliezar Alexander, 2 tracts 150 A on Cane Creek surveyed for James Adamson 7 Sept 1756 adj. John Arnold Pender, Gills Creek and granted to Eleanor Adamson 10 Nov 1761, conveyed to Thomas Simpson, conveyed by exrs. James Patton and Robert Patton, to William Simpson and then to sd. Doctor John Cantzon decd., and also 100 A adj. the aforesd. 150 A granted to Dr. John Cantzon 28 Aug 1767, being the place whereon the sd. Eliezar Alexander now lives in Lancaster County, & Waxhaw Settlement, and whereas the said Doctor John Cantzon (Father of the sd. Moses) died intestate and his eldest son William Cantzon dying also intestate and without issue, the sd. Moses Cantzon became heir , now for Ł 125...Moses Cantzon (Seal), Sarah Harper (Seal), Wit: RobertKer, Joseph McMeen, A. Alexander. Prov. by Joseph Lee J. P., 11 Feb 1794.

Pp. 138-139: 2 Aug 1775, Samuel Dunlap & wife Elizabeth of St. Bartholomews Parish, Bekley Co., to John McElhany of St. Marks Parish, Craven Co., for Ł 45 south currency...300 A on S side Cane Creek in Craven Co., adj. Thomas McMeen, John Cantzon, David Adams, granted to sd. Dunlap 1 Feb 1768...Saml Dunlap, Elizabeth Dunlap, Wit: Richard Cousart, Alexdr Thompson, John Dunlap.

James McElhany late of County of Chester, for $300, to Eliezar Alexander, 300 A on E side Cane Creek on both sides of the Road called the Lands ford Road adj. Eliezar Alexander, Elizabeth and William McMeen, John Simpson, Benjamin Cudworth, David Adams, 21 June 1799. James McElhenny (LS), Wit: Alexdr Moore, Thos McElhenny. Agness McElheney (X), relinquished dower 21 June 1799, before Alexr Moore, J. C. C. Prov. by Thomas McElheney, 2 July 1799, before John Simpson, J. L. C. Pp. 139-140.

Pp. 141-5 Blank.

Pp. 146-147: S. C., Lancaster County: Whereas George King of Rocky
branch, a branch of Cedar creek, did obtain a plat
and grant for 200 Acres dated 12 Oct 1770 and died about 16 years
ago intestate, so that Bennet King his eldest son became his sole
heir, now 14 Jan 1797, Bennet King for Ł 50 to Samuel Dunlap Senr
of the Catawba River, 42 A on Rocky creek adj. Mr. Carlisle, adj.
to 100 A sold by Bennet King to Thomas Glaze, and land sold to
William Steel and afterwards sold to sd. Samuel Dunlap, and is
now sold by deed 4 June 1795...Bennet King (X), Wit: Jas Bredin,
John Richardson. (plat included showing adj. Capt Tilman, Wm.
Allen, 11 Feb 1796, also adj. Thomas Glaze and Lewis Hudson....
Prov. by Jas Bredin, 24 March 1797, before Nathan Barr, J. P.

Pp. 147-148: 15 Nov 1791, Bennet King and wife Sarah of Lancaster
Co., to Thomas Glaze of same, , by grant dated 12
Oct 1770 to George King, 200 A, 100 A conveyed to Thomas Glaze
15 Nov 1791, now for Ł 10 sterling...Bennet King (X) (LS), Sarah
King (X) (LS), Wit: Joel Carlisle (X), Elisabeth King. Prov. by
Joel Carlisle and Elisabeth King 8 Feb 1792, before Jesse Tillman,
J. P.

Pp. 148-149: 7 March 1795, Thomas Glaze of Lancaster Co., to Sam-
uel Dunlap, part of 200 A granted 12 Oct 1770...
Thomas Glaze (Seal), Wit: W. Morrison, Will. Steel, Lewis Hudson.
Prov. by William Steel, 31 May 1797, before E. Alexander, C. L. C.

Page 149: William McDonald of Chester Co., planter, for Ł 60
sterling, to Daniel Wade of Lancaster Co, planter, 100
A on E side Catawba adj. Daniel McDonald, granted to Daniel
McDonald and by him bequeathed in his L. W. & T. to sd. William
McDonald, 30 June 1798. William McDonald (Seal), Wit: Wm. McDon-
ald Junr, James Gaston.

Pp. 150-151: 20 Feb 1797, Abdon Alexander, Sheriff of Lancaster
Co., to John Chesnut of Camden, 200 A in the Waxhaw
settlement on both sides of Gills creek granted to Robert day, on
which David Adams late deceased lived and owned previously and
at the time of his death...by virtue of the last will and testament of sd. David Adams...whereas William Adams became indebted
to sd. John Chesnut Ł 20, case in July term 1791...A. Alexander
Shff, Lancaster (Seal), Wit: James Clack, Margaret Alexander.
Prov. by James Clack, 18 Aug 1797, before Elir Alexander, J. P.
John Chesnut transferred for Ł 26 s 12 sterling to James Cowsar,
5 July 1798, Wit: Joseph Brevard, Ely Kershaw. Prov. by Joseph
Brevard, in Lancaster Court July Term 1798.

Page 152: 6 Feb 1796, Adam Heath of Lancaster Co., to William
Davies of Mecklinburgh Co., N. C., for Ł 100 sterling,
63 A part of grant to Samuel Dunlap, 3 Feb 1754...Adam Heath (X)
(Seal), Wit: Joseph Baker, Jesse Heathe, James Cureton. Prov.
in Court Jly term 1796.

Pp. 152-153: 29 May 1797, Middleton McDonald Senr & wife Eliza-
beth, to Guilliam Ezell, for Ł 75 sterling...200 A,
½ of grant to James Moffat 5 Mar 1770, along the old path to
Camp Creek...Middleton McDonald (Seal), Elizabeth McDonald (X)
(Seal), Wit: Lewis Ezell, Betsey Sherrenstokes, John Hicklin.
Prov. by Lewis Ezell and John Hicklin, 5 Sept 1797, before Elir.
Alexander, J. P.

Page 153: 29 May 1797, Gillam Ezel & wife Nancy of Lancaster Co.,
        to Benjamin Croxton of same, for Ł 75...200 A, ½ of
grant to James Moffat 5 Mar 1770...Gillam Ezell (Seal), Nancy
Ezell (X) (Seal), Wit: Lewis Ezell, John Croxton, Jno Hicklin (J).
Prov. by Lewis Ezell, John Hicklin & John Croxton, 5 Sept 1797,
before Elir. Alexander, J. P.

Pp. 153-154: 3 Mar 1797, Capt. William Ingrem of Lancaster Co.,
        to Samuel Love, for Ł 10...50 A, part of 200 A
granted to Alexander Ingrem, 6 Apr 1773, on branches of Little
Lynches Creek adj. Moses and Wm. Ingrem, Countrman...William
Ingrem (Seal), Wit: Danl Monaghan, John Love, Levy Strickland.
Prov. by John Love, before William Ward, J. P., 17 May 1797.

Page 154: Plat for 80 acres on waters of Gills creek, adj. Nathan
        Barr, Robert Dunlap, William McMeen, David Adams,
granted 5 Dec 1796 to John Barkley, for $3 transferred to Alex-
ander Craig, 24 Dec 1798. John Barkley (Seal), Wit: John Simpson,
William Barkley, John May.

For $40 to James Cowsart...26 Dec 1798. Alexr Craig (Seal), Wit:
Jno. Simpson, John May, William Gibson. Ack. by Craig 30 Jan
1799.

Page 155: John Simpson of Lancaster Co., for $100 to James Cowser
        and David Cowser, land near Lancaster court house public
ground, 1/2 of 2 lots...15 Feb 1799. Jno Simpson (Seal), Wit:
Elir. Alexander, James Douglass. Prov. by Capt. James Douglass,
15 Feb 1799,before Elir. Alexander, J. P.

William Coffin, planter, for titles for one hundred acres of land,
to Charles Barber of Kershaw Co., 100 A adj. Mr.Howel, John Best
adj. Paul Howel, granted to Holzendorf, purchased by sd. John
Best conveyed by him to William Cauthan, 11 Jan 1799. William
Cathan (X) (LS), Wit: Sherrod Sims, Martha Innes (X), Jesse Dunkin
(X). Prov. in Kershaw Co., by Sherrod Sims Junr, before Thos
Ballard, J. P.

Page 156: Blank.

Pp. 157-158: 21 Dec 1798, Abdon Alexander Sheriff of Lancaster
        Co., to James Cowser of Kershaw Co., merchant, 200
A adj. on both sides Gills creek adj. Nathan Barr, Alexander
Craig, Robert Dunlap, William McMeen, it being the plantation
on which sd. David Adams died, and since the death of sd. David
Adams 1/3 of plantation or at least so much thereof as William
Adams one of the Legatees under the L. W. & T. of sd. deceased
was sold to satisfy an execution in favor of John Chesnut of
Camden, and also the deceased became indebted to Sarah Robinson
Ł 44 s 1 d 4 sterling, whereof she commenced an action against
William Adams...A Alexander Sheriff of Lancaster (Seal), Wit:
Henry Vallandingham, Alir. Alexander. Prov. by Henry Vallanding-
ham, 25 Dec 1798, before Elir. Alexander, J. P. Plat included
showing the land surveyed for Robert Day 12 Nov 1756.

Page 158: Edward Kennington of Lancaster Co., for Ł 5 to Tully
        Biggs, 10 A on waters of Lick Creek adj. Edward Canning-
ton, Tully Gibbs, 2 March 1798. Edward Kennington Wit: Richmon
Terrell, Catharine Terrell (X). Prov. 21 March 1798 by Richmond
Terrell, before Thos Welch, J. P.

Pp. 158-159: 2 Jan 1798, John Farrow to Abraham Merryman of Lancaster Co., for Ł 10...25 A, part of 5000 A granted to Thomas Sumter 23 Mar 1795, waters of Buffaloe a branch of Lynches creek...John Farrow (X), Wit: Richmond Terrell, William Terrell. Prov. by Richmond Terrell, before Thomas Welsh, J. P., 21 March 1798.

Page 159: 30 Oct 1799, John Freeman to Mark Merryman of Co. of Lancaster, for Ł 30 sterling, 240 A, part of 5000 A granted to Thomas Sumter...John Freeman Wit: Richmond Terrell, Joshua Merryman (X). Prov. by Richmon Terrell, 21 March 1798 before John Welsh.

Pp. 159-160: 27 June 1798, Samuel Johnston of Lancaster Co., to Jesse Masho, for Ł 20 sterling...250 A adj. to a survey for Samuel Johnston 1 Dec 1794, Minor Winn, John Caston... Samuel Jonson (Seal), Wit: William Chambers, Susanna Chambers (M). Prov. by William Chambers, before R. Hunley, J. P., 4 Feb 1799.

Pp. 160-161: 9 July 1796, Alexander Craig of Lancaster Co., to Patrick Kenny, for Ł 35 sterling, 100 A surveyed for John Neely 10 Nov 1785 on a branch of bear creek, a prong of cane creek NE side Catawba River, granted to sd. Alexander Craig, 1 Oct 1787...Alexander Craig (O), Kettrin Craig (O), Wit: William Graves, Joseph Graves. Proved in Court July 28th 1796.

Page 161: 4 Sept 1797, Jethro Weaver, planter, to John Weaver, for Ł 10 sterling, land on waters courses of Wild Cat Creek 150 A part of 460 A the sd. Jethro Weaver purchased of Esqr. John Welsh, adj. Robert Welsh...Jethrew Weaver (X) (LS), Wit: James Holliman, John Welsh. Prov. by James Holliman, 30 Jan 1798, before John Welsh, J. P.

Page 162: William Simpson of Davidson County, Tennessee, for Ł 40 to William Rowel of the Chinkapine Ridge in Lancaster Co., SC, 100 A on the head drains of Rocky Creek, 1/2 of survey granted to William Simpson (Grandfather to the sd. William Simpson) 12 Oct 1770, by the L. W. & T. of William Simpson decd, bequeathed to sd. William Simpson...16 Nov 1797. William Simpson (Seal), Wit: A. Alexander, Elir. Alexander. Prov. by Abdon Alexander, before Elir. Alexander, J. P., 16 Nov 1797.

Pp. 162-163: William Simpson of Davidson Co., Tenn., for Ł 40 to John Massey of Chinkapine Ridge in Lancaster Co., half of survey granted to William Simpson grandfather to sd. William Simpson 12 Oct 1770...William Simpson (Seal), Wit: Elir Alexander, A. Alexander. Prov. by Abdon Alexander, before Elir Alexander, J. P., 16 Nov 1797.

Page 163: Jan 1799, Micaijah Crenshaw of Lancaster Co., to William Rowel, for Ł 60 sterling...100 A, part of a tract 202 A granted to Micaijah Crenshaw 7 Nov 1791, on a branch of Rocky creek a prong of Cedar Creek on NE side Catawba, adj. plantation whereon sd. Micaijah Crenshaw Senr now lives... Micaijah Crenshaw (Seal), Wit: William Curry Esqr., Isaac Stuart, Joseph Coile. Prov. by Isaac Stuart, 12 July 1799, before Elir. Alexander, J. P.

Page 164: John Caston of Lancaster Co., for Ł 50 sterling to
John Fowler of same, 100 A, part of 800 A granted to
sd. John Caston, on waters of Camp Creek adj. Charles Mackey,
against the head of school house branch adj. Peter Perry, Izzard,
Mary Watson, 29 Nov 1797. John Caster (Seal), Wit: Charles
Mackey (X), Elijah Ratley (X), Danl Wade. Prov. by Elijah Ratley,
before Danl Wade, J. L. C., 29 Nov 1797. Frances Caston, wife
of John relinquished dower, 29 Nov 1797.

Pp. 164-165: 28 Apr 1798, James Holliman of Lancaster Co., to
Nathaniel Bibbe, for Ł 8 sterling, tract on both
sides of fork of Wild Cat creek, part of 15000 A granted to
Gen. Sumter, 2 Apr 1787. James Holliman (Seal), Wit: Bennet
Highfield, Robert Chappel (X). Prov. by Bennet Highfield, before
Jno Welsh, J. P. 19 May 1798.

Page 165: 1 Dec 1794, John Fegan of Sullivan Co., North Carolina,
to William Rogers of Lancaster Co., for Ł 150 sterling
340 A on a branch of Hanging rock creek adj. land once belonging
to John Ellerby & land belonging to Thomas Wade, James Tribble,
James Gaston, granted to sd. John Fegan 1 May 1786...John Fegan
(LS), Wit: John Ingrem, John David (X), Wm. Ingrem. Prov. before
James Ingrem, 19 Oct 1795, by John David.

Pp. 165-166: 19 Dec 1797, William Rogers of Lancaster Co., To
Richard Elkins, 1/2 of 340 A granted to John Fegan,
1784 on Hanging Rock Creek adj. James Tribble, John Creighton,
William Rogers...William Rogers (LS), Wit: Cordner Ingrem, John
Ingrem. Prov. 22 Feb 1798, by Cordner Ingram, before James
Ingrem, J. P.

Pp. 166-167: 19 Dec 1797, William Rogers to Robert Stringfellow
for Ł 35...1/2 of 340 A granted to John Fegan...
(Same wit., sign., and proof).

Page 167: 7 Apr 1797, James Nickle, on Hanging Rock creek to
William McDonald, land granted Sept 1774 to Robert
Love, and lastly sold to sd. James Nickles by Deed, now for $50
...James Nickles (N) (LS), Wit: Philip Mathis (X), Nancy McDonald,
Alexdr Wm. McDonald. Prov. by Philip Mathis, 7 Apr 1797, before
Jas. Ingrem, J. P.

Page 168: David Read Evans of Fairfield county, for Ł 15 sterling,
to John Artis of Kershaw County, 150 A in Kershaw
Co., on waters of Lynches Creek adj. Chambers, originally granted
to Robert Craig & David Reed Evans 5 Aug 1793...22 Sept 1798.
D. R. Evans (LS), Wit: Robert McCulloch, James Barkley. Prov. in
Fairfield District, 22 Sept 1798, before S. W. Yongue, C. C., by
James Barkley.

17 Sept 1797, John Night planter to Thomas Farmer, for Ł 30...60
A, part of 150 A granted to Samuel Lundy 7 May 1773...John Night
(X) Wit: Daniel Monaghon Senr, Danl Monaghon, Jason Peats (X).
Prov. by Jason Pate, 26 Sept 1797, before B. Hale, J. P.

Page 169: S. C. Kershaw County: 17 Dec 1791, Ephraim Ponder &
Susanna Ponder his mother, both of co. afsd., to John
Night, planter, for(s 10, lease; Ł 40 release)...100 A granted
to William Shepherd 29 May 1762, and obtain in May 24 1764, a
memorial entered 17 Dec 1764, and by lawful authority conveyed in
to the property of Robert Gardner and so by virtue of a deed

into the possession of Ephraim Ponder and by heirship into the
possession of Ephraim Ponder his son...Ephraim Ponder (LS), Susanna Ponder (LS), Wit: Daniel Monaghon, RobertJones (X). Prov. by
Daniel Monaghon, 1 Feb 1794, before Ben Hale, J. P.

Page 170: Blank.

Page 171: 21 Nov 1790, Benjamin Haile Esqr. of Lancaster Co., to
John Faulkenberry Senr of same, planter, for s 10...
part of 2869 A granted to John Marshel 1 Jan 1789, on both sides
Flat Creek adj. William Meyers, John Night Senr, Isaac Faulken-
berry...250 A. Benn. Haile (LS), Wit: Ferguson Hale (X), Benjn
Ladd.

7 March 1795, David Faulkenberry of Lancaster Co., to John Faul-
kenberry of same, planter, for Ł 5...100 A part of 2869 A
surveyed 20 Jan 1787,granted to John Marshel adj. Night Night...
David Faulkenberry (LS), Wit: John Artis, Jacob Faulkenberry (X),
Danl Monaghon. Prov. by John Artis, 5 Aug 1797, before Ben
Haile.

Page 172: Tully Biggs of Lancaster Co., for Ł 5 to Benjamin Ladd
Senr., tract in Lancaster Co., on waters of Lick Creek
9 March 1798. Tully Biggs (LS), Wit: Benjamin Ladd (B), Robert
Hodge (X). Prov. by Benjamin Ladd Junr, before Thomas Welsh,
21 March 1798.

Kershaw County: William Bracey of Camden, to Benjamin Ladd Junr.,
negro girl named Nance. 24 May 1798. William Bracey. Wit: Tully
Biggs. Prov. by Tully Biggs 21 March 1798, before John Welsh.

Pp. 172-173: 19 Jan 1798, James Holliman to Jacob Funderburk,
tract, part of 15,000 A granted to Thomas Sumer,
in the fork of Wild Cat Creek adj. John Bibbes, Jacob Carnes,
Titus Laney, David Usher, Robert Welsh...James Holliman (LS),
Wit: Archd McCorkle, Henry Funderburk. Prov. by Henry Funderburk, 19 May 1798, before John Welsh, J. P.

Page 173: 29 Nov 1787, David Robinson of Dist. of Camden. (deed
left incomplete)

Page 174: Articles of Agreement between Thomas Dunlap and Elener
Thomson, sd. Thomas Dunlap is to maintain sd. Elener
during life with sufficient food and raiment, etc, when sd.
Thomson deceased said Dunlap engages to give her corps a decent
burial and set a decent tombstone to her grave and to her father
and Mothers grave, and agrees to keep two negroes, if they live
for two of her brother John Thomson's children, the young
negro named Rose for Margaret and negro named Tansy for Benjamin
...31 Dec 1793. Thomas Dunlap (LS), Wit: Robert Montgomery, Benjamin Thomson, Walter Carson. In consideration I give sd. Thomas
Dunalp negreso Cussander, Pembo Luce and Phillice...Elener
Thompson (℈) (LS), Same wit. Prov. by Robert Montomgery and
Walter Carson, 29 Oct.

Page 175: Blank.

Page 176: 4 Feb 1796, Robert Crawford and wife Jane of Lancaster
Co., to John Tomlinson, for Ł 83 sterling...166 A in Lan-
caster Co., adj. Robert Lockhart, Guy Wallace, Nathan Tomlinson,
Robert Hancock...Robert Crawford (Seal), Jane Crawford (0) (Seal)

Wit: Wm. Crawford, Robt Hancock, Robt Crawford. Prov. by Robert
Hancock before Henry Massey, J. P., 7 Sept 1796.

Pp. 176-177: 27 Oct 1794, William Barnett Esqr. Sheriff of Lan-
              caster Co., to Benjamin Harper, planter, whereas
John Bibby was seized of a plantation of 150 A on waters of
Lynches Creek and was indebted to Benjamin Harper, and recovered
Ł 41 s 17 d 5 sterling in court, by writ of fiere facias 1 May
1794...William Barnett S. L. C. (Seal), Wit: William Blair,
Alexdr. Craig. Ack. in open Court.

Pp. 177-178: 2 Apr 1794, Andrew Herron of Mecklinburg Co., NC,
              to William Simpson Senior of Lancaster Co., for
natural love and affection the sd. Andrew Herron hath for his
daughter Sally Donnom Herron and for s 5 sterling...one Mulatto
girl about 12 years of age named Sophy, in trust...Andrew Heron
(Seal), Wit: Elir Alexander, Margret Alexander, Jane McMeen (X).

Pp. 178-179: 3 Nov 1795, John Scott of Lancaster Co., planter,
              to George Vickery of same, planter, by grant 5 Dec
1785, to William Caston, 640 A on a branch of Turkey Quarter
waters of Kane Creek on each side of the great Road to Charleston,
200 A, for Ł 30...John Scott (Seal), Wit: Wm Graves, Wm. Moore,
Andw Walker. Prov. by Andrew Walker, 25 Feb 1797, before Elir
Alexander, C. C.

Page 180: 17 Jan 1797, Henry Shaver of Lancaster Co., to James
           Purdy, for 506 A of land and a Horse, 100 A on Rum
Creek a prong of Cane Creek adj. at time of survey, Morris
Roney, Mr. Adams, granted to Henry Shaver 1 Oct 1787, land on
Great Road from Landsford to Camden, part of 200 A granted to
John Graved 5 Dec 1785, which said tract fell by descent to Patrick
Graves son and heir of John Graves, and sold to John Thompson
by sd. Thompson conveyed to William Graves and sd. 100 A sold by
William Graves & wife to Henry Shaver 17 Nov 1794...Henry Shaver
(Seal), Wit: William Nisbet, George Vickory. Prov. by William
Nisbet, 17 Jan 1797, before Elir. Alexander, C. L. Ct.

Page 181: 13 Dec 1797, John Welsh of Lancaster Co., to Leonard
           Cagle, for Ł 50, 500 A in Dist. of Camden, on waters
of Lynches Creek adj. Boston Hagler, George McManus, Turkey Creek,
part of grant to Thomas Sumter 2 Apr 1787...John Welsh (Seal),
Wit: Abraham Hagler (X), Charles McManus. Prov. by Charles
McManus, 18 Dec 1797, before John Welsh, J. P.

Pp. 181-182: 9 Sept 1795, John Lockahrt and wife Catharine of
              Orangeburgh County, to George McManus of Lancaster
Co., for Ł 40...land on Turkey Creek adj. Hugh McManus, by
plat annexed to grant dated 10 May 1787, John Lockhart being the
Pantetee...John Lockhart (Seal), Catharine Lockahrt (X) (Seal),
Wit: John Welsh, Lewis Faile. Prov. by Lewis Faile, 9 Sept
1795, before John Welsh, J. P.

Page 182: 6 Sept 1796, John Cagle & wife Lucy of Lancaster Co.,
           to Jacob Hagler of Lancaster Co., for Ł 30 sterling,
50 A on W side Big Lynches Creek adj. sd. Hagler, Pate, plat
dated 1750 to James McManus the Pantentee...John Cagle (X)
(Seal), Lucy Cagle (X), Wit: Charles McManus, Leonard Cagle (+)
Prov. by Charles McManus, 6 Sept 1796, before John Welsh,J. P.

Pp. 182-183: Benjamin Ladd, Taylor, of Lancaster Co., for Ł 70
to Andrew Baker, 50 A on waters of Flat Creek,
Lick Creek...28 Feb 1799. Benjn Ladd Senr (Seal), Wit: Richmond
Terrel, Isaac Mallet, Providence Mallet (X). Prov. 29 March
17-9, by Richmond Terrel, before R Hunlep, J. P.

Page 184: Isaac Mallet of Lancaster Co., for Ł 35 to Joseph
Haile, land belonging to a plat of Henry Gracy,
granted "ninety one" deed by Thomas Frizzle and then to sd. Mal-
let, adj. McDonald, Kennington, 150 A...7 Mar 1799. Isaac
Mallet (Seal), Wit: Saml Fields, R. Hunley, Randal McDonald (X).
Prov. by Isaac Mallet, ack. in open Court6 Mar 1799, before R.
Hunlep, J. P.

Pp. 184-185: 6 Jan 1797, James McVey of Lancaster Co., to Jason
Peat, for Ł16...land where Dicey Fuller formerly
lived according to a line that Benjn. Haile & Margaret Bishop
made, 50 A pattend to Henry Massey, conveyed to Margaret Bishop,
by Benj Haile 29 Aug 1788... James McVey (Seal), Wit: R. Hunley,
Wm McVey (X), James Farguson. Prov. by Richard Hunley Esqr.,
28 Mar 1799, before Elir. Alexander, J. P.

Page 185: 26 July 1798, Jason Pate of Lancaster Co., to Benjamin
Johnston of same, for Ł16...same land in above deed...
Jason Pate (X) (Seal), Elizabeth Pate (X) (Seal), Wit: R. Hunley,
Absalom Hunley, George McVey. Prov. by George McVey, 5 Nov 1798
before John Welsh, J. P.

Pp. 185-186: 4 Nov 1793, Henry Gracy of Lancaster Co., planter,
to Thomas Frizzle, planter, by granted 5 Sept 1791
to Henry Gracey 400 A in Lick Creek adj. Richmond Terrell, William Narramore, Elisha White, Edmund McKenny, now for Ł 30...
Henry Gracey (Seal), Wit: Benjamin Deason , John Frisel (H), Susanna Johnston (X). Prov. before B. Haile, J. P., by Benjamin
Deason, 15 Feb 1794.

Pp. 186-187: 25 May 1793, Henry Gracy, planter, to David Johnston,
(lease & release) 218 A granted to Henry Gracey
5 Sept 1791 on waters of Flat Creek, Lick Creek adj. Benjn Ladd
Senr, Benjn Ladd Junr, Henry Peebles, Wm. Terrell. Henry Gracy
(Seal), Wit: Richmond Terrell, Benjamin Deason, Hester Ladd (X)
Prov. by Richmond Terrell, 20 Sept 1793, before _____

Pp. 188-189: Blank.

Pp. 190-191: 15 Jan 1791, Clement Gardner of Chesterfield Co.,
planter, to Elisha White of Lancaster co., by grant
10 Apr 1771 to Abraham Deason, 100 A on Flat Creek, adj. William
Elliott, William Bratton, for Ł 8 s 11 sd. Clement Gardner & wife
Sarah...Clement Gardner (C) (Seal), Sarah Gardner (X) (Seal),
Wit: Benjamin Deason, Jonathan Deason (O), Joanna Massey (X).
Prov. by Ben. Deason, 13 Apr 1793, before B. Haile, J. P.

Page 191: 10 Mar 1796, Thomas Frizzle of Lancaster co., to Isaac
Mallet of same, by grant 5 Sept 1790 to Henry Gracey,
400 A, adj. Edmund McKenny, now for Ł 5....Thomas Frizzle(O)
(Seal), Wit: William Hull, John Knight (X), Stephen Mallet. Prov.
by John Knight before Richard Hunlep, J. P., 6 Mar 1799.

Page 192: Blank.

Page 193: 4 Dec 1797, Night Night of Lancaster Co., to Daniel
        Fuller of same, planter, for Ꝟ 20...part of 2869 A
granted to John Marshel 20 Jan 1787, on waters of Flat Creek,
became property of Benjamin Haile and by L & R to Night Night....
Night Night (R) (Seal), Wit: Thomas Hopkins, Richard Night Senr,
Prov. in Chesterfield Co., by Thomas Hopkins, before Richard
Bettis, J. P., 16 Dec 1797.

Page 194: S. C. Lancaster Co.: Colden Williams, planter, of co.
        afsd., to David Johnston, 50 A on waters of Flat Creek
adj. sd. Johnston, John Welsh, John Johnston, cut off by a survey
of Gen. Sumter...11 March 1799. Colden Williams (Seal), Wit:
Benjamin Deason, William Ferguson, Gale Frizzle (O), Ack. by
Colden Williams, 27 Mar 1799, before B. Haile, J. P.

(March 28th 1799) Appeared personally before me Absalom Hunley
and made oath that he was present at Capt. John Welsh's Muster
Ground in the County aforesaid on the 23d day of Feb last being
Muster day when and where a Squabble enowed (?) between Robert
Moore and John Baker Junr. of Flat Creek in which scuffle or
fight the said Moore bit off a piece of the upper part of said
John Bakers Right Ear. Sworn to and subscribed March 29th 1799
before me Elir Alexander, J. P.   Absalom Hunley.

Pp. 195-199: Blank.

Page 200: Samuel Farr Junr. yeoman of Lancaster Co., for $362
        to John McMurray Senr of Lancaster Co., tract on N side
Cain Creek in Lancaster Co., whereon sd. Saml Farr Junr. now lives
...29 Aug 1798. Samuel Farr (Seal), Wit: James Craig, John Mc-
Murray Junr, John Stewart. Prov. 19 Feb 1799 by John McMurray
Junr, before John Craig, J. P.

S. C. Kershaw County: William Bracey of Camden, to Richmond Ter-
rell, negro wench Molly about 26 years old...24 Jan 1798. William
Bracey Junr. Wit: Tully Biggs, Benjn Ladd (B). Prov. by Tully
Biggs, 21 Mar 1798, before Thos Welsh, J. P.

John Wisenor of Lancaster Co., for Ꝟ 5 to Richmond Terrell, 50 A
in Lancaster Co., adj. William Denman, John Baker, John Evans,
granted to John Hewit on Flat Creek 300 A...26 Aug 1799. John
Wisenor, Wit: William Baker (X), Eley Narramore (X). Prov. by
Eley Narramore, 17 Sept 1799 before Richard Hunley.

Pp. 200-201: James Walnut of Mecklinburgh Co., N. C., for $300
        to Samuel Farr Junr of Lancaster Co., tract whereon
Saml Farr Senr and said Junior now lives on N side Cain Creek,
125 A...11 Aug 1797. James Walnut (Seal), Wit: Bruce Livington,
David Farr, William Crocket. Prov. by David Farr of North
Carolina, 13 Feb 1799, before Robert Montgomery, J. P.

Page 201: William Terrell of Lancaster Co., for Ꝟ 20 to Randal
        McDonald, 100 A in Lancaster Co., on Lick Creek, adj.
land granted to William Terrell...14 Apr 1798. William Terrell
(Seal), Wit: Richmond Terrell, Isaac Mallet. Prov. by Richmond
Terrell, 27 Mar 1799, before Richd. Hunly, J. P.

Isaac Mallet of Lancaster Co., for Ꝟ 20 to Randal McDonald, 50 A
on waters of Lick Creek granted to Henry Gracey...6 Mar 1799. Isaac Mallet (LS), Wit: Richmond Terrell, James Ferguson, Samuel
Fields. Ack. by Isaac Mallet, before R. Hunley, 6 March 1799.

Page 202: S. C. Lancaster Co.: John Caston of co. afsd., farmer,
         for Ł 200 sterling to John Osburn of North Carolina,
Mecklinburgh Co., farmer, 50 A surveyed for Daniel Williams decd.
part of 250 A near the head of little Lynches creek granted to
Daniel Williams, dated 19 Sept 1758, which fell to John Williams
being the heir at law then bid off at the vendue of John Williams
decd by Isam Shurling then conveyed by Isam Shurling by a deed
15 Apr 1793, conveyed from John Caston to John Osburn 5 Aug
1799 adj. Isam Shurling, James Blackman, William Ward...John
Caston Junr (Seal), Wit: William Ward, James Blackman, John Barkley. Mildred Caston (1) relinquished dower, 5 Aug 1799. Prov.
by William Ward, 24 Jan 1800, before Elir Alexander, C. L. D.

Page 203: (Sept 17 1799) On or before the 1st May 1800 I promise
         to pay to Titus Laney of Lancaster Co., $88.66 with law-
ful interest, 5 June 1799. John Shepherd (J), Wit: James Craig,
William Craig. N. B. Proof Whiskey to be taken at 3/6 pr Gallon
if tendered.

John Shepherd of Lancaster Co., by note bound to Titus Laney
$88.66, mortgage of two tracts, 150 A adj. the new meeting house
in the Waxhaw Settlement on Camp Creek, the other tract of 11 A
on N side Camp Creek...5 June 1799. John Shepherd (J) (Seal),
Wit: James Craig, William Craig,. Prov. 6 June 1799 by James
Craig, before John Craig, J. P.

Page 204: 27 Feb 1794, Benjamin Haile of Lancaster Co., to Wil-
         liam Reeder of same, for Ł 10 sterling, land on E side
Gills branch, 200 A above Catey Bridges old place...Ben Haile
Wit: Richard Hunley, Peter Andrews, Susanna Philip (X).

Pp. 204-205: 20 Mar 1794, William Reader of Lancaster Co., to
            William Danzy of same, for Ł 10 sterling, land on E
side Gills branch above Catey Bridges old place...William Reader
(Seal), Wit: Benjn Haile Sr., Benjamin Haile Junr. Catey Haile
(X). Ack. 20 Mar 1794, before Ben Haile, J. P.

Page 205: 13 Dec 1798, William Danzy of Lancaster Co., planter,
         to Kitchen Killebraw of Robinson Co., N. C., planter,
for Ł 100 sterling...450 A adj. John Ferguson, Ferguson Haile,
William Denman, William Covey, granted to Francis Bettis 965 A
adj. James Ball...William Danzy (Seal), Pamelia Danzy (Seal),
Wit: R Hunley, Tully Biggs, James Killebrew. Prov. by James
Killebrew, 27 Mar 1799, before Rich. Hunley, J. P.

Pp. 205-206: Abraham Merryman & Mark Merryman, for Ł 8 to Tully
            Biggs, 50 A in the Dist. of Camden, waters of Lick
Creek, near Mark Merrymans spring, adj. sd. Tully Biggs, near the
race paths...4 Feb 1799. Abm Merriman (X), Mark Merriman (X)
Wit: Richmond Terrell, James Denman. Prov. by Richmond Terrell,
27 Mar 1799, before Richd Hunley, J. P.

Page 206: 26 Jan 1793, Thomas Frizzle to William Ferguson, for Ł
         5 sterling, land on prongs of Flat Creek adj. William
Ferguson, Thomas Frizzle, on s side land that William Deason now
lives on...Thomas Frizzle (O), Mishaba (?) Frizzle (X). Wit:
Colden Williams, John Gale Frizzle (J). Prov. by John Gale
Frizzle before Benjn Hale, J. P., 6 Apr 1793.

Page 207: William Ferguson of Fairfield Co., planter, for Ł 20

to Jonathan Blackman of Lancaster Co., 195 A on the Rocky River
Road, adj. James Blackman, John Blackman, granted to William Robinson...3 Dec 1798. William Ferguson (Seal), Wit: William Ferguson Junr, John Stogner, William Blackman (X). Prov. by Wm
Ferguson Junr, 12 Apr 1799, before Elir. Alexander, J. P.

Pp. 207-208: Susanna White admx. of Henry White decd. of St.
             Lukes parish, S. C., for L 125 to George White of
Lancaster Co., 250 A adj. Catawba River part of grant to Henry
White Senr., adj. Hugh White...15 Dec 1797. Susanna White (LS),
Wit: David Ferguson,Robt White, William Simpson. Prov. by Capt.
William Simpson, 8 Oct 1798, before Elir. Alexander, J. P.

Pp. 208-209: 28 Dec 1791, John Ingrem of Kershaw Co., to James
             Ingrem, whereas the lands herein after mentioned
on 18 Jan 1765 granted to Humphrey Barnett, and directed by his
will that the tract be sold by his exrs. Michal Barnet and James
Hester, and Michal Barnet acting exr. did on 27 Dec 1791 by deed
of feoffment convey 50 A on the Broad road to Charleston below
Hanging Tock to John Ingrem, now for L 18 s 5 ...John Ingrem (LS),
Wit: Elir Alexander, James Miller, Michal Barnet. Prov. by
James Miller. (plat included)

Page 209: 22 Mar 1797, William Ingrem and John Ingram both of
          Lancaster Co., to James Ingrem Esqr. of same, 300 A in
two separate tracts granted to Alexander Ingrem 25 Aug 1769,
which was left by the last will and testament to be equally divided
between his four children by name James & William and John &
Ann Ingrem, and now the sd. William and John do by virtue of this
deed convey their fourth parts...John Ingrem (LS), William Ingrem
(LS), Wit: Danl Monaghon, Arthur Ingrem, Samuel Helton. Prov. by
Samuel Helton 22 Mar 1797, before Jas. Ingrem, J. P.

Page 210: 22 Mar 1797, John Ingrem of Lancaster Co., to James
          Ingrem Esqr, John Ingrem who being executor to his
father Alexander Ingrem....John Ingrem Wit: Danl Monaghon,
Arthur Ingrem, Samuel Helton. Prov. by Samuel Helton, 22 Mar
1797, before James Ingrem, J. P.

Pp. 210-211: Middleton McDonald of Lancaster Co., planter, for L
             50 to James Clifton, planter, 150 A including the
Graveyard ½ of plantation of 300 A on E side Catawba River
granted to George Platt conveyed to James Denton Decd., and sold
by virtue of fi fa in favor the the admx. of Col. William
Farrell agianst the estate of sd. James Denton, and conveyed
by John Simpson Esqr. then Sheriff to Middleton McDonald...on
Camp Creek adj. Tilman...10 May 1797. Midn. McDonald (LS), Wit:
Benjn Clifton, Shadrach Ratley (X). Elizabeth McDonald, wife
of Middlton, relinquished dower 27 June 1797, before Danl Wade,
J. L. C. Prov. by Benjamin Clifton, 10 May 1797.

Page 216: Blank.

Page 217: 1 Dec 1793, Gen. Thomas Sumter of Claremont County,
          to John Laney of Lancaster Co., for s 10 sterling...
175 A, on W side Big Lynches Creek adj. John Lany, Holliman,
Titus and Laney, part of 15,000 A granted to sd. Sumter, Wit:
Josiah Cantey, Samuel Tynes. Prov. by Saml Tynes in Chesterfield
Co., beofre Richard Bettis, 25 Mar 1795.

Pp. 217-218: 2 Sept 1793, Gen. Thomas Sumter of Claremont Co.,
        to John Lany of Lancaster Co., for ₺ 50..175 A
on SW side Lynches Creek. Same wit, sign., and proof. (plat included, 21 Oct 1793, by John Barron, D. S.

Pp. 219-225: Blank.

Page 226: 12 Jan 1799, William Tomlinson and wife Mary to Joseph
        Baker, for ₺ 50...land on S side twelve miles creek
adj. George Wrenn, 100 A;...William Tomlinson (Seal), Mary Tomlinson (X) (Seal), Wit: John Tomlinson, Natl. Tomlinson (X),
Arthur Collier. Prov. by John Tomlinson, 14 Jan 1799, before Samuel C. Dunlap, J. P., plat included.

Pp. 226-227: S. C. Lancaster Co.: John Belk, farmer, for ₺ 20 to
        Joseph Montgomery,farmer, 385 A (surveyed for him 25
Jan 1789) on drains of Bear cr-ek, a prong of Cane Creek adj.
Glass Caston...31 July 1799. John Belk (X), Wit: A. Alexander,
Tho Dunlap, Saml Dunlap. Hannah Belk, wife of John, relinquished
dower, 31 July 1799, before Robt Dunlap, J. L. C. Ack. in open
court 31 July 1799.

Page 228: Blank.

Page 229: John Gallespy of Chester Co., for $100 to George Weir
        of same, 350 A on Shingletons Creek NE side Wateree
River granted to John Gillaspy 5 June 1786...3 May 1798. John
Gillespy, Wit: John Jones, John McCreary. Prov. in Chester Co.,
by John Jones, before John McCreary, J. P., 3 May 1798.

Pp. 229-230: Tully Biggs of Lancaster Co., for ₺ 5 to Edward
        Kennington (Cannington), 10 A in Lancaster Co.,
2 March 1798. Tully Biggs (Seal), Wit: Richmond Terrel, Catharine
Terrell (X). Prov. by Richmond Terrel, 21 Mar 1798, before
John Welsh.

Pp. 230-231: S. C. Lancaster Co,: 19 Dec 1796, Edmund McKinney to
        William Cannington, for ₺ 20 sterling...land on
Lick Creek, adj. Henry Peebles, 100 A, granted to Henry Gracey,
5 Sept 1791, adj. land granted to Widow McKinney, William Narramore...Edmund McKenny (X), Elizabeth McKinny (X) Wit: William
Bridges, Edwd Narramor, William Baker. Prov. by Edward Narramore,
15 March 1797, before John Welsh, J. P.

Page 232: ____ 1798, John Best of Lancaster Co., to William
        Cawthorn of same, for ₺ 60 sterling...400 A granted
to Thomas Lehre 5 Mar 1787, ½ of sd. tract. John Best (X) (Seal),
Wit: Benedict Best, Joseph Coile, John Weaver. Prov. by John
Weaver, 28 Jan 1799, before Elir. Alexander, J. P.

Pp. 232-233: S. C. Lancaster County, Camden District: Charles
        Barber of Kershaw Co., planter, for title to 100 A
made by William Coffin, 100 A on a branch of Cedar Creek at Orums
branch, adj. James Hood, Archibald Hood, William Fleningham, part
of grant to Charles Barber 775 A...11 Jan 1799. Charles Barber
(Seal), Wit: Arthur Innes (X), Jesse Duncan (X). Prov. by Jesse
Dunken, 28 Jan 1799, before Elir. Alexander, J. P.

Page 233: John Best of Lancaster Co., planter for ₺ 20, to William
        Cauthorn, 100 A adj. Charles Barber...17 Mar 1798.
John Best (X) (Seal), Wit: Benedict Best, Jos Coile, Winn Twitty.

Prov. by Benedict Best, 28 Jan 1799, before Wm Barkley, J. P.
Pp. 233-234: John Best of Lancaster Co., for Ł 20 to James
         Cothren, 100 A adj. Charles Barber, Weaver, Cauthrens
old tract, Linn...17 Mar 1798. John Best (X), Same wit. and proof.

Page 234: 10 Mar 1798, James Purdy of Lancaster to Richard
         Ussery of same, for Ł 60...100 A on Hanging Rock Creek,
part of 300 A granted to Robert Love and that has deceas'd fell
to his son and heir James Love, conveyed to James Nickle, adj.
William McDonald, road from the Mill to the meeting house,
Thomas Gaston, Henry Horton...James Purdy (Seal), Wit: Richard
Elkins . (X), Robert Stringellow. Prov. by Richard Elkins before
James Ingrem, J. P. 17 Nov 1798.

Pp. 234-235: 16 Nov 1799, Benjamin Croxton and wife Mary of Lan-
         caster Co., to John Croxton, for Ł 80 sterling...
200 A, ½ of 400 A on waters of lower Camp Creek granted to James
Maffet 5 Mar 1770...Benjamin Croxton (Seal), Mary Croxton (Seal),
Wit: Philip Hawkins, James Croxton, Allen Croxton. Prov. by
James Croxton, 24 Jan 1800, before Elir. Alexander, C. L. C.

Pp. 235-236: William Barnet of Chester Co.,for $130½, to Alexander
         Craig and James Douglas, 71 A granted to William
Barnet 1 Dec 1794 near Lancaster Court House, adj. John White,
John Simpson,Nathan Barr, and the Estate of David Adams...16 Oct
1799. William Barnett (Seal), Wit: Eliezar Alexander, Thomas
Edwards. Prov. by Thomas Edwards, 16 Oct 1799, before Eliezar
Alexander, J. P.

Page 236: Articles of Agreement made 6 May 1791 between William
         Barton Junr and William Barton Senr. doth agree to give
up the land at this time to William Barton Junr. all his stock but
two cows and all his land, for his part William Barton Junr. to
maintain William Barton Senr. and his wife, and furnish him a
house to live in, and support two cows to give them milk.
Both signed by mark. Wit: John Barkley, John Taylor. Prov. by
John Barkley, 29 Oct 1799.

Page 237: 27 June 1796, Samuel Graham to John Scott, both of
         Lancaster Co., for Ł 40 s 13 sterling, 200 A on SW
side George Vickrey, Elir. Alexander, Scott, William Graham...
Saml Graham (LS), Wit: E. Alexander, William Gibson. Prov. by
William Gibson, 28 June 1796, before Elir. Alexander, C. L. C.

Pp. 238-239: 1 Mar 1794, Joseph Singleton, merchant of Camden
         Dist., to Stewart Dickey, planter, of Georgetown
Dist., whereas sd. Singleton standeth justly indebted to sd.
Dickey by two notes...mortgage 1936 A grant in Camden Dist.,
1080 A on Camp Creek adj. Amos Riches, Jas McCamons, Ringor
Montgomery, Mr. Cousar, and another tract on both sides Rocky
River road, adj. Genl Sumter, Jacob Plylar, Paul Plyler, John
White, Wm. Tates...Joseph Singleton (Seal), Wit: John Mills (X),
George Dickey. Prov. in Georgetown Dist., by John Mill, before
Robt Ervin, J. P., 25 May 1794.

Pp. 239-240: __ Aug 1791, William Johnston planter of Lancaster
     Co. , to Samuel and Charles Dotson of same, release of claim
to 200 A on Rocky Creek adj. Arthur Hicklin, 200 A...William
Johnston (Seal), Wit: Daniel Glaze, William Maddox (X). Prov. by
Danl Glaze, 13 Mar 1799, before Elir. Alexander.

Pp. 240-241: John Ezell of Lancaster Co., for love and good will
and affections to grandson Lewis Ezell of same,
negroes Surry and Pleasant, 4 Mar 1796. John Ezell (+) (Seal),
Wit: Gillim Ezell, James Leeton, Zacchariah Bell (X). Prov. by
Gillim Ezell and Zachariah Bell, 17 Apr 1797, before Elir Alexander, C. L. C.

Pp. 241-242: 29 Jan 1799, Jesse Mesho of Lancaster Co., planter,
to William Eastridge, planter, for Ł 10 sterling,
160 A tract on Little Linches Creek surveyed for him 7 Dec 1794,
adj. Enoch Anderson, John Williams, Joseph Caston, Jesse Mesho
(T), Elizabeth Mesho (X), Wit: Joseph Eastridge (V), William
Chambers. Prov. before Richard Hunley, J. P., 14 Mar 1799, by
Wm. Chambers.

Pp. 243-245: 29 Aug 1796, Robert McDow, wheelwright, and wife
Mary, of Lancaster Co., to William McDow, by grant
3 Apr 1752 to Thomas McElhenny, by Gov. Johnston of N. C., 300
A on E side Catawba in the Waxhaws now called Lancaster Co.,
and by sd. Thomas Mcelhenny's last will to Thomas McDow, and
the afsd. Robert McDow and by a survey of John McClenahan 19 Nov
1795 who was appointed to law off the 100 A for Robert McDow
agreeable to the will of afsd. testator, on cat tail branch, adj.
George Dunlap, John McDow...Robert McDow (Seal), Maria McDow
(Seal), Wit: Moses Cantzon, Jane Carryl, Thos Lee. Prov. by
Moses Cantzon, 29 Aug 1796, before Joseph Lee, J. P.

Pp. 245-247: 29 Aug 1796, Robert McDow wheelwright, and wife
Mary, to William McDow, student, of Lancaster Co.,
by grant 27 Aug 1764 by Gov. Bull of S. C. to John Hudson, 100 A
near the Waterree river adj. Mathew Wilson, and sd. John Hudson
and wife Ann conveyed by deed 29 Feb 1767 to Moses Dick, and by
heirs of said. Moses conveyed 7 May 1790 to John McDow, and on
26 Feb 1793 conveyed to RobertMcDow, now for $400...75 A...
Same wign & wit and proof.

Pp. 247-249: 28 Nov 1797, William McDow Student of Lancaster Co.,
to Samuel Dunlap, of same, by grant 27 Aug 1764, 100
A above Cane Creek near Wateree River adj. Matthew Wilson...
same land as preceding deed...Wm. McDow (seal), Wit: Saml Dunlap,
Agnes Ferrell, Mary Dunlap. Prov. by Saml Dunlap, 24 Aug 1798
before Robert Dunlap, J. L. C.

Pp. 249-251: 28 Nov 1797, William McDow, student, to Samuel
Dunlap, planter, by grant 3 Apr 1752 to Thomas
McElhenny (same land as above)...Wm. McDow (Seal), Saml Dunlap,
Agnes Ferrell, Mary Dunlap. Prov. 24 Aug 1798, by Samuel Dunlap.

Pp.252-253: 11 Dec 1796, John Craton of Kershaw Co., to James
Gaston, for Ł 20, ½ of tract of 150 A granted to sd.
John Craton, by Gov. Arnoldus Vanderhorst, on waters of Little
Linches Creek and on a branch of Hanging Rock Creek ...Jno
Creighton (Seal), Nancy Creighton (O) (Seal), Wit: Robert String-
fellow, James Purdy. Prov. by Robert Stringefllow, 22 Mar 1797,
before Elir. Alexander, J. P.

Pp. 253-255: 13 Apr 1795, William Blair of Lancaster Co., to
John Simpson, whereas James Yancey Attorney at
law late of Lancaster decd. was possessed of two tracts of land
300 A on waters of Cane Creek adj. Benjamin Cudworth, John Mc-
Ilhaney, David Adams, John Carrin, by execution of Wm. Barnett

Sheriff to William Blair...William Blair (Seal), Wit: Elir Alexander, A. Alexander. Prov. by Elizar Alexander, 27 Oct 1795,
before Robert Dunlap, J. L. C.

Pp. 255-256: 2 Feb 1796, William Mothershed of Lancaster Co., for
          Ł 60 sterling, to Mary Glaze widow of same, negro
woman Sall about 16 or 17 years old, for Ł 60 sterling at 4/8
per dollar...William Mothershead (Seal), Wit: Joseph Coile,
Thos McKey, Christo. Mothershead. Prov. by Jos. Coile, before
Robert Bratney, J. P. 15 Feb 1796.

Page 256: Contract or articles of a contract between John
          Johnston Widower and Jane Johnston widow both of Lan-
caster co., before marriage that John Johnston doth agree that I
wi-1 never claim any part of her dowery which fell to her by Law
of the estate of John Johnston decd...3 Jan 1799. John Johnston
(Seal), Wit: John Craig, James Johnston.

Pp. 256-257: 27 Jan 1797, John Hood of Kershaw Co., to Benedict
          Best of Lancaster Co., whereas the sd. John Hood
did obtain Letters of admn. on the goods and chattles, etc. of
Luke Pettis deceased from Henry Hampton Esqr. ordinary for the
Dist. of Camden, and bond with Benedict Best as his Surety...
two negroes Peg, Tom, and cattle, etc. 300 bushels of corn...
John Hood (Seal), Wit: Jno Simpson, A. Alexander.
(N. B. For papers of above Luke Petty,see Camden District, S. C.
Wills and Administrations 1781-1787, by Brent H. Holcomb and
Elmer O. Parker)

Page 258: Joseph Findley of Green Co., State of Georgia, appoint
          Samuel Phar (Farr) attorney, to receive from Thomas
Blair what is due to me for carpenter and joint work...7 Apr 1791
Joseph Findly (Seal), Wit: Jno Lumpkin, J. P., John Kennedy, Lucy
Lumpkin. Prov. by John Kennedy 27 May 1795, before Elir. Alex-
ander, J. P.

Pp. 258-260: 15 Oct 1796, James Simpson, of Lancaster Co., to
          Kanady Bailey of same, for Ł 160...150 A part of
200 A granted to Fedrick Touchston 14 Sept 1771, adj. to land sold
by James Simpson to Harriss Rice, part of survey now held by
James Sprunt on Touchstone branch, 150 A conveyed by James
Simpson to Kanady Bailey, the remainder of sd. tract, adj. Wm.
Bailey, Absalom Clark, Widow Clark...James Simpson (Seal), Martha
Simpson. Wit: Jos Coile, Henry Hudson, Allston Clark. Prov. by
Joseph Coile, before Wm Barkley, 15 Feb 1799.

Pp. 260-262: 30 Dec 1797, Kanady Bailey of Lancaster Co., to Ely
          Clark of same, for $50...50 A, part of 123 A granted
to sd. Ely Clark 5 Mar 1792...(error obviously, land was conveyed
from Ely Clark to Kanady Bailey)...Ely Clark (Seal), Wit: William
Bailey, Joseph Coile, Wm. Oweings (X). Prov. by Joseph Coile,
15 Jan 1799, before Wm. Barkley, J. P.

Pp. 262-263: 17 Mar 1798, John Best of Lancaster Co., to John
          Weaver for Ł 30 sterling, 100 A on NE side Catawba
River adj. James Oram, Arthur Henessee, William Chewthrows,
land on N end of tract of 640 A granted to John Best 15 Feb by Wade
Hampton high Sheriff of Camden Dist., 1798...John Best (X) (Seal),
Wit: Jos Coile, Winn Twitty, William Chewthron. Prov. by William
Cauthorn, 28 Jan 1799, before Elir. Alexander.

Pp. 263-265: 6 Mar 1790, Robert Crawford and wife Jane of Lancaster Co., to Samuel Dunlap of same, for Ł 60...
land in Waxhaws, bounded with land formerly the property of
John Hood, Samuel Thompson, 100 A, granted to Jane Grierson 21
June 1765 being her bounty land, and by sd. Jane Grierson and
husband Archibald Clearke, made over to George Grier 5 Dec 1772,
and by sd. Greir to Jno Kelloh, 28 Mar 1777, by sd. Jno Kellsoh
(?) to Thomas Henderson, 5 Aug 1782, by sd. Thomas Henderson to
Robert Crawford 21 Apr 1787....Robert Crawford (Seal), Jane Crawford (O) (Seal), Wit: David Dunlap, Daniel Carnes, James Crawford.
Prov. by James Crawford, 9 Oct 1798 before Samuel C. Dunlap, J.
P.

Pp. 265-266: 17 Nov 1795, William Starks of Lancaster Co., plan-
ter, for Ł 60 to Reubin Starks, 100 A adj. William
Harison, originally granted to William Harrison 29 Oct 1766...
William Starke (Seal), Wit: Gray Briggs, Elizabeth Pickett, Saml
Starke.

END OF VOLUME.

BOOK F

Pp. 1-2: 12 Feb 1800, James Gaston of Dist. of Lancaser, planter,
stands indebted to Enoch Anderson, for $350...two adj. tracts
on Lynches little creek, granted to John Peter 18 Aug 1763, & sold
by L & R 25 & 26 Nov 1763 to Robert Simpson & conveyed by him 29
& 30 Nov 1764 to William Welsh, & conveyed 18 & 19 Apr 1768
to Patrick Hennis, and by Hennis 18 & 19 Aug 1768 to Glass Caston
and 27 & 27 May 1771, to Richard Anderson; the other granted to
Jasper Rogers 24 Aug 1770 & by L & R __ Aug 1772, to Richard
Anderson, & Richard Anderson dying intestate, became vested in
Enock Anderson (son & heir to sd. Richard, who conveyed said
tracts to James Gaston) adj. John Murphey, Robert McKain, Samuel
Johnson & John Love...James Gaston (Seal), Wit: Jonathan Johnson,
Joseph Clerk. Prov. by Johnson before Andrew Baskins, J. P., 6
Aug ___. Rec. Aug 1800.

Page 3: John Parker (atty for George Dickinson formerly of Charleston now of London) for Ł 140 to William McDonald Sr.,
150 A part of tract formerly in Anson County, NC, on N side Catawba, adj. Francis Ellisons entry...24 May 1800. Jno Parker
(atty for George Dickinson), Wit: Alexr Mathison, Henry Kerr.
Prov. in Kershaw Dist., by Alexander Mathison, before Jno Brown,
J. P. 5 Aug 1800.

Page 4: Richard Hatfield Homan of Richland District, for s 5
sterling, to Andrew Boddan, 562 A in Camden Dist., on a
branch of Cane Creek adj. John Coffee, James Mcatur, James Craig,
Hugh Coffee, John Hood, Saml Martin, James Montgomery, originally
surveyed for Rev. Brice Miller, 15 Feb 1793, granted to sd. Homan
3 Nov 1794; also 1355 A on both sides Turkey Quarter Creek, adj.
James Douglass, William Johnston, Glass Caston, William Thompson,
William Caston, Robt Robinson, 25 Apr 1800. Richd H Homan Wit:
Danl Wade, Saml Dunlap. Prov. by Danl Wade before Jno Simpson,
8 Nov 1800.

Page 5: S. C., Lancaster County: John Caston & wife Milly farmer
to John Clark, farmer, for Ł 20 sterling, land granted to
John Caston, 5 Dec 1795, 465 A, 30 Jan 1800. John Caston (Seal)
Mildred Caston (X) (Seal), Wit: Jas Blackman, William Ward,
Gabriel Caston. Prov. 15 Apr 1800 by Wm Ward, before Andrew
Baskin.

Page 6: Richard Stringfellow of Lancaster District, for love,
good will, to son in law John Isom (Or Icorn?), negro
Kitt, mare, etc. 29 Dec 1800. Richard Stringfellow (Seal), Wit:
Thomas Cauthorn, Henry Hudson, John Cauthorn. Ack. 3 Mar 1801

Richard Stringfellow, ton so Ruben, negro Pompely, carpenter tools
and blacksmith tools, etc. 39 Dec. 1800. Same wit, signature,
and proving as above.

Pp. 7-9: 14 & 15 Mar 1774, John Fortenberry of Parish of St.
Mark, S. C., planter, to Isaac Fortenberry of same, plan-
ter, 150 A on a branch of Linches Creek, granted 19 Nov 1760 to
Patrick McCormack; John Fortenbery (I) (Seal), Wit: David Miers,
Jacob Fortenberry. Prov. by David Myers, before John Marshell,
7 June 1788.

Page 9: Article of agreement between John Foster of Lancaster
District, and Alexander Orr of Mecklenburg Co., N. C.,the
sd. Alexander having been lately married to the daughter of John

117

Foster, and in consequence gotten in possession of cattle, negroes
etc., having since lost by death his wife...disclaimed negroes...6
Jan 1801. John Foster (Seal), Alexander Orr (Seal), Wit: Samuel
C. Dunlap, Moses White. Prov. by Moses White, 6 Jan 1801, before
Samuel C. Dunlap, J. P.

Page 10: 20 Aug 1790 Benjn Haile of Lancaster Co., to James
        Falkenberry, son of Isaac Falkenberry of same, for Ł 5;
40 A, part of 2869 granted to col. John Marshal, adj. his fathers
line, opposite the spring formerly called the widow Faulkenberrys
spring, Jacob Faulkenberry. Ben Haile (Seal), Wit: John Faulkenberry, Knight Night (R). Prov. in Chesterfield County, 17 Jan
1798, by Night Night, before Richard Bettis, J. P.

Page 11: 18 March 1797, Andrew Falkenberry, of Kershaw Co., to
        James Faulkenberry son of Isaac, 40 A, part of 2869 A
granted to John Marshel. Andrew Faulkenberry (X), Wit: John
Artis, Joel Jordan (X), Prov. in Chesterfield Co., 17 Jan 1798
by Joel Jordan, before Richard Bettis, J. P.

Pp. 11-12: 1800, Edmond Hull & wife Jane of Camden Dist., to
        Samuel Caskey, by granted 5 Mar 1787, for 150 A on
Gills Creek, for Ł 20...Edmond Hull (E) (Seal), Jane Hull (A)
(Seal), Wit: Hugh Cofey, Nathaniel Cousart, Joseph Strain. Prov.
in Lancaster District by Hugh Coffey, before Wm. Woods, J. P. 7
Nov 1800.

Page 13: 2 May 1800, John Clark of Dist. of Lancaster, planter,
        to John Clark, son of John Clark, for s 35...465 A
granted to John Caston, 29 Jan 1785, conveyed by deed for 132 A,
30 Jan 1800 by sd. John Caston & wife near head of Little Linches
Creek; also 400 A in the State of Virginia, bedford Co., on Otter
River, about 12 miles from Bedford town near one Mr. Owty & sd.
John Clark purchased sd. land from Mr. John Burk, tavern keeper in
Caroline Co., Va., also 513 A on bug swamp in Georgetown Dist.,
conveyed by Moses Floid & wife in 1792...John Clark (Seal), Wit:
Joseph Clark, William Baskin. 13 May 1800, prov. by Joseph Clark,
before Andrew Baskin.

Page 14: 3 May 1800, John Clark, of Lancaster District, planter,
        to daughter Mary, for natural love, etc. cattle, sheep...
John Clark (Seal), Wit: Same as above. Same proving.

Pp. 14-15: William Belfour of the County of _____ North Carolina,
        to Colain Williams of Lancaster Co., for 250 silver
dollars negro Noel...17 Apr 1800. Wit: Joseph Deland. William
Belfour (Seal), Prov. 18 Apr 1800, by Joseph Deland.

Pp. 15-16: 7 Apr 1797, James Bredin of rocky creek, a branch of
        Ceder Creek, reputy surveyor, to William Allen of sd.
creek, for Ł 4...between 12 and 14 acres on both sides turkey
creek, a prong of Cedar Creek, adj. James Bredins survey, 150 A
granted 4 Sept 1786, and said part also claimed by the widow
Pendergrass and her children, adj. land granted to John Shubert,
now sd. William Allens...James Bredin (Seal), Wit: Philip Shubard,
John Richardson. Prov. by Philip Shewbert, 12 Apr 1800, before
Jno. Simpson, clerk.

Page 16: William Ferguson of Fairfield County, to William Reaves
        of Lancaster Co., for Ł 25...land adj. William Ward,

118

BOOK F

Baslines, Barnards...William Ferguson (Seal), Wit: William Ferguson Junr, David Williams, Moses Barnard, Prov. by Wm Ferguson, before Andrew Baskin, J. P.

Page 17: Mary Williams of Lancaster County, cooper, for Ŀ 16, to
      Colden Williams, 250 acres granted to John Roberson, conveyed to William Deason, conveyed from Deason, to William Williams, and willed to sd. Mary...Mary Williams (X), Wit: John Williams, David Williams. Prov. by John Williams, before Andrew Baskin, J. P.

Page 18: Whereas William Steel obtained a grant for 217 acres, 6
      Feb 1792, now William Steel and wife Martha, for Ŀ 10, to Philip Shewbart of Rocky Creek, sd. 217 acres, adj. Philip Shewbart, Widow Pendergrass, Widow Carlil....William Steel (LS), Martha (ꙅ) Steel (LS), Wit: James Breden, Danl. Glaze, Charles Shewbart (X). Proved by Daniel Glaze, before Jesse Tilman, J. P.

Page 19: William and Mary Tomlinson, to Churchwell Anderson, for
      $300...land on S side Twelve mile creek, 110 acres granted by Andrew McCorkle to Thomas Eliot, in 1781, left by Thomas Eliot decd to James Eliot his son, conveyed to William Tomlinson, 6 Jan 1795 adj. Robert Crockett...5 Dec 1799; William Tomlinson (Seal), Mary (X) Tomlinson (Seal), Wit: Joseph Doby, Joseph Baker, Arthur Collier. Prov. by Joseph Dobey, 1 Apr 1800, before Jno Simpson, C. C. L. D.

Page 20: Starling Degges of Edgemba [Edgecombe]County, N. C. to
      Colden Williams, of Lancaster Co., negro Norell, 22 Feb 1800. Starling Degges (Seal), Wit: Joseph Dillard. Prov. by Joseph Dillard before Andrew Baskin, J. P.

Pp. 20-21: Robert Hodges, of Lancaster District, for $350 to John
      Kennington, land on S side Flat Creek, near head of flat creek adj. Benja. Haile, James Ferguson, Ferguson Haile, Robert Hodges, Edward Narramore...7 Feb 1801. Robert Hodges (X), Caron Hodges (X). Wit: John Kennington, Edw. Narromore, Prov. by John Kennington, 14 March 1801, before R. Hunley, J. P.

Page 21: Robert Hodges of Dist. of Lancaster, for $27.50 to Edward
      Narramore, 25 acres adj. Ferguson, Haile, John Kennington,
. Robert Hodges (+) (Seal), Wit: John Keavenport, Selah (X) Kennington . Prov. by Selah Kennington, before R. Hunley, J. P.

Pp. 21-22: 12 Sept 1791, Thomas Frisel & wife Elishaba of Lancas-
      ter Co., to Colden Williams, yourman (sic), for Ŀ 18...
75 acres on flat creek adj. Robertson line. Thomas Frisel (θ), Elishaba (+) Frisell, Wit: Benjamin Deason, William Ferguson, Prudence Frisel (+). Prov. by William Ferguson, 15 Apr 1793, before Ben. Haile.

Pp. 22-23: 28 Oct 1799, Felix Kennedy of Lancaster County, to
      Joseph White of same, for $1000, 1/2 of tract on waters of Cataba adj. Benjamin Cowan, 273 A...Felix Kennedy (Seal) Wit: Archibald McCorkle, Robert McCorkle, Robert McCorkle. Prov. by Archibald McCorkle, 29 March 1800, beofre Wm. Woods, J. P.

Pp. 23-24: 17 Oct 1800, James Douglas to Charles Cox, both of
      Lancaster Dist., 240 A adj. Carsons, granted to James Douglas, 3 Feb 1800, adj. Beard, Lewis Ezel; land granted to Benjamin Thompson 1754, sold to Alexr Thompson, and by Benj.

119

Thompson and wife Margaret, 1757...James Douglas (Seal), Wit:
William Baker, William Richardson. Prov. by Wm. Richardson, 11
Apr 1801.

Pp. 24-25: 1 June 1799, Charles McManus of Lancaster Co., to
            Joseph Hough, planter, for Ł 50 sterling, part of 500
acres granted to James McManus decd., 8 Jan 1760, and being in
Chesterfield County, on NE side Big Lynches Creek adj. Joseph
Hough, John Blakney, Widenor...Charles McManus (Seal), Wit: John
Welsh, William Voel. Prov. 26 March 1800, by John Welsh, before
Andrew Baskin, J. P.

Pp. 25-26: William Myers of Chesterfield Co., for Ł 31, to Neal
            Johnston, of Lancaster Co., 180 A on S side Wild
Cat Creek, granted to Benjamin Harper, 200 A, 4 June 1787...
William Myers (X) (Seal), Wit: Benjamin Deason, John Myers.
Prov. by Beanjamin Deason, before Andrew Baskin, J. P.

Pp. 26-27: 30 Dec 1799, John Shepherd of Lancaster Co., for $300
            to Lewis Kirk, land on both sides 12 mile creek, the
Indian claim excepted...John Shepherd (X) (Seal), Wit: Henry
Massey, David Crenshaw, John Dobey. Prov. by Henry Massey, 1
Apr 1800, before John Simpson, C. C. L. D.

Page 27: Randol McDonald of Lancaster Co., to Joseph Dillard of
          same, cabinet maker, two tracts, 150 acres on Lick
Creek adj. William Terrill, the other tract adj. to it...Randol
(R) McDonald, Nancy (X) McDonald, Wit: Moses Barnard, Colden
Williams, John Williams. Prov. by Colden Williams, 25 Jan 1800,
before R. Hunley, J. P.

Page 28: 16 Feb 1799, William Blackman, of Lancaster Co., to Jame
          Blackman, for Ł 20 sterling, 70 A, part of granted to
William Blackman, on Little Linches Creek adj. Joseph Blackman,
Thomas Small...William Blackman (X), Wit: William Ward, Joseph
Johnston. Prov. 2 May 1800 before Jno Simpson, by Joseph Johnston.

Pp. 29-30: 1795, Francis Adams & wife Margret of Lancaster Co.,
            to Hugh Black, by a grant 26 July 1774 to William
Adams, 150 acres on the head of Lambs branch, waters of Wateree
River, the sd. William Adams, being deceased, this said land being
bequeathed to sd. Francis Adams his son, now for Ł 21 s 8 d 8 to
Hugh Black....Francis Adams (Seal), Margret Adams (X) (Seal), Wit:
Thos Niell, John Strain, Alexander Black. Proved by John Strain,
5 May 1800, before John Simpson, Clerk.

Pp. 30-31: 16 Apr 1800, Thomas Pulley & wife Lydia of Lancaster
            Dist., to Andrew McIlwain, for Ł 50, 100 acres on rum
Creek...Thomas Pulley (Seal), Lydia Pulley (X) (Seal), Wit: William
McIlwain, Andrew McIlwain, Proved by Wm McIlwain, 15 April 1800,
before William Barkley, J. P.

Pp. 31-32: Thomas Latta of Chester District, for Ł 12 to John
            Foster of Lancaster Dist., 200 acres on NE side Catawba
River & Waxhaw Creek, being a tract of land bequeathed to Thomas
Latta, by the last will & testament of his father John Latta
decd., dated 1 August 1796...12 May 1801. Thomas Latta (Seal)
Wit: William Barkley, William Simpson, Jno Simpson. Plat included
shows adj. John Foster. Proved by William Barkley, 12 May 1801

Pp. 32-33: 10 Jan 1800, Sanders Redin of Lancaster Co., to Elias
        Tylor of same, for Ŀ 30 sterling, 100 acres on head
of the branches of Linches Creek, adj. Robert Gaston...Sanders
Redden (+) (Seal), Wit: James Hase (X), John Green (Ɨ). Proved
by John Green, 26 April 1800, before John Ingram, J. P.

Page 33: Dempsy Bryan of Edgecombe County, N. C., for 400 silver
        dollars, to Colain Williams of Lancaster Co., S. C.,
negro slave Lucy, 5 December 1799   Dempsy Bryan (Seal), Wit:
Joseph Dillard, Smyth Bryan. Proved by Joseph Dillard, 8 March
1800 before Andrew Baskin.

Pp. 34-35: Lancaster District: James Montgomery the elder of Camp
        Creek waters, Dist., of Lancaster, planter, for $365,
to Hugh McMillian & Thomas Quigley of the Town of Lancaster, 150
acres granted to myself, adj. William Gamble, Robert Dunlap,
James Cowsar, & Nathan Barr...30 Aug 1800. James Montgomery (LS)
Wit: Thos Dunlap, Jno May. Plat included. Susana Montgomery,
wife of James, relinquished dower, 19 Sept 1800.

Pp. 35-36: William Barton & wife Agness of Lancaster Co., for
        $120, to John Taylor, part of a tract granted to
William Barton decd.,adj. Richd Cowsart, 28 Feb 1800...William
Barton (Seal), Anges Barton (X) (Seal), Wit: William Adams,
Abram Niell, James Adams. Proved by James Adams, 7 April 1800.

Page 36: 13 May 1801, William Huston, of the Dist. of Lancaster,
        to Arthur Ingrem Senr & Arthur Ingram Junr, for $50...
lot in Lancaster town...William Huston (Seal), Wit: Elir. Alexander, John May. 14 May 1801, Tabitha, wife of William Huston,
relinquished dower; Proved by Elir. Alexander, 14 May 1801.

Page 37: 3 July 1800, John Tomlinson & wife Rebecca of the County
        of Lancaster to William Tomlinson Junr. of same, for Ŀ 41
s 10 sterling, part of a grant to Samuel Burnet, 83 acres...John
Tomlinson, Rebekah Tomlinson (X) Wit: Joseph White, Nathaniel
Tomlinson (+), Elizabeth Tomlinson (X). Proved by Nathaniel Tomlinson, 18 Feb 1801.

Pp. 37-38: Samuel Dunlap & wife Lydia of Lancaster Co., planter,
        for $257.16 to David Cowsart of same, yeoman, 100 acres
in the Waxhaws...19 Sept 1798. Samuel Dunlap (Seal), Lydia Dunlap (O) (Seal), Wit: James Craig, Willm Craig, Thomas Cowsart.
Proved by Thomas Cowsart, 30 March 1801, before Robert Montgomery,
J. P.

Pp. 38-39: Saml Dunlap & wife Ludia of Lancaster Co., for $635,
        to Thomas Cowsart, all that tract whereon Saml Dunlap
lived, 174½ acres in the Waxhaws, adj. John Barnett...(Same
signatures as preceding deed). Wit: Jas Craig, Willm Craig,
David Cowsart. Proved by David Cowsart, 30 March 1801, before
Robert Montgomery, J. P.

Pp. 39-40: Benjamin Haile & wife Mary of Kershaw Co., for 500
        silver dollars, to Jesse Fly, 900 acres, part of 2869
acres granted to Benj. Haile Senr decd, 13 Dec 1788 adj. Francis
Bettis corner, on Flat Creek, Michael Miller, Thomas Farmer, Isaac
Faulkenbury, John Knight...20 Dec 1800. Bn Haile (Seal), Mary
Haile (+) (Seal), Wit: Daniel Monaghan Junr, Jesse Fly. Proved
by Daniel Monaghan, 29 Jan 1801, before Andrew Baskin, J. P.

BOOK F

Page 40: 29 May 1799, John Funderburk of Chesterfield Co., to
          Adam Team for 150 silver dollars, part of a tract gran-
ted to Daniel Funderburk, 6 Aug 1787...John Funderburk (Seal)
Wit: Koonrod Pliler (X), James Hollena. Proved by Koonrod Plyler,
before John Craig, 22 Feb 1800.

Page 41: Middleton McDonald of Lancaster Co., planter, for s 5
          sterling, to Wm McDonald Junr of Chester County, four
tracts (1) 40 acres, part of 100 acres granted to Daniel McDonald
on E side Catawba River (2) 83 Acres granted to Geo. Wade, adj.
land granted to William Ford (3) 100 acres granted to Wm Ford (4)
100 acres known as Featherston old place...29 June 1798
Wit: Daniel McDonald, John Cornelius,   Middleton McDonald (Seal)
     Danl Wade.
Proved by Danl McDonald, 29 June 1798, beofre Danl Wade, J. L. C.

Page 42: James Henderson of Lancaster Co., for Ł 61 sterling to
          Midtn. McDonald, planter of same, all right of lands
purchased jointly by sd. Middleton McDonald of Smith,Desaussure
and Darrel, 200 acres granted to Thomas Adams, and 300 acres
surv. for George Wade and granted to Daniel Wade, and 100 acres
granted to George Wade, sold by executors...6 May 1797.
Wit: Thos J. Wade,   James Henderson (Seal)
Wade Kimbell. Proved by Wade Kimbell, 6 May 1797, before Danl.
Wade, J. L. C.

Pp. 42-43: Charles & Agness Montgomery of Lancaster Dist., for 16
            silver dollars to Benjamin Nesbet of same, land on
waters of Cane Creek, 13 Nov 1800.   Charles Montgomery (Seal)
Wit: Andrew Taylor, John Nisbet.   Agness Montgomery (*) (Seal)
Proved by John Nisbet before Robert Montgomery, 31 March 1801.
(plat included in deed).

Pp. 43-44: James Hogg and wife Nancy of Lancaster Co., for $10 to
            Archibald Kimball, 45 acres, part of 236 acres, granted
to James Hogg, 5 Aug 1799, adj. Moses Cantzon, William Simpson,
dated 1 Dec 1800. James Hogg (Seal), Nancy Hogg (Seal), Wit: John
Davies, Henry Turner, Robert Davies. Proved by R. Davis, 25 May
1801, before Jno Simpson, clerk.

Pp. 44-45: Adam McWillie of Kershaw District, for $11.30 to John
            Gamble of Lancaster Dist., land on both sides Camp
Creek, adj. John Gamble, John Davis, John Lasly, James Montgomery,
Nath Barr, granted to myself 5 May 1800, 154 acres...Adm McWillie
(Seal), Wit: Arthur Hicklin, Stephen Gamble, J. Hicklin.
Proved by Arthur Hicklin, Stephem Gamble, Jason Hicklin, before
Saml Dunlap, J. Q. (no date)

Page 45: 6 Jan 1801, Harcules & James Hoey, of Lancaster Co.,
          to John Myers of Chesterfield Co., 200 Acres, for $300...
on a branch of Wilcat...   Hercules Hewey (Seal)
Wit: Jno Hoey, Edward Kennington.   James Hewey (Seal)
Proved 27 March 1801, before R. Hunly, J. P.

Pp. 45-46: 1 Jan 1797, Thomas Sumpter to Saml Widene of Lancaster
            Co., for Ł 20 sterling, 200 acres on S side Great Lynches
Creek, part of 15000 A granted 2 Apr 1787. Wit: Jacob Shofner,
Middleton Belk. Proved by Jacob Shofner, before John Craig, J. P.

122

Pp. 46-47: 1 Feb 1800, Francis Adams of Carshaw Dist., to James
            Purdy of Lancaster Dist., for Ł 20 sterling, 100 acres
on Cain(?) Creek adj. Shaver, granted to Francis Adams, 1774.
Wit: James Douglas, Edmond Rains   Francis Adams (Seal)
     Samuel Douglas.
Proved 16 May 1800 by James Douglas.

Pp. 47-48: 24 June 1800, Jeremiah Simmons & William Simmons (son
            of afsd. Jeremiah aged about 16 years) of Lancaster
Dist., to John May Esqr., William Simmons apprenticed for 4 years
to teach the art of farming....

Pp. 48-49: 27 Feb 1800, Thomas Kelly of Lancaster Co., to David
            Laney for Ł 20 sterling, 100 acres on wild cat waters,
surv. for James Harper by William Carson, sold to sd. Kelly
1 Jan 1794...   Thomas Kelly (𝒜) (Seal)
Wit: James Holliman
     John McManus (X).
Proved 22 March 1800 by Jas McManus before John Craig, J. P.

Page 49: John Gillaspy of Chester County, for $100 to Benjamin
          Perry, land in Lancaster Co., on a branch of Cattaba River,
Wit: Thomas Gillaspy   John Gillaspy (Seal)
     John Orr
Sarah Gillaspy, wife of John, relinquished dower, 18 Jan 1800.
Proved by Thomas Gillaspy, 5 March 1800.

Pp. 49-50: John Osburn, farmer, and wife Rebecca to James Black-
            man, farmer, 50 acres surveyed for Daniel Williams
decd, part of 250 acres on head of Little Linches Creek, granted
to Danl Williams, 19 Sept 1758, which fell to John Williams decd.,
being the heir by law, then bid at the vandue of John Williams
decd. by Isom Shirling, then conveyed to John Caston, 15 Apr
1793, then to John Osburn, 5 Aug 1799, now to James Blackman, 7
Jan 1800...   John Osburn (Seal)
Wit: William Ward   Rebecca Osburn (/) (Seal)
     Burrel Clark
     Joseph Johnson.
Proved by William Ward, 31 March 1800.

Page 50: South Carolina, Fairfield Dist: James and Benjamin Heart
          sold a negro slave Molly to Benjamin Perry, living in
Lancaster Dist.,   (no date)   James Hart, Benjamin
Hart; Wit: Jesse Havis. D--Washington. Proved 21 July 1800

Pp. 50-51: 7 March 1800, John Stewart of Chester Co., to Wike Ivey
            of Lancaster Co., for $234, tract on 12 mile creek..
Wit: James Patton   John Steward (Seal)
     Saml Shiteside
Proved 12 March 1800, by James Patton, before Hugh Whiteside, J.
Q.

Pp. 51-52: 10 June 1776, William Patton & wife Elizabeth of St.
            Marks Parish, Craven County, to John Ferrell of same,
for Ł 100...part of land whereon sd. Patton now lives, adj.
William White, 117 acres...   William Patton (Seal)
Wit: Robert Stewart   Elizabeth Patton (Seal)
     Jno Johnston (O)
     Joseph McCulah.
Proved by Joseph McCulah, 12 June 1777, before Jno Drennon, J. P.

BOOK F

Pp. 52-54: 12 June 1777, John Ferrel of St. Marks Parish, Craven
          Co., to Robert Stewart of Mecklinburg Co., N. C., for
Ł 17 s 10, part of land William Patton now lives on, purchased
by Ferrel from Patton...   John Ferrel (Seal)
Wit: Jos Doulass
     Jno Drennon
     Thomas Rogers
Proved in York Co., SC by John Drennan, before Hugh White, J. P.,
8 Aug 1797.

Pp. 54-55: 10 Aug 1799, James McTeer of Lancaster Co., to Hugh
          Montgomery for Ł 42 sterling...100 acres granted to
Mary Campbell, 2 Oct 1767 in the Waxhaw Settlement, adj. Jas.
Huey, John Nisbet, Thoas Hart(?).   James McAteer (Seal)
Wit: John Nisbet, Francis McAteer. Proved by Nisbet, 21 July
1800, before Wm. Woods, J. P.

Pp. 55-56: Minor Winn of Fairfield Co., to John McMurry of Lan-
          caster Co., for $57...land on waters of Cain Creek,
surveyed for John Nisbet, granted to James Winn, 17 Jan 1787,
adj. Saml Wahop, widow Nisbet, and others, 25 Feb 1800.
Wit: James McCreight, Josh. Evans.   M. Winn
Proved by James McCreight, 25 Feb 1800, before S. W. Yongue, J.
P.

Page 56: 12 Nov 1783, John Coffey and wife Susannah of Camden
          Dist., planter, to Hugh Montgomery of same, for Ł 14 s
6 sterling, 20 acres on Cane Creek, Waxhaw Settlement, part of
grant to James Walker, 17 Aug 1654, conveyed to William Walker,
then to John Coffey (not completed).

(no page 57)

Page 58: Mark Stevens sold to George Hayes, for $150 one mulatto
          boy Ely, 20 Apr 1801. Mark Stevens (Seal), Wit: Baptist
Cole, William Curry, J. P. Proved by William Curry, 28 Apr 1801.

Page 58: S. C. Lancaster Dist.: William Mothershead to Mark Stevens,
          for Ł 50 one mulatto boy Ely, going on three years old...
30 June 1800.   William Mothershead (Seal)
Wit: Thos Middleton, William Bailey.
Proved by William Bailey, 1 Aug 1801, before Wm Curry, J. P.

Pp. 59-60: S. C., Lancaster County: Abraham Eastridge and Johseph
          Eastridge Sr., farmer, for Ł 10 sterling, to Joseph
Johnson of same, 25 acres surveyed for William Johnson now decd.,
part of 200 acres near the head of Little Linches Creek, granted
to William Johnson, 3 July 1772, and conveyed part to Edward
Williams, 23 Sept 1776, supposed to contain 50 acres, and conveyed
to Abraham Eastridge, and Samuel Johnston and wife Christian
assigned a lease & release as heirs of Wm Johnston decd unto
Abraham Eastridge, 21 Aug 1789, and the sd. Abraham Eastridge,
and Joseph his son conveyed part of 50 acres,25 May 1800....
Wit: William Ward   Abraham Eastridge (O) (Seal)
     Samuel Johnsto-   Joseph Eastridge (X) (Seal)
     Joseph Eastridge Junr (Ɱ)
Mary, wife of Abraham Eastridge, and Suphia, wife of Joseph
Eastridge, relinquished dower,19 March 1801, before Andrew Baskin,
J. P. Proved by William Ward,19 March 1801.

124

Pp. 60-63: 28 Aug 1789, Samuel Johnston and wife Christian, plan-
          ters, of Lancaster Co., to Abraham Eastridge, planter,
for s 10...25 acres (land in preceding deed)...adj. Daniel
Williams, John Murphy, Richard Anderson.   Samuel Johnson (X) (Seal)
Wit: John Williams   Christian Johnson (X)
     Edward Williams
     William Adams.

Pp. 63-64: 17 April 1801, John Brown of Lancaster Dist., to
          Baxter Thrower, for $255, tract on E side Can Creek
126 acres, adj. Thomas Douglas, John Stephenson, part of a grant
to William Moore...   John Brown (Seal)
Wit: Henry Foster   Mary Brown (Seal)
     Andrew Thompson
     Robert McCorkle
Mary Brown, wife of John, relinquished dower, 16 July 1801
Proved by Robert McCorkle, 16 July 1801.

Page 64: South Carolina, Lancaster District, James Walles, for
          59 third milled dollars to Peter Perry, one brown bay
horse, 1 year old. (bond or mortgage)...24 Jan 1801.
Wit: Middleton Joyner, John Stephens.   James Walles (Z) (Seal)
Proved by John Stephens, 21 Sept 1801.

Page 65: Camden District: Trespass to try title of three tracts
          of land, 21 April 1797, cause is settled between
Francis Adams and Rose Adams, 350 acres on Run Creek originally
measured to Francis Adams decd., and granted to him 11 Aug 1774,
to above Francis Adams; to Rose Adams, 350 acres on Capres(?)
Creek, granted to William Jones, 3 June 1774; the other tract in
dispute, 100 acres on Buffelow branch granted to Agnes Wilson,
11 Aug 1774, to be equally divided....   Francis Adams (Seal)
Wit: Saml Mathis   Rose Adams (X) (Seal)
     Thomas McCrory.

Pp. 65-66: Articles of agreement between James Bredin and wife
          Mary, that all past grievances shall be buried in
Eternal oblivion(?) and never to be repeated...to assure her
dower, and lands to be divided by William Hicklin, Thomas Houze,
and Jesse Tilman..22 Feb 1800.   James Bredin
Wit: William Hicklin   Mary Bredin(X)
     Arthur Hicklin
Proved, by Wm. Hicklin, 1 Aug 1800

Pp. 66-67: 8 Dec 1796, Thos Sumpter to John Welch of Lancaster
          Co., for Ł 210 sterling, 3500 acres on SW side
Big Lynches Creek. Wit: William White, John Sumter. Proved by
William White, 11 March 1797.

Pp. 67-68: S. C. Lancaster County: John Coffey, to Hugh Montgomery,
          for Ł 3 s 1 sterling, land on E side Cane Creek,
adj. Samuel Martain, 13 Dec 1799.   John Coffey (Seal)
Wit: John Nisbet, James McAteer, Proved by John Nisbet, before
William Woods, J. P., 21 July 1800.

Page 68: John Best of the Dist. of Lancaster, planter to James
          Oram, of same, for Ł 40...cows, calves, etc. 29 June
1800.   John Best (X) (Seal)
Wit: Wm Thompson, Tignel Perry. Proved by Tignel Perry, 30
June 1800.

Pp. 69-70: 11 Feb 1800, Enoch Anderson, of Lancaster Dist., plan-
        ter, to James Gaston, of same, planter, $550....
Enoch Anderson (Seal), Wit: Jonathan Johnson, Joseph Clark.
Proved by Jonathan Johnson, 6 Aug 1800, before Andrew Baskin.

Pp. 70-71: William Brewer of Lancaster Co., for $560 to Richmond
        Terrell, land on flat creek adj. John Baker, John
Kennington, Ferguson Hail, the old tract possessed of Jacob
Wisner decd., granted 8 May 1758, 100 Acres and the upper part
of tract granted to Francis Bettis, 7 Jan 1788, 270 acres...
Wit: Samuel Johnson (X)   William Brewer (Seal)
     Edward Kennington (X).
Proved by Edward Kennington, 29 Sept 1800.

Page 71: John McMaster of Lancaster Dist., planter, for love,
        good will & affection, to sons Thomas and William Mc-
Master, 250 acres, land I now live on surveyed for Thomas Mc-
Master, 1772, and granted 1773, Book FFF, p. 239, adj. Jas Love.
10 Jan 1801.   John McMaster (Seal)
Wit: William Mounce Junr.   Elizabeth McMaster (+) (Seal)
     William Mounce
Prov. 30 May 1801, before Jas Douglas, J. P.

Pp. 72-73: William Montgomery of Lancaster Dist., for $800, to
        John Craig Junr, plantation of 215 acres in the Waxhaw
Settlement on both sides Camp Creek, 11 acres sold to Thomas
Wells decd, part of tract of 302 acres granted to John Linn, 17
May 1754, by Mathew Rowan, Gov. of N. C., conveyed to Hugh Mont-
gomery, 10 Jan 1755, and to William Montgomery; dated 24 Aug 1801.
Wit: James Faulkner,   William Montgomery (Seal)
     William Draffin,   Agnes Montgomery (+) (Seal)
     John Johnston.
Agnes, wife of William, relinquished dower, before John Montgomery,
3 Sept 1801. Proved by James Faulkner, 3 Sept 1801.

Pp. 73-74: William Montgomery of Lancaster Dist., for $300 to John
        Craig Junr, 100 acres between Camp Creek and Gills
Creek, a branch of Watree River, 100 acres granted to John McCrory,
17 March 1775; dated 17 Aug 1801.
Same signatures, witnesses, and proof as above.

Pp. 74-75: James Simpson Senr of Lancaster Dist., for $200 to
        James Simpson Junr of same, 250 acres on E side Cataba
River, both sides Cane and Rum Creek adj. David Dunlap, Wm Baird,
and William Simpson, part of 1000 A granted to Thomas Simpson, and
by the last will & testament of Thomas Simpson to William Simpson
Senr, and by last will & testament of Wm Simpson Senr to me...
Wit: Patrick Graves   Jas Simpson (X) (Seal)
     Andrew McIlwain
     Mary White   Proved by Patrick Graves, 27 Oct 1801.

Pp. 75-76: 13 Aug 1790, Joseph Caston of Lancaster Co., planter,
        to George Bottoms, farmer, for Ƚ 7 sterling, part of
land on Rocky Road laid out for sd. Joseph Caston, 6 Feb 1786,
50 acres adj. Glass Caston, commonly called James Douglas land.
Wit: Glass Caston, Wm Caston,   Joseph Caston (Seal)
     Seth Caston.
Proved by Glass Caston, 1801.

BOOK F

Pp. 76-77: 3 Nov 1801, William Tomlinson Junr of Lancaster Dist.,
        to Wiley Dossey for $350, 83 acres...Wm Tomlinson (Seal)
Wit: Wm Dossey, Jesse Roper Junr, Nathaniel Tomlinson (+)
Proved by Wm Dossey, 3 Nov 1801.

Pp. 77-78: 22 Jan 1801, William Miers of Chesterfield Co., to
        John Faulkenberry Sr of Lancaster Co., for £ 14 SC
money, 100 acres of Joseph Williams being the patentee, adj.
Prittiman Berry, Wm Taylor.   William Miers (X) (Seal)
Wit: Little Berry Ozburn, William Taylor.
Proved by Taylor, 17 Oct 1801.

Pp. 78-79: 19 Sept 1801, Isaac Gardner to John McNutt for £ 10,
        50 acres granted to Thos Sumpter Senr, 2 Apr 1787,
on Faulkenberrys mill creek adj. John Gardner, Robert Gardner(?).
Wit: John Gardner,   Isaac Gardner (X) (Seal)
     Wm Gardner (X).   Aberilla Gardner (X) (Seal)
Proved by John Gardner, 31 Oct 1801.

Pp. 79-80: John Wever of the State of Georgia, for £ 30 sterling,
        to Jacob Englet of Lancaster Dist., 30 Jan 1801...land
on waters of Wild Cat Creek, 150 acres where sd. Jacob Enlet now
lives, and part of 460 acres that Tathrow Wever purchased of John
Wels, adj. Robert Welsh...   John Weaver (Seal)
Wit: Peter Andrews, Tathrow Weaver. Proved by Peter Andrews,
11 Feb 1801.

Page 81: S. C., Lancaster District: 25 Aug 1801, John Cantzon
        of Lancaster Dist., to William Harper, farmer, for $100,
100 acres near Cane Creek, on N side of Wateree River...John
Cantzon (Seal), Wit: Abbigail Yancey, Richard Graves. Proved by
Graves, 25 Aug 1801, before Jos. Lee, J. Q.

Pp. 82-83: Whereas John Caston Jr. of Lancaster Dist., planter,
        was seized of 123 acres on Little Linches Creek, granted
to sd. Caston, and sd. John Caston Jr. and Joseph Caston, was
indebted to Gibbs Lamb, and action brought in County Court in
Lancaster, case renewed by Daniel Brown, sd. Lamb's lawyer, and
land sold by shff to James Blackman, planter, for $80...1 June
1801.   Thos H Wade (LS)
Wit: Jno Simpson,William Huston. Proved by Wm. Huston, 1 June 1801.

Pp. 83-84: S. C., Lancaster County: 27 Sept 1793, Benjamin Haile
        Esqr., of Lancaster Co., to William Denman of same,
270 acres on waters of Flat Creek, land granted to Francis Bettis,
7 Jan 1788, and conveyed to sd. Haile by deed 2 May 1791....
Wit: Ferguson Haile, Richard   Benjamin Haile (Seal)
     Knight. Proved by Richard Knight, 26 Dec 1799, before R.
Hunley, J. P.

Pp. 84-85: Glass Caston, of Lancaster Dist., to William Nutt, for
        $300, 100 acres granted to George Campbell and conveyed
to Glass Caston, 24 Aug 1800....Glass Caston (Seal), Wit: Joseph
Caston, Gabriel Caston. Elizabeth Caston, wife of Glass Caston,
relinquished dower, 1 Oct ____. Proved by Joseph Caston, 24
Aug 1801.

Pp. 85-86: Colden Williams of Lancaster Dist., planter, for £ 20
        to John Williams, 100 acres on Flat Creek, adj. William
Williams, land granted to sd. Colden Williams, 12 July 1793....

Colden Williams (Seal), Wit: Daniel Williams, Benjamin Reaves (+).
Proved by Daniel Williams, 16 Jan 1801.

Pp. 86-87: S. C. Lancaster County: William Brewer of Lancaster
Co., for $560, to Richard Terrell of same, land adj.
John Baker, John Kennington, Ferguson Hail, lower part of Jacob
Wesner decd grant 8 May 1758, 100 acres on Flat Creek, upper
part of land granted 7 Jan 1788 to Francis Bettis...Wm Brewer
(Seal), Wit: Samuel Johnson (X), Edward Kennington (X); Proved
by Edward Kennington, 29 Sept 1800, before R. Hunley, J. P.

Pp. 87-88: James Gaston, farmer to Burrell Clark, 100 acres on
head branches of Little Linches Creek, granted to
John Peters, 18 Aug 1763, then conveyed to Robert Simpson, then
to Wm Welch, to Patrick Hennis, to Glass Caston, to Richard
Anderson, which became vested in Enoch Anderson, to James Gaston,
11 Feb 1800....dated __ July 1801. James Gaston (Seal), Wit:
Joseph Clark, William Baskins. Cathrin, wife of James Gaston,
relinquished dower, 18 July 1801. Proved by Joseph Clark, 18
July 1801.

Page 89: 26 June 1801, Elias Tyler, of Lancaster Co., to Samuel
Lee, 100 acres on branch of Linches Creek adj. Robert
Gaston...Elias Tyler (Seal), Wit: Fredk Williams, John Tyler,
Proved by John Tyler, 18 July 1801, before Jno Ingrem, J. P.

Pp. 90-92: 27 Nov 1783, Marshal Jones of Craven County, Camden
Dist., Blacksmith, to James Thompson of same, planter,
150 acres on Turkey Quarter, adj. Middleton McDonald, granted
to William Carson, 2 June 1769...Marshal Jones (Seal), Martha
Jones (X) (Seal), Wit: Joseph Coile, Isaiah Thompson. Proved
by Isaiah Thompson, 4 Aug 1789, before Robert Dunlap.

Pp. 93-94: 15 Apr 1777, William Carson, of Camden Dist., to Mar-
shell Jones, by grant 2 June 1769, 150 acres on Turkey
Quarter...William Carson (Seal), Wit: James Kell, Agnes Carsen.
Proved by Agnes Ferrell, before Robert Dunlap,J. P., 15 Oct 1788.

Pp. 94-95: James Barnett of York Dist., for $520, to John Gettys
of Lancaster Dist., adj. John McDow, Doctor Dunlap,
William Massey, Robert Thompson...28 July 1801. James Barnett (LS)
Wit: James Collins, Hugh Rogers. Margaret Barnett, wife of James,
relinquished dower, 28 July 1801, before John McClenachan, J. Q.
Proved by James Collins, 10 Nov 1801, before Wm Wood, J. P.

Pp. 95-96: Sarah Ladd of Lancaster Dist., to Benjamin Ladd of
same, for Ь 10, land on Lick Creek adj. Richard Hunley,
David Johnson,dated 25 Feb 1800...Sarah Ladd (X) (Seal), Wit:
John Ferguson, Absalom Hunley. Proved by Absalom Hunley, 17 March
1800.

Pp. 96-97: Tully Biggs of Lancaster Co., for $350, to Richard Hun-
ley, land on Lick Creek adj. Wm Narramore, Benj. Ladd
...28 Jan 1800. Tully Biggs (Seal), Mary Biggs (X) (Seal), Wit:
John Kennington Jr., John Ferguson. Proved by John Ferguson, 7
May 1800, before James Blakeney, J. Q.

Page 97: Thomas Niell of Lancaster District, does free and emancipate
negro wench Judith, aged about 42 years, who has been
adjudged by a justice and free holders to be of good character &
capable of gaining a livelihood...17 Nov 1801. Thomas Niell (Seal)
Wit: John McMurray, Samuel McMurray. Proved by John McMurry Senr,
9 Nov 1801, before John Craige, J. P.

Page 98: Charles Cox to George Hayes of Lancaster District, for
          $1050, a negro wench Milly and her five children, the
oldest Rose, the 2 Chany, 3 a boy named Clincherin, the 4
Franklin, the 5 Sally, the oldest about 8 years old, and the
youngest better than one...7 Dec 1801. Charles Cox (Seal)
Wit: Joel Circils (+), Mary Hays, George Hays. Proved by Joel
Carliles, and George Hays, Jr., 7 Dec 1801, before Jas Douglas,
J. P.

Pp. 98-99: 25 Jan 1789, Benjamin Haile of Lancaster Co., to Francis
          Bettis, for ₺ 10 sterling, half of a tract on Lick Run,
granted to Henry Massey, 3 Apr 1786, and 640 acres, conveyed by
Massey to Haile...Ben Haile (Seal), Wit: Ben Therman (B), Francis
Ferguson, Elijah Philips (E). Proved in Chesterfield County,
by James Ferguson, before Richard Bettis, J. P., 28 July 1798.

Pp. 99-100: South Carolina, Orangeburgh District.: Abraham Rush
          Sr., to Abraham Rush Jr., for love, and good will,
100 acres in Craven County, grant recorded in Book QQQ, p. 704,
15 Feb 1800. Abraham Rush (A), Wit: Jacob Rush, Daniel Syfritt,
Susannah Syfritt (S). Proved by Jacob Rush in Orangeburg Dist.,
19 Feb 1801, before Henry D. Ward, J. Q.

Pp. 100-101: 25 Dec 1799, John Coffe of Lancaster Co., to James
          Craig, for ₺ 10 sterling, 78 acres on Cane Creek adj.
James Huge, Hugh Montgomery, granted to James Walker, 17 Aug 1764,
and by the heirs of James Walker to John Coffey, 1 Feb 1783....
John Coffey (Seal), Wit: James Huey, James McAteer; proved by
James McAteer, 18 Oct 1800, before John Craig, J.P.

Pp. 102-103: John Caston of Lancaster Dist., planter, was seized,
          of land on Little Linches Creek, part of 495 acres
granted to sd. Caston, and divided by him, 132 acres conveyed to
John Clark, and sd. Caston was indebted to John McCrary and Thomas
Gaston, exrs. of Robert Gaston, decd., and action commenced in
county court, Thos Wade shff. sells to John Clark, 1 June 1801...
Thos H. Wade (Seal), Wit: James Pursey, Jno Simpson. Proved by
Jno Simpson,20 Jan 1802, before Nathan Barr, J. P.

Page 103: State of North Carolina, Rutherford. Sary Ray of co.
          afsd., for ₺ 50 to Thomas Cockerham of same, 200 acres in
Dist. of Camden, on the branch of Flat Creek, 2 Feb 1801...Sary
Ray (Z), Wit: Joshua Fisher, Sary Cockram. Proved by Joshua
Fisher, 9 Feb 1801, in Lancaster Dist., before Andrew Baskin, J. P.

Page 104: Personally appeared before James Douglas, J. P., Elay
          Clark and Mark Stevens, and saith that on 4 July 1801,
Capt. Kennedy Bailey and William Stevens were in a fray, and Capt.
Bailey had his ear bit off...1 Feb 1802. Ealey (X) Clark, Mark
Stevens.

Pp. 104-105: S. C., District of Lancaster, 29 Aug 1801, William
          Kenny and Jonathan Emanuel Steeples of Chester Dist.,
to Charles Cox of Lancaster Dist., for ₺ 70 sterling, 250 acres on
waters of Rum Creek, granted to Alexander Kenney, 1768...William
Kenney (Seal), Jonathan Amanuel Steeples (O) (Seal), Wit: James
Purdy, Isaiah Haggwood (X). Proved by James Purdy, 1 Feb 1802.

Page 105: S. C., Lancaster County: William Denman for $560 to Wm
        Brewer, land on Flat Creek adj. John Baker, John Ken-
nington, Ferguson Haile, granted to Jacob Wisner decd., 8 May
1758, 100 acres and tract adj. to it, granted to Francis Bettis
17___ 1788, 270 acres...6 Jan 1800.   William Denman (Seal)
Wit: John Ferguson   her
     Richard Bullock   Sarah ⊬ Denman (Seal)
                                          mark
Proved by Ferguson, 8 Oct 1800.

Page 106: James Douglas of the Dist. of Lancaster, for $128.56 to
        Samuel Balding, 218 acres on Cane Creek, adj. William
Johnston, Joseph Caston, Glass Caston, 22 Oct 1800.
Wit: Hugh McMullin   James Douglas (LS)
     Robert Harman (X).

Pp. 106-107: Samuel Balding being indebted to James Douglas,
        (mortgage of said 218 acres)...22 Oct 1800.
Proved by Robert Harman, before Wm Barkley, J.P., 22 Oct 1800.

Pp. 107-109: 18 Jan 1800, William McMeen Junr, of Lancaster Dist.,
        to William Harper, mortgage for debt of $90.78,
100 acres in the fork of Cane Creek in the Waxhaw Settlement, adj
Robert Dunlap, William McMeen Sr., and lands lately transferred
by Eliazar Alexander to John Edwards & whereon Joseph McMeen
decd lived and at the time of his Deseazure and which said Joseph
McMeen by his last will & testament did bequeath to William
McMeen party to these presents, and James McMeen Junr and Joseph
McMeen Junr three of the sons of sd. decd...William McMeen Junr (Seal)
Wit: John Edwards
     Elir. Alexander
Proved by Eliazer Alexander, 2 Apr 1800.

Pp. 109-110: 17 Jan 1799, Thomas Frisel of Lancaster Co., to
        Moses Barnard for Ł 10 sterling, land in Lancaster
Co., part of granted to sd. Frisel, adj. Colden Williams,
Moses Barnard, Wm Reaves...   Thomas Frizle (O) (Seal)
Wit: Gale Frizzle, William Ferguson.
Proved by William Ferguson, 26 Dec 1799.

Page 110: Matthew Nutt and wife Elizabeth of Lancaster Dist.,
        for Ł 75 to Hollinsworth Trusdale, 100 acres on Camp
Creek adj. George Smith, Patrick Glass, granted to Mary Watson,
1 Dec 1768...21 Oct 1800.   Matthew Nutt (Seal)
Wit: Jno Trusdel,   Elizabeth Nutt (X) (Seal)
     Henry Hudson
Proved by Jno Trusdel, 24 Feb 1802, before Wm Barkley, J. P.

Pp. 110-112: 22 Nov 1794, Matthew Kirk of Lancaster Co., to
        Thomas Small, land granted to Thomas Smith, 350
acres, 12 Sept 1768, on Little Linches Creek, conveyed by Thomas
Smith to sd. Kirk, 13 March 1794, for Ł 50... Matthew Kirk (Seal)
Wit: William Graves   Grace Kirk (+) (Seal)
     Charles Small (X).
Proved by Christopher Small, 23 July 1795, before Jas Ingram,
J. P.

Pp. 112-113: Saml Vermillion of Lancaster Dist., planter, was
        seized of 196 acres on waters of big Linches
Creek adj. Hector Hoover(?), Eliazar Alexander, James Breden,

Jacob Carnes, James Carter, granted to Joseph Singleton, and laid off for Vermillion, 9 March 1797, and sd. Vermillion was indebted to sd. Eliazer Alexander, sold by Shff to Robert Kerr, merchant, dated 1 March 1802. Wit: Eliazer Alexander, Stephen Barr, D. S. (Plat included). Proved by Alexander, 3 March 1802.

Pp. 113-114: 8 Sept 1796, Nancy Carnes of Lancaster Co., to Sanders Reddin, for £ 10 sterling, 100 acres on Linches Creek adj. Robert Gaston...   Nancy Carnes (X) (Seal)
Wit: James Avent, Daniel Carnes. Proved by James Avent, 3 Jan 1800, before Samuel Dunlap, J. P.

Page 114: Isom Shirling of Lancaster Dist., for $200 to Solomon McKey, negro girl Marsha...18 March 1800.
Wit: William Barkley   Isom Shurling (LS)
     William Couser.
Proved by Barkley, 11 Aug ___, before John Simpson, clerk.

Page 115: Thomas Small, planter of Lancaster Dist., for $300 to Christopher Small, planter, 200 acres on a branch of Little Linches Creek and Flat Creek, part of a grant to Thomas Smith, 350 acres, granted 12 Sept 1768, conveyed from sd. Smith to Mathew Kirk, by L & R 4 March 1794, then to Thos Small, 22 Nov 1794...11 Oct 1800.   Thomas Small (X) (Seal)
Wit: Joel Blackman, William Ward, John Stogner.
Syntha Small, wife of Thomas Small, relinquished dower, 11 Oct 1800. Proved by William Ward, 11 Oct 1800.

Pp. 116-117: John Hill of Lancaster District, for $300 to Thomas Small, 150 acres in two tracts, conveyed by Mathew Kirk 14 March 1794, to Thomas Small, 22 Nov 1794, to John Hill, 85 acres, 23 July 1796, between John Hill & Mat Stephens, & the other granted to Barnett Johnston, 200 acres, 5 May 1773, conveyed to James Blackman, 30 March 1795, then to John Hill, 70 acres...dated 11 Oct 1800.   John Hill (ʃʃ) (Seal)
Wit: William Ward, Joel Blackman, John Stogner.
Margaret Hill, wife of John, relinquished dower, 11 Oct 1800.

Page 117: Lancaster County, 4 January 1800: on Nov 10, 1792, James Houze for certain reasons did record to his children certain deed of gift of all his property, the children listed below have given up said deed as if it had never been made.   Clabon Houze
Wit: Benja Clifton   Eliza'h (X) House
     William Tillman   Henry House
                                Sarah (X) Houze
                                Littleont Houze
                                Bregt (X-his mark) Pace
                                Pene'y Pace (X)
                                Anderson Houze
                                Polley (X) Houze
                                Jincy Houze
                                Isaac (X) Houze
Proved by Benja Clifton, 19 Feb 1802, before Samuel Dunlap, J. P.

Pp. 117-118: William Stuart for love and good will to daughter Charlotte, bay mare and colt etc. and $39 in cash...
8 March 1802.   William Stuart (X) (Seal)
Wit: Robert Williams
     James Maddox (X). Proved 15 March 1802, before James Douglas, J. P.

Page 118: Eliazer Alexander of Lancaster Dist., for $1000 to John
        May, 3 negroes, Isaac about 21, Jin (Isaac's wife),
and child Onus(?), aged about 6 or 7 months...21 Nov 1801
Wit: Hugh McMullin, Patrick Graves.   Eliezar Alexander (Seal)
Proved 20 Feb 1802, by Hugh McMullin.

Page 119: 22 May 1798, Richard Knight, planter, of Chesterfield
        Co., to Lewis Faile of Lancaster Co., for Ł 40...land
adj. Genl. Thomas Sumpter, Benjamin Haile, Matthew Sigley, granted
7 Aug 1797...   Richard Knight (X) (Seal)
Wit: Matthew Sigler (X)
    John Faile, Jacob Faile.

Page 120: For $350 pd. by Messrs McMullin & Quigley of Lancaster
        Dist., Wm Johnston of George Town District, sells
negro Peter, 35 years of age...   Willm P. Johnston (Seal)
Wit: Jno Simpson, James Isom (X). Proved by James Isom, 14
Jan 1802.

Page 120: 5 Jan 1802, William Hicklin Senr of Lancaster Dist.,
        to Zach. Hicklin, 100 acres part of tract of Andrew
McKenney, 4 July 1754...   William Hicklin (Seal)
Wit: William Hicklin, Hugh Hicklin,
    J. Hicklin.
Proved by Hugh Hicklin, before Wm Curry, J. P.

Page 121: 8 Feb 1791, Benjamin Haile, planter of Lancaster Co.,
        to Lewis Faile of same, for Ł 30, land on Nealings branch,
part of 2869 acres granted to John Marshall, 1 Jan 1789...
                    Benjamin Haile (Seal)
Wit: Michael Miller (M), Wm. Bridges, Benjn Haile, Junr.
Proved by Michael Miller, 13 Apr 1793.

Page 122: John Blair of Lancaster Co., planter, for Ł 47, to John
        Rogers, 140 acres on Catawba River, adj. William Taylor,
13 Jan 1798.   John Blair (Seal)
Wit: Wm. A. Harper, Thos Lee,
    E. Alexander. Proved by E. Alexander, 13 Jan 1798.

Pp. 122-123: John Caskey, planter, for $1 to James Caskey of
        Lancaster Dist., 100 acres on W side of John Caskeys,
adj. Wm Graham, John Taylor, Minor Will, 13 April 1802.
Wit: James Foster, William Graham (8),   John Caskey (Seal)
Margaret Caskey, wife of John, relinquished dower, 13 Apr 1802.
Proved by James Foster, 22 April 1802.

Page 123: 28 Jan 1801, Jethrow Weaver of Lancaster Co, to Josiah
        Hancock, for $317, 350 acres where sd. Weaver now lives
part of 500 acres sd. Weaver purchased of John Welsh...
                    Jethrow Weaver (X) (Seal)
Wit: James Wilkinson, Charles McManus. Proved by Charles McManus
26 Sept 1801.

Page 124: Saml Widener of Lancaster Co., to Josiah Hancock, 2 acres
        on bank of Great Linches Creek,opposite Higgses Mill
seat, for 5 shillings...29 Oct 1798.   Saml Widener (Seal)
Wit: James Holliman, John Hough. Proved by John Hough, 26 Sept
1801.

BOOK F

Pp. 124-126: 3 Jan 1776, Israel Moor & Saml Moore, both of Camden
             Dist., Craven Co., plantesr, to Drury Campbell, of
same, for Ł 86...100 acres on S fork Little Linches Creek, adj.
William Starnes, granted 12 Dec 1768...Israel Moor (Seal)
Wit: Robert Mchaffy, Israel Moor,   Saml Moor   (Seal)
     John Campbell.
Proved by Israel Moore, 27 May 1780.

Pp. 126-127: 16 Apr 1798, John Welsh of Lancaster Co., Esqr., to
             George Harris, 150 acres part of tract purchased from
Genl. Thos Sumter...   Jno Welsh
Wit: Edmund Ballard, John Beesely.
Proved by John Beesely, 21 Feb 1802, before R. Hunley, J. P.

Page 127: Charles Cox, to George Hays of Lancaster Dist., for
          $1050, negro Milly and five children...(same deed as
book F, page 98)....

Page 127: Roger Cannon of Kershaw Dist., for $200, to William
          Huston, negro wench Silly...3 June 1802.
Wit: Thos Quigley, John Quigley.   Roger Cannon (Seal)

Page 128: Roger Cannon, of Dist. of Kershaw for $85 to William
          Huston, negro girl Rose, 10 years old and raise in this
state...3 June 1802. (same signature and wit. as preceding).

Pp. 128-129: Joseph Montgomery, farmer, for $450, to Jacob Shof-
             ner, 385 acres surveyed for John Belk, 25 Jan 1789,
on a prong of Cane Creek adj. Glass Caston...17 May 1802
Wit: John May,Robert Harman.   Joseph Montgomery (Seal)
Proved by John May, 30 March 1802.   Mary Montgomery (Seal)

Page 129: John Clark of Lancaster Dist., to Jonathan Blackman,
          for $150, 20 acres, part of 465 acres granted to John
Caston, then conveyed to John Clark, on Little Linches Creek and
sold at sheriff sale, 21 Jan 1802...   John Clark (Seal)
Wit: William Ward, Joel Blackman. Proved by William Ward, 30 March
1802.

Page 130: Thomas Sumter of Claremont Co., for Ł 75 sterling, to
          Jacob Shofner of Lancaster Co., land on head branches
of Little Linches Creek, 6 Oct 1797. Wit: Peter Rape, Anna
Shofner (X). Proved by Anna Shofner, 30 March 1802.

Pp. 130-131: 23 July 1795, Thomas Small of Lancaster Co., for
             Ł 30 sterling, to John Hill, land granted to Thos
Smith, 12 Sept 1768, part of 350 acres, 85 acres...
Wit: Williwm Ward, Philip Ward.   Thomas (T) Small
Proved by William Ward, 23 July 1795, **Setha** (P) Small
before Jas Ingram, J. P.

Page 132: Owen Reid of Lancaster Dist., for $119 to George Miller
          of Kershaw Dist., 100 acres where sd. Reid now lives,
part of 200 acres granted to Matthew Hood, conveyed to Charles
Carter, then to Owen Reid, adj. John Chesnut, Charles Carter,
Nathaniel Barber...13 June 1801   Owen Reid (R)
Wit: Robert Baird, John Duren.
Proved by John Duren, 18 June 1802, before Thomas Creighton, J. P.

133

BOOK F

Pp. 132-133: Bryce Miller did by virtue of a warrant in my name
have surveyed 267 acres on Bear Creek adj. William
Graves, Daniel Blackman, Bryce Miller, Thomas Miller, 1 Feb 1796,
and I have given Bryce Miller a quit claim and he transferred to
James Miller of Franklin County, Virginia, by bond 12 Sept 1799,
and the said deed is lost, that I, William Graves, of Lancaster
District, for $1 sell to sd. James Miller, all my right...9 Sept
1802.   Wm Graves (Seal)
Wit: Wm Barkley, Thos Quigley, Jno Simpson.
Proved by William Barkley, 9 Sept 1802.

Page 133: 20 Jan 1802, Jane Baker, widow of Joseph Baker, decd.,
of Lancaster District, to William Anderson, for $350, land
on waters of Twelve Mile Creek, 100 acres, adj. Charles Miller,
John Anderson, William Tomlinson, George Wren, granted to
William White, and conveyed by William Tomlinson, to Joseph Baker,
and in consequence of a petition of Jane Baker for her lawful
dowry, 2 Nov 1801...   Jane Baker (Seal)
Wit: Jno Brown, John Anderson (X), George Anderson (X). Proved
by John Anderson, 8 May 1802, before Saml Dunlap, J. P.

Page 134: James Barnett of York County, for $500 to Joseph Massey,
of Lancaster County, 150 acres in Lancaster Co., on
waters of Waxhaw Creek adj. John Grader, William Massey's land
purchased of John Haggans, near Ebenezer Miller's old cabbin,
part of a grant to John Barnett, and resurveyed for William
Barnett...7 Oct 1799.   James Barnett (Seal)
Wit: Hugh Rodgers,   Margarett Barnett (Seal)
John Rodgers, Martha Rodgers.
Proved by Hugh Rodgers, 22 May 1802, before Saml Dunlap, J. P.

Pp. 134-135: John McDole of Charleston, for Ŀ 150 sterling to Robert
Hancock, of Lancaster District, planter, 200 acres on
North side Waxhaw Creek, 1 May 1801.   John McDowell (Seal)
Wit: James Johnston, Archibald McCorkle, John Johnston. Proved
by Archibald McCorkle, 22 Aug 1801.
Barbara McDowell, wife of John, relinquished dower, in Charleston
District, 4 Feb 1802, before William Turpin, J. Q.

Page 135: Plat: Certified for Robert Lockhart, 200 acres granted
by Mathew Rowan, president of N. C., to John Lynch,
and since purchased by and in possession of sd. Lockhart, on N
side Waxhaw Creek, 7 Feb 1755. James Carter, D. S.

Pp. 135-137: __ Aug 1799, George Wren and Allatha his wife of
Lancaster Co., to Robert Hancock, John Tomlinson,
Mark Meacham, Nathaniel Tomlinson, Nathan Tomlinson, Jesse Roper
Senr., for $4.50, all the right of property adj. Robert Lockert,
1½ acres to build a house of worship for the use of members of the
Methodist Episcopal Church...   George Wren (Seal)
Wit: Jas Avent, Guy Wallace,   Allatha Wren (X) (Seal)
William Cousar.
Proved by William Couser, 10 Feb 1801, beofre Samuel Dunlap, J.P.

Pp. 137-138: Patrick Graves of Lancaster District, silver smith,
for Ŀ 5 sterling, to Joseph Lee, of Lancaster Co.,
5 acres on N side Cane Creek, granted to William Gamble, conveyed
to Barr, then to Saml McClelan, to John Dunlap, to John May, to
to Patrick Graves, 4 Feb 1802.   Patrick Graves
Wit: John Cantzon, Abigail Yancey, Mary Lee. Proved by John
Cantzon, 20 Sept 1802, before Nathan Barr, J. P.

Page 138: South Carolina, Lancaster County: William A. Harper,
          doctor of physic of Chester County, for Ł 25 sterling,
to JosephLee, Esqr., of Lancaster Co., 100 acres on both sides
of Caen Creek adj. James Simpson, Saml McClellan, Wm Gamble,
granted 6 Apr 1768 to Sarah Lindsay, and conveyed by lease and
release 1 May 1769, to Wm Carsen, and 25 Aug 1771, to Harper
decd., which fell to William A. Harper, heir....8 June 1799.
                              William A. Harper (Seal)
Wit: John Cantzon, Mary Lee, Richard Graves. Proved by John
Cantzon, 20 Sept 1802.

Page 139: 27 Sept 1801, Jonathan Johnston, of Lancaster Dist.,
          planter, to James Johnston, planter, for $50...part
of 160 acres granted to Jesse Mesho, 7 Dec 1794, and conveyed
to William Eastridge, then to Jonathan Johnston.
Wit: Samuel Johnson, John   Jonathan Johnston (Seal)
     Winn Brown (X).   Barbara Johnston (Ƚ) (Seal)
Proved by John Winn Brown, 20 Oct 1802.

Pp.139-140: 13 Nov 1801, Patrick Graves of Lancaster Dist., sil-
            ver smith, to John May, Inn keeper, whereas by a
promissary note, indebted to John May, for $383.25, 12 Nov 1801...
150 acres on Cane Creek in the Waxhaw Settlement...
Wit: Eleazar Alexander;   Patrick Graves (Seal)
Proved 17 Nov 1801, before Wm Barkley, J. P.

Pp. 140-141: John Simpson of Lancaster County, for $60 to Alexander
             Craig, of same, shop keeper, 2 lots in Barnetts
Ville, alias Lancaster, 20 Apr 1797.   Jno Simpson (Seal)
Wit: John May, A. Alexander.
Assigned 20 July 1798 to William Stephens of Charleston, by Alexr
Craig. David Couser swore to the handwriting of Jno Simpson and
Alexr. Craig.

Page 141: 22 Oct 1802, David Russel to Mark Stevens Jr., for
          $107, 52 acres granted to David Russel, 3 Oct 1791, on
Cedar Creek adj. William Johnston.   David Russel (X)
Wit: Peter Twitty, Samuel Marder. Proved by Peter Twitty, 3 Nov
1802.

Page 142: William Myers of Chesterfield District, for Ł 100
          sterling, to Jepthah Gynn, of Lancaster District,
40 acres on SW side of Great Lynches Creek adj. Thomas Scott
Weims, George Hail, George Taylor...8 Dec 1802.
Wit: Archibald Finlay,   William Myers (X) (Seal)
     Myer Magee (Ꝑ).
Proved by Myer Magee, before William Ward, J. P.

Page 142: 4 March 1798, John Welsh Esqr. of South Carolina, Lan-
          caster Co., to Elisha Baker of same, for Ł 20 sterling,
150 acres, part of a tract purchased of Genl Thomas Sumter...
Wit: Knight Knight (R)   Jno Welsh (Seal)
     Josiah Hancock.
Proved by Knight Knight, 5 March 1801.

Page 143: John Craig Esqr & wife Elizabeth of Lancaster Co., for
          $193 to Averet Yerby of same, 100 acres on Flat Rock...
10 Jan 1798.   John Craig (Seal)
Wit: Willm Craig,   Elisabeth Criag (/) (Seal)
     Benjamin Nisbit.
Proved by Benjamin Nisbit, 2 Nov 1802.

Page 143: 1 Aug 1801, Kenedy Bailey of Lancaster District, South
          Carolina, to Mark Stevens, for $500, 365 acres granted
12 Aug 1797...   Kenada Bailey (Seal)
Wit: John Johnston, John Bell, Daniel Glaze. Proved 1 Aug 1801
before Wm Currey, J. P.

Page 144: Andrew McIlwain of the Dist. of Lancaster, for $700,
          to Charles Cox, three tracts (1) 200 acres granted to
Andrew McKewen, 19 Sept 1758 on Rum Creek, a branch of Cane
Creek (2) 100 acres granted to Sarah Bottoms, 3 Apr 1786 (3)
123 acres granted to myself, 3 Nov 1788...22 July 1802.
Wit: John May, Eliezar Alexander.   Andrew McIlwain (LS)
                                     Margret McIlwain
Proved by Eliezar Alexander, 22 Oct 1802.

Page 145: Isaac Barr and wife Margret of Lancaster Dist., planter,
          for $100 to Robert Kirk, 100 acres, part of a grant
to Isaac Barr, 1772, on Hannah's Creek, adj. Francis Gillins(?)...
22 Oct 1802.   Isaac Barr (Seal)
Wit: Jno Kirk, John Caskey.   Margret Barr (Ѻ)(Seal)
Proved by John Kirk, 23 Oct 1802.

Page 145: James Montgomery and wife Francis of Lancaster Co., for
          $271 to John McMurry Senr, two tracts, total 136½ acres
on SE side Cane Creek adj. Benjamin Nisbet, John Nisbet, Samuel
Martin...19 Oct 1802.   James Montgomery (Seal)
Wit: Joseph Nisbet,   Francis Montgomery (Seal)
Samuel McMurray. Proved by Joseph Nisbet, before John Craig,
J. P., 8 Jan 1803.

Page 145: Bayly Fleming, of the Dist. of Lancaster, for natural
          love and affection to daughter Jemimah Ingrum, tract
adj. Samuel Maddox, William Warters....11 Oct 1802.
Wit: James Pritchard, Samuel Martin.   Bailey Fleming (Seal)
Proved by Samuel Martin, 12 Oct 1802.

Page 146: Whereas Thomas Thompson of Lancaster Dist., planter, was
          seized of 100 acres on N side Catawba adj. William
Harrison, granted to William Harrison, and sd. Thomas Thompson
was indebted to William Sprunt, and action was commenced...now
for $181, sold by Shff to Clement Aldridge (Arledge) of Fairfield
District, with the crop of corn & cotton...3 Nov 1802.
Wit: David Cowsar   Thos H. Wade, S. L. D.
     William L. Connell, Daniel Kirkland.
Proved by David Cowsar, 3 Nov 1802.

Page 146: Samuel Widener of Lancaster Co., transfers to Josiah
          Hancock, two acres on bank of Great Lynches Creek,
opposite Higgses mill, for five shillings. 29 Oct 1798.
Wit: James Holliman, John Hough.   Saml Widener (ᐯ) (Seal)
Proved by John Hough, 26 Sept 1801, before Rd. Hunley, J. P.

Page 147: 4 Sept 1802, John McMaster to Amos Horton, for $400,
          249 acres on Hanging Rock, surveyed for Thomas McMaster,
1772....   John McMaster (Seal)
Wit: William Horton,Sterling Horton. Proved by William Horton,
27 Jan 1803, before William Ward, J. P.

Page 147: Thomas Cockrum of Rutherford County, N. C., farmer,
          for $150 to Britain Blackman, farmer, 200 acres on head
branches of Flat Creek granted to William Roy, __ Jan 1773, then

conveyed from the widow of Thomas Cock<u>man</u> (<u>sic</u>) who appears to
be the heir of William Roy by his last will and testament, the
deed from the widow bearing date 2 Feb 1801...9 Feb 1801
Wit: Jonathan Blackman,   Thomas Cockrum (C) (Seal)
     Nathan Blackman.
Mary, wife of Thomas Cockrum, relinquished dower, __ Feb 1801
Proved by Jonathan Blackman, 9 Feb 1801.

Page 148: 9 Oct 1802, William Ingram Senr of Lancaster Co., to
          William Ingram Junr, of same, for Ł 20, 80 acres, the
north part of a survey of 150 acres, granted to William Welsh,
1762, adj. More, James Ingram...   Wm Ingram (Seal)
Wit: Jordan Ashley, James Ingram, John Williams.
Proved by James Ingram, 1 March 1803, before John Ingram, J. P.

22 March 1797, James Ingram Esq., of Lancaster Co., to Wm Ingram,
for Ł 10, 200 acres on Little Lynches Creek adj. Countryman,
granted to Alexander Ingram, 6 April 1773, and became property of
sd. James by virtue of his fathers Abraham Ingrams last will and
testament...   Jas Ingram (Seal)
Wit: Danl Monaghan, Arthur Ingram, Samell Kilton. Proved by
Saml Kilton, 22 March 1797.

Pp. 148-149: 27 Sept 1800, William Ingram, Captain of Lancaster
             Co., to James Ingram Jr., his son, for Ł 40 sterling,
80 acres, part of 100 acres granted to John Ingram, adj. Saml Mc-
Clure Senr, on waters of Little Linches Creek, 596 acres granted
to sd. William Ingram, 13 Apr 1793...   Wm Ingram (Seal)
Wit: Danl Monaghan, Hanah Johnson (X),   Jean Ingram (Seal)
     Danl Monaghan Senr.
Proved by Danl Monaghan Junr, 27 Sept 1800, before John Ingram,
J. P.

Page 149: 9 Oct 1802, William Ingram Senr of Lancaster Co., to
          Alexander Ingram Junr, for Ł 20...200 acres granted to
Alexander Ingram, 1775, and Danl Monaghan Junr, and some of another
survey granted to William Welch, 1762...   Wm Ingram (Seal)
Wit: Jordan Ashley, James Ingram, Danl Monaghan. Proved by
James Ingram, 1 March 1803, before John Ingram.

Page 150: 9 Oct 1802, William Ingram Senr of Lancaster Co., to
          James Ingram, for Ł 20...75 acres, 35 acres of a survey
of John Ingram of 100 acres adj. William Ingram, Woods, Saml
McClure, and remainder, 40 acres of a surveye of 150 acres granted
to William Welch, adj. James Ingram.   Wm Ingram (Seal)
Wit: Jordan Ashley, Alexander Ingram, Danl Monaghan. Proved by
Alexander Ingram, 1 March 1803.

Page 150: South Carolina, Lancaster District, Jordan Ashly, to
          William Ingram Senr., 170 acres, part of a grant to
sd. Ashley, 534 acres, 14 Aug 1792...9 Oct 1802.   Jordan Ashly
(Seal), Wit: Danl Monaghan Senr, James Ingram, John Williams.
Proved by James Ingram, 1 March 1803, before John Ingram.

Pp. 150-151: 22 March 1797, John Ingram of Lancaster Co., to
             William Ingram, Capt., for Ł10, 100 acres surveyed by
John Ingram, adj. Saml McClure...   Jno Ingram (LS)
Wit: Saml Kilton, Danl Monaghan, Arthur Ingram.

Page 151: 7 Nov 1802, Alexander Douglass, of Lancaster Dist.,
        to Andrew McIlwain, for $65, 50 acres, part of 640
acres adj. Andw McIlwain, Allr. Douglass, waters of lower Camp
Creek, granted to Douglass, 15 March 1785....Allexr Douglass
(Seal), Wit: Robt McIlwain, James Douglass. Proved by James
Douglass, 7 Feb 1803.
        6 March 1797, Saml Hammond of Kershaw County, to Wil-
liam Ingram of Lancaster Co., for Ł 10 sterling, 100 acres adj.
David Tombs, on school house branch...   Saml Hammond (Seal)
Wit: Samuel Hilton, John Love, Wm Brewer.
Proved by Hilton, 6 March 1797, before James Ingram, J. P.

Page 152: Hugh McMullen and Thomas Quigley, merchants, of Lan-
        caster, for $1600 to Samuel Dunlap, Inn Keeper, lot in
town of Lancaster, adj. public ground for Jail & Court house,
John May, Capt. Simpson, 4 April 1803.   Hugh McMullen (Seal)
                              and for Thos Quigley (Seal)
Wit: Eleazar Alexander, William Howe, William McMeen.
Proved by E. Alexander, 1 July 1803, before John Simpson, Not.
Pub.
        Abraham Adams of Cester (sic) Dist., planter, for $40 to
Colden Williams, of Lancaster Dist., 50 acres on Flat Creek,
granted to Abraham Adams, plat dated 11 Aug 1774....9 Feb 1802
Wit: John Craig, J. P.   Abrm Adams (Seal)
    Joseph Dillard.
Proved 28 __ 1803, before William Ward, J. P.

Pp. 152-153: John Ingram, of Lancaster Dist., for Ł 55 s 10 to
        Richard Ussery, planter, 111 acres, part of a grant
to William Cato, 3 Dec 1785, 675 acres on hanging rock Creek,
conveyed by Cato to William Ingram 9 Oct 1796, and to John Ingram
22 March 1797, and to Richard Ussery, 20 Oct 1800, adj. James
Nicols.   27 Jan 1803.   John Ingram (Seal)
Wit: Robert Ashly, J. P. Clark. Proved 19 March 1803, before
John Ingrem, J. P.

Page 153: Abraham Adams and James Adams of Chester Dist., plan-
        ters, for $200 to Colden Williams, of Lancaster Dist.,
200 acres on Flat Creek, granted to Abraham Adams, 20 Jan 1773...
9 Feb 1802.   Abrm Adams (Seal)
Wit: John Craig, J. P., Joseph   James Adams (Seal)
    Dillard. Proved by Joseph Dillard, 28 March 1803,
before William Ward, J. P.

        2 Jan 1802, Catharine Howard of Lancaster Dist., to Moses
Dicky, of same, for Ł 180, 180 acres, part of 261 acres granted
to Stephen White on N side Waxhaw Creek...   Catharine Howard (Seal)
Wit: Robt Hancock, John Tomlinson, Thomas Howard. Proved by Robt
Hancock, 22 Jan 1802, before Samuel C. Dunlap, J. P.

Page 154: John Ingrem of Lancaster Dist., planter, for $224 to
        George Cook, 112 acres granted to Wm Cato, 5 Dec 1785
on Hanging Rock Creek...5 Feb 1803.   John Ingrem (Seal)
Wit: None. Plat included, 12 Feb 1803, by J. P. Clark, shows
adj. Richard Ussery, John McMaster, Green branch.

        Francis Bettis of Lancaster Dist., for $300 to Reuben
Cook, part of 640 acres granted to Henry Massey, 3 Apr 1786, on
lick run of Flat Creek, 22 July 1802.   Francis Bettis (Seal)
Wit: Ferguson Haile, John Ferguson, James Killebrue. Proved by
Ferguson Haile, before Colden Williams, J. P. 2 Apr 1803.

BOOK F

Page 155: 2 Jan 1802, Catharine Howard of Lancaster Dist., to
         Thomas Howard of same, for Ł 180, ½ of 260 acres
granted to Stephen White, adj. Moses Heath, James Crawford,
Robert Crawford...   Catharine Howard (Seal)
Wit: Robt Hancock, John Tomlinson, Moses Dickey. Proved by Robt
Hancock, 22 Jan 1802, before Saml C. Dunlap, J. P.

         7 May 1796, William Baily of Lancaster Co., to Solomon
Mackey of same, for Ł 30 sterling, land on waters of Rockey
Creek, adj. Isaac Stewart...   William Bailey (Seal)
Wit: Jos Coile, Arthur Hicklin, John Ballard.
Proved by Joseph Coile, 7 May 1796, before Robert Brutney, J. P.

Pp. 155-156: John Shepherd of Lancaster Dist., for $50 to John
         Carig Jr., 11 acres in the Waxhaw Settlement, on N
side Camp Creek part of a grant to John Linn, by Gov. Roan of
N. C., 17 May 1754, conveyed to Hugh Montgomery, 10 Jan 1757, and
by the L. W. & T. of Hugh Montgomery, to William Montgomery, to
Thomas Wells, by deed 22 Oct 1785, and 16 Dec 1795 to John Shepherd...3 Nov 1802.   John Shepherd (Ɖ) (Seal)
Wit: Wm Craig, Alexander Nisbet, Thomas Cothron (X). Proved
by Nesbit, 22 March 1803, before Wm Woods, J. P.
    [N. B. The grant to John Linn is abstracted in my <u>North Carolina
    Land Grants in South Carolina 1745-1773</u>]

Pp. 156-157: 4 June 1779, John Wyly Esqr., Sheriff of the District
         or Precinct of Camden, to Robert Barnet of the
Waxhaws; whereas Joseph Barnet was lately seized of 200 acres on
a branch of Cain Creek, on both sides the great road to Salisbury
in North Carolina, adj. William Barnet, William Hood, Adams,
surveyed for sd. Barnet 12 years past, and whereas Wm Hamilton
in the Court of Common Pleas against sd. Joseph Barnett....
Wit: Samuel Wyly, John Rushbrook Hutchins;John Wyly (Seal)
    William Wyly.

Page 157: South Carolina, Union District: 25 Dec 1800, Joseph
         Kelso of the Dist. afsd., to James Hogge of Lancaster
District, for Ł 50 sterling,125 acres, part of a tract granted to
Joseph Kelso Senr, 7 Oct 1764, on a branch of Catawba...Joseph
Kelso (Seal), Wit: Thos Patton, Thomas Park, Hugh Means.
Isabella Kelso, wife of Joseph, relinquished dower, 14 July ____,
before Andrew Terrance, J. Q. Proved by Thomas Patton, before
Hugh Means, J. P., 25 Dec 1800.

Pp. 157-158: Thomas Wells of Lancaster Co., Blacksmith, to John
         Shepherd, of same, yoeman, for Ł 30 sterling, 11
acres in the Waxhaw settlement, on N side Camp Creek, part of
302 acres, granted to John Linn, by the Gov. of N. C., 17 May
1754...16 Dec 1795.   Thomas Wells (Seal)
 Wit: William Draffen,   Jane Wells (ᴄᴣ) (Seal)
    William Wells, William Taylor.
Proved by William Taylor, 1 Jan 1796, before Robert Montgomery.

Page 158: James Macantire, for $60 to William Hood, part of a
         grant to James Macantire, 1801, adj. sd. Hood, James
Ramsey...21 Aug 1802.   James Mcantire (Seal)
Wit: Wm Nisbet, Francis McAteer, Thomas Hood. Proved by Wm
Nisbet, 5 Feb 1803.

Pp. 158-159: John May of Lancaster Town, for $750 to Hugh Mc
          Millen and Thomas Quigley, lot in Lancaster Town,
titles made by John Simpson, lot #15, 20 Apr 1797...5 Feb 1800.
Wit: Wm Huston, Thomas Edwards,   John May (Seal)
     Elir. Alexander.
Proved by Eliazer Alexander, 22 Jan 1803.

Page 159: 9 Nov 1799, John Ramsey and wife Ellenor of Lancaster
          Co., to William Hood of Mecklenburg Co., N. C., for Ł
60, part of grant of 100 acres to Mary Ann McCullough, 19 Aug
1774, and in the Waxhaw Settlement adj. James Ramsey, Wm Woods...
Wit: James Taylor, Jas Hagins,   John Ramsey (Seal)
     Benjamin Nisbet.   Ellenor Ramsey (ᛘᛜ) (Seal)
Proved by James Taylor, 24 July 1801, before Wm Woods, J.P.

Pp. 159-160: Thomas Wells of Lancaster Co., to John Shepherd of
          same, 150 acres near the new meeting house, granted
to Archibald Davie, 1 June 1767, made over to Thos Wells, 24 Aug
1789...dated 18 Apr 1795.   Thos Wells (Seal)
Wit: James Faulkner, George   Jane Wells (+) (Seal)
     Lassley, William Taylor.
Proved 26 Aug 1802, by James Faulkner, before John Montgomery,
J. Q.

Page 160: Lancaster District; John Shepherd for $150 to Titus Laney,
          150 acres near the new meeting house...27 Aug 1802.
                              John Shepherd (X).
Wit: James Faulkner, John Johnston, David Laney (X). Proved by
John Johnston, 26 Aug 1802, before John Montgomery.

     11 March 1802, Sherrod Henderson and wife Elizabeth and
William Marler and wife Elisabeth to George Hicklin, for $50...
100 acres on Bear Branch, adj. George Hicklin, John Burden,
George Wade, granted to James Mackey, 31 Oct 1769 and by his
lease & release to Nathaniel Henderson, to his son Sherrod
Henderson and his daughter Elizabeth Henderson by his last will
& testament....   Sherrod Henderson (Seal)
Wit: Thomas Glaze, Thomas Houze Jr.,   Wm Marler (Seal)
     Elisabeth Henderson.   Elizabeth Marler (Seal)
Proved by Thomas Houze Junr.,12 Aug 1803, before James Douglas,
J. P.
[N. B. The will of the above named Nathaniel Henderson can be
     found in my Camden District, S. C. Wills & Administrations
     1781-1787]

Page 161: William Narrimore of the Dist. of Lancaster for $70
          to Benjamin Maddox, 75 acres on waters of Flat Creek,
adj. William Kennington, Wm Narrimore, Edward Kennington, John
Right...5 Nov 1801   William Narrimore (X) (Seal)
Wit: Richmond Terrell, Benjamin Ladd (B). Proved by Terrell,
4 March 1802, before R. Hunley, J. P.

     John Johnston, of Lancaster Dist., for $150 to Andrew
Johnston, an undivided third of the real estate of John Johnston
decd., it being the legal dower of my present wife Jane Johnston
out of said estate, 23 March 1801....   John Johnston (Seal)
Wit: John Craig, William Draffin. Proved by John Craig, 4 April
1803, befoer Joseph Lee. Jane Johnston, wife of John, relinquished
dower,20 Apr 1803, before Saml Dunlap, J. P.

Page 162: John Edwards of Lancaster District, for $150, to Eliezar
            Alexander of same, land in the fork of Cane & Bear Creek
in the Waxhaw Settlement, 70 acres purchased from Moses Cantzon,
5 Dec 1799, whereon I now live...10 March 1802. John Edwards (Seal)
Wit: Thos Quigley, William Blair. Proved by Thos Quigley, before
Wm. Barkly, J. P., 20 Sept 1802.

John Brown of Lancaster District, to Lewis Kirk, 11 Oct 1802, for
$370, 33 acres on S side 12 Mile Creek, adj. Jane Yong, on the
Road leading from the place where Joseph Duglass formerly lived
to John Drannons old place, on Tomas Drennans spring branch...
Wit: John Tomlinson, Thomas Tomlinson (X),   John Brown (Seal)
       Rebecah Romlinson (X).
Proved by John Tomlinson, 12 July 1803 before Samuel C. Dunlap,
J. P.

Pp. 162-163: James Mcateer, Scool master, of Lancaster Dist., to
            John Hoey of North Carolina, for Ł 63 sterling, land
on Moores branch on E side Cain Creek, Waxhaw settlement...James
Mcateer and wife Nelly...2 Oct 1802.   James Mcateer
                                    Ellenor Mcateer (ᘐ)
Wit: Hugh Montgomery, Francis Mcateer. Proved by Francis Mcateer
10 Aug 1803, before Wm Woods, J. P.

Page 163: John Welsh, of Lancaster Dist., for $40 to John Tunston,
            150 acres adj. David Johnstons line, 26 March 1803...
Wit: Benjamin Deason, Joseph Hough.   John Welsh (Seal)

Pp. 163-164: 24 July 1794, James Blackman of Lancaster Co., to
            Joseph Blackman of same, tract granted to Peter Leger,
3 April 1775, 250 acres, conveyed by heirs to Blackman, 6 Feb
1793, namely the heirs of Peter Leger, Elizabeth Leger and Elizabeth
Love Hutchinson, 140 acres.... James Blackman (Seal)
                                    Anna Blackman (1) (Seal)
Wit: William Ward, Mark Ward, Joseph Eastridge (X). Proved by
Wm Ward, 23 May 1795, before Thos Welch, J. P.

Page 164: Richard Bettis of the Dist. of Chesterfield for $725 to
            James Carrel of North Carolina, part of 1000 acres granted
to Richard Bettis, 3 June 1799...8 Feb 1803. Richard Bettis (Seal)
Wit: Irvine McIntosh, Alexr Carrel. Proved by Alexr. Carrell before
Colden Williams, J. P., 1 Oct 1803.

9 Dec 1802, Thos Pully of Lancaster Dist., to Holden Wade for
Ł 50 sterling...300 acres granted to Arthur Cunningham, 138 acres,
part of sd. tract... Thos Pully (Seal)
Wit: James Fudge, A. Perry. Proved by Abraham Perry, 25 Oct 1803.

Page 165: Margaret Johnson of Lancaster Dist., for $60 to
            Johnson, my right to the real estate of my father John
Johnson decd, 12 March 1803.   Margaret Johnson (X)
Wit: John McClenchan, James Johnson

John Simpson of Lancaster Dist., for $100 to Hugh McMullen &
Thomas Quigley of town of Lancaster, lots in sd. town, 22 Jan
1803.   Jno Simpson (Seal)
Wit: Eliezar Alexander, John Kirk.

Pp. 165-166: Henry Shaver Senr of Lancaster Dist., for a good
                    horse to William Grann, 100 acres adj. Alexr Craigs
land, 3 Nov 1801.   Henry Shaver (Seal)
Wit: Jno Simpson, Wm. Barkley. Elizabeth Shaver, wife of Henry,
relinquished dower 3 Nov 1801.

Page 166: John Simpson of Lancaster Dist., for $160 to James Purdy
                    of same, lots in Lancaster village, 12 Sept 1803. Wit:
Hugh McMullen, David Cowsar.

Pp. 166-167: John Simpson to John May, lot on Dunlap St., Lancaster
                    town, 26 Feb 1803. Wit: James Purdy, Thos Quigley.

Page 167: John Simpson to James Blackman, lot in Lancaster, 14
                    Aug 1802, no wit.

Pp. 167-168: Britain Blackman of Lancaster Dist., farmer, to Nathan
                    Blackman, for $125, 100 acres granted to William Roy,
1773 on flat Creek, 200 acres, conveyed from the widow Roy to Thomas
Cockeran, who appears to be the heir of William Roy decd., by
the last will & testament of widow Roy to Thomas Cochran, 2 Feb 1803,
then conveyed to Britain Blackman, 23 Dec 1801. Britain Blackman.
Wit: William Ward, Jonathan Blackman. Proved 31 Oct 1803 before
William Ward by Jonathan Blackman.

Page 168: Hugh McMullen for $50 to William Huston of Rocky Mount
                    in the Dist. of Fairfield, lot by him now occupied on
Broad St., #41...25 May 1803.   Hugh McMullen (Seal)
Wit: Robt Stinson, Eliezar Alexander.

18 Dec 1773, Abraham Peebles of Craven Co., planter, to William
Brewer, planter for s 3...150 acres, part of the plantation of
250 acres on south fork Lynches Creek adj. James Brinkley, William
Horton, Lewis Peebles...Abraham Peebles (Seal), Kezia Peebles (X)
(Seal), Wit: Richard Burnet, Amos Horton.

Page 169: Patrick Graves of the Catawba River, at the mouth of
                    Cedar Creek, Lancaster Dist., Gunsmith, for $1000 to
James Breden, of Cedar Creek, planter, slave Rose girl about 10
years, and boy Sandy about 4 or 5 years old, 28 Oct 1803.
                                        Patrick Graves (Seal)
Wit: Jeremiah Graves, John Graves. Proved by Jeremiah Graves,
before Wm Woods, J. P.

Pp. 169-170: 29 Nov 1796, William Prewer of Lancaster Co., to
                    Rawleigh Hammond of Kershaw Co., for Ł 28 sterling...
50 acres on Beaver Creek, on the North side of Laurel Branch,
part of 200 acres...   William Prewet (W) (Seal)
Wit: Philip Burford, William Cawthon, Henry Vallandingham. Proved
by Henry Vallandingham, 12 Dec 1803.

Page 170: 20 Nov 1790, Benjamin Haile Senr of Lancaster Co., to
                    William Scarbrough of same, planter, part of 2869 acres
granted to John Marshal 1 Jan 1789 adj. John Faulkenberry, Benj.
Haile, that lies between where sd. Scarbrough now lives and Henry
Faulkenbrough, 200 acres on Great Linches Creek. B. Haile (Seal)
Wit: Danl Monagham, Robert Jones (R), Ephraim Ponder. Proved by
Danl Monagham, 23 July 1793, before Andrew Baskin, J. P.

Pp. 170-171: Abraham Rush of the dist. of Lancaster, planter, for
$200 to Paul Plyler, planter, 100 acres onboth sides
Oter Creek, a branch of Great Lynches Creek, Abraham Rush (X).
Wit: John Hancock, Coonrod Plyler (X). Proved by John Hancock,
15 July 1802, before John Craig, J. P.

Page 171: John Mosman of Lancaster Dist., for $150 to Paul Plyler,
planter, land on a branch of linches creek, called
Little Oter, 100 acres, part of 200 acres that sd. Mosman bought
from Jacob Rush...20 July 1801   John Mossman (X) (Seal)
Wit: John Hancock, John Sides.

20 Nov 1790, Benjamin Haile of Lancaster Co., to William Scarbrough
of same, for s 10, part of 2869 acres granted to John Marshall
(lease with above deed), same wit.

Page 172: 7 Feb 1789, John Baker and wife Frances of Lancaster Co.,
to Peter Perry of same, for Ł 16 sterling, 150 acres,
part of 300 acres granted to John Baker, 5 June 1786 on Camp Cr.
Wit: Joseph Coile,   John Baker (Seal)
Daniel Fleming, Sarah Webster (X).   Frances Baker (X) (Seal)
Proved by Joseph Coile, 7 Nov 1803, before Jas Douglas, J. P.

Page 173: 30 Sept 1803, James Bredin & wife Mary, near the mouth
of Cedar Creek on Catawba River, Lancaster Dist., to
George Hays, $150, 100 acres on Tyres branch adj. Mary Anderson,
James Glaze, Willm Smyth, Carlisle, Nathaniel Pendergrass, Jno or
widow Pendergrass, George Hays...   James Bredin (Seal)
Wit: Jos Graves, George Hayes,   Mary Bredin (X) (Seal)
James Douglas, J. P.
Mary Bredin, wife of James Bredin, relinquished dower, 1 Nov 1803.
Proved by George Hayes Junr., before Wm Curry, J. P., 2 Jan 1803.

Pp. 173-174: James Holleman Senr. of North Carolina, & McLingburg
(Mecklenburg) Co., for $40 to James Holleman Junr.,
land in Lancaster Co., in the upper corner of Genl. Sumter's sur-
vey, granted 2 April 1786 adj. Jacob Plyler, Koonrod Plyler, Henry
Shoots, Paul Plyler, John Mausmon, 30 Sept 1803. James Holliman
(Seal), Wit: Joshua Walters, Susanna Waters (X). Proved by Joshua
Walters, 31 Dec 1803, before John Crowder, J. P.

Page 174: 1 Aug 1797, William Baily of Lancaster Co., to Richard
Perry, for Ł 10 sterling...40 acres, part of 340 acres,
granted to Wm Baily, 2 June 1788...   William Baily (Seal)
Wit: Wm. S. Linton, Joseph Coile, John Perry.

Page 175: 24 March 1803; Jacob Funderburk of Lancaster Dist., to
James Runnels of same, 150 acres on waters of Wild Cat
Creek, adj. Zekiel Chester...   Jacob Funderburk (Seal)
Wit: David Funderburk (F), Zekiel Chester (C).

This day sold, Mrs. Mary Glaze, a negro girl named Tab for Ł 55
Camden, 22 Nov 1796   McRa & Canty.

Lancaster District: George Bell, turner, for $150, to John Cantzon...
horses, etc. _____ 1803.   George Bell (Seal)
Wit: Thomas Lee

Pp. 175-176: 16 Oct 1801; Anne Brewer & John Cato of Lancaster &
Kershaw Co., exrs. of William Brewer decd.,to John
Brewer, 100 acres, part of 250 acres on Little Linches Creek,

granted to Abraham Pebles, 1 April 1768, adj. Dinniss Quinley,
William Brewer, on Studstills branch...   Anne Brewer (X) (Seal)
Wit: James Ferguson, Wm. Brewer   John Cato (Seal)
Proved by James Ferguson, 4 March 1802, before R. Hunley, J. P.

Page 176: Josiah Hancock of Lancaster Dist., planter, to James
        Blakeny of Chesterfield Dist., land on waters of Wildcat
Creek, adj. Jackson Legate, now Robt Welsh, 400 acres...3 Aug 1803
Wit: Wm Shepherd, J. John Hancock.   Josiah Hancock (Seal)
Proved by Joseph J. Hancock, 3 Sept 1803; Elizabeth, wife of
Josiah Hancock, relinquished dower, 31 Jan 1804.

Pp. 176-177: 22 Nov 1802, Jacob Engles of Chesterfield Dist., to
        Josiah Hancock of Lancaster Dist., 150 acres on Wild
Cat Creek, part of tract that Jethrew Weaver purchased of John
Welsh, Thomas Sumter being patentee...   Jacob Engles (+)
Wit: George McManus (W), John Welch.

Page 177: Charles Cox of Lancaster Dist., for $700 to Andrew Mc-
        Ilwain, of same, three tracts on Rum Creek, 200 acres
granted to Andrew McKaven, 19 Sept 1758, 100 acres granted to
Sarah Bottons, 3 April 1786 and 123 acres granted to Andrew McIlwain,
3 Nov 1788...deed dated 9 Dec 1803.   Charles Cox (Seal)
Wit: Wm. Barkley, Wm. Simpson, Eleazar Alexander. Proved by Wm.
Barkley, 9 Dec 1803.

5 April 1803; Thomas Pully of Dist. of Lancaster to Thomas H. Wade,
for $500, 290 acres...   Thomas Pully (Seal)
Wit: Saml Dunlap Junr., Wm. Curry, Wm. L. Connell.
Proved by Wm. L. Connell, 10 Feb 1803.

Page 178: 27 Dec 1792, John Marshel Esqr of Kershaw Co., to William
        Welsh, for ₺ 54 sterling; 2014 acres on waters of Little
Linches Creek, adj. William Welsh, Gray, Samuel Mathis...
Wit: Thomas Welsh   John Marshel (Seal)
    Jacob Gray.
receipt signed by John & Tabitha Marshel. Proved by Jacob Gray,
1 Nov 1803, before Nathan Barr, J. P.

Page 179: James Strane of Lancaster Dist.,planter, for $50 to Joseph
        Strane, of same, planter, land adj. John McDow, James
Strane...10 Nov 1803.   James Strane (J) (LS)
Wit: Sarah Dunlap, James Collins, James Hood. Proved by Saml
Dunlap, 9 Feb 1804, before J. Tempson, Not. Pub.

S. C., Lancaster Dist.: By bill of sale unto James Taylor decd a
        certain negro Sarah, made over to the use & service of Jane
Blair, and as the heirs of Taylor have relinquished claim, I Thomas
McDow have sold to Dr. Robert D. Montgomery & John Clennachan
Esqr., trustees to Jane, wife of Thomas Blair...4 Jan 1802.
                        Thomas McDow (LS)
Wit: Elizabeth Montgomery (C), Josh. Lee. Proved by Elizabeth
Montgomery, 27 Dec 1803, before Saml. C. Dunlap, J. P.

Pp. 179-180: S. C., Lancaster Dist., Jesse Mesho for $100 to Joseph
        Johnson, 25 acres, part of 200 acres, granted to Wil-
liam Johnson, 3 July 1722, adj. Samuel Johnson...14 Dec 1802
Wit; William Ward Esqr., Starling Cato (J). Jesse Mesho (Seal)
proved by Starling Cato, 14 Dec 1802. Elizabeth Mesho, wife of
Jesse, relinquished dower, 20 Nov 1803, before John Welsh, J. Q.

Page 180: William Barton of Lancaster Dist., for $105 to Robert
                Kerr of same, 100 acres on N side Gills Creek adj. John
Barkley, Richd Cousar, 1 Dec 1803.   William Barton (Seal)
Wit: Jno Simpson, Wm. Barkley.
Proved by Wm. Barkly. Agness Barton, wife of William, relinquished
dower, 1 Dec 1803.

Pp. 181-182: 1 Oct 1787, John Duglass, doctor, heir to George Duglass,
                decd.,of Claremont Co., to James Faulkender of Lan-
caster Co., for ⅃ 23 s 4...tract granted to George Duglass, 20 Aug
1767...   Jno Douglass (Seal)
Wit: Hugh Milligan (O),   Sarah Douglass (X) (Seal)
James Johnston, Thomas Blair.
Proved 13 Sept 1788, before Robt Dunlap, J. P., by James Johnston.

Page 182: John Caskel (Caskey) of Lancaster Dist., planter for $1
                to James Faulkner, planter, 91 acres granted to sd. Caskey,
on Cane Creek, adj. William Faulkner, James Johnston, John Stevenson,
Thomas Douglass...6 April 1802.   John Caskey (Seal)
Wit: John Craig, William Nesbet, Charles Lethom. Margaret, wife of
John Caskey, relinquished dower, 6 April 1802.

Pp. 182-183: Hugh Montgomery of Lancaster Dist., for $700 to Jonas
                Vick, of North Carolina, Mecklenburg Co., land on S
side Cane Creek, Lancaster Dist., 260 acres adj. James Huey, Thomas
Hart, 15 March 1804...   Hugh Montgomery (Seal)
Wit: James Rogers, James McAteer. Proved by James Rogers, 16 March
1804.

Page 183: Hugh Montgomery of Lanc Dist., for $180 to James Vick of
                Meck Co., NC, land on Cane Creek where sd. Montgomery
now lives...__ March 1804. Same wit & sign.

Pp. 183-184: Hugh Montgomery of Lancaster Dist., for $80 to John
                Berry of same, 40 acres on N side Cane Creek, Waxhaw
Settlement, part of 100 acres granted to Mary Campbell, 7 Oct 1767
adj. Jas Huey, Thos Hart, 29 Dec 1802.   Hugh Montgomery (Seal)
Wit: James Montgomery, James McAteer. Proved by McAteer, 27 Dec
1802.

Page 184: S. C., Lancaster Dist., George Smith of York Dist., for
                $40.87½ to Thomas Knox of York Dist., 100 acres in Lan-
caster Dist., adj. Andrew Shaw...30 June 1803   George C. Smith (Seal)
Wit: John Bales Junr, John Crocket. Proved by John Crocket, 7 March
1804.

Pp. 184-185: William and Jane Foster of Lancaster Co.,for ⅃ 40 to
                Allen Anderson of same, 150 acres, part of tract
conveyed to Wm Foster, adj. Capt. Wm. Simpson, 29 Sept 1791.
Wit: Thos Dunlap, Samuel Dunlap,   William Foster (Seal)
     William Dunlap.   Jane Foster (Seal)
Proved by Samuel Dunlap, 17 Feb 1804.

Page 185: 19 Oct 1774, Cornelius Anderson of the Waxhaws in Craven
                Co., SC to Allen Anderson his son for ⅃ 5 SC currency...
200 acres where the sd. Cornelius Anderson now lives, part of 400
acres granted to Samuel Makelvene, then of Anson Co., and by North
patton, conveyed. to Hamilton Ross, then by sd. Ross in Mecklenburg
Co., to Cornelius Anderson...   Cornelius Anderson (Seal)
Wit: John Kennedy, Timothy Anderson, Lida Anderson (O). Proved by
John Kennedy, 11 Nov 1802, before Robert Patton, J. P.

Pp. 185-186: Britain Blackman, of Lancaster Dist., farmer, for $75
to Nathan Blackman, farmer, 100 acres granted to
William Roy, Jan 1773, on head waters of Flat Creek, 200 acres
conveyed by widow Roy to Thomas Cockman, who appears to be the
heir of sd. William Roy decd., will dated 2 Feb 1801, by Cockman
to Britain Blackman, 9 Feb 1801...21 Dec 1801
Wit: William Ward, Jonathan Blackman.   Britain Blackman (Seal)
Proved by Jonathan Blackman, 31 Oct 1803.

Pp. 186-187: 15 Jan 1778, John Chesnut & Ely Kershaw of Craven Co.,
Parish of St. Mark, merchants, to John Bell for Ł 600;
250 acres on Cedar Creek, N side Wateree, adj. Edward Davis, granted
to Patrick Brady, 10 Sept 1765, conveyed to Chesnut & Kershaw,
9 & 10 Oct 1765...   John Chesnut (Seal)
Wit: Duncan McRa, Francis Boykin,   Ely Kershaw (Seal)
Richard Sutton.
Proved 29 Jan 1778 by Duncan McRae, before John Newman Oglethorpe,
J. P. Proved again by Duncan McRa, 10 Nov 1803.

Page 187: Patrick Graves to James Graves, negro boy Sandy, 6 years
old for $200...21 Feb 1804   Patrick Graves
Wit: Jesse Vanwinkel.
Proved 23 Feb 1804, be Jesse Vanwinkel, before Wm. Curry, J. P.

Pp. 187-88: 5 March 1804, John Montgomery of Lancaster Dist., to
John House of same, land granted 10 April 1771 to
Thomas Adams, 200 acres adj. Daniel McDonald, conveyed to George
Wade, then to John & James Montgomery...   John Montgomery (X)
Wit: Thos H. Wade, Middleton McDonald, Wyley Crook. Proved by
Thos H. Wade, 5 March 1804.

Page 188: Claborne Houze, planter & Middleton McDonald, planter,
bound to John Houze, planter, 29 Feb 1804...Tabitha
Houze and Isham Houze, children of sd. Claborne Houze, by the
L. W. & T. of their grandfather Thomas Houze are entitled to pro-
perty, two slaves (named)...   Clabon Houze
                                    Middleton McDonald
Wit; Jas Denton, Jno Cheves

Pp. 188-189: S. C., Lancaster Dist.: Clabon Houze, agreed with
the exrs. of Thomas Houze, to wit James Houze, John
Houze, & William Houze, by the L. W. & T. of Thomas Houze, 12
April 1798, bequeathed to Tabitha & Isham House...9 Jan 1804.
Wit: Thomas Houze   Clabon Houze (Seal)

Page 189: 16 Sept 1803, James Douglas of Lancaster Dist., to Wiley
Crook of Chester Dist., for $100, part of tract in
Lancaster Dist., adj. Charles Cox, Benjamin Thompson & old survey
for Benjamin Maddox, part of a grant to Benjamin Thompson, 1754
sold to Alex. Thompson, conveyed by Benjamin Thompson & wife Mary,
1757, willd by sd. Alexr Thompson to Robert & Samuel Thompson,
in 1800, 40 acres...   James Douglass (Seal)
Wit: Henry McIlwain, Joseph Coile, Joshua Crook. Proved by Joseph
Coile, 16 Sept 1803.

Pp. 189-190: 16 Sept 1803, George Hicklin of Lancaster Dist., planter to Wiley Crook of Chester Dist., for $200...land on
Rum Creek adj. Charles Cox, James Douglas, Alexander Kenney, granted
to George Hicklin, 1 Sept 1785, 60 acres...   George Hicklin (Seal)
Wit; Henry McIlwain, Joseph Coile, Joshua Crook.

146

BOOK F

Pp. 190-191: 5 April 1804; Moses Cantzon to Thomas Lee, for $500,
400 acres on both sides Cane Creek, on the road from
Land's ford to McCenachan's (sic) ferry, 100 acres taken up by
Stephen Gambel, the other 300 acres taken up by Dr. John Cantzon
decd., the land sd. Cantzon livd. upon when in the Waxsaws...
Wit: Elizabeth Montgomery, Richard   Moses Cantzon (Seal)
Cousart, Robt. D. Montgomery.
Proved by Richard Cousart, 5 April 1804. Margaret Curry Cantzon,
wife of Moses, relinquished dower, 5 April 1804, before Josh. Lee,
J. Q.

Pp. 191-193: 28 & 29 Sept 1803, Eliezar Alexander of the Dist. of
Lancaster, to Elizabeth Cousar, relict of James
Cousar, decd...6 tracts, 670½ acres, on Cane Creek where Land's
ford road crosses...150 acres granted to Eleanor Adamson, 10 Nov
1761, and conveyed 11 & 12 June 1762 to Thomas Simpson Esqr., and
by exrs. of sd. Simpson (James Patton & Robert Patton), 10 Jan
1765, to William Simpson, & 10 June 1765 to Dr. John Cantzon, and
by Moses Cantzon and Sarah Harper(the one being the son, the
other relict of sd. Dr. John Cantzon), conveyed to Eliezar Alexander,
11 Feb 1794; 100 acres granted to Dr. John Cantzon, 28 Aug 1767;
300 acres granted to Samuel Dunlap, 1 Jan 1768, and Saml Dunlap
and wife Elizabeth conveyed to John McIlhaney, 2 Aug 1775, and by
James McIlhany (son of John McIlhany decd), to E. Alexander, 21
June 1799; 20½ acres granted to E. Alexander, 5 Nov 1792; 26 acres
granted to Joseph McMeen, 1 Dec 1794, and by his L. W. & T. conveyed
to E. Alexander, 2 April 1803; 70 acres granted to sd. Alexander,
5 Jan 1801....   Eliezar Alexander (Seal)
Wit: Jno Simpson, David Cowsar.
Proved by David Cousart, 23 March 1804.

Page 194: S. C., Lancaster District, John Best of Lanc. Dist., for
$325 to John Cauthon, 100 acres on waters of Camp Creek,
part of 800 acres belonging to John Caston Senr., adj. Holis
Trusdal, Charles Mackey Senr...3 Jan 1804   John Best (X) (Seal)
Wit: Thomas Cauthon, Joseph Coile, James Cauthon (X).
Proved by Joseph Coile, 3 April 1804.

Jeptha Guin of Lancaster Dist., for Ł 100 sterling, to John Pace
of Chesterfield District, 40 acres on SW side Great Linches Creek,
adj. land laid out for Thos Scot Wren, and George Hail, George
Taylor, William Taylor, 5 Dec 1803.   Jephthah Gynn (X)
Wit: Richd Todd, David Cockran. Proved in Anson district (sic)
by Richd. Todd, before James Blakeney, J. Q.

Pp. 194-195: John Tunstor and wife Sarah for $200 to Henry Tunstor,
50 acres on double branch of Flat Creek, part of a grant
to William Desen, 28 May 1803...   John Tunstor (∼)
Wit: Benjamin Deason, John Francis (X).   Saray Tunstor (X)

Page 195: John Fowler of Lancaster Co., for $300 to John Best, 100
acres on N side Catawba on waters of Camp Creek, part of
800 acres belonging to John Caston Sr., adj. John Hicklin, on
schoolhouse branch...11 Sept 1802.   John Fowler (Seal)
Wit: Joseph Coile, Henry Oram Senr., Burgess Isom (X). Proved by
Joseph Coile, 3 April 1804.

10 feb 1804, John King of Lancaster Dist., to Thomas Cauthon Senr,
for $50, 20 acres part of 200 acres on waters of lower Camp Creek,
made over to John King by John Hicklin, 6 Feb 1804....John King
(Seal), Wit: Henry Oram, James Cornelius (ŦC), Joseph Coile.

147

BOOK F

Pp. 195-196: Joseph Duglass of Mecklenburg County, Salisbury Dist.,
for $444 to James Faulkner of Lancaster District,
planter, 111 acres originally granted to George Duglass decd on
both sides Cane Creek adj. John Brown, Thos Duglass...7 March 1804
Wit: George Duglass,   Joseph Duglass (Seal)
    Thos Duglass, John Countryman.

Page 196: Jonas Vick of Lancaster District, to James Haings, negro
girl Reiny, for $180...22 March 1804. Jonas Vick (Seal)
Wit: John McMeen, Jas. Hagins. Proved by John McMeen, 3 April
1804 before Jno. Simpson, Not. Pub.

John Coffey of Lancaster Co., planter, for $261 to Elizabeth
Coffey, spinster...negro girl Flora, 9 March 1797. John Coffey (Seal
Wit: James Craig, Henry Taylor.
Proved by Henry Taylor, before Nathan Barr, J. P., 6 Feb 1798.

Pp. 196-197: S. C., Lancaster District, Elizabeth McDonald, Robin
Stringfellow, and John Truesdal, exrs. of the estate
of William McDonald, decd., for $800 to Owen Slaughter of Richmond
Co., N. C., planter, land granted to Robert Love, 1762, in N. C.
on both sides Hanging Rock Creek...____ 1802. Elizabeth McDonald
(X), Robert Stringfellow, John Truesdal. Wit: Harburd Horton,
Alexander William McDonald.
Proved by Alexander William McDonald, 5 March 1803.

Page 197: Same to same, six acres on Haning Rock Creek, granted
to Robert Love, 12 April 1802....(same signatures and
wit.)

5 Sept 1801, Alexander Logan, of Lancaster Co., yeoman, to William
Harrison, planter, for $150...180 acres on waters of Cedar Creek,
granted to Archibald McAfee, 1799...Alexander Logan (A)
Wit: Peter Twitty, Archibald Hood, John Ballard.
Proved by Archible Hood, 3 April 1804, before Jas. Douglas, J. P.

Pp. 197-198: John Baker of Lancaster District, for $665, to William
Baker, 100 acres which was bequeathed to Henry Wisener,
on waters of great linches Creek, adj. Richmond Terrell. 8 Dec
1802...   John Baker (X) (Seal)
Wit: Richmond Terrell, Benjamin Deason. Proved by Benjamin Deason,
28 Jan 1804.

Page 198: 2 Jan 1804, Micajah Cranshaw of Lancaster district, to
Micajah Cranshaw Jr.,for love & affection, 150 acres on
S side Dry Creek...   Micajah Cranshaw (Seal)
Wit: Wm. Curry, J. P.

18 Aug 1801, James Purdy to John Mcdonald, for $200, 184 acres on
Hanging Rock Creek, part of a survey to William Cato, 1795...
Wit: William Mothershead,   James Purdy (Seal)
    Elizabeth Cragg (X).
Proved by William Mothershead, 18 Aug 1801.

Page 199: Hugh Montgomery of dist. of Lancaster to James Rodgers
of Mecklenburg County, N. C., for $180...grist mill on
Cane Creek, 18 Feb 1804.   Hugh Montgomery (Seal)
Wit: James McAteer, Samuel McMurry.

Hugh Montgomery to James Rodgers, for $145, land adj. Samuel Martins
field...18 Feb 1804. (same signatures and wit.)

148

Pp. 199-200: John Coffey of the district of Lancaster set free
a mulatto wench Tenner aged about 40, and Milly aged
about 10...11 March 1804.   John Coffey (Seal)
Wit: Wm Robinson, Hugh Coffey, Hercules Huey.
Proved by William Robertson, 24 March 1804.
We certify that Tenna 40 years about 4' 8" high, guinea born, and
Millie about 9 years old, mixed bllod, country born, all of
good character, 26 March 1804: John Montgomery, Wm Robinson,
Hercules Huey, William Taylor, John Johnston.

Page 200: Henry Vallandingham of Dist. of Lancaster, by promissary
notes am indebted to James Purdy...land on waggon road
from Lands fork to Catawba, known as Barkleys old mill, adj.
Ponder, 100 acres; part of land purchased by James Purdy from
Francis Adams; and land purchased by James Purdy from Henry
Shaver...6 Dec 1803.   Henry Vallandingham (Seal)
Wit: Wm Howe, Eliezar Alexander. Proved by Howe, 26 May 1804.

Page 201: John Linn bound to his brother Andrew Linn for $2800
18 June 1804 to make title to the land whereon their
father lived and died, 321½ acres on Waxhaw Creek...John Linn (Seal)
Wit: Josh Lee, J. Q., Andrew Johnston.

Pp. 201-202: John McMurrey of Lancaster Dist., for $500 to John
McMurrey Jr. of same, land on N side Cane Creek,
where John McMurrey Jr. now lives, 81 A, originally surveyed for
John Nisbett, granted to James Winn, 17 Jan 1787 adj. William
Nisbet...4 Feb 1804;   John McMurry (Seal)
Wit: Samuel McMurry,   Martha McMurry (M) (Seal)
    John Steel.
Proved by John Steel, 6 Aug 1804, before Wm Woods, J.P.

Page 202: George Wade and wife Sarah of Lancaster Dist. to William
McDonald Sr. of Chester Dist., for $2000, 600 acres on
N side Catawba, 28 Nov 1803; George Wade (Seal) Salley Wade (Seal)
Wit: William Richardson, John Richardson, Abraham Perry. Proved
by John Richardson, 20 Dec 1803.

John Welsh of Lancaster Dist., planter, for $150 to John Smith,
land on waters of Wild Cat Creek, adj. Josiah Hancock...30 Aug
1803.   John Welsh (Seal)
Wit: John Lennox, Richmond Terrell. Proved by Richmond Terrell,
30 Aug 1803, before John Welsh, J. P.

Page 203: Jacob Champion, planter of Lancaster Dist., for $100 to
Robert Champion, of same, planter, 100 A, ½ of 200 A
on a branch of Camp Creek, granted to James Hawkins, 2 Sept 1772,
deed dated 26 Aug 1804.   Jacob Champion (111)
Wit: Jesse Hood, Jesse Giles.
Proved by Jesse Giles, 26 Aug 1804 before Adam McWillie, J. Q.

John Anderson of Lancaster Dist., for $250 to Joseph Lawrence,
land adj. Mrs. Carns (the burying ground excepted)...29 Feb
1804.   John Anderson (X) (Seal)
Wit: Charles Miller, Stephen Miller. Proved by Stephen Miller,
8 Oct 1804.

Pp. 203-204: 8 Dec 1792, James Simpson of Lancaster Co., to
Ely Clerk of same, for ₤ 50, land on the race path
branch, 215 acres granted to sd. Simpson, 5 March 1792...James
Simpson (Seal), Wit: John McDowl (8), Absalom Clark, Jos. Coile.

Page 204: Gilson Foote of Dist. of Chester to Rebekah Bell of
          Lancaster Dist., a sorrel mare, 14 hands high, 11 years
old, for $70...11 March 1804.   Gilson Foote
Wit: Saml McManahen, Joseph Loving.

Walter Bell of Lancaster Dist., to Rebekah Bell, cow & calf, bed
steds, etc., for $40...2 Feb 1804.   Walter Bell.
Test: Sarah Bell (L)

Kintchen Killbrugh & Marthew Killbrugh of Lancaster Dist., for
$90 to Shadrach Howard of same, 250 acres part of 2 tracts
granted to Benjamin Hail, conveyed to William Reader, to William
Drurey, then to Killbrugh, 23 Dec 1798, deed dated 25 Feb 1804.
Wit: Nelson Kennedy,   Kinchen Killebrew (Seal)
Harmon Howard.   Marthew Killebrew (+) (Seal)
Proved by Harmon Howard, 6 June 1804.

Pp. 204-205: John White of Lancaster Dist., bound to Abraham
             Perry Junr, for $3000, 4 Aug 1804, to make title to
tract where I now live, 134 acres, and 190 acres westward of
Lancaster Court House, adj. John May, James Grave, John Johnson,
James Coward...   John White (Seal)
Wit: Jno Simpson, Robert Stinson; proved by Robert Stinson, 18
Aug 1804.

Page 205: Joseph Breden of Madison County, Kentucky, bound to
          James Anderson of Lancaster Dist., $250, 1 Nov 1803 to
make titles to land on N side Cedar Creek adj. William Johnston,
Robert Bells, James Bredin, land where sd. James Anderson hath
now made an improvement...   Joseph Bredin (Seal)
Wit: Jesse Vanwinkle, Eliezar Alexander.

Pp. 205-206: John Love, planter, for $2000 to Burrel Clark, 400
             acres on branches of Little Linches Creek adj. John
Murphy, granted to John Williams, 3 May 1790, sold by Abdon
Alexander shff of Lancaster Co., 3 Sept 1796 to Daniel Clark,
then to John Love; 21 July 1804   John Love (Seal)
Wit: Robert Gaston, Wyly Horton.
Jane Love, wife of John, relinquished dower, 21 July 1804.
Proved by Wyly Horton, 21 July 1804.

Page 206: Edward Kennington of Lancaster Dist., for £ 10 to Wil-
          liam Kennington Junr., son of William Kennington Sr.,
86 acres on each side Lick Creek, 13 April 1801.
Wit: Edwd Narramore,   Edward Kennington (X) (Seal)
     Richmon Terrell. (plat included) Proved by Edward Narramore,
28 July 1804.

Page 207: Lancaster District: John Baker, for $100 to Joseph Baker,
          land on E side Flatt Creek adj. Gen. Sumter...8 Dec
1802.   John Baker (X) (Seal)
Wit: Richmon Terrell, Benjamin Deason. Proved by Benjamin Deason,
28 Jan 1804.

John Baker, for $665 to Joseph Baker, part of land that did
belong to Martain Wisenor, 8 Dec 1802 (same signatures and wit.).

Pp. 207-208: Andrew Baker to Benjamin Deason, for $200, land adj.
             Colder Williams, John Night, Richard Bullock, part
of 400 acres granted to Thomas Frizzell; 21 Feb 1804
Wit: Joseh Hough, Benjamin Ladd (B),   Andrew Baker (X)

Amos Hough (A). Proved by Joseph Hough, 25 Oct 1804.

Page 208: Agreement between Samuel Balding and James Douglas &
        Eliezar Alexander...sd. Balding purchased 218 acres
from Douglas on a branch of Bear Creek for Ł 30 sterling...it
appears that an elder grant exists for some of this land in the
name of Joseph Montgomery, and also a grant to Richard Hatfield
Homan, sd. Douglass and Alexander agree to take a lesser sum...
5 Nov 1804   Samuel Balding (Seal)
Wit: Wm McIlwain, Stephen Barr. Proved by William McIlwane, 5
Nov 1804.

Pp. 208-209: Thomas Frizzle, of the state of Georgia, for $200
            to Andrew Baker, land on S side Flat Creek adj.
Colden Williams, John Knight, Richard Bullock, 31 Oct 1800
Wit: John Smith, Nathan Weaver.   Thomas Frizzle (B)
Proved by John Smith, 31 Oct 1800.

Page 209: Cageby Duling (Dowling) of South Carolina, Orangeburgh
          District, to Amos Hough of Camden District, 60 acres
surveyed for William Duling, 25 July 1771 on Flat Creek adj.
Widow Gibson, Wm Bratton...29 Nov 1797.   Cageby Dowling (Seal)
Wit: Benjamin Deason, Joseph Hough. Proved by Benjamin Deason,
25 Oct 1804.

Pp. 209-210: Elisha White of Lancaster, planter, for $450 to Amos
            Hough, 175 acres part of 3 adjacent surveys, granted
to Elisha White, 1790 on Flat Creek adj. Benjamin Maddox, William
Deason, 125 acres; a tract granted to Abraham Deason, and transferred to Clement Gardner, then to Elisha White, 20 acres; and
30 acres part of 200 acres granted to William Bratton...23 Feb
1802.   Elisha White (X) (Seal)
Wit: Benjamin Deason, Joseph   Marget White (0) (Seal)
        Hough, John Wisnor.
Proved by Benjamin Deason, 25 Oct 1804.

Page 210: Gillam Ezell of Lancaster Dist., planter, for $334,
          to Amos Hough, 130 acres on Flat Creek granted to
James Bratton, part of 400 acres; and part of a tract of John
Tunston, adj. George Chrisman...9 Aug 1802.   Gilliam Ezell (Seal)
Wit: Benjamin Deason, Joseph Hough, John Hough. Proved 25 Oct
1804 by Benjamin Deason.

Joseph Gracey of Lancaster Co., planter, to Amos Hough of same,
for Ł 10; 100 acres on waters of Flatt Creek, part of 713 acres
granted to Joseph Gracey, 1792...23 July 1799   Joseph Gracey (Seal)
Wit: Benjamin Deason, Joseph Hough, William Lett. Proved by
Benjamin Deason, 25 Oct 1804.

Page 211: 9 Jan 1798, Jacob and Catharine Englet of Lancaster Co.,
          to Paul Hagler of same, for Ł 32, 155 acres on a branch
of Turkey hoe, waters of Linches Creek, granted 3 April 1786...
Wit: Charles McManus, John   Jacob Englet (X) (Seal)
        Cagle (   )   Catharine Englet (X) (Seal)
Proved by Charles McManus, 30 July 1803.

Page 211: Robert Kirkpatrick of Lancaster Dist., planter for
          $912.50 to David Letham of same, 100 acres on waters of
Cane Creek, surveyed 26 July 1768 for Joseph Moore, and granted
2 Feb 1771 to James Wood, and conveyed to Joseph McMeen, 2 Feb
1771, and by McMeen and wife to Alexander Galloway, 22 July 1778

adj. William Moore, Thomas Wright, Henry Hays, John Greer...25
Oct 1804.   Robert Kirkpatrick (Seal)
Wit: John Johnson,   Martha Kirkpatrick (X) (Seal)
John Lessley.
Martha Kirkpatrick, wife of Robert, relinquished dower, 25 Oct
1804. Proved by John Johnson, 25 Oct 1804.

Pp. 212-213: To Messrs James Massey, John Doby, Jeremiah Cureton,
             Daniel Carnes, and Isham Shirling...whereas Mary
Couser, admx. & William Couser, admr., on the estate of Archibald
Couser, late of Lancaster County, decd., and John Couser, James
Couser, Nancy Crawford, Martha Couser, Mary Couser Junr., Jane
Kirk, Sarah Couser, Letticia Couser, Archibald Couser Junr., and
Richard Couser, children and heirs of the estate of sd. Archibald
Couser decd., have made choice of you to divided the estate real
and personal...23 Jan 1804.
Division and inventory included: Mary Couser widow, Agnes Crawford
wife of James Crawford, Rev. John Couser, William Couser, Martha
Couser, James Couser, Mary Couser Junr., Jane Kirk,wife of Joshua
Kirk, children of mature age, and Archibald Couser, Sarah Couser,
Letticia Couser, and Richard Couser, minor children...15 Nov 1804.

Page 213: Moses Cantzon hath heretofore sold me a tract of 400
          acres which fell to him by the decease of his father
and brother, where his father resided when in the Waxhaws, and made
titles to his brother John Cantzon, and was under execution by
Thomas Wade, sheriff of Lancaster Co., by widow Eaves...I relinquish title 2 June 1804.   Thomas Lee (Seal)
Wit: Mary Blair, Mary Titus (M).
Mary Lee, wife of Thomas, relinquished dower 19 Dec 1804. Proved
by Mary Blair.

Pp. 213-214: 10 Oct 1801, John Philips of Lancaster District, to
             William Runnals of same, for $50, land on waters of
Wild Cat adj. Robert Welsh, Johnson, 200 acres....John Philips (Seal)
Wit: Daniel Clark, John Lennox. Proved by Daniel Clark, 17 Jan
1805 before Jno Crowder, J. P.

Page 214: John McDow to James McDow for $500, 149 acres adj. James
          Hood, Charles Miller, Andrew Boyd, Robert Thompson, 26
Oct 1804.   John McDow (Seal)
Wit: Fenney McClenahan, William Dunlap. Proved by William Dunlap,
26 Oct 1804.

Pp. 214-215: 29 Dec 1803, Adam Thompson of Kershaw Dist., planter,
             to Arthur Cunningham, planter, for $500, 200 acres
on both sides Cedar Creek, granted to sd. Thompson, 15 March 1771,
adj. James Smith...   Adam Tomson (Seal)
Wit: Wm Curry, Robert Cunningham, Joseph Cunningham. Proved by
Wm Curry, 4 Dec 1804.

Page 215: John Simpson of Lancaster Dist., for $100 to James
          Blackburn of same, lot #99 in Lancaster C. H., adj.
Jefferson St., 14 Aug 1802...Wit: Abraham Perry, Middleton Mc-
Donald. Proved by Abraham Perry, 30 Jan 1805.

          Jacob Shoffner of Lancaster Dist.,for $500 to Andrew
Walker, two tracts of 385 acres surveyd for John Belk, on Bear
Creek, adj .Glass Caston, and 100 acres on head of Big Lynches
Creek, 10 Jan 1805...Jacob Shoffner, (Seal), wit: Abraham Perry,
John Simpson. Proved by Abraham Perry, 30 Jan 1805.

BOOK F

Page 216: James McMeen Jr. and Joseph McMeen both of Barnwell
          Dist., for $230 to William McMeen Sr. of Lancaster
Dist., 100 acres in forks of Cane and Bear Creek, adj. Robert
Dunlap, William McMeen, Eliazar Alexander, & Messrs Cousar &
Connely, known as plantation of Joseph McMeens decd, 3 Jan 1805.
Wit: Eliezar Alexander,   James McMeen (Seal)
     James McMeen.   Joseph McMeen (Seal)
Proved by Eliezar Alexander, 3 Jan 1805.

Pp. 216-217: Joseph Bredin of Madison County, Kentucky, bound
             to James Anderson of Lancaster Dist., for $250...
sd. Bredin has sold to sd. Anderson land adj. John Shewbart,
William Johnston, Robert Betis, James Bredin, land where James
Anderson hath now made an improvement...there is now an action
in Lancaster District Court wherein Robert Bell is plantiff &
Jesse Vanwinkle deft. in which action the improvement of James
Anderson may be materially affection, and as a large portion of
100 acres is claimed by Robert Bell...Joseph Bredin (Seal)
Wit: Jesse Vanwinkle, Eliezar Alexander.

Page 217: John Clark for $100 to Richard Yancy, part of a grant
          to John Caston, 29 January 1785, 465 acres, on Indian
Branch, 29 Nov 1802...John Clark (Seal) Wit: William Barker, William Ward, J. P. Proved by Wm. Ward, 29 Nov 1802.

Pp. 217-218: Richard Yancy of Lancaster Dist., for $400 to Samuel
             Humphries, 112 acres where Richard Yancy now lives,
adj. Jonathan Blackman, part of a grant to John Caston, and part
of grant to John Wyly 3 April 1772, on Little Linches Creek,
28 Dec 1804. Richard Yancy (R), Wit: John Stogner, William
Baskin. Proved by William Baskin, 26 Jan 1805.

Page 218: 19 March 1799, William Ransom Davis, Esq., Sheriff, to
          Richard Yancy...whereas John Wyly was seized of 100
acres on west branch of Little Linches Creek granted to sd. Wyly
3 April 1772, adj. Samuel Wyly, and being indebted to Powell, Hopton & Co. of Charleston, for ₤ 50,000 former currency... Wit:
R. L. Champion, Ben Bineham. Proved by Ben Bineham, 25 July 1800.

Page 219: Jordan Ashly of Lancaster District, planter, for $100
          to John Bowers of same, 25 acres, part of 534 acres
granted to Jordan Ashly, 5 March 1792, adj. James Love, Alexander
Tom, William Ingram, 8 Nov 1804.   Jordan Ashly (Seal)
Wit: Richard Ussery, William   Sarah Ashly (X) (Seal)
     Keziah, Thos Gaston.
Proved by Wm. Keziah before Thomas Gaston, J. P., 15 Nov 1804.

Whereas James Hutchinson of the Dist. of Lancaster by notes of
hand bearing date 19 Nov 1804 and 20 March 1805 stands indebted
to John Hutchinson of York District, for $206...mortgage land
on Indian boundary, McCorpins Creek adj. Thomas Black, Abm. Miller,
Chas Knowlen, Jas Gribble, 100 acres being the plantation where
James Hutchinson now lives, also 2 horses, 20 March 1805....
                              James Hutchinson (X) (Seal)
Wit: Jno Simpson, Thomas Lee. Proved by Thomas Lee, 20 March
1805.

Page 220: John Cantzon late of Lancaster Dist. was seized of a
          plantation, 300 acres on NW side Cane Creek in the
Waxhaw Settlement, on both sides Lands Ford Road, granted to

John Cantzon, father of the aforesaid John Cantzon, whereon sd.
John lately resided, and said John Cantzon being indebted to
Robert Robinson of Chester District, and recoevered in 1804 in
Lancaster Court, $166.95...Thomas Holden Wade, Sheriff, sells
to David Cowsar and James Connell, 22 Oct 1804...Thos H Wade (Seal)
Wit: Jno Simpson, James Clancy. Proved by Simpson, before William
Barkley, J. P., 12 Nov 1804.

Page 221: 14 June 1789, William McDonald of Chester County, to
          Thomas Holden Wade of Lancaster Co., for Ŀ 100, land
on E side Catawba River, granted to Daniel McDonald, 7 June 1767...
Wt: Isom Pully (X),   William McDonald (Seal)
    Daniel Wade. Proved by Daniel Wade, 1 March 1805.

     Josiah Smith as surviving copartner of the late house of
Smith, Desaussure & Darrell of Charleston, certified the bond of
Daniel Wade, Wm. McDonald & Middleton McDonald to Daniel Jennings
& John Woddrop & Josiah Smith,David DeSaussure & Edward Darrell,
dated 11 Dec 1790 for Ŀ 324 9/4 was in the year 1795 delivered
over into the hands of Nathaniel Russell....April 8, 1801.
Wit: D. Remington.

Pp. 221-222: Frankey Black of Lancaster Co., for $40 to Alexander
          Black, 30 acres, part of plantation on which Frankey
Black now lives...23 Feb 1805.   Frankey Black (Λ) (Seal)
Wit: Robert Kirk, Agness Kirk.

Pp. 222-223: 26 July 1785, George Sleeker of Camden District,
          admr. of John Jacob Webbers estate, to John Arnold
Bender, for Ŀ 43 sterling, 100 acres granted to John Jacob Webber,
6 Feb 1773 adj. Andrew Shaver...   George Sleeker (X) (Seal)
Wit: Robert Thompson, John Foster, Wm. Day. Proved by Robert
Thompson, 26 July 1785, before Andrew Foster, J. P.
(For additional information on the above John Jacob Webber and
George Sleeker, see Camden District Wills & Administrations
1781-1787, the estate of Jacob Weaver, George Slicker, admr.)

Page 223: S. C., York District: George Carlisle Smith for $100 to
          Richard Sessions of Lancaster District, 100 acres gran-
ted to John Jacob Webber, transferred by George Sleeker to John
Arnold Pender, and by the last will & testament of John Arnold
Pender to sd. George Carlisle Smith, 28 Jan 1805. George C.
Smith (Seal), Wit: Joseph Davie, John Crockett; Proved by Davie
in York District, 31 Jan 1805, before Robert Crockett, J. P.

     Jonas Vick by note of hand stands indebted to David Cowsar
for $200...mortgage tract on N side Cane Creek, 260 acres where
Hugh Montgomery has formerly resided adj. James Hays, Thomas Hail,
John Nisbet...16 March 1804.   Jonas Vick (Seal)
Wit: Jonathan Coffee, Jn Simpson. Proved by Jno Simpson.

Page 224: John Harper of Chester District & Eleanor Carson of
          Lancaster District, for $400, to James Purdy, merchant
of Lancaster, 100 acres a tract granted to Grace & Eleanor Carson,
178 acres adj. James Graves, John White, John Simpson, Isaiah
Thompson...1 Feb 1805.   John Harper (Seal)
                                    Ellonder Carson (X) (Seal)
Wit: William Howe, Saml Dunlap, John Barkley.
Gracey Harper, wife of John Harper, relinquished dower, 8 Feb
1805. Proved by Dunlap, 21 March 1805.

Pp. 224-225: James Purdy indebted to Eleanor Carson & John Har-
        per, for $330 and $335...mortgage two tracts,
granted to Grace and Eleanor Carson, 2 Feb 1805.   James Purdy
(Seal), Wit: Saml Dunlap, William Hower, John Barkley.

Page 225: Andrew Boyd of Lancaster District, for $100 to William
        Nutt, negro boy George, 8 years old...20 May 1805.
Wit: Jonas Vick, John Gettys.   And Boyd (LS)
Proved by John Gettys, 27 May 1805.

Page 226: 5 Dec 1804: Jonathan Johnston of Lancaster Dist., to
        James Johnston of same, for $100, 75 acres on branches
of Little Lynches Creek, part of 160 acres granted to Jesse Mesho,
7 Dec 1794, conveyed to William Estridge, and to Jonathan Johnston...
Wit: James Gaston,   Jonathan Johnston (Seal)
    Susannah Johnson
Proved by James Gaston, 5 Dec 1804, before Wm Ward, J. P.

    John White of Gills Creek, Lancaster District, for $900, to
Saml Dunlap of Lancaster Ville, several tracts: 133 acres on
Gills Creek whereon I presently reside on the Salisbury Road near
Lancasterville, part of 302 acres granted to Richard Cowsart 24
Sept 1754, adj. Nathan Barr, Robert Davis, Mr. Craig, Nathaniel
Cowsert, 190 acres in the fork of Gills Creek and Bear Creek,
granted to Simon Baird, 200 acres 5 Jan 1786, adj. John Simpson,
the representatives of Alexander Craig decd., perhaps James Doug-
las, the representatives of James Cowsar decd., the representa-
tives of Thos McMeen decd., ditto of John Cowsar decd., & James
Graves, John May, 18 April 1805.   John White (Seal)
Wit: William Howie, James Purdy, Andw White. Proved by Howie,
1 July 1805.

Page 227: Burrel Clark of Lancaster Dist., to James Johnston, 40
        acres on a branch of Little Lynches Creek adj. Guy
Wallace, part of 800 acres granted to John Williams, sold by
sheriff to DanielClark, then to John Love, then to Burrel Clark,
3 Dec 1804.   Burrel Clark (Seal)
Wit: Samuel Johnson, James Gaston. Proved by Samuel Johnson,
25 May 1805. Sarah Clark, wife of Burrel Clark, relinquished
dower, 25 May 1805.

    Moses Cantzon of Lancaster Co., for Ь 5 sterling to nephew
Daniel Cantzon, minor, 100 acres near Cane Creek, granted to Ste-
phen Gamble, 14 Feb 1762 and conveyed to my fahter Dr. John
Cantzon, 6 Oct 1764, also 300 acresadj. to it, granted to my
father Dr. John Cantzon, 28 May 1797... Moses Cantzon (Seal)
Wit: James Davis, Robert McDow, Robert Otridge. Proved by
Robert McDow, 8 June 1805.

Page 228: 26 March 1805, James Strain and wife Lucinthy of Lan-
        caster Dist., to James Hagins, for $100, 103 acres,
part of 300 acres granted to Martin Climes...James Strane (T)
(Seal), Wit: Saml Dunlap, Richd Cousar, William Howe. Proved by
Samuel Dunlap, 4 April 1805. Lucinthy, wife of James Strain,
relinquished dower 2 April 1805.

Pp. 228-229: Thomas Douglas of Lancaster Dist., planter, for $345,
        to Nat Stephenson, land granted to James Crow, 7
Nov 1770, the said James Crow dying intestate, granted to Grace
Crow (the wife of Thomas Douglas) 8 Nov 1793, the lawful heir of
John Crow decd., her father, who was the proper heir of James

Crow, 164 acres...15 April 1805.   Thos H Douglass (Seal)
Wit: George Douglass, Jesse   Gracey Douglas (&) (Seal)
     Douglass, Margret Douglass (X).
Gracey, wife of Thomas Doulgas, relinquished dower, 10 May 1805.

Page 229: William Ware, house joiner, to Samuel Dunlap, 3 feather
     beds & furniture, mare, cows & calves, other furniture,
etc., for $100...19 Dec 1804. Wm Ware (Seal), Wit: William HOwe,
Elizabeth Dunlap, Isbelle Howe. Proved by Wm Howe, 13 June 1805.

     James Bredin of Cedar Creek, Lancaster Dist., for $1000 bond
to make titles to land on mouth of Cedar Creek to Patrick Graves,
18 Oct 1802...Jno Bredin (Seal), Wit: John Bavart, Littleberry
Champion.

Pp. 229-230: William Adams of Lancaster Dist., stands indebted to
     Mary Bard of same for $61.82, mortgage of 150 acres
on Camp Creek whereon Rosey Adams now lives, adj. James Boyd,
James Wilson, John Strain, 18 Feb 1805...William Adams (Seal)
Wit: David Montgomery, John Adams.

Page 230: 11 May 1805, Jesse Roper and wife Piddy to Isaac Ander-
     son, for $400, 62 acres on lower side Catawba River,
Waxhaw Creek...   Jesse Roper (Seal), Biddy Roper
(X) (Seal), Wit: George Wren, Thos Vincent, Guy Wallace. Proved
by Wren, 31 July 1805.

Pp. 230-231: Joseph Strain cf Lancaster Dist., for $90 to James
     Collins, merchant, 30 acres adj. James Strain,
Joseph Strain, James Collins, George Glenn, 14 Feb 1804.
Wit: Saml Dunlap, Wm. Woods,   Josep Strain (Seal)
     Andw Boyd. (Plat included)

Page 231: Mary Cowsar Senr, James Crawford, John Cousaw, Martha
     Cowsar, William Cowsar, James Couser, Mary Cowser Junr.,
Joshua Kirk and Mary Cowsar Senior and John Cowsar as guardians
for Archibald Cowsar, Richard Cowsar and Letitia Cowser, minors,
of Lancaster Dist., to Jeremiah Cureton, of Mecklenburg County,
North Carolina, for $292, 106 acres adj. Absalom Ivey, 30 Nov 1804.
Wit: Saml C. Dunlap, Robt Crawford, Moses Heath.

Pp. 231-232: Ferguson Haile of Lancaster Dist., for $1600 to Richard
     Kennon of Chatham County, North Carolina, 300 acres
on both sides flat Creek granted to Robert Harper, 22 Jan 1759,
from Benjamin Haile to Ferguson Haile, 18 May 1793 and also land
deeded from William Bridges and Caty Bridges to sd. Ferguson Haile,
3 Nov 1795. (plat included) 19 Feb 1805.   Ferguson Haile (Seal)
Wit: Lovick Young, John Bird (X).   Jemima Haile (X) (Seal)

Page 232: Dorcas Young of Lancaster Dist. for $300 to Mary Blair,
     negro gril Nann, 5 Dec 1804...Dorcas Young (O) (Seal)
Wit: Robert Davis, James Faulkner.

     Archibald Kimball of Lancaster Dist., planter, for ₺ 510
sterling, to Moses Cantzon of Dist. of Lancaster, part of a
grant to Joseph Kelso, plat Oct 1767, survey made by John Gaston,
125 acres conveyed by Thomas Jackson and Sarah his wife to
Archibald Kimball, 3 Nov 1803...18 Oct 1804. Archibald Kimball
(Seal), Wit: Robt D. Montgomery, John Weaver, John F. Cousert.
Proved by Dr. Robert D. Montgomery, 15 April 1805.
Elizabeth Kimbell, wife of Archibald, relinquished dower 15 April

1805.
(This land was sold by William Kelso and wife Joannah to
Thomas Jackson. See Spartanburg County Deed Book F, pp.
213-214).

Pp. 232-233: Benjamin Scarborough of Lancaster District, to
Abraham Hagler of same, for $150, land on head
branches of Turkey Creek, waters of Big Lynches Creek, 200 acres
granted to Joseph Ferguson...10 Nov 1804. Benjamin Scarborough
(X) (Seal), Wit: John Baker, John Welsh Jr. Proved by John Baker,
10 Nov 1804.

Page 233: 31 Jan 1804, Jane Avent of Lancaster Dist., to Thomas
Pair of Mecklenburg County, North Carolina, for $55,
20½ acres...Jane Avent (A) (Seal), Wit: Charity Wallace, Wm Dossey,
Benjamin Avent.

James Howze of Lancaster Dist., planter, for $100, to Littleton
Howze, 238 acres... 30 Jan 1805. James Houze (Seal), Wit: William
Dunavant, John Houze. Milly House, wife of James, relinquished
dower, 30 Jan 1805.

Pp. 233-234: James Houze of Lancaster Dist., planter for $100 to
Henry Houze, 111 acres at the mouth of Canoe branch,
adj. Henry Houze, Clayton Houze, part of 300 acres granted to
Thomas Singleton...29 Jan 1805.
Wit: Nathaniel Pendergrass, John Pendergrass. Milly Houze, wife
of James, relinquished dower, 29 Jan 1805.

Page 234: Jacob Rush of Lancaster Dist., planter, was seized of
235 acres on both sides Flat Creek adj. John Gale Friz-
zle, John Belk, John Masters, and sd. Rush was indebted to James
Holliman for $57, and suit was brought by Holliman; Thomas H.
Wade, Sheriff sells for $51 to John Stogner...21 May 1803...
Thomas H. Wade S. L. D.
Wit: Saml Caston, Jonathan Blackman (X).

Pp. 234-235: William Barkly of Lancaster Dist., for $180 to
Abraham Perry, lot in Lancaster Town, adj. Gay St.,
Capt. James Douglass, Arthur Ingram, 19 Jan 1805. Wm Barkley
Wit: Robert Stinson, Isiah Hagwood (X).
Elizabeth Barkley, wife of William, relinquished dower, 19 Jan
1805.

Page 235: Jesse Mesho for $200 to Joseph Johnston, 100 acres adj.
Edmund Hull, William Ward, Joseph Johnston, Samuel
Johnston, 5 Jan 1805. Jesse Mesho (Seal), Wit: Jacob Shafner,
Elizabeth Ward (X).

Pp. 235-236: James Howze of Lancaster Dist., planter, to William
Dunnovant, planter, 110 acres, part of 500 acres
granted to Thomas Singleton, 8 Nov 1769, adj. Henry Houze, Clabon
Houze, 14 Jan 1805. James Houze (Seal)
Wit: Wm Curry, Henry Horton, Clabon Houze.

Page 236: John Caston was seized of 140 acres, part of 465 acres
granted to sd. Caston, and was indebted to Samuel Caston
for $63...Thos H. Wade sheriff sells to Jonathan Blackman, for
$23...21 May 1803...
Wit: John Stogner, Dempsey Haile.

Pp. 236-237: Andrew Boyd of Lancaster Dist., for $50 to James
Collins, 72 acres in Lancaster Dist., adj. Joseph
Strain, John McDow, Andrew Boyd, George Glenn, 10 Nov 1803.
Wit: Wm Woods, James Hood,   Andw Boyd (SL)
Saml Dunlap Junr.

Page 237: 29 July 1805, Wiley Crook to George Cox, for $270,
100 acres on Rum Creek, part of an old survey formerly
belonging to Alexander Thompson, and part of another survey
granted to George Hicklin...   Wiley Crook (Seal)
Wit: Joseph Cox, Sarah Daniel (X).

Pp. 237-238: 12 Jan 1805, Henry Massey of Mecklenburg Co., N. C.,
to Moses Heath of same, for $300, 425 acres in
Lancaster Dist., adj. James Elliot...   Henry Massey (Seal)
                                         Elizabeth Massey (X) (Seal)
Wit: Jereh. Cureton, Elizabeth Wiggins (X). Proved by Jeremiah
Cureton, 26 Feb 1805.

Page 238: Frankey Black of Lancaster Dist., for $100 to Alexander
Black of Mecklenburg Co., N. C., 115 acres granted to
Ananias Black, 3 June 1793 on Hannahs Creek of Gills Creek, 24
Aug 1804.   Frankey Black (X)
Wit: Samuel Martin (O), James McAteer. Proved by Samuel Martin,
15 Feb 1805.

Page 239: S. C., Lancaster District: William McMeen Jr., son of
Joseph McMeen decd., sell my right in the estate of
the above mentioned deceased to my second Brother James McMeen,
for $76.62½ in the fork of Cane and Bare Creek adj. Robert Dun-
lap, Wm McMeen Sr., James McMeen Sr., Eliazar Alexander, John
Cantzon, 30 Oct 1804...   William McMeen
Wit: Thomas Carson.

William Claudius Ingrem of Lancaster Dist., for $160 to
Cordner Ingrem and John Ingrem of same, 1/4 part of 440 acres on
Hanging Rock Creek, the only part left to sd. William C. Ingrem
by the last will & testament of Alexander Ingrem decd., adj.
Charles Barton, Jno Fuguson (sic), 28 Feb 1805... Wm. C. Ingrem
(Seal), Wit: Alexander Ingrem, Saml Douglas. Proved by Alexander
Ingrem, 23 March 1805.

Pp. 239-240: Jacob Shofner of Lancaster Dist., for $500 to Andrew
Walker, two plantations of 385 acres surveyed for
John Belk on drains of Bare Creek adj. Glass Caston, and 100
acres on head branches of Big Linches Creek, called pole cat
branch, 10 Jan 1805...   Jacob Shafner (Seal)
Wit: Abraham Perry, John Simpson.
Proved by Abraham Perry, 30 Jan 1805.

Page 240: 12 Nov 1800, James Douglass of Lancaster Dist., for
Ł 30 sterling to Lodawick Thompson, 200 acres adj.
George Correy, near to where Solomon Smith raise a house, part
of a grant to sd. Douglass, 986 acres, 1787...James Douglass
(Seal), Wit: James Anderson, George Vickery (T). Proved by
James Anderson, 3 April 1804.

Pp. 240-241: Archibald Crocket for $650 to Robert Stinson, a
negro woman Peggy and her two chilrdren Julius &
Will...3 Nov 1804. Archibald Crocket (Seal), Wit: Hugh McMullen

Page 241: South Carolina, Lancaster Dist., Drury Watson of Cum-
    berland County, Virginia, to James Morrow of Lancaster
Dist., a negro woman Agg and boy London, and child Ambris, for
$500...27 Aug 1804.   Drury Watson (Seal)
Wit: Eli Crocket, Jonathan Coffey.

Pp. 241-242: 2 March 1805, Daniel Wade of Richland District, to
    Thomas Holden Wade of Lancaster Dist., for $2500...
several tracts (1) 200 acres half of 400 acres granted to Daniel
McDonald now decd., 13 Dec 1756, willed to sd. Wade by sd. McDonald
(2) 100 acres adj. or near sd. tract, granted to Alexander McKown,
19 Aug 1774, conveyed by L & R 8 & 9 May 1785 to sd. Wade   (3)
100 acres near sd. tract surveyed for Daniel McDonald and bequeathed
to William McDonald & by him conveyed 30 June 1798....
Wit: James Cheves, William McDonald,   Danl Wade (Seal)
    John Richardson.
Proved 21 March 1805 by James Cheves.

Pp. 242-243: 4 March 1805, Thomas Holden Wade to Daniel Wade,
    of Richland Dist., miller, for $1 (same land as
preceding deed). Same wit. and proving date.

Pp. 243-246: 5 March 1805, Thomas Holden Wade of Lancaster Dist.,
    planter, to Daniel Wade of Richland Dist., for
$1010, mortgage of above tracts. same signature and wit, prov.
date.

Pp. 246-247: 30 Sept 1805, William Ware of Lancaster Dist., car-
    penter, to George Currey, weaver, land conveyed to
secure note for $194.88...250 acres granted to George Currey in
1774...   William Ware (Seal)
Wit: William Rowel, Wm. Curry. Proved by Wm. Curry, 7 Oct 1805.

Page 247: 7 June 1805, John Chesnut of Kershaw Dist., planter,
    to James Crenshaw of Lancaster Dist., for $300, 200
acres on Kemp Creek, waters of Catawba, adj. Benjamin Cook,
Elizabeth Cornelius, granted to William Shaley, 4 Nov 1772, conveyed
to sd. Chesnut...   John Chesnut (Seal)
Wit: Micajah Crenshaw, Ben Carter. Proved 27 July 1805 by
Micajah Crenshaw.

        19 Nov 1804, Andrew Boyd of Lancaster Dist., sold to James
Collins of same, 4 negroes; Ester, Leth, Grace & Sara...Andw
Boyd Wit: Robt Thompson. Proved 12 Sept 1805.

Page 248: 7 Oct 1801, James Simpson Sr. of Lancaster Dist., to
    James Simpson Jr., for $200, 250 acres on both sides
Cane Creek & Rum Creek adj. David Dunlap, William Baird, William
Simpson; part of 1000 acres granted to Thomas Simpson and willed
to William Simpson Sr.,and by him willed to James Simpson...
                            James Simpson (X) (Seal)
Wit: Patrick Graves, Andrew McIlwain Jr. Proved 27 Oct 1801 by
Patrick Graves.

Pp. 248-249: 19 Sept 1793, William Scarborough of Lancaster Co.,
    planter, to John Scarborough for Ł 40 sterling, 200
acres, part of 2869 acres granted to John Marshall, 1 Jan 1789
adj. John Faulkenburgh, on Great Lynches Creek, Henry Faulkenburgh
...   Wm. Scarborough (Seal)
Wit: Thomas Kirkley, George Kirkley. Proved by Thomas Kirkley,
7 March 1804.

BOOK F

Page 249: 1 Nov 1803, Joseph Bredin of Madison County, Kentucky,
          to brother in law James Anderson of Lancaster Dist.,
power of attorney to purchase 100 acres on N side Cedar Creek adj.
Robert Bell...   Joseph Bredin (Seal)
Wit: Jesse Vanwinkle, Eliazer Alexander. Proved by E. Alexander,
1 March 1805.

Pp. 249-250: James Adams of Lancaster Dist., to Andrew McIlwain
             of same, for $130, 100 acres granted to William
Adams Jr., 4 May 1775 on Turkey Quarter, branch of Berkleys Creek,
sd. William Adams willed to Rosey, Wm. Frances & John Adams,
and sd. James...   1805.   James Adams
Wit: John Scott, William Barkley. Proved by William Barkley, 5
Aug 1805.
Agnes Adams, wife of James, relinquished dower, 5 Aug 1805.

Page 250: 2 Nov 1805,Arther Cuningham of Kershaw District, to
          Robert Cunningham of Lancaster Dist., for $1500, 200
acres on both sides Cedar Creek adj. land that Henry Hudson now
lives on, granted to Adam Thompson, __ March 1771.
                                   Arter Cuningham (Seal)
Wit: John Gooch, William Stover. Proved by William Stover, 4 Nov
1805.

Pp. 250-251: 19 Oct 1803, Jesse Roper Jr. and wife Hannah of
             Lancaster Dist., to Jane Avent, for $40, 20½ acres.
                                   Jesse Roper Junr (Seal)
Wit: Thomas Pair (T),   Hannah (X) Roper (Seal)
     Edward Shepard (X).
Proved by Thomas Pairs, 21 Jan 1804.

Page 251: 1 Nov 1805, Edward Kennington of Lick Creek, waters of
          Flat Creek, Lancaster Dist., planter, to David Johnston,
formerly of Flat Creek, for s 10 sterling, 2 acres, the upper part
of his new survey whereon John Baker now lives, the house & stables
...   Edward Kennington (X) (Seal)
Wit: Edward Terrell, John Baker. Proved by John Baker, 4 Nov
1805.

Pp. 251-252: 28 Nov 1804, John Welsh of Lancaster Dist., planter,
             for $70 to David Johnston of same, 350 acres lying
on double branch, waters of Flat Creek... John Welsh (Seal)
Wit: Harrison Baird, Burrel Welsh. Proved by Burrel Welsh, 28
Nov 1804.

Page 252: 6 Oct 1804, Lewis Kirk & wife Polly of Lancaster Dist.,
          planter, to William Tomlinson of same, planter, for
$400, 50 acres conveyed from John Brown, and part of tract from
John Sheper (sic), adj. Jane Young, on road leading from Joseph
Douglas's former place to John Drennens old place, and on Thomas
Drennon's spring branch...   Lewis Kirk (Seal)
Wit: John Tomlinson,   Mary Kirk (X) (Seal)
     Charles Miller, Jereh. Cureton.
Proved by John Tomlinson, 3 July 1805.

Pp. 252-253: 22 Sept 1804, Richard Elkins of Lancaster Dist.,
             planter, to William Vallandingham of same, 1/2 of
340 acres granted to John Tagon(?), by a resurey reduced to 285
acres, waters of Haning Rock, Lynches Creek adj. James Trible,
John Craton.   Richard Elkins (X)
Wit: Zach Ellis, Daniel McDonald. Proved by McDonald, 5 Nov 1805.

BOOK F

Page 253: 22 Sept 1804, Richard Elkins of William Vallandingham
for $50, 50 acres part of grant to John Craton, conveyed
to James Caston, to James McClure, to Richard Elkins....
(same signature and witnesses)

Page 254: Henry Oram Junr of Lancaster Co. bound to Henry Oram
Senr, father of Henry Oram Junr, for Ł 100...to keep
him from want during his natural life, tract of land of 100 acres,
26 March 1795.   Henry Oram (C) (Seal)
Wit: Joseph Coile. Proved 28 Feb 1801, before Jas Douglas, J. P.

        S. C. Lancaster District: Richard Springs to son Ely, negro
boy Ben 7 years old, and Dame(?) 5 years old; to daughter Margaret
2 negroes Philis 5 years old and George 4 years old; to daughter
Harriot, negro boy Charles 3 years old; when said children are
of age, 21 August 1805.   Richard Springs (Seal)
Wit: Andw Springs, Fredrick Dinkins.

        Richard Springs to daughter Jean, 2 negroes Mime aged 13 years,
and Nelly 3 years old; to daughter Sophia, 2 girls Penny 8 years
old and Lucy, 6 months old; when said children are of age, 21
August 1805. Wit: Andw Springs, Jno Springs.

Page 255: Patrick Graves and wife Elizh., give interest in a tract
I purchased by recorded bond from James Bredin of
Cedar Creek, for giving up a bill of sale for negroes, in Mr.
Matthews hands...19 Aug 1805.   Pat Graves
                                      Elizabeth Graves
Wit: Wm Brown, Charles Paley(?), James Anderson. Proved by James
Anderson, 17 Feb 1806, before Ebenr. Elliott, J. P.

Pp. 255-256: Recd of John Kenedy, the full amount of our part of
a tract of land originally held by Felix Kenedy,
passing into the hands of John Kenedy senior & at his death fell
to us the heirs of his estate...10 Dec 1805. Agness McCain,
Margret Findly (X), Willm Perry, Mary Perry (X), Felix Kenedy,
Dorcas Kenedy (X).
Wit: George W. McGaughey, Banner Shields, Robert McCorkle.
State of Tennessee, Blount County: Proved by Banner Shields, 7
Jan 1806, before John Woods, J. P.
James Houston, clerk of Court of Pleas and Quarter Sessions of
said county, certify that Banner Shields is a J. P., 7 Jan 1806.

S. C., Lancaster Dist.: Archibald McCorkle by power of attorney
by Felix Kenedy of Clount Co., Tenn., and for $1450 pd. by John
Foster, sell 200 acres, the plantation formerly to Felix Kenedy
decd., adj. James Stephenson...10 Feb 1806. Archible McCorkle
Wit: J. McClenahan, Joseph McCorkle, John Foster Junr. (plat
included).

Pp. 256-257: William Nutt of Lancaster Dist., for $442 to James
Scott of same, 150 acres adj. Robert McIlwain, on
waters of Lynches Creek, on waters of Bear Creek on both sides
Rocky River road, conveyed to Joseph Caston, then to sd. Nutt...
7 Jan 1806.   William Nutt
Wit: John Johnston, Jno Scott.
Proved by John Johnston, 12 Feb 1806. Mary Nutt, wife of William,
relinquished dower, 6 March 1806.

Page 257: William Ezel of Lancaster County, for $200 to Elijah
          Philips of the Dist. of Lancaster, 328 acres adj.
Braders line, Eliazar Alexander, under a title & resurvey of two
tracts granted to Joseph Singleton of 2000 acres each....24 Nov
1804.   William Ezell (Seal)
Wit: John Myers, Alexr Bowen (X). Proved by John Myers, 30 March
1805.

Pp. 257-258: John Kenedy of Blunt Co., Tenn., appoint Archibald
             McCorkle of Lancaster Dist., attorney..to sell
tract in the Waxhaws, 4 Sept 1805.   John Kenedy (Seal)
Wit: Robert McCorkle, Robert M. Crockett.
Proved by Robert McCorkle in Lancaster Dist., 17 Sept 1805.

Page 258: 13 Feb 1797, Joseph Findly of Oglethorp County, Ga.,
          to Felix Kenedy of Craven County, S. C., for Ł 7
sterling, part of two tracts of 570 acres adj. John Foster and
Felix Kenedy decd., James Blair, which part of said lands I
fell heir to by the death of John Kennedy late decd of Lancaster
Co., S. C...   Joseph Findly (Seal)
Wit: John Davies, Robert Davies, William Davies. Proved by
Robert Davies, 9 Jan 1805.
[N. B. The use of the term of Craven County in the above deed
 is obviously a reference to the colonial county. By 1797 that
 term was anachronistic, as there was no Craven County after
 1785.]

Pp. 258-259: 10 Nov 1805, Thomas Cawthorn Snr of Lancaster Dist.,
             to John Cawthorn (Chewthorn) for $60...200 acres
on waters of lower Camp Creek, 20 acres sold by John Chewthorn to
Thomas Chewthorn Sr., 10 Feb 1804 adj. Hollis Trusdale...
Wit: Joseph Coile.   Thomas Cawthorn (Seal)
Proved 11 Nov 1805 by Joseph Coile.

Page 259: James Carrol of Moore County, North Carolina, for $1200
          to Duncan Patterson of same, 540 acres on S side Lynches
Creek, adj. Fuller, Falkenborough, & Scarborough...20 Oct 1805
                                        James Carrol (Seal)
Wit: John McIver, Allan Morison, John Buchan. Proved by John
Buchan, 7 Feb 1806.

Page 260: Andrew Faulkenberry of Lancaster Dist., planter to
          Oliver Massey of Carshaw [Kershaw] Dist., 100 acres
on hanging rock creek adj. Henry Horton, on the old road from
James Love's old place to linches creek....15 Dec 1804.
                           Andrew Faulkenberry (X)
                           Caronhappage Faulkenberry (X)
Wit: Readick Mosley, Joacom Faulkinbury. Proved by Readick Mosley, 4 Nov 1805.

    Francis Gibbins for $60 to Lewis Cook, 2 cows, one calf, 2
feather beds, etc...8 Jan 1806.   Francis Gibbins
Wit: J. Harford.   Susanah Gibbins (X)

Page 261: Jonathan Blackman of Lancaster Dist., for $150 to
          Bedford Garris, 60 acres part of 465 acres granted to
John Caston, conveyed to John Clark decd., & John Clark sold to
Blackman...and a tract bought by Sheriffs sale by sd. Clark,
granted to William Ferguson, 195 acres adj. Joseph Hail...23
May 1805.   Jonathan Blackman (X)
Wit: William Ward, J. P., Henry Shaver. Proved by Henry Shaver

Sr., 23 May 1805. Sarah Blackman, wife of Jonathan, relinquished dower, 25 Oct 1805.

Pp. 262-263: John Chesnut of Kershaw Co., planter for $402 to
          Richard Elkins of Lancaster Dist., 201 acres being
subject to dower of Eleanor, _____ Farrell, the said Stubby, late
Mrs. Farrall (this portion of deed is not clear), part of 350
acres granted to Thomas Lide, 2 Nov 1761 on Hanging Rock Creek,
on the main road from Camden to the Waxaws, adj. land granted to
William McKee, widow Ingram, John Ingram, conveyed to sd. Chesnut by Henry Hunter, Esqr., Sheriff of Camden District, 1 May
1788...30 June 1805.   John Chesnut (Seal)
Wit: Thomas Brown, John Cantey.
Proved by Thomas Brown, 13 June 1805, before Jas Brown, J. P.
(Plat included, shows widow Stubs house).

Page 263: Jordan Ashley of Lancaster Dist., planter, for Ł 8 to
          Andrew Faulkenbury of same, planter...100 acres, part of
534 acres, granted to sd. Ashley, adj. Hanerly Horton, on road
from John Love's old place...20 July 1801.   Jordan Ashley (Seal)
Wit: Wiley Horton, James Trusdel.   Sary Ashley (X) (Seal)
Proved by James Truesdel, 22 Jan 1805.

Pp. 263-264: 4 Feb 1797, John McCain and John Kennedy of Blunt
          Co., Tenn., & Mary Kennedy of Lancaster Co., S. C.,
to Felix Kennedy of Lancaster Co., for Ł 34 sterling, our part of
two parcels of land...   John McCain (Seal)
                              John Kennedy (Seal)
                              Mary Kennedy (X) (Seal)
Wit: John Davis, Robert Davis, William Davis.

Page 264: Thomas Douglas of Lancaster Dist., planter, for $900
          to Isaiah Thompson of same, land granted to Ralph Jones,
conveyed to John Douglas, to George Douglas, to Thomas Douglas
his son by his last will & testament adj. James Faulkner, George
Douglas, Baxter Thowar, John Brown...30 July 1805.
Wit: James Faulkner, John   Thos H. Douglas (Seal)
     Gettys, John Thompson.
Grace Douglas, wife of Thomas, relinquished dower, 13 Nov 1805.

Pp. 264-265: Alexander Carrol of Moore County, N. C., to Duncan
          Patterson for $200...200 acres on Flat Creek, 12
Oct 1805.   Alexander Carrol (Seal)
Wit: James Carrell, Allen Morison, John Buchan. Proved by John
Buchan, 7 Feb 1806.

Pp. 265-266: Martha White exx. & Hugh White exr. of the last will
          & testament of Joseph White, both of York Dist.,
for $840 to Revd. James W. Stephenson of Williamborough (sic)
Dist., S. C.,200 acres in Lancaster Dist., part of two original
tracts, 325 acres granted to Stephen White, 9 April 1753, & 400
acres granted to John Kennedy, 1 Feb 1768; the former conveyed
from Stephen White to Felix Kennedy, part of which Felix Kennedy
Sr. conveyed to John Kennedy Sr., 1 Sept 1771, which on the death
of John Kennedy fell to John McCain, Joseph Findly, John Kennedy,
Jr., Felix Kennedy and Mary Kennedy, and conveyed to Felix Kennedy
Jr., 4 Feb 1797, and said Felix 28 Oct 1799, plat certified by
James Massey, Oct 14, 1805, adj. John Foster...15 Oct 1805.
                              Martha White
Wit: Archible McCorkle,   Hugh White
Nat Stephenson, Joseph McCorkle.

Page 266: John Horton of Kershaw Dist., for $5 to John Paterson
of Lancaster Dist., 20 acres, part of 300 acres granted
to Daniel Horton, on waters of Hanging Rock Creek...7 June 1805.
John Horton (Seal)
Wit: William Chambers, James Hamilton.

Matthew Nutt for $5 to John Simpson, negro woman Sue about 35
years of age...   4 March 1806.
Wit: Andrew McIlwain, J. P.

Wm Bass of Hancock County, Ga., to Abraham Perry of Lancaster
Dist., for $315, negro wench Butt(?)...   Wm Bass
Wit: Thomas Lee

Page 267: Andrew McIlwain of Lancaster Dist., to Samuel Dunlap
of Lancaster Court House, for $250...100 acres on
springs of Rum Creek, granted to Sarah Bottoms, 11 Nov 1784,
conveyed to Thomas Pully, 10 March 1795, to sd. McIlwain, 16
April 1800...4 Sept 1805.   Andw McIlwain
Wit: Wm Ross, William How.
Margraet, wife of Andrew McIlwain, relinquished dower, 11 Jan
1806.

Pp. 267-268: 11 Jan 1804, Adam Heath of Chester Dist., to Peter
Vincent of Lancaster Dist., for $1000, land on
waggon road, 162 acres...   Adam Heath (X)
Lucy Heath (X)
Wit: Everard Curton, Jessey Heath, Thomas Curton.
Proved by E. Cureton, 12 April 1806. Lucy Heath, wife of Adam,
relinquished dower, 14 April 1806.

Page 268: Davault Funderburk of Lancaster Dist., for $150, to
Jeremiah Funderburk, land on N side Polecat Creek,
part of a grant to William Woods, for 200 acres, 100 acres;
29 July 1805   Davault Funderburk.
Wit: John Funderburk, Abel Funderburk.

Pp. 268-269: ____ 1806, John Cowsart & wife Mary to Hugh McCrorey,
by grant 15 July 1768 to sd. John Cowsart, 150
acres on branches of Gills Creek...   John Cowsart (Seal)
Wit: Robert Dunlap,   Mary Cowsart (X) (Seal)
David Montgomery, John McCrory.

Page 269: Recd of Andrew Johnston the surviving agent of the estate
of John Johnston, $331.57 for the copartnership of James
& John Johnston....13 March 1806.   Samuel C. Dunlap, O. L. D.
Recorded 21 April 1806.

Recd, 1 Feb 1806 of Benjamin Croxton, $425 for negro fellow Punch
...   Thos H. Wade (Seal)
Wit: Robert Barkley, Allen Croxton. Proved by Allen Croxton,
4 Feb 1806.

END OF VOLUME.

Page 1: John Holley to Jacob Holly, negroes Cato about 18 years
and Arey about 16 years old, for $400...5 May 1777.
Wit: Benjamin Holly,   John Holly (X) (Seal)
    Sarah Jones.
Proved by Benjamin Holly, 25 May 1777.

Pp. 1-2: S. C., Lancaster County, Jacob Holly of Lancaster Co.,
    to Richard Holley of Chesterfield County, negroes Cato
and Arey, left in possession of his father John Holley, and were
plundered and taken away from him in 1782, and carried to the
Indian nation...2 6 May 1806.
Wit: Benjamin Evans, Zachariah Holly. Proved by Benjamin Evans
in Kershaw District, 26 June 1806, before William Cato, J. P.

Pp. 2-3: Jordan Ashly of Lancaster, planter, for $130 to John
    Graham, of same, planter, 100 acres, part of 434 acres
granted to sd. Ashly, 5 March 1792, adj. James Corr, 9 Feb 1803.
Wit: Andrew Falkenberry (X).   Jordan Ashly
    Robert Ashly.   Sary (X) Ashly
Proved by Robert Ashly, 25 Feb 1803, before John Ingrem, J. P.

Pp. 3-4: Robert Dunlap of Lancaster Dist., planter,to Samuel C.
    Dunlap, physician, for $914...209 acres on Cane Creek, 6
May 1806.   Robert Dunlap (Seal)
Wit: Wm Ross, Robert D. Montgomery, Samuel Dunlap.
Mary, wife of Robert Dunlap, relinquished dower,16 May 1806,
before William Ross, J. Q. Proved by Wm Ross, before Jno Simpson.

Pp. 4-5: 28 Dec 1778, Gilbert Kennedy & wife Sarah of Craven Co.,
    S. C., to Amos Richard, for Ł 100, 100 acres granted to
sd. Kennedy, 23 June 1774...   Gilbert Kennedy (Seal)
Wit: John Davies,   Sarah (X) Kennedy (Seal)
    Samuel Burnet, Felix Davis.
Proved by John Davies, 8 Oct 1779 before John Gaston, J. P.

Pp. 5-7: 15 Dec 1766, William Hall of Roan (Rowan) County, N. C.,
    farmer, to John Barkly of Craven Co., S. C., in the Waxhaw
Settlement, by north patton, 24 Sept 1754, to sd. William Hall,
300 acres...   William Hall (Seal)
Wit: John How, Samuel Dunlap, John White.
Proved by John Howe, before John Cantzon, J. P.

Pp. 7-8: 20 July 1795, Gustavous Rape of South Carolina, Lancaster
    Co., to Henry Kee, of same, for Ł 12 s 6, part of a
granted 15 July 1795 in little Cedar Creek, 149 acres...
Wit: J. Holliman, Coonrod Aron,   Gustavous Rape (X)
    James McDonald.
Proved by Coonrod Aron, 8 Oct 1796, before John Welsh.

Page 8: William Tomlinson, and wife Polly of Lancaster Dist.,
    planter, to Nathan Tomlinson, land adj. Charles Miller,
Jane Carns, George Wren, William Anderson... William Tomlinson
Wit: Robert Hancock, Clem Hancock,   Polley (X) Tomlinson.
    William Hancock. Proved by all three wit., 25 Jan 1804,
before Saml. C. Dunlap, J. P.

Pp. 8-9: Gilliam Ezell of Lancaster Dist., for $112 to Demsey
    Haile, 150 acres, part of two surveys on Lick Creek,
granted to Grace Crow, 18 Dec 1805...   Gillian Ezell (Seal)
Wit: Moab Stevens, Dudley Haile. Proved by Dudley Haile, 8 April
1806 before Saml Caston, J. P.

BOOK G

Pp. 9-10: 17 May 1797, William Barnet of Chester County, late
          sheriff of Lancaster Co., to Eleazar Alexander, of
Lancaster Co., whereas Joseph Singelton, late of Lancaster co.,
aws seized of land on Wild Cat Creek, 2610 acres, part of 4000
acres granted in two grants, adj. Jacob Kern, Genl. Sumter, James
Braden...sd. Singelton became indebted to James Person, late of
Camden...for Ł 14 s 15, land sold...   Willm Barnett (Seal)
Wit: John May, Alexr. Craig.
Proved by John May, 28 July 1806, before Benjn Boyd, city warden
of Charleston.

Pp. 10-11: S. C., Lancaster Dist: Nathaniel Stephenson, planter for
           $620 to James H. Witherspoon, land granted to James
Crow, 27 Nov 1770, the said Crow dying intestate, it being granted
to Grace Crow, wife of Thomas Douglass, 8 Nov 1793, lawful heir
of John Crow her father, adj. David Cowser, Hugh Wills, and 100
acres conveyed by John Foster to sd. Stephenson, granted to
John Hood...27 June 1806.   Nat Stephenson (Seal)
Wit: I. Dunnom, Wm. Howel (X), John Foster.
Elizabeth Stephenson, wife of Nathaniel, relinquished dower,
15 Aug 1806. Proved by Isaac Donnom, 16 Aug 1806.

Page 12: Richard Sessions of Lancaster District, for $174 to Henry
         Vallandingham of same, 100 acres on waters of Rum Creek,
granted to John Jacob Webber; by George Decker (Hecker?), the
legal representative of John Jacob Webber, to John Arnold Bender,
and by his last will & testament to George Carlisle Smith, then
to sd. Richard Sessions...20 Oct 1806.   Richard Sessions (Seal)
Wit: Edmund Raines, Jno Simpson. Proved by Edmund Raines, 20
Oct 1806.

Pp. 12-13: Mark & Winney Meacham of the District of Lancaster,
           planter, for Ł 49 s 8 d 4 sterling, to John Collier,
planter, 53 acres, part of 376 acres granted to Samuel Burnet on
N side Waxhaw Creek, on E side Catawba River, 3 Dec 1801.
Wit: George Wren,   Mark Meacham (X) (Seal)
Nathaniel Tomlinson (X),   Winnefred Meacham (X) (Seal)
Moses Heth.
Acknowledged by Mark Maecham, 8 Feb 1806.

Pp. 13-14: Alexander Wren & wife Mary of the dist. of Lancaster,
           for $151 to John Collier, planter, 41½ acres, part of
a granted to Saml Burnett adj. Thomas Vincent, the sd. John Collier,
& Winneyfred Wren hers being part of a tract conveyed to George
Wren to John Tomlinson, 4 Feb 1806.   Alexr Wren (Seal)
Wit: Guy Wallace, George Wren,   Mary Wren (X) (Seal)
     Clem Hancock. Proved by Guy Wallace, 8 Feb 1806.

Page 14: Lewis Kirk and wife Polly of Dist. of Lancaster, for $270
         to John Porter of same, planter, 60 acres conveyed by
John Shepherd, to Lewis Kirk, 6 Oct 1804.   Lewis Kirk (Seal)
Wit: John Tomlinson,   Mary Kirk (X) (Seal)
     Mary Davis, Rece Porter.
Proved by Rees Porter, 15 April 1806.

Pp. 15-16: James Bredin of Lancaster Dist for $1000 to Andrew
           McIlwain, land on both sides mouth of Cedar Creek, 389
acres adj. George Hayes, James Bredin, Jesse Vanwinkle, the
Catawba Company, plat 15 March 1803 for Patrick Graves...18 July
1806. Jas Bredin (Seal) Wit: Thomas Edwards, William McIlwain.
Proved by Thomas Edwards, 22 Aug 1806. Plat by Thos Archer, D. S.

166

Pp. 16-17: 31 Aug 1806: William Waller of Lancaster Dist., for
$100 to George Marler, land on NE side Cedar Creek,
Suck branch and cols. branch, part of a tract granted to Benedict
Best...   William Waller (X) (Seal)
Wit: Henry Horton,   Mary Waller (X) (Seal)
Thomas Johnston, Jessey Johnston (X). Proved by Henry Horton,
4 Dec 1806, before Jas. Douglas, J. P.

Page 17: George Maler for $180 to Thomas Cawthron Jr., both of
Lancaster Dist., land on N side Catawbaw River on waters
of Cedar Creek, Coles branch, part of a grant to Benedict Best,
and sold by Best to William Waller, then to George Marler, 31
Aug 1802, (see above deed), adj. William Howel, sd. Marler,
Wynn Twety, John Baker...4 Jan 1804. George Marler (Seal)
Wit: Wynne Twitty, Joseph Coile. Proved by Joseph Coile, 11
Nov 1805 before James Douglas, J. P.

Page 18: James Purdy of Lancaster, for $500 to Henry Vallandingham,
land on waggon road from Lands ford to Catawba River,
near Graves old fields, Barkley old mill road, Penders corner,
purchased from Francis Adams, 4 Feb 1800, and Henry Shaver, granted
to sd. Shaver 1 Oct 1787, and part of 100 acres granted to John
Graves, 5 Dec 1785, last conveyance to myself, 17 Jan 1797, also
part of 50 acres granted to myself 3 July 1797...5 Dec 1803
Wit: Elezar Alexander,   James Purdy (Seal)
      William Howe.
Proved by E. Alexander, 28 Oct 1806.

Page 19: William Adams by promissary note indebted to William
Taylor, for $446.15 payable 25 Dec 1807, mortgage negro
Rachel about 25 years old and son Tom near 3 years old...21 Aug
1806.   William Adams (Seal)
Wit: William Caskey, John Adams. Proved by William Caskey, 21
Aug 1806.

Page 20: John Voyles of Anson Co., N. C., exr. of the L. W. & T.
of James Holleman Jr. decd., agreeable to sd. will, I
was directed to sell tract in Lancaster Co., SC, part of 15,000
acres granted to Genl. Sumter, 2 April 1787, 200 acres...sold to
Aaron Arant, for $39 adj. Martain Smith, 15 June 1804.
Wit: James Holleman Sr.,   John Voyles (Seal)
      William Reaves (X). Proved by James Holleman Sr., 27 April
1805.

Pp. 20-21: 30 Dec 1805, William Hicklin Sr. of Lancaster Co.,
planter, to James Cole, for $400, 200 acres on Bare
branch, where William Hicklin Sr. now lives, adj. William Gibson,
Widow Addison, Zachariah Hicklin, Robt McDowls spring branch...
Wit: Hugh Hicklin,   William Hicklin (Seal)
      Zach Hicklin.   Sarah Hicklin (X) (Seal)
Proved by Zachariah Hicklin, 9 April 1806.

Pp. 21-22: 7 Dec 1803, David Laney to Reubin Wingate, both of
Lancaster Dist., for Ł 30, 100 acres on waters of
Wild Cat Creek surveyd by Wm Carson for James Harper, and conveyed
to Thomas Kelly, 10 Jan 1794....   David Laney (X) (Seal)
Wit: John Crowder, J. P., Milley Crowder (X).
Proved by John Crowder, 26 May 1805.

Page 22: 7 March 1804, Samuel Kerr of Sullivan County, Tenn.,
        planter, to James Ingram of Lancaster Dist., for $120,
150 acres on both sides Cedar Creek, a branch of Wateree River,
adj. Andrew Nutt, Cunningham, Thomas Cothian, John Hood, Clark,
granted to sd. Kerr 11 Feb 1773...   Samuel Kerr (Seal)
Wit: William Chambers, John Baker, James Ingram Junr.

Pp. 22-23: 10 Aug 1805, James Ingram of Lancaster Dist., planter,
        to Thomas Cothian of same, planter, for $2 per acre, 55
acres granted to Samuel Kerr, 11 Feb 1773, lying on Cedar Creek
(same land as preceding)...   Jas Ingram (Seal)
Wit: Jas. Bredin, John Cauthorn; ¨ Margaret Ingram (X) (Seal)
Wm Barrett. (plat included)

Page 24: 16 Feb 1805, Davolt Funderburk of Lancaster Dist.,
        planter, to Abel Funderburk of same, planter, for $300,
186 acres part of two gracts, one of 150 acres surv. for Funderburk 13 Feb 1772, on branches of Linches Creek which other part
he sold to Daniel Hunter; other tract of 36 acres, from tract of
Gen. Thomas Sumpter adj. Coonrod Plyler...Davolt Funderburk (Seal)
Wit: John Hancock, Henry Funderburk (X).

Pp. 25-26: 16 Sept 1806, William Ingram Sr. of Lancaster Dist.,
        planter, to William Robertson, for $840, 600 acres
adj. Kimbrels road, Hanging Rock Meeting House road, and lands
of James Ingram Jr., Countreman, John Stevens, Jordan Ashley, Amos
Horton, James Love Sr., John Bowers, Alexander Tombs, Giden Petty,
Samuel Love and Alexander Ingram.   Wm. Ingram (Seal)
Wit: Wm. Currey, John Ingram.
Jean Ingram, wife of William, relinquished dower.

Page 26: 16 Oct 1801, James Curtis of Lancaster Dist., to
        Edward Brumbelow of Chesterfield District, hatter, for
$200, 196½ acres on Wild Cat Creek being part of two surveyed of
2000 acres each, granted to Joseph Singleton, 6 May 1793, and
sold by execution to Eliezar Alexander and then to Curtis...
Wit: Hugh Blackney, Kader Gervin (X).   James Curtis (Seal)

Pp. 27-28: 4 July 1799, Abdon Alexander, Sheriff of Lancaster
        Dist., to James Douglass, for $10 all interest that
Bryce Miller has or had in several tracts, viz 1000 acres, 200
acres and 337 acres all lying in Turkey Quarter and sold to
satisfy a judgment obtained by James Huston of North Carolina
against Bryce Miller for debt.   Ad: Alexander, Sheriff
L. D. (Seal), Wit: John May, Elizar Alexander.

Page 28: 3 April 1806, James Cothran of Lancaster Dist., planter,
        to John Clanton of same, planter, for $62.50, 12½ acres
on N side Hanging Rock Creek...   James Cothran (Seal)
Wit: Rhodam Cole, Guilford Green Smith.

Page 29: 16 Jan 1806, Alexander Wm. McDonald, of Lancaster Dist.,
        planter, to James Cothran of same, planter for $125...
25 acres whereon McDonald lives in the fork of Hanging Rock
Creek and George Miller's Spring branch... Alexander Wm. McDonald
(Seal), Wit: Rhodam Cole, Gilfred G. Smith.

Pp. 29-30: 5 Feb 1796, The Sheriff of Lancaster County was comman-
        ded to levy of the goods of Rev. Bryce Miller, Ł 10
sterling which James Huston recovered against him for debt, and also
Ł 0 35 9 damages....Execution issued in York Co., for Ł 9, 1 Aug 1797.

Pp. 30-31: 7 Dec 1796, Abdon Alexander, Sheriff of Lancaster Co., to James Douglass for 30 silver dollars, 822 acres called Alexander Douglass' land on lower Camp Creek adj. Henry McIlwain, Turner Pace, William McGarrah, Joseph Coile, Bailey Fleming, Farril's Quarter, Adam Carnahan, Pender, Blair, said land sold to satisfy a judgment of Ł 10 sterling which Daniel Brown recovered against Alexander Douglass, and damages of Ł 4 5 6. Wit: Geo. Alexander, Eliezar Alexander.

Page 32: 24 Nov 1806, David Morrow of Lancaster Dist., to James Morrow of same, for $450, sold one negro woman Cloe and her negro child.   David Morros (LS)
Wit; Jonathan Coffey.

Pp. 32-33: 20 Sept 1803, John Baker of Lancaster Dist., to Mathew Hood of same, for $300, 200 acres on NW side Catawba River on Dry Creek, part of grant to Bailey Fleming Jr., 2 Aug 1784 adj. Samuel Nutt, George Marlow's spring branch, Joseph Coil...   John Baker (Seal)
Wit: James Oram, James Pritchard.

Pp. 33-34: 23 Dec 1806, John Barkley of Lancaster Dist., to Abraham Perry to satisfy a debt of $185, deeds three negroes wench named Beck, boy Nathan and boy Will...John Barkley (LS), Wit: Wm Ross, Robert Stinson.

Pp. 34-35: 8 Nov 1805, John Miller of Rutherford Co., N. C. to James Trusdel of Lancaster Dist.,for $60, 100 acres on Little Lynches Creek, granted 17 March 1775 by S. C....
Wit: Holinsworth Trusdel,   John Miller (Seal)
     Robert McAfa.

Page 35: Recd 24 July 1806 of James Anderson, $74 for negro woman Hager about 30 years old...   William Stevens
Wit: Arthur Hicklin.   Jean (O) (Stevens)

Pp. 35-37: 16 Aug 1806, William Ingrim Senr of Lancaster Co., to Elexander Ingrim of same, for Ł 30, land on south prong of Little Lynches Creek, part of 150 acres granted to William Welch...   Wm Ingram (Seal)
Wit: Samuel McClure, James Ingram.   Jean Ingram (Seal)
Proved by Samuel McClure, 13 Jan 1807 by Alexander Ingrem, J. P.

Pp. 37-38: 12 Aug 1806, William Ingrem Senr to his son James Ingrem, for Ł 30, 100 acres, part of 150 acres granted to William Welch, & Part of a grant to Wilm. Ingrem, adj. Wm. Ingrem Jr...   Wm. Ingrem
Wit: Saml McClure,   Jean Ingrem
     Alexander Ingram.
Proved by Saml McClure, 13 Jan 1807.

Pp. 38-39: John Parker of Charleston, merchant, appoints Robert Barkley of Winnsborough, as attorney for John Harford and George Dickinson, of London, merchants, by their power of attorney, 14 Sept 1797...9 Jan 1805.   Jno Parker (Seal)
Wit: Wm Wilkie Junior.

Pp. 39-40: Jessey Hodd for $400 to John King, 180 acres on waters of Lower Camp Creek adj. John Croxton, John Cawthorn, 23 Feb 1807...   Jesse Hood
Wit: Benj. Byram, Jas. Byram, Jos. Coile. Proved by Coile.

BOOK G

Pp. 40-41: George Wade of Daverson County, Tenn, for s 5 to James
            Cheves of Lancaster District, 150 acres granted to
Mary Kell, 7 Aug 1772 on NE side Cataba... ___ March 1805.
Wit: James Cheves Jr,   George Wade (Seal)
     Amelia Cheves (X), Mary Cheves (X).

Pp. 41-42: Edward Kennington of Lancaster District, for $800
            to Abraham Deason, 200 acres granted 7 June 1788 on
N side Flat Creek adj. John Baker, 19 Feb 1807.
Wit: Richmond Terrell,   Edward Kennington (X)
     Edmund Terrell.
Proved by Richmond Terrell, before Saml Caston, J. P., 20 Feb
1806.

Pp. 42-43: James McKown of Willson County, Tenn., for love and
            affection to sister Mary Nutt, wife of William Nutt,
of Lancaster Dist., one negro boy Peter about 16 years of age...
2 Jan 1807.   James McCown (Seal)
Wit: Joseph Johnston, George McCown. Proved by Joseph Johnston,
before James McKown, J. P., 3 Jan 1806.

Pp. 43-44: John Caston of Lancaster Dist., for $150 to William
            McDonald of Chester Dist., 100 acres adj. James
Moor, being a tract originally surveyed for sd. John Caston, 6 Nov
1767 and granted 16 Sept 1774...3 June 1807John Caston (Seal)
Wit: Charles Mackey (L), Fedrick Joyner (X).
Frances Caston, wife of John, relinquished dower, 3 ___1807,
before Wm. Currey, J. Q.   Proved by Charles Mackey and Fedrick
Joyner, 3 June 1807, before Wm. Currey, J. Q.

Page 44: Thomas Lee, Shff of Lanc Dist., appoint Abram Perry
         deputy (document not completed).

Page 45: William Adams of Lancaster Dist., by note of hand stands
         indebted to Francis Adams in the District of Caster (sic
for Chester), for $126.30...150 acres on Camp Creek, being the
plantation whereon Rosey Adams now lives adj. James Boyd, James
Wilson, John Strain...4 April 1807.   William Adams (Seal)
Wit; John Adams, Rosana Adams (X). Proved by Rosanna Adams,
13 May 1807 before Jn. Simpson, J. Qu.

Pp. 46-48: Samuel Balding of Lanc. Dist., by note of hand indebted
            to James Montgomery late of Chester Dist., for $88 payable
25 Dec 1807...sell to George Vickery Sr., 237 acres...11 Feb 1807
Wit: Jas Scott,   Samuel Balding (Seal)
     Samuel Balding Junr (S). Proved by James Scott, 3 Aug 1807
before Jno. Simpson, J. Qu.

Pp. 48-49: 8 May 1801, James McEwen of Rowan, Andrew Davis of
            Mecklenburg, and Henry Davis of Lincoln Countys, exrs.
of the estate of William Davis decd, to John Davis of the County
of Mecklenburg, both parties being of the state of North Carolina,
land in Lancaster County, S. C., on the waters of Waxhaw Creek
134 acres, now for $545....   Jas McEwen (Seal)
Wit: D. Beary   Henry Davis (Seal)
     John Sims(?)   Andw Davis (Seal)
     James Collins.
Proved by James Collins, 24 Oct 1806, before Wm. Woods, J. P.

170

Pp. 49-50: 15 April 1806, John Davis of Mecklenburg Co., N. C. to
John Steel of Lancaster Dist., John Davis and wife
Esther, for $540...land originally granted to William Davis,
on the dividing ridge between the Waxhaw Creek and Cane Creek,
adj. James Cureton....   John Davis (Seal)
Wit: James Collins,   Esther Davis (Seal)
     James Steel, Nath. Stephenson. Proved by James Collins,
10 Nov 1806, before Wm. Woods, J. P.

Pp. 50-51: George White of Lancaster Dist., for $650 to Isaac
Donnom of same, 129 acres on the Cataba River, part of
grant to Henry White Senr, adj. James White...29 Dec 1801.
Wit: Archibald McCorkle,   George White (Seal)
     Andw. Johnston, Andrew Linn.
Proved by all three wit., 31 March 1806, before Lamuel C. Dunlap,
J. P. Mary White, wife of George, relinquished dower, 24 June
1802, before John McClenahan, J. Q.

Page 51: William Harper of Lancaster Dist., for $200 to John
Keey of Chesterfield Dist., 200 acres on Wild Cat Creek,
waters of Big Lynches Creek, granted to John Harper...9 Sept
1805.   William Harper (W)
Wit: John Carns, Jacob Kern. Proved by John Carnes, 29 March
1806, before Jno. Crowder, J. P.

Pp. 51-52: Robert Stringfellow of Lancaster Dist., Blacksmith,
for $700, to John Robinson of Kershaw Dist.,planter,
170 acres part of 340 acres, also 76 acres, and another tract
of 14 acres, on waters of Hanging Rock Creek...__ Dec 1805.
Wit: Sherrod Sims Junr.,   Robert Stringfellow
James Croxton,   Margaret Stringfellow (X)
William Vallandingham (X). Proved by William Flandingham, 2
Oct 1806 before Alexander Ingrem, J. P.

Page 52: John Berry of Lancaster Dist., for $40 to Jonas Vick
of Lancaster Dist., 40 acres part of 100 acres granted
to Mary Campbel, 17 Oct 1767 in the Waxhaw Settlement...27 Feb
1806.   John Berry (X) (Seal)
Wit: Jon. Coffey, Hugh Coffey. Proved by Jonathan Coffey, 10
Nov 1806, before William Woods, J. P.

Pp. 52-53: 6 Aug 1806, Samuel Moses of Lancaster Dist., to Jacob
Vickory of same, for $220, land on N side Catawba
River, adj. a tract of land called Adams land, adj. John Carnahan,
Adam Carnahan; granted to James Douglass by patent, 1787....
                                          Samuel Moses (X) (Seal)
Wit: Samuel Douglas, William Stevens. Proved by Saml. Douglas,
6 Aug 1806, before Jas. Douglas, J. P.

Page 53: James Douglass of Lancaster Dist., for Ŀ 40 sterling to
Thomas Pender now deceased, now to Charlotte Pender,
Elizabeth Pender, Ann Pender & Patsy Burgess late Patsy Pender,
land on Rum Creek known as Shavers land,150 acres, adj. by lands
then the property of James Purdy(?), Edmund Raines, the Waggon
Road...4 Jan 1807.   Jas. Douglas (Seal)
Wit: Nathan Barr, J. P., Wm. Ross. Proved by William Ross, 8 July
1807, before Jno. Simpson, J. Q.

Pp. 53-54: S. C.,Lancaster & Kershaw Districts: Claudius Ingrem, of
Georgia, Burk County, for $30 to Alexander Ingrem of
Lancaster Dist., his part of Dowry of land of Mary Ingrem decd.,

the tract containing 440 acres on waters of Beaver Creek...4
March 1806.   Clauds. Ingram (Seal)
Wit: Richard Elkins (X), Wm. Claudius Ingrem. Proved by Wm. C.
Ingrem, before James Douglas, J. P., 13 June 1806.

Page 54: Alexander Galloway and William Galloway of York Dist.,
        for and in consideration of John Ushart helping William
Galloway to move over the Catawba River, 100 acres the land said
Ushar now liveth upon, on a branch of Gills Creek, Lancaster
Dist...11 Feb 1807.   Alexdr. Galloway (Seal)
Wit; William Galloway, John Rainey.   William Galloway (Seal)
Proved by Wm. Galloway, 25 Feb 1807, before Joseph Draffin, J. P.

12 Jan 1807, William Galloway to Sarah Moore, for $280, 238 acres
on a branch of Gills Creek being the land she now liveth on, by
plat made by Samuel Dunlap, granted to John Baker, 24 June 1774;
the other granted to William Galloway, 4 Aug 1788...Elizabeth
Galloway, the lawful wife of said William Galloway....
Wit: Alexdr. Galloway,   William Galloway (Seal)
     Thomas Niell, John Usher.   Elizabeth Galloway (O) (Seal)
Proved by John Usher, 31 July 1807, before W. Ross, Q. U.

Page 55: 20 March 1802(?), Mark Stevens of Lancaster Dist., to
        William Walker, for $500, 315 acres, part of grant to
Kennedy Bailey, 12 Aug 1797, adj. William Curry, Jesse Tilman,
George King....   Mark Stevens (Seal)
Wit: Saml. Johnston,Jeremiah Walker, Rebekah Walker. Proved
by Jeremiah Walker, 25 March 1802 , before Wm. Curry, J. P.

William Walker of Lancaster Dist., for $100 to John Dunnavant, five
head of cattle, one ox, one horse, etc...21 July 1807.
Wit: Wm. Curry, Jesse Moore.   William Walker (W) (LS)
Proved by Wm. Currey, 3 Aug 1807 before Jno. Simpson, J. Qu.

William Walker of Lancaster Dist., for $500 to John Dunnovant,
315 acres originally granted to Kennedy Bailey adj. William
Curry....21 July 1807.   William Walker (W) (LS)
Wit: William Dunnavant, Rebekah Walker. Proved by William Dunnovant, before Wm. Currey, J. P., 21 July 1807.

Page 56: 13 June 1807, John Hunter, planter, of Chesterfield
        County, to Michal Miller of Lancaster, for ₺ 5 sterling,
33 acres on Great Lynches Creek adj. Eliza Miller, John Cannington,
Barbara Miller...   John Hunter (Seal)
Wit: John Faile,   Milley Hunter (X)
     William Miller.
Proved by John Faile, 5 Sept 1807, before John Welsh, J. Q.

13 June 1807, Barber Miller, planter, of Chesterfield County, to
Michael Miller, of Lancaster County, 33 acres on Great Lynches
Creek, adj. John Kennington, Eliza Miller...
Wit: George Taylor (T)   Barbara Miller (11)
     John Faile.
Proved by John Faile, 5 Sept 1807, before John Welsh, J. Q.

Pp. 56-57: Elizabeth Miller of Lancaster Dist., for $5 to Michael
           Miller, 228 acres on N side Lynches Creek, adj. Jacob
Miller, part of two surveys, one deeded by Benjamin Haile, the
other by Michael Miller...21 Sept 1806. Elizabeth Miller (X) (Seal)
Wit: John Faile, James McVey, Caty Faile. Proved by John Faile,
21 Sept 1806, before John Welsh, J. Q., 21 Sept 1806.

Page 57: Thomas Sumter of S. C., for Ƚ 8 s 10 to Coonrod Ployler, of Lancaster Dist., 85 acres, part of 15,000 acres granted to sd. Sumter 2 April 1787, admeasured to sd. Ployler by Saml Kelly, 25 March 1793....25 April 1795.   Thos Sumter (LS) Wit: Mary Belk, Martin Smith. Proved by Martin Smith, 25 Aug 1807, before Thos Nelson, J. P.

Thomas Sumter for Ƚ 21 s 14 sterling to Koonrod Ployler, 248 acres, part of 15,000 acres...   27 Sept 1793   Thos Sumter Wit: Mary Belk, Martin Smith. Proved by Martin Smith, 25 Aug 1807, before Thos Nelson, J. P.

Page 58: John Collier and wife Mary of Lancaster Dist., planter, to William Porter, of same, planter, for $300, one tract of 53 acres, part of 376 acres granted to Richard Burnett, on N side Waxhaw Creek, also 41½ acres, part of grant to Samuel Burnett, adj.Thomas Vincent and Winefred Wrenn...   John Collier (Seal) Wit: William Hancock,   Mary Collier (X) (Seal)
     Thomas Thrower, Peter Watts. Proved by William Hancock, 30 May 1807, before Samuel C. Dunlap, J. Q.

Pp. 58-59: S. C. Lancaster Dist: Peter Vincent, late of the dist. aforesaid, was in his life time and at the time of his death seized of a plantation on the N side Catawba River adj. lands of Andred Pickens, William Davis, and William Hood, granted to Samuel Dunlap, 23 Feb 1754, 313 acres, and sd. Peter Vincent departed this life intestate leaving Ann Vincent, Edmund Vincent, Henry Vincent, Peter Vincent, Thomas Vincent, William Vincent, Rebecca Vincent and Edmund Williamson heirs at law, and whereas Thomas Vincent petitioned the associate Justices of the court of common pleas October 1807 to grant a writ of partition...Ann Vincent the widow shall have her third part....Thomas Lee, sheriff sold to Henry Vincent, __ Aug 1807.   Thomas Lee (LS) Wit: William Ross, Saml. Dunlap. Proved by Wm. Ross, before William Barkley, 19 Sept 1807.

Page 59: James Orum of Lancaster Dist., to William McIlwain, for $480, 130 acres granted to Charles Barber, 6 Feb 1792, on a branch of Dry Creek a prong of Camp Creek adj. William Isom, William Stubbs, John Baker, Charles Barber, Bailey Fleming... 2 Oct 1806.   James Orum (Seal) Wit: Eliezar Alexander, John Best (X). Proved by Eliezar Alexander, 6 Nov 1807 before Wil. Ross, J. Q.

Pp. 59-60: Charles Barber, planter, of Kershaw Dist., for $85, to Rolly Weaver, planter of Lancaster Dist., 100 acres part of 775 acres granted to sd. Barber, adj. William Walker, Arthur Ingrem, Col. Linton...24 Jan 1805. Charles Barber (Seal) Wit: Saml Dunlap, William Cauthorn, Federick Joiner. Proved by Saml Dunlap, 6 Nov 1807 before Wm. Barkley, J. P.

Page 60: This day came Richd Sessions who being duly sworn saith that in an affray between James Denton and John Musten, the John Musten lost part of his left ear....12 Dec 1807.
     I do hereby certify that James Denton did this day come before me and acknowledge that in the affray between him and John Mustin in the month of November last, Mustin lost part of his ear in which I have been the cause.   James Denton Wm. Ross, Q. U.

Pp. 60-61: S. C. Lancaster Dist.: Whereas Richard Cowsar the elder
in his life time and at the time of his death was
possessed of a certain tract on Gills Creek formerly Craven County
now Lancaster Dist., 400 acres, and the said Richard Cowsar by his
L. W. & T. dated 1 Oct 1779 bequeathed to Richard Cowsar son of
Nathaniel Cowsar, 100 acres of sd. tract, to be taken off the
from James Cowsars sons land, now, Nathaniel Cowsar, acting exr.
of sd. will, to sell to sd. Richard Cowsar sd. 100 acres...28
Jan 1807...   Nathaniel Cowsar (Seal)
Wit: Wm. Ross, Saml. Dunlap. Proved by Wm. Ross, 2 Feb 1807,
before Jno. Simpson, J. Q.

Pp. 61-62: William Marlow Senr. of Lancaster Dist., for love to
Mary Johnson, my daughter wife of John Johnson, land
on Camp Creek on NE side Catabaw River...2 March 1805.
Wit: Henry McIlwain,   William Marlow (X) (Seal)
Joseph Coil.
Proved by Henry McIlwain, 9 Feb 1807, before Wm. Currey, J. Q.

Page 62: William Robinsons ear mark for his stock an half crop
in the left ear and a slit in the right ear.

Pp. 62-63: John B. Davies, Preacher of the Gospel of Chester Dist.,
for $375 to William Robinson of Lancaster Dist., land
on both sides Camp Creek, Waxhaw Settlement, 120 acres, granted
to John B. Davies, 1796...29 July 1806.   John B. Davies
Wit: James Gill, John Miller. (Plat included shows land sold
to Stephen Gamble, land of John Montgomery). Polley Davies, wife
of John B. Davies, relinquished dower, before Geo. Gill, J. Q.
for Chester County, 29 July 1806. Proved by James Gill, 29 July
1806, before Geo. Gill, J. Q.

Page 63: Recd from Grace Ferrel, $300 in full for a negro woman
Lucy and her child Sam...20 Feb 1807.
Wit: Thomas Welch, Richard Rutledge.   William Narrimore (X)
Proved by Richard Rutledge, 8 May 1807, before Saml Caston, J. P.

Pp. 63-65: James Ferrell of Lancaster Dist., to Mary Shingleton,
widow of same, for $40 of a note of hand, two beds,
household furniture, cattle, horses, etc...5 March 1808.
Wit: John Ingram Junr.,   James Ferrell (Seal)
Cordner Ingrem.
Proved by both wit. before Alexr. Ingram, J. P., 5 March 1808.

Pp. 65-66: James Hogg of York Dist., for $660 to Walcot Evans of
Chester Dist., 330 acres in the Dist. of Lancaster,
adj. Robert Davis, the late William Taylor...1 Aug 1807.
Wit: Nancy Bates. Proved in York Dist,   James Hogge (Seal)
before Jno. Bates, J. Qu.
Plat included shows land adj. William Simpson, by Saml Dunlap,
D. S.,29 Dec 1806.

Pp. 67-68: Thos McDow of Lancaster Dist., for $40 to William
Ferrell of same, 20 acres in Lancaster Dist., adj.
sd. McDow and Ferrell, 9 Nov 1801.   Thomas McDow (Seal)
Wit: John Cantzon, Henrietta Lee, Richard Graves. Plat included.
Elizabeth McDow, wife of Thomas, relinquished, dower, 24 Jan 1803.
Proved by John Cantzon, 9 Nov 1801, before Jos. Lee, J. Q.

Pp. 68-71: 18 Nov 1771, Thomas Harrington of Craven County, S. C.,
to Andrew Nut of same, for Ł 300 S. C. currency, 150
acres on Cedar Creek, ½ of tract granted to sd. Harrington, 25
June 1771...   Thomas Harenton
Wit: Zedn. Gibson   Sarah Harrinton (+)
     Elijah Clark (X)
     Hannah Clark (H)
Proved in Wilks County, Georgia by General Elijah Clark, 26 Feb 1791,
before Tho. C. Russell, J. P.

Pp. 72-73: 10 Sept 1806, Samuel Nutt of Lancaster Dist., to Henry
Hudson Senr of same, for $650, land on Ceder Creek,
300 acres granted to Thomas Harrington, 25 Jan 1771, divided
in two parts, and was conveyed to Andrew Nutt Senr....
Wit: Jos Coile, John Hood.   Samuel Nutt (Seal)
Proved by both wit., 10 Sept 1806 by Wm. Currey, J. Q.

Page 73: Elizabeth Cowsar Exx of David Cowsar decd., of Lancaster
Dist., for $450 to William McKenna of Lancaster Dist.,
½ of all lots and houses that was the property of David Cowsar
belonging to the late firm of James & David Cowsar, in Lancaster
Ville...4 Jan 1808.   Elizabeth Cowsar (Seal)
Wit: Wm. Ross, Samuel C. Dunlap. Proved by Samuel C. Dunlap,
before Wm. Ross, 4 Jan 1808.

Page 74: William McKenna of Lancaster Dist., for $440 to Eliza-
beth Cowsar, half of lots in Lancaster Ville...4 Jan
1808. Same wit.

Page 75: 3 March 1806, Hugh McManus to John McManus, a son of
sd. Hugh, for $100, tract on both sides of big linches
creek, in the county of lancaster and Chesterfield, 200 acres...
Wit: Richmon Terrell,   Hugh McManus (Seal)
     Edward Terrell. Proved by Richmon Terrell, 4 Aug 1808,
before Jno. Simpson, J. Q.

Pp. 75-76: 3 Nov 1800, Jackson Ligget of McLingburg (sic) Co.,
N. C., to Robert Welch of Lancaster County, for $100
land on both sides of Diesbanda smal prong of wild Cat Creek,
granted to Thos Neel, deeded from Neel to Christian Shy...
Wit: James Holliman,   Jackson Liggett (Seal)
     James Belk, John Rone (R). Proved by James Belk, before
Jno. Crowder, J. P.

Pp. 76-77: Samuel Cranshaw of Jackson County, Ga·., planter, for
$200 to Henry Horton of Lancaster Dist., planter, land
on waters of Dry Creek adj. Wm. McGarrak, James Rogers, David
Nelson, Robt Dukes, granted to Frances Boykin, 5 June 1786...
19 March 1807.   Samuel Cranshaw (LS)
Wit: George Hicklin, William Stevens. Proved by both wit, 19
March 1807 before Wm. Currey, J.P.

Pp. 77-78: Nimrod Pendergrass of Lancaster Dist., planter, for
$40 to John Pendergrass, half of tract willed to sd.
John and myself by my grand father John Powell, 17 Jan 1785, and
conveyed to him by Thomas Charlton, granted 3 April 1775 to
Thomas Charlton...17 Jan 1807.   Nimrod Pendergrass (Seal)
Wit: Nathl. Pendergrass, Philip Shewbart. Martha Pendergrass,
wife of Nimrod, relinquished dower. Proved by both wit, 17 Jan
1808.

Pp. 78-79: William McBride of Lancaster Dist., for $70 to Leonard
          Rush of same, 100 acres on E side of the main road
that leads to Rockey River, adj. Jacob Pliler, James Bredin, part
of grant to Joseph Shingelton, 19 Feb 1791, 856 acres, sold by
Wm. McBride...24 Aug 1805.   William McBride (LS)
Wit: Jacob Plieler, Joab Nelson, John Philips. Proved by Thos.
Nelson, 24 Aug 1805.

Pp. 79-80: James Gasten of Lancaster Dist., for $230 to Thomas
          Carson of same, 100 acres on head branches of Little
Linches Creek, granted 24 Aug 1770 to Jasper Rogers, & conveyed
to Richardson who died intestate and then conveyed by Enoch
Anderson, the lawful heir, to James Gasten, being the plantation
whereon sd. James Gasten now resides...12 Nov 1807.
Wit: John Clark (C), James Scott.   James Gaston (Seal)
No proof or dower.

Page 81: Whereas our Father Joseph McMeen decd. allowed Eliezar
          Alexander to use a land warrant of his, by which the
said Alexander obtained a grant for 26 acres dated 1 Dec 1794
on S side Cane Creek adj. sd. Alexander, John Mays, William Harper, James McIlhaney in the name of Joseph our father, and whereas
by his last will directed his exrs. to make titles for the same
or quit claim to the same in favor of the sd. Alexander...2 April
1803.   James McMeen Junr. (LS)
Wit: William McMeen   Joseph McMeen Junr. (LS)
     James McMeen.
Proved by James McMeen, 16 March 1808, before John Simpson, J. Q.

Pp. 82-83: 5 Jan 1808, Thomas Lee, Esqr. Sheriff of Lancaster
          Dist., to James Douglass of same, Esqr...whereas
Alexander Douglass was seized of a tract of 100 acres on both
sides Lower Camp Creek adj. lands granted to Samuel Lamp, John
Mackey; granted to William Carson, plat 23 Feb 1773, and sd.
Alexander Douglass became indebted to Ebenezer Elliot as admr.
of the goods and chattels of William Elliott decd., for $69.79
...sold for $111.   Thomas Lee, S. L. D.
Wit: A. Perry, John Gorrah. Proved by A. Perry, 23 Jan 1808.

Page 84: 3 Jan 1800, John Hood of Lancaster Co., planter, to Tho-
          mas Cauthorn, planter, for 8 Spanish Mill Dollars, land
on S side Rockey Creek...   John Hood (H) (LS)
Wit: Willm. Thomson, John Ingrem, Henry Hudson.
Proved 10 Nov 1807 by Henry Hudson, before Wm. Currey, J. P.

Pp. 84-85: 11 April 1788, Samuel Shy of Macklinburg Co., N. C.,
          to Jack Sion Ligit for Ƚ 50, land surveyed for Thomas
Neel, formerly Craven County, 150 acres on Dils branch, waters
of Pedee, adj. land granted to Jacksin Leget... Samuel Shy (LS)
Wit: John Belk, Darling Belk. Proved by Darling Belk, before
Jno. Crowder, J. P., 1806.

Page 86: Mary Brown, Extx and heir at law of Daniel Brown Esqr.,
          decd. of Camden, for $120 to Robert Cunningham, planter,
100 acres on Cedar Creek, adj. Robert Bratney, Adam Thomson,
Widow Summervell, sold by Sheriff of Camden Dist., as the property
of David Russell, and purchased by sd. Daniel Brown...10 June
1805.   Mary Brown (LS)
Wit: R. Brown, R. L. Champion. Proved by Richard Champion, __
Sept 1806, before Abram Blanding, J. P.

Pp. 86-87: John Simpson of Lancaster Dist., for $100 to William
McKenna of same, lot at Lancaster Court House, adj.
lot owned by James Douglass, Abraham Perry...9 April 1807.
Wit: Wm. Barkley, A. Perry.   John Simson (LS)
Proved by Abraham Perry, 9 April 1807, before John Simpson, J. Q.
Jane Simpson, wife of John, relinquished dower, 1 March 1808.

Page 88: Fredrick Karns, for $1000 to Daniel Shehan, my plantation
of 755 acres in four different tracts whereon I now live
150 acres surveyed 26 Oct 1784; 375 acres surveyed 9 Jan 1788;
150 acres surveyed for sd. Daniel Shehan, and 60 acres which the
sd. Frederick Kerns bought of James Holliman, part of 1500 acres
surveyed for Thomas Sumter, 2 April 1787...17 March 1808.
Wit: John Hancock, Nathaniel Bibbe.   Frederick Karns (LS)
Proved by Nathaniel Bibbe, 17 March 1808, before Jno. Crowder,
J. P.

Page 89: William Mothershead for $500 to John Graham, negro wench
Jude...14 Jan 1808.   William Mothershead (LS)
Wit: John Breeden, Robert McDowell. Proved by Robert McDowell,
before Nathl. Pendergrass, J. P., 30 April 1808.

Pp. 89-90: Alexander Black of Lancaster Dist., for $200 to James
Purdy of Lancaster Ville, merchant, tract on Hannahs
Creek of Gills Creek, adj. Adam Carnahan, Richard Cousart, Edmond
Hull, Ananias Black, John Barkley, Robert Kirk, 150 acres granted
to Ananias Black, and conveyed to Frankey Black his wife by will
and from her to Alexander Black, also a tract adj. to it, 30 acres.
4 Oct 1807.   Alexander Black (LS)
Wit: William Ross, John Richardson. Proved by Wm. Ross, 11 Feb 1807
before Jno Simpson, J. Q.
Isabella Black, wife of Alexander, relinquished dower, 11 Oct
1807, before W. Ross, Q. U.

Pp. 91-92: 14 No 1792, John Roper of Richmon County, N. C., to
Crenshaw Duke of Lancaster Co., S. C., for Ł 35...
250 acres on Sou. side Cataba River, being made over as a deed
of gift from his brother John Rogers(sic)...John Roper (Seal)
Wit: Micajah Crenshaw, Button Capel, Rober Duke. Proved by
Micager Cranshaw, 19 Dec 1797 before Jesse Tillman.

Pp. 92-93: Amos Horton and wife Sarah of Lancaster Dist., for
$400 to Thomas Chewthrow Junr., 186½ acres on waters
of Hanging Rock, part of tract granted to Thomas McMaster, 6 Feb
1773, on a line made between Amos Horton and John Stevens...15
Dec 1806.   Amos Horton (Seal)
Wit: Jos. Coile,   Sarah Horton (X) (Seal)
     Samuel Maddon (Maddox?) (X).
Proved by Joseph Coile, before Wm. Barkley, J. P.

Pp. 93-94: Fanny Black of Lancaster Dist., for $50 to Annecus
Neely of same, land on N side Hannahs Creek, whereon
I now live, 60 acres, part of tract of 100 acres granted to
Ananias Black 29 Sept 1772 adj. Robert Kirk, Edmond Hull, James
Craige, Jas. Purdey...25 Jan 1808.   Fanny Black (X) (Seal)
Wit: James McAteer, John Nelly (4). Proved by John Neely, 25
Feb 1808, before Jno. Simpson, J. Q.

Page 94: John Barkly of Lancaster Dist., is indebted to Abraham Perry
$185, negro boy wench Beck and boy Nathan, and boy Will...
23 Dec 1806. John Barkley (Seal), Wit: Wm Ross, Robert Stinson.

Page 95: Lodewick Thomson of Lancaster Dist. for $355 to Andrew
        McIlwain, two bay mares, beds & furnature, hoggs, etc...
9 April 1808.   Lodewick Thomson (L) (Seal)
Wit: Robert McIlwain. Proved by Robert McIlwain, 15 March 1808,
before Jno Simpson, J. Q.

Pp. 95-96: ___ 1803, 29 Sept, William Steel of Lancaster County,
        planter, to Jno. R. Marshall, for Ł 40...100 acres
granted to John Dunn, 1787 on Cedar Creek...   Wm. Steel (Seal)
Wit: Samuel McKenny, Joseph McAdams, Thomas Stewart (X), William
Watson. Proved by Thomas Stewart, 19 Dec 1807, before R. D.
Montgomery, U. Q.

Page 96: Frederick Karns of Lancaster Dist., to Daniel Shehane,
        horses, cattle, hogs, etc. 17 March 1808.   Frederick
Kerns, Wit: John Hancock, Nathaniel Bibbe. Proved by Nathaniel
Bibbe, 17 March 1808, before Jno Crowder, J. P.

Page 97: Rosey Adams of Lancaster Dist., stands indebted to Fran-
        cis Adams of Chester Dist., 126 dollars, payable 1 Jan
1809, mortgage horse, cattle, etc...5 Jan 1808. Rosey Adams (X)
Wit: William Adams, John Adams. Proved by John Adams, 11 March
1808.

Pp. 97-98: William McIlwain of Lancaster Dist., for $480 to Andrew
        McIlwain Junr, 130 acres granted to Charles Barber, 6
Feb 1792, on a branch of dry Creek a prong of Camp Creek adj.
William Isams, William Stubbs, John Baker, Charles Barber; granted
to Charles Barber, conveyed to George Marlow, to Elijah Pettey, to
Tignal Perry, to James Oram, to William Ilwain...2 Feb 1808.
Wit: Robert McIlwain,   William McIlwain (Seal)
        Mary McIlwain. Proved by Robert McIlwain, 15 April 1808,
before Jno Simpson, J. Q.

Page 99: Whereas the parties herein named have heretofore purchased
        lands adjoining each other to wit Eliezar Alexander a
plantation known as McIlhanys old place on Lands ford road and
Johnson, a plantation denominated Hall's old place consisting
of two adjoining tracts one granted to Jenet Patterson the other
to sd. Hall, two grants containing 300 acres eastward of the sd.
McIlhany tract, and these parties have agreed to a line...14 Feb
1808.   Eliezar Alexander (Seal)
Wit: John McClenahan, Thos Carsen. Proved by Thos Carsen, 31
May 1808, before John Simpson, J. Q.

Page 100: Same as preceding, John Simpson a plantation of 300 acres
        granted to Janet Patterson and James Hall, known as
Hall's old place...adj. Cudworth...14 Feb 1808. Jno Simpson (LS)
Wit: John McClenahan, Thos Carsen.

Page 101: John Barkley has given note of hand to pay Robert
        Barkley or order $205, 300 acres granted to William
Hall and conveyed to John Barkley Senr, and by will conveyed to
the present mortgagee...3 Feb 1808.   John Barkley
Wit: A. Perry.

Pp. 102-103: James Bredin of Cedar Creek, Lancaster Dist., did
        bargain to make a gift to daughter Mary Anderson who
was then a widow and in distress with an orphan little boy, 75
acres of land on Tyres (Tyces?) branch of Cataba river, and now
being called upon by the Mary Anderson and her present husband

James Anderson to make a deed to said orphan boy James Bredin Glaze my grandson, now James and Mary Bredin, to James Bredin Glaze, 2 May 1807, 75 acres on Tyces branch adj. George Hays.... Jas. Bredin (LS), Mary Bredin (LS), Wit: Jesse Vanwinkel, Anne Vanwinkel. Proved by Jesse Vanwinkel, 10 Nov 1807, before Wm. Barkley, J. P.

Pp. 104-105: Whereas James Bredin Glaze a minor and orphan sur-
            vived into the 17th year of his age and does with
the advice of his grand father who is intended to be his guardian...
the said orphan's mother Mary Bredin Glaze, widow, did obtain a
bond from James Anderson her intended second husband for ₤ 41
15 4 ster, 2 March 1801 which sum was the orphans share of the
notes of the vendue of his father estate.... James Anderson (LS)
Wit: Jesse Vanwinkel.   Mary Anderson (LS)

Pp. 105-106: Charles Mesho of Lancaster Dist., farmer, for $26
            paid by James Johnston farmer, of same, 100 acres
granted to Samuel Johnston, 1 Dec 1794, then part of sd. survey
was conveyed to Jess Mesho, by deed 27 June 1798, 250 acres,
then part of sd. 250 acres was conveyed from Jesse Mesho to
Henrey Love, then to James Johnston, 100 acres adj. Edmon Hull,5
Aug 1806.   Charles Mesho (Seal)
Wit: Wm. Ingrem, James Ingrem.   Elizabeth Mesho (X) (Seal)
Proved by James Ingrem, before Alexander Ingrem, J. P., 13 Jan
1807.

Pp. 106-107: 13 Jan 1807, John Robertson of County of Lancaster
            to Gayden Pettey of same, for $750, 125 acres part
of 170 acres, laid out for John Haggins, 1 July 1784 adj. Wade...
Wit: Robt Goldsberry,   John Robertson (6) (Seal)
    Thomas Hilliard.
Proved by Robert Goaldsberrey, 6 June 1807, before Alexander Ingrem,
J. P.

Pp. 107-108: Alexander Duglass of Lancaster Dist., for $100 to
            Thomas Mackey, planter, part of a tract granted to
Alexander Duglas, 25 March 1784 or 1785, on S side Camp Creek
on Wates branch, on a grant to Hennery Clark...29 June 1807.
Wit: John Hagon, Saml Dunlap.   Alexander Douglas (Seal)
Proved 28 Dec 1807 by Samuel Dunlap, before Wm. Barkley, J. P.

Page 108: John Murfey of Lancaster Dist., for $16.41 to James
          Blackman, all the intrest or title in or to any
execution in Lancaster Dist. Sherifs office of which is Gibs
Lamb vs. John & Joseph Caston....7 Sept 1801. John Murfey (+).
Wit: Elir. Alexander, William Hustan.

Pp. 108-109: Mary Cousart & James Cousart of Lancaster Dist.,
            to William Taylor, planter, for $723, 11 Aug 1807,
bond to make title to tract of 145 acres on Gills Creek.
James Taylor, James Hood, wit.   Marey Cousart (LS)
Proved by James Taylor, 9 Dec 1806,   James Cousart (LS)
before Wm. Ross, Q. U.

Pp. 109-110: S. C., Lancaster Dist: William M. Nelson indebted
            to John Adams and Rosana Adams, for $496, 12 April
1808, bond for all kinds of demands, costs and charges for and on
account of a certain Eligitimate Bastard child of sd. Elizabeth
Nelson, wife of William M. Nelson, and formerly called Elizabeth
Barten, which said Bastard child is named and called Leander Adams,

and is the reputed son of sd. John Adams...   William M. Nelson (X)
Wit: John Barkley, Hugh McCrorey.   Elizabeth Nelson (ℓ)
Proved by John Barkley, 17 June 1808,   John Adams (LS)
before Jno Simpson, J. Q.

Page 110: Dunning Kesiah of Lancaster Dist., for love to my step
          son William Webb, one feather bed & furniture, cups and
saucers, one chest, 1 dozen of Delf plates, etc...20 Oct 1807.
Wit: Saml Dunlap.   Dunning Kesiah (LS)
Proved by Samuel Dunlap, __ Oct 1807, before Wm.Ross, Q. U.

Pp. 110-111: William Tomlison and wife Cattey of Lancaster Dist.,
             to Churchil Anderson of same, 50 acres, being a tract
from Brown and part of a tract from John Sheperd to Lewis Kirk,
on the road leading from the place where Joseph Duglass formerly
lived to John Drennes auld place...18 Jan 1806.
Wit: Jas Ellot,   Wm Tomilinson (LS)
     Jesse Fincher,   Cathrine Tomilinson (X) (LS)
     James McCorkile.
Proved by James McCorkel, 11 Aug 1806 before Jno Simpson, J. Q.

Page 111: S. C., Lancaster Dist: Henry Valandingham and Agnes
          Valangdingham of Lancaster Dist., for $500 to Isaac
Donnom of same, negro wench Sarah aged 22 and negro boy Bob of
age of 3 months...5 March 1806.   Henry Valandingham (LS)
Wit: Wm. Ross,   Agnes Valandingham (X) (LS)
     James Cousar.
Proved by James Cousar, 5 March 1806, by Wm. Ross, J. Q.

Pp. 111-112: 6 Aug 1800, John Doby of Lancaster Dist., to John
             Brown of same, for $200, land in the Waxhaws on the
waters of Cain Creek, 200 acres, adj. James Moor, George Day(?),
Alexander Nesbit, originally granted to John Greer, 15 March
1771, and conveyed to John Doby 19 Nov ____.   John Doby (LS)
Wit: Alex Carns, Joseph Baker, Samuel Baker. Proved by Samuel
Baker, 14 July 1807 to Jno Nesebit, J. P.

Pp. 112-113: Lodwick Thompson of Lancaster Dist., for $150 to
             Andrew McIlwean of same, 200 acres at the Waggon
Road near Mary Watson, adj. George Currey, near to where Solomon
Smith raised a house, along the road known by McDonalds Road,
part of a grant to James Duglas, 966 acres, 1787...26 Sept 1807.
Wt: Wm Ross, Elias Caston.   Loddwick Thompson (L) (LS)
Proved by Wm Ross, 10 Nov 1806 before Jno Crowder, J. P.

Pp. 113-114: Jonas Vick of Lancaster Dist., for $50 to John
             Hisbet, 51 acres on waters of Cain Creek, Lancaster
Dist., part of two diffrent survays of land, first granted to
Thomas Walker, 7 March 1767, the other to Marey Cambel, 3 July
1767....6 June 1806.   Jonas Vick (LS)
Wit: James McAteer, George A. Nesbett. Proved by James McAteer,
27 Nov 1806, before Wm. Woods, J. P.

Pp. 114-115: John May of the City of Charleston, for $175 to
             Thomas Lee, Esqr.,Sheriff of Lancaster Dist., 145
acres on both sides Cain Creek adj. Joseph and Thomas Lee, adj.
land late John Cantzons, Elizar Alexander, and is the plantation
whereon Patrick Graves lately resided, surveyed by Stephen Gamble...
13 Sept 1806. .   John May
Wit: David Loughridge, Jno Simpson. Proved in Lancaster Dist.
by David Loughridge, 13 Sept 1806, before Jno Simpson, J. Q.

BOOK G

Pp. 115-117: William Taylor of Lancaster Dist., planter, for
              $225 to John Craig Jr. of same, planter, 100 acres
on waters of Camp Creek, part of a tract granted to James Sormer(?)
26 March 1755 and conveyed to Hugh Coffey decd., and from Henry
Coffey to Grace Taylor, and then by Grace Taylor's last will &
testament to William Taylor her son...7 Aug 1806. William Taylor.
Wit: John Gattys, James Taylor, Nathaniel Craig.
Sarah Taylor, wife of William, relinquished dower, 9 Dec 1806.
Proved by James Taylor, 9 Dec 1806, before Wm. Ross, Q. U.

Pp. 117-118: William Nutt of Lancaster Dist. for $450, 100 acres
              on a branch of Bear Creek, to Jacob Shofner...except
a small piece of said tract sold to Samuel Baldan whereon he now
lives, 10 acres...tract granted to George Campbell, conveyed to
Glass Caston, then to William Nutt...1 Oct 1806. William Nutt (Seal)
Wit: Elizabeth Shofner, James Scott. Mary Nutt, wife of William,
relinquished dower, 15 April 1807. Proved by both wit, 15 April
1807, before Wm. Currey, J. Q.

Page 118: Thomas Edwards late of Kershaw Dist., but now of Lan-
           caster Dist., for $20 to AbrahamPerry of Lancasterville,
yellow bay gelding about 9 years old... Thomas Edwards (Seal)
Wit: Eliezar Alexander, John Barkley. Proved by John Barkley,
8 Nov 1806, before John Simpson, J. Q. U.

Pp. 119-120: Andrew McIlwain of Lancaster Dist., planter, for
              $600, to Henry Shaver Senr., planter, of same,
tract on Rum Creek granted to Andrew McIlwain, 6 Dec 1757, also
a tract certified 8 Oct 1788...18 Aug 1806. Andrew McIlwain (Seal)
Wit: Wm. Ross, Thomas Edwards. Margaret McIlwain, wife of Andrew,
relinquished dower, 1 Sept 1806.

Pp. 120-121: John Brown of South Carolina, Montgomery County, for
              $725, to James Faulkner of Lancaster Dist., 285 acres
on west side Cane Creek, part of grant to William Moore, and
the whole of a tract granted to John Green, adj. Cane Creek...19
Feb 1807.   John Brown (Seal)
Wit: Saml Dunlap, Tho. Faulkner, Saml. Faulkner. Proved by Saml
Dunlap, 20 Feb 1807, before Wm. Ross, Q. U. Mary Brown, wife
of Rev. John Brown, appears before Maxwell Chambers and David Woodson, J. P.'s for Rowan County, N. C., relinquished dower.

Page 122: John Welsh of Wild Cat Creek, Lancaster Dist., planter,
           for $50 to Joseph Baker of Flat Creek, same dist.,
100 acres adj. Richmon Terrell, Elijah Baker, Abraham Hagler,
on the road that leads to David Thomsons old place...29 March
1806.   John Welsh Senr (Seal)
Wit: Benjamin Deason, George Fuller (X). Proved by Benjamin Deason,
29 March 1806.

Pp. 123-124: Robert Wilson of Lancaster Dist., for $150, to Hugh
              McMullin of same, tract on waters of Bear Creek,
200 acres adj. Amos Richards, Isaac Barr, granted to me 5 Sept
1790...5 Nov 1806.   Robert Wilson (Seal)
Wit: Saml Dunlap, James Clancy. Jane Wilson, wife of Robert,
relinquished dower 22 Nov 1806,before Wm. Ross, J. Q.
Proved by James Clancy, 22 Nov 1806, before Wm. Ross, J. Q.

Page 124: William Marler Senr of Lancaster Dist., for love and
           good will to Nancy Johnson, my daughter, wife of James
Johnson, land on Camp Creek, adj. Little Berry Champion, Garret

181

BOOK G

Branch...31 March 1808.   William Marler (X) (Seal)
Wit: John Marler, John Johnson. Proved by John Johnson, 9 May
1808.

Pp. 125-126: Middleton McDonald of Lancaster Dist., for s 5 ster-
            ling to James Cheves of same, planter, 300 acres
whereon sd. Cheves now liveth, adj. William McDonald, Danl Wade,
20 March 1805.   Middleton McDonald (Seal)
Wit: Thos H. Wade, James Cheves Junr., Wm. Richardson. Proved by
Thomas Holden Wade, 21 March 1805, before Wm. Barkley, J. P.

Pp. 126-127: George Wade of Daverson County, Tenn., for s 5
            to James Cheves of Lancaster Dist., 150 acres
granted to Mary Kell, 7 Aug 1772... __ March 1805.
Wit: Amelia Cheves (+), James Cheves Junr.   George Wade (Seal)
    Mary Cheves (+). Proved by James Chves Junr, 5 Feb 1807
before Jno Simpson, J. Q.

Pp. 127-128: Danl Wade of Richland Dist., for s 5 to James Cheves
            of Lancaster Dist., planter, tract of 300 acres
surveyed for George Wade, and granted to sd. Daniel Wade, 6
Aug 1792 adj. George Wade, Middleton McDonald, James Kell...
7 March 1805.   Danl Wade (Seal)
Wite; Benjn Boothe, James Cheves Junr.,Wm. McDonald.   Proved by
James Cheves, Junr., 5 Feb1807, before Jno Simpson, J. Q.

Pp. 128-129: Middleton McDonald of Lancaster Dist., for $50 to
            James Cheves, 13 acres adj. John Burden, being a
tract surveyed for Middleton McDonald Senr 19 Feb 179_...20 March
1805.   Middleton McDonald (Seal)
Wit: Thos H. Wade, James Cheves Junr., Wm. Richardson. Proved by
Thos H. Wade, 21 March 1805, before Wm. Barkley, J. P.

Pp. 129-130: Middleton McDonald of Lancaster Dist., to James
            Cheves, 150 acres adj. Thomas Houze, Fisher spring
branch, granted to Minor Winn 29 Nov 1785, conveyed to sd.
McDonald, 3 June 1797 ...20 March 1805.   Middleton McDonald (Sea
Wit: Thos H. Wade, James Cheves Junr., Wm. Richardson. Proved
by James Cheves Junr, 6 Feb 1807, before Jno Simpson, J. Q.

Pp. 130-131: Benjajin Johnson of Lancaster Dist., for $150 to
            Isaac Faulkenbury, 50 acres on branches of Flat
Creek, 7 Jan 1808...Benj Son (X) (Seal),
Wit: John Faile, John Faulkenberry. Proved by John Faile, 19
Feb 1808, before John Welch, Q. U.

Pp. 131-133: Whereas Patrick Graves late of Dist. of Lancaster,
            but now of State of Tennessee, was seized of a tract
of 45 acres adj. John Cantzon, Joseph and Thomas Lee, whereon
sd. Patrick Graves latest resided, originally surveyed for
Stephen Gamble...was indebted to John May, late of the village
of Lancaster but now of Charleston...Thomas Lee sells to John
May, 13 Sept 1806.   Thomas Lee, S. L. D. (Seal)
Wit: David Loughridge, Jno Simpson. Proved by David Loughridge,
13 Sept 1806, before Jno Simpson, J. Q.

Pp. 133- 134: Samuel Dunlap, merchant in the Dist. of Lancaster,
            for $600 to William Howe of same, 133 acres on Gills
Creek, where sd. Howe now resides,part of 302 acres granted to
Richard Cousar, 24 Sept 1754 adj. Nathan Barr, Robert Davis, and
the estate of Alexander Craig, decd., 9 April 1808. Samuel Dunlap

182

Wit: Wm. Ross, Nathan Barr. Proved by Nathan Barr, 8 April 1808, before Wm. Ross, Q. U. Elizabeth Dunlap, wife of Samuel, relinquished dower, 28 April 1808.

Page 135: William Massey of Lancaster Dist., for $225, to William Hood, land on waters of Cain Creek, 11 Jan 1806.
Wit: Alen Hood,   William Massey (LS)
     Joseph Massey. Proved by Allen Hood, 24 March 1808, before Joseph Draffen, J. P.

Pp. 135-36: James McAteer of Lancaster Dist., S. C., for $50 to William Hood, part of grant to James McAteer, 2 March 1801, 30 acres adj. William Woods, William Hoods...11 Jan 1806.   James McAteer (Seal)
Wit: B. Massey, Alen Hood, William Massey. Proved by Alen Hood, 24 March 1808, before Jos. Draffen, J. P.

Pp. 136-137: John B. Davies of Chester Dist.,Minister of the Gospel, for $582, to Stephen Gamble, planter of Lancaster Dist., 154 acres part of 274 acres granted to sd. John B. Davis, 1796, adj. John Johnston...6 April 1808. John B. Davies
Wit: James Gill, Mary Gill. Proved in Chester Dist., by James Gill, before Geo. Gill, J. Q. Polley Davies, wife of John B. Davies, relinquished dower, 6 April 1808.

Pp. 137-139: Agnes Nesbit, William Nesbit, John Nisbet, Alexander Nesbit, James Nesbit, Benjamin Nesbit and Joseph Nesbit, all in Lancaster County, are bound unto each other in the sum of Ł 500, 20 July 1791, to accept the final determination of John Craig Esqr., Robt Montgomery Esqr, John Kirk, John Lata, Robert Dunlap Esqr., Alexander Carnes, and John Craig, chosen to divide the estate...7 Nov (no year)....   Agnes Nesbit (*)
Wit: Richard Wright,   Wm Nesbit
     Robert Lockhart   John Nesbit
                                       James Nesbit
Proved by Robert Lockhart, 15 April   Benjamin Nesbit
1801, before James Jordan, J. Q.   Joseph Nesbit

Pp. 139-140: Above mentioned person divide the estate of Alexander Nesbit decd, adjudge it to be worth Ł 210...5 Sept 1791 Jno Kirk, Jno Craig Senr, John Craig, John Latta, Robert Dunlap, Robt Montgomery, Alexander Carnes.

Page 140: I have received from my Brother JohnNesbit full compensation...13 Jan 1794.   Alexander Nesbit.
Wit: Robert Montgomery, Robt White. Proved by Robt D. Montgomery, 7 March 1807, before Thomas Nelson,J. P.

Page 141: John Anderson of Lancaster Dist., planter, for $800 to Isaac Anderson, two negroes Ben and Sam...20 Feb 1800.
Wit: James Massy, George Wren,   Jno Anderson (X)
     Allethia Wren.
Proved by George Wren, 5 March 1808, before Saml C. Dunlap, Q. U.

Pp. 142-143: George Cresman of Flat Creek Lancaster Dist., for $700 to Amos Hough, planter, 275 acres, part of two adj. surveys 225 acres of Wm. Bre---, and 50 acres, part of grant to Eliza White...19 Sept 1805.   George Cresman
Wit: Benjamin Deason,   Elizabeth Christman (X)
     Joseph Hough. Proved by B. Deason, 30 Jan 1808, before Jno Crowder, J. P.

Page 143: Archibald Kell & Jennet Kell of Chester Dist., for
$168.75 to George Wade of Lancaster Dist., planter,
150 acres, being a tract granted to Mary Kell 7 Aug 1772... 8
March 1803.   A. Kell
Wit: John Joiner, Thos H. Wade.

Pp. 144-145: John Robertson of Lancaster Co., to Gayden Petty of
            same, for $750, 170 acres laid out for John Tagins,
21 July 1784...   John Robertson (X)
Wit: Robt Goldsberry, Thomas Hilliard. Proved by Robt Goldsberry,
6 June 1807, before Alexr. Ingrem, J. P.

Pp. 146-148: William McMeen of Lancaster Dist., for $1000 to
            Samuel Dunlap, Esqr., of Lancasterville, the whole
of the plantation whereon I now reside, and consisting of three
adj. parcels on Gills Creek and in the forks of Cain Creek, 256
acres, 120 acres as 2/5 of a distrubtive share of the real estate
of my father Thomas McMeen decd., who died during the operation
of the laws of primogeniture, and I as elder son; one other tract
of 61 acres part of 228 acres granted to Joseph McMeen decd., 1
Dec 1794, also 100 acres in the fork of Bear & Cain Creeks adj.
Robt Dunlap, Eliazar Alexander...20 Jan 1808. William McMeen (Seal)
Wit: Eliezar Alexander, Robt Dunlap. (Plat included). Proved
by Robert Dunlap, 9 July 1808.

Pp. 148-149: 24 March 1808, Lewis Hudson to James Hudson, for
            $400, 480 acres in two surveyes, one granted to
Thomas Glaze, for 250 acres 5 June 1797, then other for 200
granted to sd. Thomas Glaze 17 Jan 1799...Lewis Hudson
Wit: George Perry, Sarah Hudson (X).
Proved by George Perry, 11 April 1808, before William Currey, J. P.

Pp. 149-150: Reuben Wingate of Lancaster Dist., for $130, to
            Humphrey Higs of Lancaster Dist., land on Wild Cat
Creek, 100 acres, surveyed for James Harper, which he conveyed to
Thomas Kelly, 15 Jan 1794, transferred to David Leany, and then
to sd. Wingate...   Reuben Wingate (Seal)
Wit: Charles Cook (X), Stephen Cook. Proved by Charles Cook,
26 March 1808, before John Welsh, J. Q.

Pp. 150-152: 7 April 1808, William Valandingham of Lancaster
            Dist., to Johnathon Thompson, for $600, on persimmon
branch of Cedar Creek, adj. Archibald Hood, adj. Tarod Sims Senr...
                        William Valandingham (X)
Wit: John Stephens, Richard Bowers. Proved by John Stephens, 12
April 1808, before H. Hudson, J. P.

Pp. 153-154: 26 Nov 1794, Jacob Free son of one of the heirs of
            the estate of Jacob Free decd., of S. C., Hatter,
to Hugh McManer of Chesterfield County, for Ł 100, paid by sd.
Mark McManus, land on both sides Big Lynches Creek, 200 acres
conveyed to Jacob Freed decd by Thomas McManer, Mary McManer, &
James McManer....   Jacob Free (Seal)
Wit: Robert Walsh,   Mary Magdelin Free (X)
    Wm. Isom (X).
Proved by Robt Walsh, 5 March 179_, before James Blakeney, J. P.,
in Chesterfield District.

Pp. 154-155: John Byrom of Lancaster Dist., for $250 to Saml
            Duglass, cows, cattle, etc, 8 Jan 1808. John Byrom
Wit: Rush Hudson,Benjamin Tribble. Proved by Rush Hudson, 2 April
1808.

Pp. 156-157: Daniel Mattox of Lancaster Dist., to Samuel Duglass,
100 acres part of tract sold by Thomas Glaze to said
Mattox, where said Mattox now lives, for $79...   Danl Mattox (X)
Wit: Stephen Sims, James Maddox (X). Proved by James Maddox,
2 April 1808. Deed dated 11 March 1808.

Pp. 157-158: S. C., Chesterfield District: John Brown for $300
to Edward Bromelow of Anson County, N. C., land on
both sides Lynches Creek in District of Chesterfield and Lancaster,
granted to Thomas McManer decd., 1794, 100 acres purchased by
Charles MackManners of John Waver adj. James McDonald... John
Brown, dated 25 Aug 1802.
Wit: Edward Brumlelow, Samuel Duffey. Proved in Chesterfield
Dist. by Samuel Duffey, 23 July 1808 before Jas. Blakeney, U. Q.

Page 158: Davold Funderburk of Lancaster Dist., planter, for
$25 to Jesse Hays of same, sold tract on Pauteat Creek
...deed not completed.

Pp. 158-159: Thomas H. Wade by note of hand stands indebted to
Robert Barkley for $260...mortgate of negro Peter,
5 Jan 1807.   Thos H. Wade
Wit: Jno Simpson.

Pp. 159-160: Isaac Dunnom of Lancaster Dist., for natural love &
affection to daughter Jane Witherspoon and grandson
Isaac Dunnom Witherspoon and Sarah Crawford Witherspoon, and also
for $5 by William Ross, negro wench Sarah Tenah and Joe...13 Jan
1808.   I. Donnom (Seal)
Wit: Hugh McMullan, Saml Moore. Proved by Hugh McMullen, 5
Sept 1808, before Jno Simpson, J. Q.

Pp. 160-161: 21 Nov 1806, John Love of Lancaster Dist., to Amos
Horton of same, for $750, land on Little Linches
Creek (1) tract of 300 acres, part of 500 acres granted to Saml
Hammons (2) 150 acres adj. it...21 Nov 1806.   John Love (Seal)
Wit: Jas Ballard, Gayden Petty. Proved by Jas Ballard, 21 Nov
1806 before Saml Caston, J. P.

Pp. 161-162: John Love of Lancaster Dist., for $750 to Gayden
Petty, 150 acres on waters of Little Linches Creek,
granted 4 Nov 1762 to Robt Moore; also 150 acres part of 596
acres adj. Hammons, W. Ingrem, J. Countreyman, Harrison, Love,
J. Alexander & Jordan Ashley, also 175 acres part of 390 acres
granted to Saml LittleJohn decd., and willed to Roberson, adj.
land granted to Robt Swan...Nick Robinson, Barbary Kinney....
21 Nov 1806.   John Love (Seal)
Wit: Amos Horton, Jas. Ballard; 21 Nov 1806 proved by Amos Horton,
before Saml. Caston, J. P.

Pp. 162-163: John Edwards of Lancaster Dist., for $400 bond
18 Dec 1804; to make titles to land adj. John Croxton,
Gibs...   John Edwards (Seal)
Wit: John Bell, James Orum. Proved by John Bell, 12 April 1808,
before H. Hudson, J. P.

Pp. 163-164: William Mounce Junr of Lancaster Dist., was seized
of 228 acres on Hangin Rock Creek granted to William
Brown, 22 Jan 1787, and William Ingrem lately recovered against
sd. Mounce....28 April 1802. Thos H. Wade Sheriff sold to John
Stevens (planter), for $302... ___ Nov 1802. Thos H. Wade

Wit: Wm. L. Connell, James McAteer, William Graves.

Pp. 164-165: Devold Funderburk of Lancaster Dist., planter, for
$325 to Jesse Hayes, of same, land on a branch of
Great Linches Creek on poulcat branch, being the plantation the
sd. Funderburk now lives on, part of tract surveyed for William
Wood, 25 Aug 1785...14 March 1806. Devold Funderburk (Seal)
Wit: John Hancock, Abel Funderburk. Proved by Able Funderburk,
29 March 1806, before John Crowder, J. P.

Page 165: Jeremiah Funderburk of Lancaster Dist., for $150 to
David Funderburk, land on NE side Poulcat Creek, 100
acres...24 March 1808   Jeremiah Funderburk (Seal)
Wit: James Holliman, Paul Pliler. Proved by James Holliman,
before J. Crowder, J. P.

Page 166: 6 April 1796, The head men of the Cattawba Nation to
Sally Newriver, parcel 15 miles square, adj. Thos
Greer, Robert Crocket....   Genl New River (N) (Seal)
                                      Collo John Ears (C) (Seal)
                                      Magor John Brown (U)
Wit: Andw Foster, Thos Spratt, Hugh White. Proved by Hugh White,
28 Jan 1808, before Sam Henderson, J. P.

Page 167: James Hood of Lancaster Dist., for $70 to John Stevens,
30 acres, part of land granted to James Hood, 7 Jan
1788 on NE side Hanging Rock Creek on Faulkners branch....25
May 1807.   James Hood (Seal)
Wit: William Flanagan (X), William Chambers, Andrew Countryman.

Pp. 167-168: William Nutt of Lancaster Dist., for $300 to John
Graves, 340 acres on waters of Bare Creek and Lynches
Creek on S side of a line made between Robert McKain & sd. Nutt,
granted to Joseph Caston, conveyed to sd. Nutt...25 March 1804.
Wit: Jas Scott, Andrew Graves,   William Nutt (Seal)
     Jonathan Montgomery. Proved by Jas Scott, 15 April 1807.
     Mary Nutt, wife of William, relinquished dower, 15
April 1807, before Wm. Curry, J. Q.

Pp. 168-169: John Neely of Lancaster Dist., for $107.50 to John
Hagans, land on Gills Creek of Cane Creek adj. late
William Barton, James Cowsar, granted 1787...30 Aug 1808.
Wit: Saml Dunlap, Thomas Lee.   John Neely (N) (Seal)
Proved by Thomas Lee, 22 Oct 1808, before Jno Simpson. Lettice
Neely, wife of John, relinquished dower 3 Sept 1808, before
Jno. Simpson.

Page 170: James Hood of Lancaster Dist., for $650 to William
Cauthon, negro man Sank...9 March 1807. James Hood (Seal)
Wit: Jacob Vickery, John Cothen. Proved by John Cathon, 1 Nov 1808.

Pp. 170-171: Annanias Neely of Lancaster Dist., for $100 to James
Purdy, land on Hannahs Creek waters of Catawba River,
60 acres, part of 100 acres granted to Annanias Black, 29 Sept
1772, and is the plantation whereon sd. Black resided at the time
of his death, adj. __ Kirk, Edmond Hull, James Purdy...18 Feb
1808.   Annanias Neely (Seal)
Wit: jno Simpson, John Richardson. Proved 2 Nov 1808 by Jno
Simpson.

BOOK G

Pp. 171-172: 29 Aug 1808, Mary Douglass otherwise Mary McMoor
and James McMoor to Samuel Douglass, for $100, land
on waters of Camp Creek, granted to Mary Douglass, 6 Feb 1773...
Wit: John McMaster,   Mary McMoor (X) (Seal)
   Thomas McMaster.   James McMoor (Seal)
Proved by John McMaster, 29 Aug 1808, before James McMaster, J. P.

Pp. 172-173: Jonathan Coffey of Lancaster Dist., for $280, to
Henry Vincent of same, two tracts (1) part of land
granted to James Walker 7 Aug 1767, 78 acres adj. James Huey,
Jonas Vick, John Coffey (2) adj. it 97 acres...1 Feb 1808
Wit: James McAteer,   Jonathan Coffey (Seal)
   James Rodgers.   Proved by James McAteer, 5 July 1808.

Pp. 173-174: Benjamin Harper of York Dist., for $262½ to Moses
White of Lancaster Dist., 94 acres laid off from his
fathers old survey by his last will & testament, adj. Moses white,
Mary Harper, Robert Harper decd...8 Oct 1806. Benjamin Harper (Seal)
Wit: Thomas Vincent, James Harper, William Blair. Elizabeth
Harper, wife of Benjamin, relinquished dower, 9 Aprl 1808.

Pp. 174-175: Thomas Cauthran of Lancaster Dist., for $600 to
William Cauthran Sr., personable property, cattle &
furniture... 13 Jan 1809.   Thomas Cauthen (Seal)
Wit: Zach Ellis, William Duke (X). Proved by Zach Ellis, 6 Feb
1809.

Pp. 175-176: William Barkley of Lancaster Dist., for $70 to Abraham
Perry, lot in Lancasterville...3 Feb 1806.
Wit: Eliezar Alexander,   Wm Barkley (Seal)
   Wm. McIlwain. Proved by Eliezar Alexander, 23 Oct 1806,
before Jno Simpson, J. Q.

Pp. 176-177: Elizabeth Cousar of Lancaster Dist., for $500 to
William McKenna of same, lot in Village of Lancaster...
7 Nov 1808.   Elisabeth Cowsar (Seal)
Wit: John McClenahan, Hugh McMullan. Proved by Hugh McMullan,
7 Nov 1808, before John McClenahan, Q. U.

Page 178: Augustavas Rape of Williamson County, Tenn., appoint
Jacob Funderburk and Jacob Shoffner both of Lancaster
Dist., S. C., attorneys... 11 Jan 1809.   Gustavas Rape (X) (Seal)
Wit: Saml Funderburk, John Carns. Proved in Lancaster Dist. by
Samuel Funderburk, before Jno Crowder, J. P.

Pp. 178-179: William Barkley of Lancaster Dist., for $120 to
William McKenna, land near Lancaster Courthouse,
22 acres which is adj. to lands which did belong to Nathaniel
Cousar, John Simpson...7 Oct 1808.   Wm. Barkley (Seal)
Wit: John Beaty, Saml Dunlap. Proved by John Beaty, 10 Oct 1808.
Elizabeth Barkley, wife of William, relinquished dower, 6 March
1809.

Pp. 179-180: Abraham Perry of Lancaster Dist., for $160 to William
McKenna, lot in Lancaster Village...23 Nov 1808.
Wit: Thos Carson, Elias Caston.   Abraham Perry (LS)
Proved by Thos Carson, 23 Nov 1808.

Pp. 180-181: Samuel Moses of Lancaster Dist., for $60 to Thos
McDonald of same, brown mare, crop of corn and cotton,
household furniture...27 Oct 1808. Saml Moses (X). Wit: Jno
Simpson, Elijah Croxton.
                         187

Pp. 181-182: Jacob Shoffner of Lancaster Dist., did by conveyance
10 Jan 1805 to Andrew Walker, 385 acres on Bear Creek
surveyed for John Belk adj. Glass Caston, 1000 acres on one of
the head branches of BigLinches Creek called polcat branch...
Andrew Walker relinquishes claim...1 Aug 1808.   Andrew Walker (Seal)
Wit: Jas Scott, Metcalf Fisher. Proved by Metcalf Fisher, 11 Oct
1808, before John Welsh, J. Q.

Pp. 182-183: 26 Oct 1807, Samuel Smith Sr. of Meclanburg County,
N. C.,to Harcules Huey of Lancaster Dist., for $50
300 acres on waters of Flat Creek adj. land granted to Benjamin
Cockran...   Samuel Smith (LS)
Wit: Alexander B. Huey.   Sarah Smith (S) (Seal)
   Samuel Huey
   Samuel Smith.
Proved by Alexander B. Huey, 11 Oct 1808, before Jno Simpson,
J. Q.

Pp. 183-185: Thomas Welsh of Lancaster Dist., for $1 to Abraham
Horton and William Horton Senr, planters, and for the
purpose of securing to my children the reversion of my estate
after my decease, plantation whereon I now live on both sides
Little Lynches Creek, granted in my own name formerly belonged to
my father William Welsh, also 13 negroes (named), household
furniture, etc...for the use of the daughters of sd. Thomas
Welsh vis: Leve Horton wife of sd. Abraham Horton, Sarah Welsh
and Nancy Welsh...13 Jan 1809.   Thomas Welsh (Seal)
Wit: James Deason, Micheal Horton, Hollis Horton. Proved by
James Deason, 13 March 1809, before B. Deason, J. P.

Pp. 185-187: Eliezar Alexander of Lancaster Dist., for $2000 to
Robert Crockett Esqr., of York Dist., land on both
sides of Cain Creek, 671½ acres but found to contain 787 acres,
from six original grants one of 150 acres to Elenor Adamson, 10
Nov 1761, one of 100 acres to John Cantzon 28 Aug 1767, one of
300 acres granted to Samuel Dunlap, 1 Feb 1763, one of 24½ acres
to Eliazar Alexander, 5 Nov 1792, 26 acres granted to Joseph
McMeans 1 Dec 1794 and 70 acres granted to Eliazar Alexander 5
Jan 1801 adj. James McMeans, Gills Creek, William McMeans, John
Cantzon, Thomas Lee, unknown, Benjamin Cudworth, and John Simpson...
16 March 1808.   Eliazar Alexander (Seal)
Wit: John Simpson, Robt. M. Crockett. Proved by Robert M. Crockett
16 March 1808. Plat included. Mrs. Margaret Alexander, wife of
Eliazar, relinquished dower, 11 April 1808, before John McClena-
han, .Q. U.

Pp. 187-88: Thomas Sumpter of Claremont County, for $500 to Miss
Mary Belk, land on road from Lancasterville to Chesterfield Court House, part of 5000 acres, by plat May 1805...25 July
1805.   Thos Sumter (Seal)
Wit: Middleton Belk, James Dixson (+). (plat included). Proved
by Middleton Belk, 16 May 1806, before John Horan, J. P. Q. U.
in Sumter District.

Page 189: Daniel Shehan of Lancaster Dist., for $435 to Jacob Carn,
three tracts, first a tract of 375 acres surveyed for
Fredrick Carns, and conveyd to Shehane, 215 acres of same; 60 acres
marked off, secondly a tract of 150 acres surveyed for Daniel
Shehan, and conveyed to Fredrick Carns, then back again, then
60 acres part of 15,000 acres to Gen. Sumter...8 Dec 1808.
Wit: Jno Hancock, John Carns.   Daniel Shehane (Seal)
Proved by Jno Hancock, 4 Feb 1809.

Page 190: Richard Stringfellow of Lancaster Dist., for $487 to
          Henery Hudson, one negro man Bob, about 45 years of age
4 Nov 1808.   Richard Stringfellow (LS)
Wit: George Wade. Proved by George Wade, 5 Nov 1808.

Nancy Welch, widow woman, of Lancaster Dist., for $1 to Thomas
Welch, land which by law belongs to me as a dowery of my deceased
husband William Welch...9 Jan 1809.   Nancy Welch (0).
Wit: Hugh Davison, Oliver Meassy, John Davison. Proved by Hugh
Davison, 13 March 1809, before James Deason, J. P.

Page 191: Charles Cox of Lancaster Dist., for $800 to Thos Cothran,
          land on Rum Creek adj. James Biere, James Duglis, Dunlap,
How, Henry Shaver, part of a survey granted to Benjamin Thompson
11 April 1754, for 200 acres, and one entire survey granted to
Alexanderh Henny 15 March 1768 for 200 acres...1 Aug 1808.
Wit: Saml Dunlap, Hn. Hudson,   Charles Cox (LS)
     Henry Vanandingham. Proved by Saml Dunlap, before Hr.
Hudson, J. P., 1 Aug 1808.

Pp. 192-193: Mary Bredin, Joseph Bredin and Jesse Vanwincle of
          Lancaster Dist., for $1881.45 to George Hays, 289
acres in Lancaster Dist. on both sides Ceder Creek and Rockey
Creek, on NE side Catabaw River, plat made out by Adam McWillie
decd., 6 Sept 1808...14 Sept 1808.   Mary Bredin (X)
(Plat included).   Joseph Bredin
                                        Jesse Vanwinkle.
Plat at the desire of Mary Bredin extx of James Bredin decd.,
part of two tracts the one granted to Robert Duke 3 June 1765 for
150 and one to James Bredin, 4 Sept ___ for 250 acres adj. George
Hays, Andrew McElwain, Jesse Vanwinkle, Robert Bell, the Catawba
Co. Wit: William Currey, Charles Hays, Mary Hayes. Proved by
William Curry, 8 Nov 1808.

Pp. 193-194: John M'Meen of Lancaster Dist., hatter, for $621
          to John Ferrel, land whereon sd. Ferrel now resides
conveyed by William M'Meen and his mother Elizabeth to Saml
Hagins, 7 May 1796, and conveyed 7 Sept 1802 to my brother James
& Self, land on both sides of Bear Creek conveyed to me by my
brother William M'Meen, 180-, 94 acres...1 feb 1808.
Wit: James McMeen, Matt Jms. Neely.   John McMeen (Seal)
 plat included. Mary Matilda McMeen, wife of John, relinquished
dower, 19 April 1808. Proved by James McMeen, 2 Sept 1808.

Page 194: Recd of Jacob Shofner a full satisfaction for a certain
          mortgage by Micheal Costillo decd., for a tract of land
on pole Cat Creek, 4 July 1808.   Thos Shepherd.

Pp. 195-196: James Collins, planter, of Lancaster Dist., for
          $489 to John Hood Junr, of same, part of tract granted
to sd. Collins, 21 Nov 1803...5 Jan 1807.   James Collins (LS)
Wit: Saml Dunlap, Wm. Ross. Plat included shows adj. to Thos
Vincent, James & Alen Hood, Joseph Stranes. Plat made 2 Jan
1807. Agness Collins, wife of James, relinquished dower 17 Jan
1807. Proved by Saml Dunlap, 2 Feb 1807, before Jno Simpson, J. Q.

Pp. 196-197: Richard Kenon of Chatham County, N. C., for $1500
          to William Caston of Kershaw Dist., land on both
sides Flat Creek, 300 acres granted to Robert Harper, 22 Jan
1759, and all that adj. tract deeded from Benj. Hail to Ferguson
Hail deed dated 18 May 1793, and land from William Bridges &

Caty Bridges to Furguson Hail, 3 Nov 1795...10 Feb 1808.
Wit: Saml Caston,   Ricd. Kenon (Seal)
     Susanna Caston (X).

Pp. 197-198: 6 Dec 1799, John Russell of Kershaw County, planter,
             to William Russell of same, planter, for Ŀ 60...
275 acres in Dist. of Camden on the drains of Ceader and Single-
tons Creeks adj. James McKee, John Gilaspie, John Davidson...
Wit: John Gayden, James Russell.   John Russell (Seal)
Proved by James Russell, 5 Feb 1800, before Thos Ballard, J. P.

Page 198: Edmond Rames of Fairfield Dist., for $300 to John
          Wade of same, land on Rum Creek adj. estate of Woods,
Gims ham(?), Widow Pender, James West, James Perdy...22 March
1808.   Edmond Ranes (LS)
Wit: Thos Duren, Hr. Hudson, William Brown.
Proved by Henry Hudson, 11 Nov 1808.

Page 199: 7 June 1808, Fredrick Cerns of Lancaster Dist., to
          Daniel Shehane of same, for $250, 150 acres on the N
fork Wild Cat Creek, granted to sd. Carns, 5 Feb 1781(sic)...
Wit: Nathaniel Bibbe,   Fredrick Kerns (LS)
     Jacob Kerns. Proved by Nathaniel Bibbe, 7 June 1808, before
John Crowdern, J. P.

Pp. 199-200: 9 March 1807, William Johnson of Lancaster Dist.,
             to Robert Welsh, for $200, 125 acres on both sides
Wild Cat Creek adj. Vaughn, Welsh, Robt Welsh...William Johnson (+).
Wit: John Welsh, Frederick Vaughn.

Page 200: John Hancock of Lancaster Dist., for $97 to Jacob
          Shofner, tract whereon I now live, 100 acres, 11 Oct
1808, mortgage, due 1 Nov 1809...   John Hancock
Wit: John Welsh.

Pp. 201-202: 26 June 1775, Thomas Chaddock of Prov. of S. C., to
             Francis Bettis of Craven Co., for Ŀ 200...land in
Craven County S. C., 550 acres on a branch of Linches Creek, Flat
Creek, granted to Patrick Doyal, 15 March 1757...
Wit: Robert Gardner (R).   Thomas Chadwick (Seal)
     Wm. Faile.
Proved by William Faile, 1 Dec 1775, before Saml. Spencer, J. P.

Page 202: Joseph Wade of Lancaster Dist., to Andrew McIlwain,
          negro man Billy about 30 years of age...20 Feb 1809
Wit: Robert McIlwain.   Jos. John Wade

Page 203: Middleton McDonald of Lancaster Co., for Ŀ 40 sterling
          to Benjamin Clifton of same, to James Denton, child
stepson of Benjamin Clifton, land whereon sd. Clfiton now lives,
150 acres adj. James Clifton, 1/2 of tract sd. McDonald sold to
James Clifton, known by the old survey of George Ratt (Platt?),
sold to James Denton decd...16 May 1798. Middleton McDonald (Seal)
Wit: James Clifton, Sally Cotton (X), Frances Hicking, (X).

James Denton of Columbia appoints Benjamin Clifton lawful attorney
to sell 150 acres on Catawba River described in a deed by Middleton
McDonald to me...22 April 1809.   James Denton (Seal)
Wit: C. Clifton, John D. Brown.

Pp. 203-204: John Love of Knox County, Tenn. for $500 to Henry
          Love of Lancaster Dist., land granted to John Williams,
adj. Glass Caston, 50 acres...13 April 1805.   John Love (Seal)
Wit: Moab Stevens, William Baskin. Proved by Moab Stevens, 13
April 1805, before William Ward, J. P.

Pp. 204-205: Jacob Shofner of Lancaster Dist., for $100 to Matcalf
          Fisher, 100 acres granted to George Campbell, and
conveyed to Glass Caston, to William Nutt to Jacob Shofner...
(no date).   Jacob Shofner (Seal)
Wit: Saml Dunlap, Andw. McIlwain. Proved by Capt. Samuel Dunlap,
13 April 1809, before Wm. Barkley, J. P.

Pp. 205-207: 14 Sept 1772, William White and wife Sarah of Craven
          Co., N. C., yeoman, to Robert Carnes, for Ł 350...
land adj. Chas Miller, 286 acres, part of tract that William White
now lives on...   William White (Seal)
Wit: John Drenan , Danl Carnes,   Sarah White (O) (Seal)
     Alex Carnes.
Proved by Daniel Carnes, 28 Dec 1808, before Jos. Draffen Esqr.

Page 207: Isaac Anderson and wife Nancy of Lancaster Dist., to
          Wike Ivy, of same, land adj. Wm. Anderson, 24 Dec 1808
Wit: Henry Massey, Henry Ivy,   Isaac Anderson (LS)
     Robert Ivy (RŁ).   Nancy Anderson (X) (LS)
Proved by Henry Massey, 29 Dec 1808, before Samuel C. Dunlap,
Q. U.

Pp. 208-209: John Hood of Lancaster Dist., planter for $250 to
          Mary Stover and Thomas Stover of Kershaw Dist., 150
acres on E side Cattawba River on waters of Rockey Creek, part
of 300 acres granted to William Mattox, adj. Wm. Stephens, Richard
Perry...22 Oct 1808.   John Hood (H) (LS)
Wit: Robert Cunningham, William Stover. Elizabeth Hood, wife of
John, relinquished dower, 22 Oct 1808, before Wm. Currey, J. Q.
Proved by both wit, 22 Oct 1808.

Pp. 209-210: William Stephens of Lancaster Dist., for $350 to
          Mary Stover, of Kershaw Dist., spinster, 141 acres
on both sides Rocky Creek part of grants to Wm Maddox and John
Chassure...25 Oct 1808.   William L. Stevens (LS)
Wit: Robert Cunningham, John Gibson. Jane Stevens, wife of Wm.
Stevens, relinquished dower, 25 Oct 1808. Proved by both wit,
25 Oct 1808.

Page 210: James Gaston of Lancaster Dist., for $230 to Thomas
          Carsen of same, 100 acres on head branches of Little
Linches Creek adj. Peters, granted 24 Aug 1770 to Jasper Rogers,
conveyed to Ricahrd Anderson who died intestate, then conveyed
by Enoch Anderson lawful heir of Richard Anderson, to James
Gaston, the plantation whereon the sd. Gaston now resides...20
Nov 1807.   James Gaston (LS)
Wit: John Clark (X), James Scott. Proved by James Scott, 3 Oct
1808, before Jno Simpson, J. Q.

Page 211: Thomas Carsen of Lancaster Dist., for $230 to John
          Langley, plantation of 100 acres on head branches of
little Linches Creek...the plantation where sd. Carsen now lives,
4 March 1809.   Thomas Carsen (Seal)
Wit: John Dunlap, John Scott. Proved by John Dunlap, 9 March
1809 before Jno Simpson, J.Q.

Pp. 211-212: John Hilliard of Hanging Rock Creek by bond to William Flandingham, for $490, for payment of $245, 194
acres on branch of Hanging Rock Creek...21 March 1809.
Wit: Gayden Pettey, Elijah Croxton.   John Hilliard (LS)
Proved by Elijah Croxton, 4 Aug 1809.

Page 213: John Love of Knox County, Tenn., exr. of Henry Loves
estate, for $1126 to Thomas Hilliard, part of a survey
to John Williams, on a branch of Little Linches creek adj. Glass
Caston...6 Aug 1805.   John Love (Seal)
Wit: Garden Pettey, Thos Hankes. Proved by John Hilliard.
Thomas Hilliard relinquished all claim to John Love, 20 July
1809.

Page 214: Charles Barber of Kershaw Dist., planter, to William
Walker, 95 acres adj. McKey, now William Cauthorn,
Halston Dorf now Thos Middleton, Arthur Ennis on Cedar Creek, part
of grant to Charles Barber 775 acres...17 Sept 1807.
Wit: Hugh Black, Thos Middleton,   Charles Barber (Seal)
William Gibson Jr. Proved by William Gibson Jr., before H.
Hudson, J. P., 24 March 1809.

Pp. 214-215: John Welsh of Lancaster Dist., for $10 to Lewis
Fail, 10 acres on Big Linches Creek adj. Knight
Knight, Elizabeth Fail, John Blackburn...25 Nov 1802.
Wit: Jacob Hagler, John Welsh Jr.   Jno Welsh (Seal)
Proved by Jacob Hagler, 26 May 1804.

Pp. 215-216: John Welsh Senr of Lancaster Dist., for $407.50 to
Daniel Clark, land on new road from Lancaster Court
House to Chesterfield Court House at the mouth of the dry branch,
450 acres...23 Nov 1808.   John Welsh Senr (Seal)
Wit: Burrel Welsh, William Welsh. Proved by Burrel Welsh, 29
Dec 1808, before Jno Crowder, J. P.

Pp. 216-217: George Harris of Lancaster Dist., for $150 to Jacob
Fail, 150 acres on a branch of Flat Creek adj. Benj.
Scarbour...25 Nov 1803.   George Harris (X) (Seal)
Wit: John Faile, Lewis Faile. Proved by Lewis Faile, 26 May
1804.

Page 217: John Hilliard for $201 to Saml Caston & William McKenna,
negro Bob, 25 years old...7 Aug 1809. John Hilliard
Wit: A Perry, Thomas Lee. Proved by Abraham Perry, 10 Aug 1809.

Pp. 217-218: John Welsh of Wilc Cat Creek in Lancaster Dist., for
$40 to George Fuller of Flat Creek, 100 acres granted
to Genl. Sumter, part of a large survey, 29 March 1806.
Wit: Benjamin Deason,   John Welsh Senr (Seal)
Joseph Baker (£).
Proved by BenjaminDeason, 29 March 1806.

Page 218: Lewis Faile of Lancaster Co., for $5 to John Faile of
same, 100 acres adj. Richard Knight, on path to the
old Waxhaw Road adj. John Modgeleg...5 Sept 1807. Lewis Faile (Seal)
Wit: Thomas Faile, Michael Miller. Proved by Michael Miller, 5
Sept 1807, before John Welsh, J. Q.

Page 219: 4 Oct 1802, Henry Roan and James Holliman to Koonrod
Plylar of Lancaster Co., for $300...tract on south
side Great Linches Creek, 105 acres...

BOOK G

Wit: Michael Oatts,   Henry Rone (H R) (Seal)
   John Meados.   James Holliman (Seal)
Proved by John Meadors, 7 April 1809.

Pp. 219-220: 3 Jan 1800, Thomas Cauthorn of Lancaster Co., plan-
       ter, to John Hood for six spanish mill'd dollars,
tract of 1½ acres...   Thomas Cawthon (Seal)
Wit: William Thomson, John Ingrem, Henry Hudson. Proved by Henry
Hudson, 11 April 1809, before Wm. Currey, J. Q.

Page 220: John Hood of Lancaster Dist., yeoman, for love, good
       will & affection to my loving grandson William Hudson,
son of Jesse & Mary Hudson, of same, one feather bed & furtniure,
cow and calf, steer...1 April 1809.   John Hood (H) (Seal)
Wit: Robt Cunningham, Thomas Cauthorn, Henry Hudson. Proved by
Thomas Cauthorn, 11 April 1809.

Page 221: Jacob Fortenbury of Chester County, for Ł 100 to Joshua
       Prout of Anson County, N. C. claim from all suits or
actions...whereas Col. Thomas Wade of Anson County, N. C. in 1782
recovered a judgment in the Court of Pleas & QS returnable to Jan.
Term 1783 against Nathaniel Ashly, John Coleson Senr, Jacob
Fortenberrgy & Isaac Fortenbury for Ł 1860, land on Jones Creek
and three negroes Venus, London & Ben, property of Isaac Fortinbury, and negroes Ben Hannah and Dick, the property of Jacob
Fortinbury, the sd. Jacob Fortinbury being the son and heir of
the said Isaac....21 April 1800.   Jacob Falcenbury (Seal)
Wit: Thos H. Wade. Proved by Thos H. Wade, 5 June 1809.

Page 222: Benjamin Thomson of Lancaster Dist., to Robert McIlwain
       negro boy Sam about 12 years old...18 April 1809...
Wit: George Dunlap,   Benjamin Thomson (Seal)
   Elizabeth Thomson (8).
Proved by George Dunlap, 4 July 1809, before Wm. Barkley, J. P.

John Morton of Lancaster Dist., for $150 to Jame Croxton of same,
bed & furniture, household furniture, black smith tools...19 Jan
1809.   John Morton
Wit: Ananias Neely, E. Croxton. Proved by _____, 17 Aug 1809.

Page 223: James Purdy of Lancaster Dist., for $200, to John
       Simpson of Lancaster Dist., tract of 23 acres on Bear
Creek adj. sd. Simpson, James Brady...13 June 1809.
Wit: Thomas Lee, A. Perry.   James Purdy (Seal)
Proved by Thomas Lee, 16 Aug 1809. Plat included, 18 May 1809.

Pp. 224-25: 19 May 1809, Thomas Lee, Sheriff of Lancaster Dist.,
       to James Douglas...whereas Andrew McIlwain was possessed
of land, 100 acres, on Catawba river on the mouth of Cedar Creek,
and indebted to Eliz Cowsar extx of David Dowsar...sold to James
Douglass, for $60...   Thomas Lee S. L. D.
Wit: John Cantzon, John Gamble. Proved by John Cantzon, 19 May
1809, before Josh. Lee, J. Q.

Page 226: Mathew Ingle of Chesterfield Dist., to John Robertson
       of Lancaster Dist., for $200, land at the fork of the
Long Branch, land granted to Jacob Isree, conveyed to sd. Mathew
Ingle...25 July 1809...   Mathew Ingle
Wit: Thomas Wimberley, John Hunter (X). Proved by Thomas Wimberley,
9 Oct 1809, before B. Deason, J. P.

Pp. 226-227: Benjamin Clifton & James Denton of Richland Dist.,
             to William Mothershead of Lancaster Dist., land
where sd. Mothershead lives (now rents), 150 acres adj. James
Clifton, sold to Denton & Clifton by Middleton McDonald, known
by the old survey of George Platts, by him sold to James Denton
decd., by Sheriff to sd. McDonald...3 May 1809. Benja Clifton (Seal)
Wit: James Kenny, Mary Kenny (X),   James Denton (Seal)
     Jesse Mothershead. Proved by James Kenny, 2 Oct 1809, before
Jno. Simpson, J. Q.

Pp. 227-228: William Ward of York Dist., for $345 to Joseph
             Johnston, tract known as Knowlin land granted to
John Caston, 180 acres, adj. James Blackman, William Tate, part
of grant to William Ward....22 Dec 1806.   William Ward (Seal)
Wit: Gustavis Haile (X), John Hill Jur. (X). Proved by Gustavis
Hill, 14 Feb 1809, before James Deason, J. P.

Pp. 228-230: 3 April 1809, Thomas McDow to Dr. Robert Montgomery
             and John McClenahan, Esqrs., admrs. of James Blair
decd., whereas partition was issued by Court of common pleas to
divide the estate of James Blair, tract of land and grist mill,
the court's opinion that the land and mill should be vested in
Mary McDow and Thomas McDow her husband, now for $1133.33 to
be paid, mortgage also slaves Jack, Lucy, Mason, Isaac, Rino &
Rachel...   Thomas McDow (Seal)
Wit: Robert Davies, John Foster. Proved by John Foster, 3 April
1809, before James H. Witherspoon, J. P.

Pp. 230-231: James Hogge of York Dist., for $390 to Thomas Dunlap
             of Lancaster Dist., 142 acres 10 Nov 1808...
Wit: Samuel Dunlap,   James Hogge (Seal)
     Samuel Dunlap Senr., Henry Duncan. Proved by Samuel Dunlap
Senr, 1 April 1809, before James H. Witherspoon, J. P.

Page 231: S. C. Lancaster Dist. John Tribble says on oath that
          the mare that John Stevens has levied on for the pro-
perty of Morris Tribble was given to his son Wyly by James
Tribble in my presence, 11 April 1809, before Alexr Ingrem.

29 July 1798, Joseph Douglass of Lancaster Co., to James Elliot,
for Ŀ 20 sterling, tract on waters of 12 Mile Creek adj. the State
line & Waggon Road, including the original improvements...
Wit: John Gettys,   Jos Douglass (Seal)
     Wm. Sprunt, Isom Scott (X). Proved by John Gettys, 6 Feb
1799, before Samuel C. Dunlap, J. P.

Page 232: George Douglass of Lancaster Dist., to John Wright of
          same, for $325 land adj. James Faulkner, James Moore,
William Draffen, 7 Oct 1808.   George Duglass (Seal)
Wit: Saml Dunlap, James Thompson, wit. Proved by Samuel Dunlap,
6 Oct 1809.

Pp. 232-234: 2 Sept 1809, Abraham Perry, Esqr., Sheriff of Lanc.
             Dist., to William McKenna...whereas Alexander Craig
late of LancasterVille, Innkeeper, decd., was seized of half of
26 acres, and was indebted to David Cowsar (in his lifetime) late
of Village of Lancaster, for Ŀ 50, and Elizabeth Cowsar, extx of
will of David Cowsar...sold for $45,   Abraham Perry S. L. Ɖ.
Wit: Benjamin F. Hampton, J. G. Martin.
Proved by Benja. F. Hampton, 8 Feb 1810, before Wm. Barkley, J. P.

Pp. 235-236: Titus Lany of Lancaster Dist., for $160 to John
Craig Junr of same, planter, 150 acres on waters of
Cane & Camp Creek near the new meeting house, adj. tract formerly
John White Junr; tract first granted to Archibald Davie , 1 June
1767, conveyed to Thomas Wells, 24 Aug 1789, to John Shepard, 8
March 1795, to Titus Laney, 7 Aug 1802...11 Jan 1809
Wit: John Funderburk, Nathaniel   Titus Laney (+) (Seal)
Craig, John Craig Jr.
Christian Laney, wife of Titus, relinquished dower, 23 Jan 1809.
Proved by Nathaniel Craig, 20 Sept 1809.

Page 236: Archibald McCorkle for $1100 to John Linn & Andrew
Linn, 160 acres on waters of Waxhaw Creek in Lancaster
Dist., adj. Dr. Samuel C. Dunlap, 21 Nov 1805. Archible McCorkle (Seal)
Wit: John Crawford, Robert McCorkle. Proved by all three wit,
21 Nov 1805, before Samuel C. Dunlap, J. P.

Page 237: John Linn and Andrew Linn for $900 to Andrew Johnston,
160½ acres on waters of Waxhaw Creek adj. Dr. Samuel C.
Dunlap...15 Sept 1809.   John Linn (Seal)
Wit: James H. Guy,   Andrew Linn (Seal)
Agnes Guy (L).
Mary Linn, wife of John, relinquished dower, 19 Feb 1810, before
Jos. Lee, Q.U. Proved by James Guy, 17 Jan 1810.

Page 238: James Neal of Lancaster Dist., to Johnston & Lee, merchants, all my chest of tools, consisting of carpenters,
house Joiners, and Cabinet makers tools, for $80....25 Aug 1809.
Wit: Jos Lee, J. Q.   James Neal (X) (Seal)

Pp. 238-239: Andrew McIlwain Senr did on 10 April 1809 give Mary
Bredin, extx of James Bradin decd., a promissory note
with Capt. William Simpson as security for $500, to be paid 12
of the same month...for being security, to sd. William Simpson,
negroes Tom, Rachel and her children Charles & Surry; Peter,
Venus, Mary and Jim....4 Oct 1809.   Andw McIlwain (Seal)
Wit: Wm. Barkley, Jno Simpson. Proved by Wm. Barkley, 4 Oct 1809.

Pp. 239-240: Burrel Clanton of Lancaster Dist., for $108 to Benja-
min Shaver, tract of 100acres adj. Alexander Craig, 13
July 1809.   Burrel Clanton (Seal)
Wit: Jer. Graves, Jonathan Montgomery. Proved 4 Nov 1809 by
Jonathan Montgomery, before Wm. Barkley, J. P.

Page 240: William Graves of Lancaster Dist., for $195, to Burrel
Clanton, 100 acres adj. Alexander Craig, 15 Dec 1807.
Wit: Benjamin Shaver,   Wm. Graves (Seal)
Henry Horton.

Page 241: James Holliman of Lancaster Co., for $6 to Drury Vinson
of same, a certain remnant of land on SW side Pole cat
Creek adj. Vinson and Daniel Hunley(?), 6 acres...25 Dec 1800
Wit: Abel Funderburk, Henry Funderburk.   James Holliman (Seal)
Proved by Abel Funderburk, 8 July 1809, before John Crowder, J. P.

Conrod Plyler of Lancaster Dist., for $400 to Obed Thompson of
same, two tracts (1) on both sides Pole Cat Creek, 89 acres adj.
Stroud, Benjamin Harper, Jacob Baker, Funderburk, plat 1 March
1787 granted to James Win; (2) 13 acres adj. the same purchased
of James Holliman as a remnant of 15,000 acres grant to Genl.
Sumter...17 Dec 1805.   Koonrod Plyler (X) (Seal)

Wit: James Holliman, Heinrich Faggot(?) (German Signature).
Proved by James Holliman, 29 Sept 1809 before Jno Crowder, J. P.

Pp. 242-243: 13 Jan 1810, Henry Dunlap of Fleming County, Kentucky,
          to Charles Barber of Kershaw Dist., S. C., 500 acres
in the fork of Cane Creek and Catawba River adj. William Simpson,
Thomas McDow, Samuel Dunlap, William Dunlap, granted to Benjamin
Thompson ____ 1754, also land granted to Samuel Dunlap, 3 April
1752 for 240 acres, and granted to Thomas Dunlap, 4 June 1787 for
183 acres...   Henry P. Dunlap (Seal)
Wit: Dm. McWillie, Nathaniel Barber, George Warlor. (Plat included).
Proved by Nathaniel Barber, __ Dec 1810.

Page 243: Charles Barber bound to George Marler for $2000, bond
          to make title to land on E side Beaver Creek adj. Mr.
Beckham, Alex McKee, Arthur Cunningham....
Wit: Jno Gregory, Rachel Nettles, William Gregory.

Pp. 243-244: Henry Shaver Senior of Lancaster Dist., planter, for
          $600 to Heartwell Sledge of Chester Dist., land gran-
ted to Andrew McKeen, 6 Dec 1767 for 200 acres, and a plantation
granted to Andrew McIlwain Senr, certified 8 Oct 1788, 123 acres
...25 Oct 1809   Henry Shaver Senr (LS)
Wit: Saml Dunlap, William Howe. Proved by Saml Dunlap, 6 Nov 1809.
Elizabeth Shaver, wife of Henry, relinquished dower, 25 Oct 1809.

Page 244: James Strain of Lancaster Dist., for natural love &
          affection, 150 acres conveyed by George Douglass and
Catherine Howard, exrs. of Robert Howard decd., on N side Cane
Creek...15 March 1810.   James Strain (X) (Seal)
Wit: Wm. McKenna, Jno Simpson. Proved by Wm. McKenna, 15 March
1810.

Page 245: Drury Vinson of Meclinburg Co., N. C., for $6 to Obed
          Thompson of Lancaster Co., land on Polecat Creek between
Thomsons own land and Daniel Hunts, 6 acres...20 Nov 1804.
Wit: Shadrac Elkins, Paul Plyler.   Drury Vinson (Seal)
Proved by Paul Plyer, 8 July 1809, before Jno Crowder, J. P.

10 Nov 1802, Edward Richardson of McLinburg Co., N. C., to Obed
Thompson, for $460, 60 acres including the plantation whereon
Drury Vinson now lives on S side pole Cat Creek, including Shofners
old Griss Mill, 100 acres granted to Benjamin Harper...
Wit: Adam Team,   Edward Richardson (Seal)
     David Funderburck.
Proved by David Funderburk, 8 July 1809.

Page 246: Joseph Gracy of Lancaster Dist., planter, for love &
          good will to Joseph T. Gracy and Polly Grace, 115 acres
part of grant to sd. Joseph Gracy, surveyed 13 July 1809...15
Jan 1810.   Joseph Gracy (Seal)
Wit: Margaret Gracy. Proved, 17 Feb 1810, before Henry Hudson, J. P.

Pp. 246-247: John Weaver, planter, of Lancaster Dist., for $600
          to Frederic Weaver, land of 100 acres...11 March
1809.   John Weaver (Seal)
Wit: Daniel Joiner, Middleton Joiner, John Reid (X).
Proved by Daniel Joiner, 3 Nov 1809, before Wm. Currey, J. Q.

Page 247: Daniel Hunter of State of Kentucky, for $60 to Obed
          Thomson, land on drains of Great Lynches Creek, part of

BOOK G

15,000 acres granted to Thos Sumpter, 2 April 1787....4 Oct 1805
                                        Daniel Hunter (Seal)
Wit: James Holliman, David Funderburk (F). Proved by David Funderburk, 8 July 1809.

Pp. 247-248: John Rodgers of Union Dist., for £ 70 to William Fann
            of Lancaster Dist., land adj. late Mr. Taylor, by
a conveyance from Abdon Alexander, late sheriff of Lancaster Dist.,
to John Blare, known as Thomas Blairs place, 140 acres...26 Jan
1803.   John Rogers (Seal)
Wit: Perry Evans, Joseph Moore. Proved in York Dist., by Joseph
Moore, 12 Feb 1810 before J. Hutchinson, J. P.
Rosey Mary (Rosanna) Rogers, wife of John, relinquished dower,
5 Feb 1803 in Union Dist., before John P. Saltor (Sartor), J. Q.

Pp. 248-249: Robert Hancock and wife Sarah of Lancaster Dist., for
            $310 to Clem Hancock of same, land on N side Waxaw
Creek, adj. Wm. Porter...23 Feb 1810.   Robert Hancock (Seal)
Wit: William Hancock, An. Anderson,   Sarah Hancock (X) (Seal)
    George Wren.
Proved by George Wren, 19 March 1810, before James H. Witherspoon,
J. Peace.

Page 249: Robert Hancock of Lancaster Dist., appoints son Clement
          Hancock attorney...26 Feb 1810. Robt Hancock (Seal)
Wit: John Crawford, Nathan Tomlinson (X). Proved by John
Crawford, 26 Feb 1810, before John McClenahan, Q. U.

Archibald McManis of Lancaster Dist., for love & affection to
my daughter Nancy McManis, negro woman Becky...30 Oct 1809.
Wit: Hugh McManis,   Archibald McManus (X) (Seal)
    Drew Massey. Proved by Drew Massey, before John Crowder, J. P.

Page 250: David Montgomery of Lancaster Dist., for $514 to William
          Taylor Jr., land on both sides Camp Creek, 209 acres,
adj. Ninion Montgomery...5 June 1809.   David Montgomery (Seal)
Wit: Wm. Graham, J. G. Mathis. (Plat included0. Proved by J. G.
Mathis, 5 June 1809. Mary Montgomery, wife of David, relinquished
dower, 5 June 1809, before Wm. Currey, J. Q.

Page 251: 5 June 1809, David Shepherd and wife Charlotte, of Lan-
          caster Dist., to Jesse Ivy, land on waters of 12 mile
creek adj. Absalom Ivy...   David Shepherd (LS)
Wit: Zechariah Ivy, John Carns,   Charlotte Shepherd (X) (LS)
    Henry Ivy.
Proved by John Carns, 9 April 1810.

Page 252: Jonathan Thompson of Butler County, Ohio, to John
          Stevens, of Lancaster Dist., 207 acres on both sides
persimmon branch of Cedar Creek adj. Sherod Sims Senr, James
Cothran, heirs of William Duke decd., William Cothan Senr, Archibald Hood, and the lands whereon Peter Twitty now lives...19 March
1810.   Jonathan Thompson (Seal)
Wit: None. Ack. before Wm. Curry, J. Q.

Pp. 252-253: Jonathan Blackman of Lancaster Dist., to Dudly
            Haile, 71 acres granted to John Caston, which sd.
Blackman bought at Sheriff sale, on Little Linches Creek....
27 Dec 1809.   Jonathan Blackman (X) (Seal)
Wit: Hardy Haile, Joseph Haile, James Strain. Proved by Joseph
Haile, 21 March 1810. by B. Deason, J. P.

Page 253: Sollomon Williams of Lancaster Dist., to John Champion,
          yeoman, of same, 260 acres, for $500, adj. James Moore,
Kennedy, granted to James McKey, on waters of Cedar Creek, also
adj. Andrew Nutt....22 Oct 1808.   Solomon Williams (Seal)
Wit: Jacob Champion (11) Wm. Moore. Proved by Wm. Moore, 9 Feb
1810. Mary Williams, wife of Solomon, relinquished dower, 9 Feb
1810.

Page 254: Mary Duke of Kershaw Dist., Agness McKee, Anderson
          Houze and his wife, to Solomon Williams of Lancaster
Dist., planter, 100 acres on branches of Cedar Creek adj. Henry
Hudson, granted to James McKee in 1773...1 March 1806.
Wit: Wm. Moore,   Mary Duke (/)
     John Davidson,   Agness McKee
     Burrel Clanton.   Anderson Houze (LS)
                                      Elizabeth House (X) (LS)

Proved by Wm. Moore, 9 Feb 1810.

William Johnston of Lancaster Dist., to Robert Cuningham, planter,
40 acres on waters of Cedar Creek adj. Adam Thompson, William
Johnston, originally granted to sd. Johnston, 1805...10 April 1810
Wit: Henry Howze, Jesse   William Johnston (LS)
     Johnston (X. Proved by both wit., 10 April 1810.

Page 255: John Champion, planter, of Lancaster Dist., for $425
          to Robert Cuningham, 260 acres adj. James Moore, Nutt...
9 Feb 1810.   John Champion (LS)
Wit: Wm Moore, Solomon Williams. Elinar Champion, wife of John,
relinquished dower 9 Feb 1810. Proved by both wit, 9 Feb 1810.

Pp. 255-256: William McGarrah Jr., planter, of Lancaster Dist.,
          for $350, to John Champion, 200 acres on Crooked
Creek adj. Rodgers, granted to Dempsey Fanney, 16 April 1795...
13 Feb 1810.   William McGarrah (LS)
Wit: George McGarrah, Moses McGarrah, Thomas Hood. Nancy McGarrah,
wife of William, relinquished dower, 13 Feb 1810. Proved by all
three wit., 13 Feb 1810.

Pp. 256-257: James Hood of Lancaster Dist., planter, for $400
          to Francis Ingram, land on Hanging Rock Creek, 200
acres excepted which is conveyed to John Stevens, surv. 21 Sept
1784, adj. John Countryman.   James Hood (LS)
Wit: Moses McGarrah, Wm. L. Connell. Proved by Wm. L. Connell,
14 April 1810, before Jno Simpson, J. Q. Mourning Hood, wife of
James, relinquished dower, 9 April 1810, before John Montgomery,
J. Q.

Page 257: 11 April 1808, Henry Vincent of Lancaster Co., to Edmond
          Vincent of same, for $950...land on main waggon road
near a large dead pine...   Henry Vincent (Seal)
Wit: John Steele, A. Perry. Proved by John Steele, 12 April 1808,
before James H. Witherspoon, J. Peace.

Page 258: John Simpson of Lancaster County, to John May of same
          for $120, lots in Barnetsville or Lancaster...20 April
1797.   John Simpson (Seal)
Wit: Eliazor Alexander, Abdon Alexander. Proved by Abdon Alexander,
21 April 1797.

Page 259: Elizabeth Gibson of Dist. of Fairfield, to Patsey Tid-
well, bed & furniture, bay mare, and an obligation on
James Anderson for $105...12 April 1810. Elizabeth Gibson (X) (LS)
Wit: D. G. Vance, William Huston. Proved by D. G. Vance in Chester
Dist., 25 April 1810, before Wm. Anderson, J. P.

Pp. 259-260: Jno Simpson of Lancaster Dist., for $125 to John
Batey, two lots in Village of Lancaster, on Catawba
St. and Meeting St...26 Oct 1808.   Jno Simpson (Seal)
Wit: Benjan. F. Hampton, Bartlett Jones. Proved by B. Hampton,
before John Simpson, J. Q.

Page 260: Miriam Russell of Lancaster Dist., to son Starling
Russell, for having entered himself as a security, negro
boy Cugoe...5 Dec 1809.   Miriam Russell (Seal)
Wit: F. Williams, Jno Coffey, Plainer Wingate. Proved by Fowler
Williams, 16 May 1810, before Jno Simpson, J. Q.

Pp. 261-262: Jeremiah Russell of Wilkinson County, Ga., bound to
William Dobie of York Dist., S. C., for $1364, whereas
William Dobie has entered as a security with said Russell & Benja-
min Culp in a note due the admrs. of William Russell decd., 4 Dec
1809.   Josh. Russell (Seal)
Wit: F. Williams. Proved by F. Williams, 4 Jan 1810.

Jeremiah Russell of Wilkinson County, Virginia, sold to William
Dobie of York Dist., negro man Ben, & my portion of the estate of
William Russell decd., for $682...4 Dec 1809. F. Williams, wit.

Pp. 262-263: 15 Jan 1810, George Taylor and wife Nancy of Kershaw
County, to George Miller, planter, of Lancaster Co.,
100 acres on both sides big Lynches Creek, conveyed 1750 from
Joseph Taylor and wife, also 100 acres purchased from Benjamin Hale
Senr, 1792, and 50 acres dated 26 Feb 1790 purchased from Samuel
West, and 100 acres 25 April 1797, purchased from Francis Bettiss.
Wit: Michael Miller,   George Taylor (T) (Seal)
     William Miller,   Nancy Taylor (C) (Seal)
     Joseph Terrell.
Proved by Michael Miller, 17 Feb1810.

Page 263: Elizabeth Miller of Lancaster Dist., for love, good
will, to son William Miller of same, all lands, stocks,
goods, etc. 10 May 1810.   Elizabeth Miller (X) (Seal)
Wit: John Kennington, Jr., George Miller. Proved by John Kennington Jr.,12 May 1810, by B. Deason, J. P.

Page 264: Charles Barber of Kershaw County, to Samuel Bowden of
Lancaster Co., for $480, land adj. ____, 180 acres...
1 March 1810.   Charles Barber (Seal)
Wit: Middleton Joyner, John Harrison (X), Berry Harrison. Proved
by Berry Harrison, 10 April 1810.

Pp. 264-265: Amey Ivey of Lancaster Dist., for $300 to David
Shepherd, 60 acres adj. Widow Cowsart...15 June
1809.   Amy Ivy (X) (LS)
Wit: Henry Massey, Zacchariah Ivy, Robert Ivy (RI). Proved by
Henry Massey, 22 Dec 1809, before Samuel C. Dunlap, Q. U.

Page 265: David Shepherd of Lancaster Dist., & wife Charlotte,
for $220, 60 acres where Amey Ivey now lives....21 Nov
1809.   David Shepherd (Seal)

Wit: Mark Edwards, S. R. Gibson, John Stevens. Charlotte Shepherd
relinquished dower, 22 Dec 1809. Mark Edward proved, 22 Dec 1809
before Samuel C. Dunlap, Q. U.

Page 266: Robert Welsh of Lancaster Dist., for $1000 to George
            Lang, land on both sides Wild Cat Creek, adj. David
Laney, 13 Feb 1809.   Robert Welsh (X) (Seal)
Wit: Elijah Clark (P), James Holliman. Milly Welsh, wife of Robert,
relinquished dower 18 June 1809. Proved by Elijah Clark, 4 Sept
1809.

Pp. 266-267: Richard Ussery of Lancaster Dist., planter, to Saml
            Ussery, for $130, land granted to William Cato, 9
Oct 1795, conveyed to William Ingram, 9 Oct 1796, to John Ingram,
22 March 1797, to Richard Ussery, 27 Jan 1801....3 March 1810
Wit: Wm. L. Connell,   Richard Ussery (Seal)
     John Kesiah (X). Proved by John Kesiah, 16 May 1810, before
B. Deason, J. P.

Page 267: 14 July 1809, Edmond Vincent of Lancaster Co., to Peter
            P. Vincent of same, for $1000, 150 acres adj. Massey,
James Cureton...   Edmond Vincent (Seal)
Wit: Henry Vincent, Thos Vincent.   Polly Vincent (Seal)
Proved by both wit, 7 Feb 1810, before Jos. Draffen, J. P.

Page 268: John Gettys of Lancaster Dist., for $600 to Joseph Massey
            175 acres on waters of Waxhaw Creek adj. Joseph Massey,
John McDow, Robert Thompson, Dr. Dunlap, granted to Robert Miller...
5 Feb 1809.   John Gettys (Seal)
Wit: B. Massey, Robert Thompson, William Hood.   4 Jan
1810, Ann Gettys, wife of John, relinquished dower. Proved 18 May
1810 by William Hood, before Jos. Draffen, J. P.

Pp. 268-269: Edward Brumloe for $270 to John Robinson, land on
            both sides Lynches Creek in the dist. of Chesterfield
and Lancaster, granted 1794, 100 acres...5 March 1805.
Wit: John Poer, Samuel Widner (X).   Edward Bumloe (X) (Seal)
Proved by John Poer, 22 Aug 1808.

Page 269: Rufus C. Rathbone of Kershaw Dist., for the security of
            $458 paid by Robert Cunningham of Lancaster Dist., 200
acres...31 March 1810.   Rufus C. Rathbone (LS)
Wit: Lemuel A. Williams, Thomas Cauthorn. Proved by both wit,
before H. Hudson,J. P., 10 May 1810.

Pp. 269-270: John White of Lancaster Dist., for $200 to Jacob
            Plylar of same, 596 acreson waters of Camp Creek,
two tracts, one of 170 acres and one of 173 acres part of grant
to Thomas Nelson, 3 Sept 1783, and also 393 acres granted to John
White, 6 May 1793, adj. Andrew Cowsart...25 Oct 1806.
Wit: Archld McCorkle, Saml McCorkle.   John White (Seal)
Proved by Saml McCorkle, 3 Nov 1809, before Thos Nelson, J. P.

Page 270: John Welsh Sr. of Chesterfield Dist., for $365 to David
            Lany of Lancaster Dist., land on both sides Wild Cat
Creek beginning at an old schoolhouse....13 Feb 18__.
Wit: James Holliman,   John Welsh (Seal)
     David McManus. Proved 11 March 1809, before Jno Crowder,
J. P., by James Holliman.

Page 271: James McIlwain and wife Sarah and Allen Croxton & wife
Mary of Lancaster Dist., for $203, to Jinny Woods,
spinster, 206 acres on Rum Creek, part of 250 acres granted to
Adam Baird, 9 Nov 1774, and a part of 60 acres deeded by James
Douglass to Isom Pulley, which land is our full part of the real
estate of Isom Pulley as Legatees of Isom Pulley decd....11 April
1810.   James McIlwain (Seal)
Wit: Lewis Croxton,   Sarah McIlwain (X) (Seal)
     Henry Vallandingham   Allen Croxton (LS)
     John Carrangham (X).   Mary Croxton (X) (LS)

Proved by Lewis Croxton, 16 May 1810.

Pp. 271-272: Mary Platt of lancaster Dist., spinster, to daughter
Lucy Platt, all my personal estate, cattle, etc...
17 Aug 1809.   Mary Platt (X)(LS)
Wit: Wm. Currey, Baptist Cole. Proved by Wm Currey, 1 Dec 1809.

Pp. 272-273: Whereas William Tate Senr decd late of the Town of
Camden did in his life time make his will, duly
proved and recorded, 12 Sept 1787, to his nephew William Tate
Jr., son of his eldest Brother Samuel Tate of the Kingdom of
Freeland (Ireland?), all estate real and personal and to his
wife Elizabeth Tate in lieu of her dower one third part of real
and personal estate...was entitled to two lots in Camden...William
Tate Junr. of Chester Dist:, to John Johnson of Lancaster Dist.
(a truestee nominated by sd. Tate) and for natural love to my
sons John Johnson Tate, Samuel Tate and James Tate now of Chester
Dist., all right in said lots...1 Aug 1809.   William Tate (Seal)
Wit: J. G. Mathis, A. Perry.

Pp. 274-275: Joseph J. Wade of Lancaster Dist., for $700 to George
Gayden, land adj. Arthur Herrin, Cedar Creek, Bailey
Fleming...1 Jan 1809.   Jos. John Wade (Seal)
Wit: Benjamin Dawson, Uriah Gaden. Proved by Uriah Gayden, 13
July 1810, before H. Hudson,J. P.

Pp. 275-276: 25 July 1809, James Harper, Henry Harper, John Linn
& Benjamin Harper, for themselves and sd. Henry
Harper as agent or trustee for the children of William Harper, to
Margaret Harper widow of Robert Harper (formerly of state and
dist. of Lancaster) whereas sd. Henry, James and Benjamin Harper
John Linn & children of William Harper are entitled to a portion
of the real estate of Robert Harper decd., for $250, 176 acres
adj. Andrew Linn, Dr. Dunlap...   Benjamin Harper (Seal)
Wit: James Blair,   Henry Harper   (Seal)
     Andw Linn,   James Harper   (Seal)
     Margaret McCorcle.   John Linn   (Seal)
Mary Linn & Rosey Harper, of Lancaster Dist., & Elizabeth Harper
and Nancy Harper of York Dist., relinquish dower, that is Mary,
wife of John Linn, Rosey wife of Henry Harper, Elizabeth wife of
Benjamin Harper, and Nancy, wife of James Harper, 27 June 1810.
Proved by Andrew Linn, 27 June 1810, before Jos. Lee, J. Q.

Pp. 276-277: John White of Lancaster Dist., for $242.52 to Moses
White, land help by Robert Harper in his life time
adj. Andrew Linn, Dr. Dunlap, 142 acres...27 June 1810.
Wit; Nancy Harper,   John White
     C. Harroh Johnston, Benjan. Harper.
Margaret White, wife of John, relinquished dower, 5 Sept 1810.
Proved by Benjamin Harper, before Josh. Lee, J. Q.

Page 278: George Petty of Kershaw Dist., planter for $150 to
          John Maxwell & Co., to say Joseph Mickle & John Maxwell
merchants of Camden, 170 acres granted to Henry Gracey, 5 Sept
1791... 27 Sept 1809.   George Petty (Seal)
Wit: Thos Salmond, Ignatius Folmer.
Proved by Thos Salmond, 27 Sept 1809, before Archelaus Watkins,
J. P.

Page 279: William McMeen son & heir of Thomas McMeen decd., of
          Lancaster Dist., and in the consideration of the desire
that my brothers & sister should have a distributive share in
the estate of my father (which I fell heir to by rights of primo-
geniture) and for $1...to James McMeen my brother, 93 acres on
Bear & Gills Creek adj. Eliezar Alexander, John Simpson, John
Farell... 16 Jan 1808.   William McMeen (Seal)
Wit: Susanna Alexander, Mary M. McMeen, Eliezar Alexander.
Proved by Eliezar Alexander, 16 Jan 1808, before Wm. Barkley, J. P.

Pp. 279-280: 16 Dec 1809, James Houze of Jackson County, Ga., to
             Henry Houze of Lancaster Co., S. C., for $20, 16 acres
on Catawba River, part of land, the point of Mountain Island and
Hill Island...   James Houze (Seal)
Wit: Josiah Carlile, Edmond Gresham, J. P. Proved in Lancaster
Dist., by Josiah Carlile, 25 Jan 1810.

Pp. 280-281: State of Georgia: 8 Oct 1806, James Miller of Camp-
             bell Co., Virginia, to George Cowen of Hancock Co.,
Ga., for $600, land on waters of Bear Creek adj. William Graves,
Bryce Miller, Thomas Miller, 267 acres, granted to William Graves.
Wit: Hugh Taylor, John Chambers,   James Miller (Seal)
     John Brodnar Jr.
Proved in Hancock Co., Ga., by John Chambers, before Jno Croder,
J. I. C.

Page 282: Alexander Montgomery of Mississippi Territory and County
          of Adams, appoint John Kirk, in Rutherford County,
Tenn., my lawful attorney, to received from John Montgomery of
Lancaster Dist., S. C., money owed to me...23 Nov 1808.
Wit: Amasa Hague.   Alexander Montgomery (Seal)
Proved in Natchez, Miss Terr., 24 Nov 1808, before John Henderson,
Not. Pub.

Pp. 283-284: John Kirk of Rutherford Co., Tenn., appoint Isaac
             Barr Junr my attorney, to received from John Mont-
gomery of Lancaster Dist., all sums due me...10 Sept 1810
Proved in Rutherford Co., Tenn., before   John Kirk (Seal)
David Fleming, J. P.

Rutherford County, Tenn: 10 Sept 1810, John Kirk personally appeared that stated that Alexander Montgomery now of Miss. Territory did in the year 1787 leave two notes in posseesion of sd.
Kirk....before John L. Jetton, J. P.

Pp. 284-285: John Welsh of Chesterfield Dist., for $15 to Abraham
             Hagler, 100 acres on waters of Lynches Creek, on
the old Waxaw Road, adj. B. Deason...20 Aug 1810. John Welsh (Seal)
Wit: John Welsh Junr., Elijah Baker. Proved by Elijah Baker, 1
Sept 1810, before B. Deason, J. P.

Page 285: John Pace of Lancaster Dist., for Ḷ 100 to George Hugh-
          banks of Chesterfield Dist., 40 acres on SW side Great

Lynches Creek, adj. Thomas Scot Wems, George Haile, George
Taylor...18 Aug 1804.   John Pace (X) (Seal)
Wit: John Eubank,   Elizabeth(?) Pace (X)
    William Griffith (W). Proved by John Hughbanks, 18 Aug
1804, before James Blakeney, J. P., Chesterfield Dist.

Pp. 285-286: John Steel of Lancaster Dist., for $650 to Thomas
            Cureton, granted to William Davis, on the dividing
ridge between Waxaw & Cane Creeks, 154 acres... John Steel (LS)
Wit: Henry Massey, William Todd, William Cureton. Proved by
Henry Massey, 23 Oct 1809, before J. Draffin, J. P.

Pp. 286-287: Matthew Ingle of Chesterfield Dist., to Joanna Mc-
            Manus of Lancaster Dist., for $200, land on S side
Big Linches Creek adj. John Robertson, 25 July 1809....
Wit: Thomas Wimberley,   Matthew Ingle (LS)
    John Hunter (X). Proved by Thomas Wimberly, 6 Jan 1810.

Pp. 287-288: 1 Sept 1809, William Rogers of Mecklenburg Co., N. C.,
            to Dudley Hail of Lancaster Dist.,for $150, 150 acres
on Lynches and Flat Creek adj. Michael McIlwrath, Nathaniel Shepherd...   William Rogers (Seal)
Wit: Joseph Hail, Abram Heill, Thos Neill.Proved by Joseph Hail,
7 Nov 1809, before B. Deason, J. P.

Pp. 288-289: Robert Dunlap of Lancaster Dist., for $1236.86 due to
            the Board of Commissioners of the poor School for
Lancaster Dist., to William Nisbet, chairman of the Board, tract
on waters of Cain and Camp Creeks, adj. John Dunlap, 100 acres
where I now reside, adj. James Montgomery, John Gamble, Benja.
Mattox, Robert McMeen, Thomas McMeen, and also five negroes (named)
...7 Nov 1810.   Robert Dunlap (Seal)
Wit: Bartlett Jones, JosephMassey, Archible Cowsar. Proved by
Bartlett Jones, 7 Nov 1810.

Page 289: Nathan Tomlinson of Lancaster Dist., for love, good
            will, to daughter Sarah Tomlinson, 14 Aug 1810...
Nathan Tomlinson (X) (SL), Wit: George Wren, Clem. Hancock, Isaac
Anderson. Proved by Isaac Anderson, 6 Nov 1810, before Jos.
Draffon, J. P.

Page 290: Nathan Tomlinson to daughter Jane Vaughan, of same, land
            on 12 mile creek, 17 Aug 1810.   Nathan Tomlinson (X)
Wit: Clem. Hancock, Brittain Gant (X), Isaac Anderson. Proved
by Isaac Anderson, 6 Nov 1810.

Nathan Tomlinson to granddaughter Nancy Gant, a negro girl Pat...
Same wit and proof.

Page 291: Nathan Tomlinson to son John Tomlinson of same, negro
            wench Mary, and her child Phill...14 Aug 1810.

Nathan Tomlinson to daughter Elizabeth Gant, negro wench Rachel,
16 Aug 1810.

Page 292: 21 Feb 1810, Robert Hancock and wife Sarah of Lancaster
            Dist., to Wm. Porter of same, 124 acres, on N side Wax-
haw Creek...   Robt Hancock (LS)
Wit: James Massey Junr.,   Sarah Hancock (X) (LS)
    Saml R. Gibson, Jas. Miller. Proved by James Massy Jr.,
6 Nov 1810.

BOOK G

Page 293: Samuel Dunlap of Lancaster Ville, merchant, for $150
        to Hartwell Sledge of Chester Dist., planter, land
granted to Sarah Bottoms, 100 acres, 8 April 1786, conveyed to
Thomas Pulley, to Andrew McIlwane, to myself....10 May 1810.
Wit: Wm. Howe, J. G. Mathis.   Saml Dunlap (LS)
Proved by J. G. Mathis, 15 May 1810. Elizabeth Dunlap, wife of
Samuel, relinquished dower, 24 Sept 1810.

Page 294: Thomas Stevens of Lancaster Dist., for $200 to John
        Gibson, 100 acres on waters of Rocky Creek, a branch of
Cedar Creek, adj. Wm. Balies...25 April 1809. Thomas Stevens (LS)
Wit: Wm. Balie, Jno Bailey, Jos. Garlick. Proved by John Bailey,
1 Oct 1810, before William Currey, J. Q.

Page 295: Robert M. Crockett of Lancaster Dist., stands indebted
        to Robert Barkley, by tw notes of hand...mortgage of
land on Gills Creek, formerly in Anson County, N. C., 477 acres
granted to Jno Barkley...2 Nov 1810   Robert M. Crockett (Seal)
Wit: Saml Dunlap, Jno Simpson, Robt. Crockett. Proved by Saml.
Dunlap, 2 Nov 1810, before Jno Simpson, J. Q.

Page 296: Middleton McDonald of Lancaster Dist., farmer, for
        good will & affection to my mulato man Thomas Fox,
he is set free and gives mare, colt, and cattle, hogs, etc...
Wit: Wm. Fudge, Wm. McDonal.   Middleton McDonald (LS)
Prov. by Wm. McDonald, 16 Jan 1811.

Pp. 296-298: Abraham Perry, Esqr.,Sheriff of Lancaster Dist.,
        by a writ of fieri facias from court of common
pleas, 4th Monday in Oct 1809 at the suit of John McCown, directed
of me to levy $277.28 of property of Jacob Shofner, 100 acres
whereon Metcalf Fisher now lives, sold to Robert Kerr...land
adj. John Johnston, John Graves...4 Feb 1811. Abraham Perry.
Wit: Jno Simpson, Robt Crockett. Proved by Robt Crockett, 4 Feb
1811.

Page 299: Robert Kerr of Lancaster Dist., for $35 to Metcalf
        Fisher, quit claim to 100 acres...4 Feb 1811.
Wit: Jno Simpson, A. Perry.   Robert Kerr (LS)
Proved by Abraham Perry, Esq., 4 Feb1811.

Pp. 299-300: Nathaniel Cousar of Lancaster Dist., for $400 to
        Hugh Hood, land on Gills & Hannahs Creek, waters of
Catawba, 156 acres, number 5 on division of the lands of Nathaniel
Cowsar Senr decd., adj. William Cowsar, estate of James Cowsar,
William Bakrley, Josah A. Cowsar...Nathl Cousar, 10 Nov 1810.
Wit: William Cousar, B. Massey, Allen Hood. Proved by Allen
Hood, 8 Dec 1810.

Pp. 300-301: Thos H. Wade of Lancaster Dist., to son Nathan C.
        Wade, for good will & affection, negro girl Rose,
aged about 30 years, child Carolina about 2 years of age...20
Feb 1811.   Thos H. Wade (Seal)
Wit: Wm. McKenna, Wm. Gibson Jr. Proved by Wm. McKenna, 26 Feb
1811.

Pp. 301-302: William Naremore by virtue of this bill of sale
        into the actual possession of Grace Terrell, all my
property, first negro woman Lucy and her child Sam, cattle, etc..
name later appears Grace Ferrell...25 Nov 1809. William Naremore (+)
Wit: John Brewer, Phebe Brewer (+). Proved 6 July 1808.
204

BOOK G

Page 302: Elijah Philips of Lancaster Dist.,to Michael Horton of
            same, 328 acres adj. Bradies, Eliazar Alexander...13
Oct 1810.   Elijah Philips (C) (LS)
Wit: Wm. R. Horton, Little Jno Belk. Proved by Little Jno Belk,
15 Oct 1810, before James Deason, J. P.

Page 303: John McMeens of Lancaster Dist., a proposer of making a
            removal to the State of Tenn., for a bay gelding about 8
years old, delived by James McMeens, 330 acres surveyed for Brice
Miller, 22 March 1794, granted to Eliezar Alexander, 1 June 1795
... ____ 1808.   John McMeens (LS)
Wit: Andrew White, Susanna Alexander. Proved by Andrew White,
2 Oct 1810.

Page 304: Titus Lany of Lancaster Dist., to David Lany, 50 acres
            for $25, ...14 Jan 1809.   Titus Laney (Ꞁ) (Seal)
Wit: James Holeman, George Lany (Ꞁ), Elijah Clark. Proved by
James Holleman.

Pp. 304-305: Thomas Sumpter Esqr. of Sumter Dist., to John Welch
            of Lancaster Dist., for $10, land on Wild Cat Creek...
3 Sept 1803.   Thos Sumter (Seal)
Wit; Middleton Belk, Robert Welch (X). Proved by Robert Welch,
6 Nov 1810.

Page 305: Thomas Sumter to Jno Welch for $300, land on Wild Cat
            Creek, adj. Daniel Clark, adj. Robert Welch...3 Sept
1803. Same wit. at preceding.

David Laney of Lancaster Dist., for $250 to Saml Funderburk...
(deed left incomplete).

Page 306: 4 Nov 1807, Robert Crawford to Joseph Fincher, of
            Mecklenburg County, for $125...50 acres part of a tract
formerly belonging to Jesse Roper, conveyed from Jesse Roper Sr.
to Jesse Roper Jr.,   Joseph Fincher (Seal)
(apparently this deed is from Joseph Fincher to Robert Crawford).
Wit: Jesse Wren, John Crawford, Archibald Crocket.

Page 307: David Laney to Saml Funderburke, land whereon Robert
            Snipes now lives, 50 acres on Wild Cat Creek, for $200
...17 Jan 1810   David Laney (+).
Wit: John Clark (X), George Laney (X). Proved by George Laney,
22 March 1811.

Pp. 307-308: Grant to Joseph Caston, for Ꞁ 14 s 18, 640 acres
            in Dist. of Camden on the Waggon road from Rockey
River to Camden...29 Sept 1784. Plat included.

Pp. 308-309: Charles Miller of Lancaster Dist., for $700 to
            Benjamin Harper, land on 12 mile creek...14 Sept
1810.   Charles Miller (Seal)
Wit: Andw Johnston, Stephen D. Miller, Henry Harper. Margaret
Miller, wife of Charles, relinquished dower, 7 March 1811. Proved
by Andrew Johnston, 7 March 1811. Plat included.

Pp. 309-310: Recd of Thomas Cauthin $400 for a negro woman Moll,
            about 19 years of age, 9 Jan 1811. James Collins
Proved by John Graves.

BOOK G

Page 310: Rozwell Byrum of Lancaster Dist., for $325 to Cleton
        Byrum, 108 acres on N side of tract of land I now live
on purchased from Charles Barber...29 May 1809. Ozwell Byrum (X)
Wit: Mathias Sims, Judy Cothon, Charles Barber. Proved by Ludy
Cothon, 28 Feb1810, before James Deason, J. P.

Pp. 310-311: Henry Houze of Lancaster Dist., to Joseph Bird of
        Chester Dist., land hel by the possesion of the sd.
Henry Houze & James Houze his father...2 Jan 1811. Henry Houze (LS)
Wit: John McCrory, Henry Horton. Sarah House, wife of Henry,
relinquished dower, 2 Jan 1811. Proved by both wit, 2 Jan 1811.

Pp. 311-312: Henry House of Lancaster Dist., for $700 to Joseph
        Bird of Chester Dist., land at the mouth of Canoe
Branch...2 Jan 1811.

Page 312: Conrod Pliler for $300 to Frederick Pliler, 205 acres
        adj. Funderburk...20 Aug 1810. Conrod Pliler (X).
Wit: John Lenox, Jacob Pliler. Proved by John Lenox.

Pp. 312-313: John Pendergrass of Lancaster Dist., to Wm. McGarrah
        Jr., tract on Dry & Lynches Creek, branches of
cedar Creek, granted to Thomas Charlton, 3 April 1775...10 Feb
1810.   John Pendergrass (LS)
Wit: Isaac Steward, Nath. Pendergrass, Robt. D. Montgomery.
Jincey, wife of John Pendergrass, relinquished dower, 10 Feb 1810.
Proved by Isaac Steward, 8 June 1810.

Pp. 313-314: Thomas S. Howard & wife Elizabeth of Lancaster Dist.,
        to Robert Stinson, of same, planter, for $1938,
263 acres on Waxhaw Creek, adj. Moses Heath, Moses Dickey...20
Nov 1809.   Thos S. Howard (Seal)
Wit: Robert White, James Bready, George White. Proved by James
Breadin , 15 Feb. Elizabeth Howard, relinquished dower.

Pp. 314-315: 24 Jan 1811, Jessee Hood & wife Elizabeth of Lancas-
        ter Dist., for $80 to Andrew McIlwain...two plantations
33 1/3 acres each on Kemp Creek adj. JohnMcKey, granted to James
Adams 8 July 1774, and one tract granted to Robt McIlwain 29 Dec
1786 adj. Alexander Douglass...   Jesse Hood
                              Elizabeth Hood (E)
Wit: George Perry, James Cunningham. Proved 10 April 1811, by
G. Perry, before Robt Crockett, J. P.

Pp. 315-316: S. C. Lancaster Dist: Charles Barber of Kershaw
        Dist., for $500 to Little Berry Harrison of Lancaster
Dist., 170 acres adj. Frederick Weaver, Sims, Kowel Jocks line...
1 March 1810...   Charles Barber (Seal)
Wit: Middleton Joiner,John Harison, Saml Bowden. Proved by Saml
Bowden, 10 April 1810, before Joseph Draffon, J. P.

Pp. 316-317: John Funderburk of Chesterfield Dist., for $100 to
        David Funderburk, 81 acres in the Dists of Lancaster
& Chesterfield, granted to sd. David Funderburk, granted 6 Aug
1787...16 March 1811.   John Funderburk (X)
Wit: John Funderburke, Jeremiah Bunderburk, Paul Pliler. Proved
by John Funderburke, before Thos Nelson,J. P., 16 March 1811.

Pp. 317-318: John Myrs of Colwell County, Kentucky for $300 to
        Amos Hough of Lancaster Dist., 200 acres on waters
of Wild Cat Creek...3 Oct 1810.

BOOK G

Proved by Saml Dunlap, before Nathan Barr, J. P., 2 Sept 1811.

Pp. 329-331: John Ferrell of Lancaster Dist., farmer, for $340
        to William Farrell, farmer, land in fork of Gills &
Bear Creek, 94½ acres, received from Jno McMeen, 1 Feb 1808...
13 June 1811.   John Farrell
Wit: Robt Crockett, Elix. Crockett. Proved by Robt Crockett,
4 July 1811.

Pp. 331-332: Evan Vaughn & wife Jenney of Lancaster Dist., to
        Benjamin Harper, two tracts on S side twelve mile
creek adj. Henry Harper...23 April 1811...   Aven Vaughan (Seal)
Wit: Henry Harper, Jeremiah Cureton,   Jane Vaughan (Seal)
    Abah Burns.
Proved by Henry Harper, before Jno Steward.

Pp. 332-334: James Crenshaw of Lancaster Dist., for $600 to
        Arthur Hicklin of Chester Dist., 200 acres granted
to William Ashly, on E side Cataba River on Camp Creek & Dry
Creek, adj. Middleton McDonald, formerly Thomas Howze, Mrs. Cor-
nelias, Jno Johnston, formerly William Tillman, Jno Brown, formerly Jesse Tillman, Henry Hortons formerly Joseph Crenshaw, conveye
to James Crenshaw by Jno Chesnut of Camden...a contract with the
exrs. of the estate of Col. Archa. Gill decd...8 April 1811.
Wit: Wm. G. Stevens,   Jas Crenshaw (Seal)
    Jason Hicklan. Proved by Wm. G. Stevens, 2 Oct 1811,
before Wm. Curry, U. Q.

Pp. 334-335: The petition of Henry Dunlap sheweth that Israel
        G. Mathis, otherwise called I. G. Mathis is justly
indebted to your petitioner for $75 with interest and refuses
payment...31 Jan 1811.

Pp. 335-336: 16 Nov 1811, John May of Charleston to John Country-
        man of Lancaster Dist., 100 acres adj. lands of
Richard Couser, John Richardson which formerly belonged to Anna-
nias Black, Wm. Barkley Esqr, for $160...promissary note....
Wit: Wilks Caston,   John Countryman (Seal)
    John Hagan. Proved by John Hagan, 18 Nov 1811.

Pp. 336-337: Wilks Caston of Lancaster Dist., by notes of hand
        indebted to JohnMay, payable 1 Nov 1813...mortgage
of lots in Village of Lancaster...5 Nov 1811.   Wilks Caston (Seal)
Wit: Wm. McKenna, Abram Perry. Proved by Wm. McKenna, 18 Nov
1811.

Pp. 337-338: William Caston of Lancaster Dist., obliged to John
        May of Charleston for $672, payable 10 Jan 1813...
mortgage of lot in Lancaster Village adj. heirs of Blackman,
James Douglass...3 Dec 1811.   Wm. Caston (Seal)
Wit: Thomas Lee, Wm. McKenna. Proved by Wm. Lee, before Jno
Simpson, J. Q.

Pp. 338-340: John Fleming of Dist. of Lancaster, planter, for
        $700 to William Carnahan, 300 acres in the fork of
Dry Creek, waters of Camp Creek, granted to Joseph Lee, and part
granted to Bailey Fleming Jr, adj. John Mackey...26 Sept 1811.
Wit: Wm. Curry,   John Fleming (Seal)
    Isaac Stuart.
Rebecca Fleming, wife of John, relinsuiqhed dower, 26 Dec 1811.
Proved by Isaac Sutart, 27 Sept 1811.

Pp. 340-341: Wm. Barkley of Lancaster Dist., for $70 to Ezra
            Merriman of Town of Cheshire, State of Connecticut,
lot in Lancaster Town, adj. William Gibson...11 Feb 1812.
Wit: Saml Dunlap, Danl McLean.   Wm. Barkley (LS)
Proved by Saml Dunlap, 24 Feb 1812, before Robert Crockett, J. P.

Pp. 341-342: Andrew McIlwain of Lancaster Dist., for $1200 to
            John Kingsburg of Fairfield Dist., land on both sides
mouth of Cedar Creek, 389 acres, adj. George Hays, James Bredin,
Jesse Vanwinkle, and the Cattawba Company, plat by Thomas Archer
15 May 1803, as laid off by Patrick Graves...14 Dec 1811.
Wit: Ezekiel Mayhew,   Andw McIlwain (Seal)
     Vincent A. Edwards, Thomas Hern.
Margaret McIlwain, wife of Andrew, relinquished dower 20 Feb
1812. Proved by Thos Hern, 1 Feb 1812.

Page 343: Daniel Harper of Lancaster Dist., for $200 to Jacob
          Carns, of Lancaster, land granted to Robert Harper...
24 Sept 1811.   Daniel Harper (Seal)
Wit: Jacob Carns, Catherine Carnes (X). Proved by Jacob Carnes,
12 Nov 1811, before B. Deason, J. P.

Page 344: Joseph Gracey, planter, for $200 to Sidney Gracey
          of same, land adj. Joseph Gracey Junr, 150 acres plat,
13 July 1809...7 Nov 1811.   Joseph Gracey (Seal)
Wit: William Powel, Mary Powel (X).

Pp. 344-345: Margary Montgomery of Lancaster Dist., sets free and
            emancipates mulatto girl Rinch about 19 years of age,
adjudged by a J. Q. & five freeholders according to an act of
assembly...28 Feb 1812.   Margary Montgomery (X)
Wit: Robert Nelson,Thomas Nelson, Hugh Coffey. Proved by Thomas
Nelson, 28 Feb1812.

Page 345: John Simpson, J. Q., certifies that Elizabeth Barkley,
          wife of William Barkley relinquishes interest in a
tract to Ezra Merriman, 16 March 1812.

We certify upon the examination of oath of Margary Montgomery,
owner of a negro slave Rinah, a mulatto, country born, about 19
years of age 5' 4 or 5" high, 28 Feb 1812, that she is of good
character and capable of gaining a livelyhood by honest means...
John Montgomery, J. Q., Thos Nelson, Hugh Coffey, William Nelson,
Robert Craig, Robert Nelson Jr.

Mary Crockett quits claim to a negro Joe disposed of by her father
to her uncle William Richardson Davie, 16 Feb 1803.
Wit: Robert Crockett.   Mary Crockett (X)

Page 346: 9 Nov 1810, Jesse Joy and wife Weeny of Lancaster Dist.,
          to John Carnes, for $165, land adj. Absolam Ivey...
Wit: Alex N. Bell, Wike Ivy,   Jesse Ivy (LS)
     Alexander Steel.   Weeny Ivy (LS)
Proved by Alexander Steel, 9 April 1811, before William Currey,
J. Q.

Pp. 347-348: Abraham Perry, Sheriff of Lancaster Dist., by
            virtue of a sum pro of fieri facias from the Court
of Common pleas, 1810, at the suit of Robert Douglass to levy from
goods of Henry Hudson and Thomas Stevens, $75.27...land sold
granted to Thomas Harrington 5 June 1771, to John Russel and

Robert Cunningham...2 March 1812.   Abraham Perry S. L. D.
Wit: Thos Williams Jr., Robert D. Montgomery.
Proved by Robert D. Montgomery.

Page 348: Margaret Isom of Lancaster Dist., for $100 to John
          Hamilton of same, 100 acres granted to John Cannington
7 Jan 1788, adj. Wm Reves Black...17 Nov 1810. Margaret Isom (LS)
Wit: Danl Harper, Nathan Cook. Proved by Daniel Harper, 29 Dec
1810, before B. Deason, J. P.

Page 349: Isaac Barr Sen of Rutherford Co., Tenn., appoints
          Nathan Barr of Lancaster Dist., attorney to receive
from John Caskey, all sums due...24 Aug 1809.Isaac Barr Senr (LS)
Wit: John L. Jetton. Ack. in Rutherford County, Tenn., before
James L. Armstrong, J. P.

Page 350: Joannah McManus of Lancaster Dist., for $70 to John
          Robinson, 175 acres, in the fork of the meadow branch
and the long branch...11 May 1811.   Joannah McManus (LS)
Wit: Drury Massey, Reuben Hough (X).
Proved by Drewry Massey, 11 May 1811, before B. Deason, J. P.

Pp. 350-351: William Howe of Lancaster Dist., for $1050 to
             Robert, James & Samuel Dunlap, 134 acres on Gills
Creek whereon sd. Howe now lives near to Lancaster Ville, on the
road from Charleston to Salisbury, part of 302 acres granted to
Richard Couser, 24 Sept 1754, adj. Nathan Barr, Robert Davis,
estate of Alexander Craig or William McKenna...5 Nov 1811.
Wit: John Montgomery, Saml Dunlap.   Wm. Howe (LS)
Isabella Howe, wife of Wm., relinquished dower, 30 March 1812.
Proved by John Montgomery, 30 March 1812, before John Stewart,
J. P.

Pp. 352-353: Saml Dunlap of Lancasterville, for $800 to Robert,
             James & Saml Dunlap, land in fork of Gills and
Bear Creek, part of grant to Simon Beard, of 200 acres 5 June
1786, 100 acres, adj. John Simpson, the representatives of
James Couser decd., John Ferrel, James Purdy, and the town of
Lancasterville...5 Nov 1811.   Saml Dunlap (LS)
Wit: John Montgomery, Wm. Howe. Proved by John Montgomery, 30
March 1812. Elizabeth C. Dunlap, wife of Saml., relinquished
dower, 30 March 1812.

Pp. 353-354: Samuel Dunlap of Lancasterville for $1500 to
             Robert, James & Samuel Dunlap, lot in Lancaster Ville
adj. Public ground for the Jail & Court house, adj. John May,
Col. Wm. Simpson, the buildings occupied by me as a store and
dwelling house and a lot adj. James Purdy...5 Nov 1811.
Wit: John Montgomery,   Samuel Dunlap (LS)
     Wm. Howe.
Elizabeth Dunlap relinquished dower, 30 March 1812. Proved by
John Montgomery.

Pp. 354-355:   1812, Daniel Clark to John Funderburk, for
             $175, land on N side N. Wildcat Creek, adj. Snipes,
Funderburk, bought from Welsh, 120 acres.... Daniel Clark.
Wit: Nathaniel Clark, John Clark. Proved by John Clark, 25
March 1812.

Page 355: 27 March 1812, John Funderburk of Lancaster Co., to
          John Funderburk of Chesterfield County, for $180...

land on N side North Wild Cat Creek, adj. Snipes, Saml. Funderburk, purchased of Daniel Clark...   John Funderburk (LS)
Wit: Jno Funderburk, Samuel Funderburk. Proved by Samuel Funderburk, 20 March 1812, before John Welsh, J. Q.

Page 356: 16 March 1811, James Fudge to Samuel Douglass, for
           $300, as security for debt...tract on waters of Camp
Creek granted 15 Sept 1795, to Pair, adj. Francis Boykin, Wm.
Ashley, Jesse Tilmon, McDonald...   James Fudge (X)
Wit: George McGarrah,   Samuel Douglass
     David B. Carnes.

Page 357: Henry Harper of Lancaster Dist., planter, for $1000 to
           Thomas Thrower, 40 acres part of 376 acres granted to
Samuel Burnett on N side Waxsaw Creek...26 July 1811.
Wit: Thomas D. Barr,   Henry Harper (LS)
     Henry Massey, William Porter. Proved by Thomas D. Barr,
2 Aug 1811, before Jos. Draffen, J. P.

Pp. 357-358: 15 Feb 1812, John McDaniel to Thomas Cauthin, for
             $400...land on Hanging Rock waters, 184 acres, part
of grant to William Cato, 1795 adj. Henry Horton,James Love,
Thomas McMasters...   John McDonald (LS)
Wit: James Stevens, John Stevens. Proved by John Stevens, 4 May
1812, before Thomas Nelson,J. P.

Pp. 358-359: John Simpson of Lancaster Dist., for $102 to William
             Simpson, land in village of Lancaster #11 on Broad
St. and Catawba St., adj. Dunlap, May and Purdy...2 May 1812.
Wit: Mary P. Simpson, Thomas Lee.   Jno Simpson (LS)
Proved by Thomas lee, 2 May 1812.
Jane Simpson, wife of John, relinquished dower, before Jos. Lee,
J. Q.

Page 359: Joseph Crenshaw of Jackson County, Ga., planter, to
           Henry Horton of the Dist. of Lancaster, planter,
on N side Dry Creek, waters of Cataba, granted to Benjamin Cook...
19 Jan 1809.   Joseph Crenshaw (Seal)
Wit: Micajah Crenshaw, Robt Champion. Proved by both wit.,19
Jan 1809, before Wm. Currey, J. Q.

Page 360: Richard Rutlege of Lancaster Dist., by bond dated 17
           Sept 1811 indebted to George Gayden for the payment
of $450....land on waters of Little Lynches Creek, granted for
100 acres adj. Lewis Peeples, Thos Welsh, Ann Brewer, James
Ferguson, Burwell Hilton....7 Nov 1811.   Richard Rutledge (LS)
Wit: Charles Miller, Uriah Gaydon.

                    End of Book G.

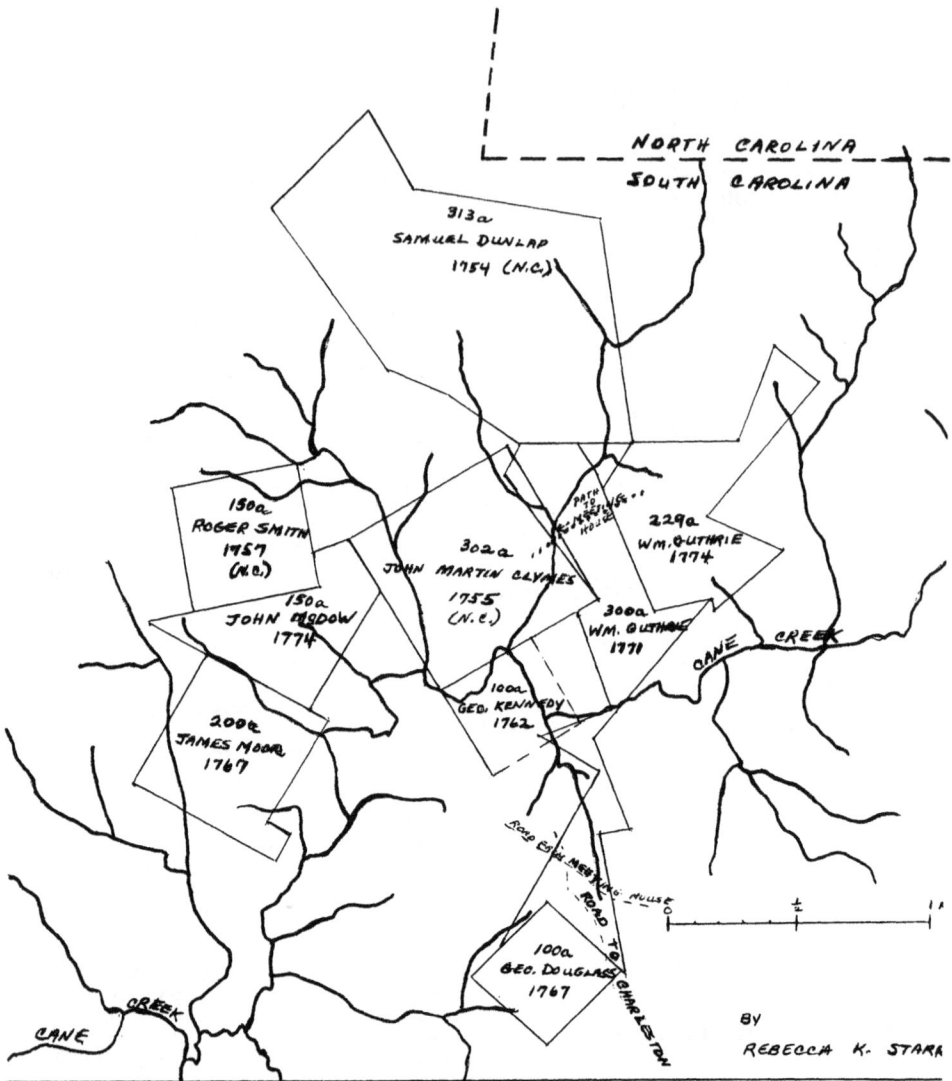

Map labels:
- NORTH CAROLINA
- SOUTH CAROLINA
- 313a SAMUEL DUNLAP 1754 (N.C.)
- 150a ROGER SMITH 1757 (N.C.)
- 302a JOHN MARTIN CLYMES 1755 (N.C.)
- PATH TO MEETING HOUSE
- 229a WM. GUTHRIE 1774
- 150a JOHN McDOW 1774
- 300a WM. GUTHRIE 1771
- CANE CREEK
- 200a JAMES MOOR 1767
- 100a GEO. KENNEDY 1762
- ROAD FROM MEETING HOUSE
- ROAD TO CHARLESTON
- 100a GEO. DOUGLASS 1767
- CANE CREEK
- BY REBECCA K. STARK

SOME EARLY LAND GRANT PLATS IN LANCASTER COUNTY

BOOK G

Wit: Daniel Harper,
    C. Cook.
John Myrs (Seal)
Frances Myers (X) (Seal)
Proved by Charles Cook, 3 Oct 1810, before B. Deason, J. P.

Pp. 318-320: 13 ___ 1808, Thos Lee, Sheriff, to Samuel Caston...
        Gustavus Rape, formerly of this state, was seized
of 375 acres on waters of Great Lynches Creek, part of grant to
Genl. Sumter, adj. Devault Funderburk...Daniel Beaver was indebted
to sd. Gustavus Rape...land of sd. Beaver was sold....Thos Lee
Wit: Thos H. Wade, Jos Lee, Q. U.

Pp. 320-321: Charles Montgomery of Lancaster Dist., for $285
        to Charles Gilaspe of same, part of land grant to
Thomas Campbell, ___ Oct 1767, transferred to Hugh Montgomery,
and bequeathed to Jas. Robt Jnr & Hugh Montgomery did sell to
John Mackey, and sd. John Mackey to Charles Montgomery, 23 Sept
1797...8 Nov 1804.   Charles Montgomery.
Wit: Frances McTeer, Robert Davis. Agness Montgomery, wife of
Charles, relinquished dower, 9 April 1811. Proved by Frances
McAteer, 9 April 1811, before Robt Crockett, J. P.

Page 322: John Chesnut of Camden, planter, for $200 to Frederick
        Weaver of Lancaster, 100 acres on head branches of
Cedar Creek, County of Craven, surveyed 9 Jan 1760 for Charles
Lowder, granted to Patrick Brady, 18 Jan 1765...15 Dec 1808.
Wit: James J. Deas,   John Chesnut (Seal)
    Rawleigh Weaver.

Pp. 323-324: ___ Nov 1806, Thomas Lee, Sheriff, to Robert Barkley
        ...whereas William Gibson was seized of 500 acres,
and was indebted to Hugh McMullen...sold for $160...Thomas Lee (Seal)
Wit: N. C. Wade, Walter Carson. Proved by N. C. Wade, 19 June
1811, before Jno Simpson, J. Q.

Pp. 324-325: John Kirk of Lancaster Dist., for $465 to William
        Harper, 200 acres held under two granteds 6 Aug 177_
and other 3 June 1793, adj. Wm. Harper, Wm. Barkley, Thomas Thom-
sen, Shaver, Mathew Kirk, on Bear Creek a prong of Cane Creek...
29 Feb 1808.   Jno Kirk (Seal)
Wit: William Harper, Mathew Kirk. Proved by William Harper, 13
Oct 1806.

Pp. 325-326: William A. Harper of Chester Dist., to William Harper
        of Lancaster Dist., for $100, 200 acres, granted to
    Robert Harper...16 Sept 1803. William A. Harper
Wit: Robert Harper, Andrew K. Harper. Proved 9 Jan 1810 by
Robert Harper, before Joseph Draffon, J. P.

Pp. 326-327: 27 Jan 1811, Jno Anderson of Lancaster Dist., to
        George Anderson, land adj. Wm Porter...
                         John Anderson (X)
Wit: Jas Miller, Wike Ivy.   Rhodah Anderson (+)
Proved by Wike Ivy, 5 Aug 1811, before Jno Simpson, J. Q.

Pp. 327-329: Isaac Barr Senr of Rutherford Co., Tenn, special
        atty for Jno Kirk of same, appointed 10 Sept 1810,
by virtue of a power of atty from Alexander Montgomery of the
Miss. Teritory, Adams County, 23 Nov 1808, for $171 to John
Montgomery of S. C., Lancaster Dist., 100 acres on both sides
Camp Creek...5 Oct 1810.   Isaac Barr (Seal)
Wit: Wm. Howe, Saml Dunlap.

Cairy, Natl. 29
Caldwell, Robert 98
Campbell also see Campbel,
  Campble
Campbel, Elizabeth 36
  Marey 180
  Mary 171
Campbell, Andrew 32
  George 181, 191
  John 133
  Mary 124, 145
  Thomas 6, 47
  William 3, 36
Campble, Alexander 48
  George 48
  Mary 61
Canmore, James 80
Cannington also see Kenn-
  ington
Cannington, Edward 28, 46,
  58(2), 67, 77(3)
  John 46, 58(2), 82,
  172, 210
  William 77, 112
Cannon, Roger 133(2)
Cant, Henry 1
Cantey, John 163
  Josiah 11, 74, 81(2),
  111
  William 11
  Zachariah 17(2), 18,
  23, 29, 33(5), 35
  (2), 37, 38, 39, 40,
  94, 95(4), 96, 97
Canteys, _____ 32
Canty, _____ 143
Cantzon, Daniel 155
  John 45, 46, 52, 53(3),
  82, 100, 101(3),
  134, 135, 143, 147,
  152, 153, 154, 155,
  158, 165, 174, 180,
  182, 188, 193
  John Jr. 127
  Margaret Curry 147
  Moses 53(2), 75, 82,
  101, 114, 122, 141,
  147, 152, 155, 156
Caot, William 63
Capel, Button 177
Carlil, Widow 119
Carliles, Joel 40, 102(2),
  129
  Josiah 201
Carlisle, _____ 143
  John 99
  Richard 99
Carn, Jacob 188
Carnahan, Adam 6, 12, 67,
  68(2), 169, 171,177
  John 171
  William 208
Carnanghan, Isabel 90
  John 68
Carnes, Alexander 183,191
  Catherine 209
  Daniel 131, 151, 152,
  191
  David 54
  David B. 211
  Frederick 55
  Jacob 106, 131, 209
  John 66, 68, 171, 209
  Nancey 131
  Rebekah 52
  Robert 99, 191
  William 68
Carnes also see Carnes
Carns, Alexander 6, 13(2),
  52, 66, 68, 180
  Daniel 5, 43, 116
  Fredick 188
  Jacob 209

Carns cont.
  Jane 165
  John 171, 187, 188,197
  Mrs. 149
Carpenter, Robertson 50
Carr, Col. John 55
Carrangham, John 201
Carrell, Alexander 141
  James 141, 163
Carrin, John 114
Carrol, Alexander 163
  James 162
Carruth, Alexander Craig-
  head 1, 3, 8, 53, 81,
  87, 91(2)
  James 1, 3, 8, 54, 91
  (2), 93
  Walter 62(2), 91(2),
  93
  William R. 62
Carryl, Jane 100, 114
Carsen also see Carson
Carsen, Agness 128
  Thomas 178, 187, 191
  William 135
Carson, Eleanor 154, 155
  Ellonder 154
  Grace 154, 155
  John 4, 71
  Thomas 158, 176
  Walter 106, 207
  William 36, 123, 128
  (2), 167, 176
Carter, Ben 159
  Benjamin 4, 18, 29(2),
  30, 96
  Charles 133
  Francis 30
  J. A. 89
  James 131, 134
  John 36, 59
  Robert 32
Cartledge, John 36, 59
Carwell, David 56
Cary, Nathaniel 30(4)
Caskel, John 145
Caskey, James 132
  John 132, 136, 145,
  210
  Margaret 132, 145
  William 167
Casky, Samuel 92
Cason, Glass 10
  John 33
Cassity, Peter 95
Caster, John 47, 105
Caston also see Gaston
Caston, Elias 180, 187
  Elizabeth 8, 127
  Frances 105, 170
  Gabriel 117, 127
  Glass 1, 7(2), 8, 10
  (2), 11, 17, 45, 60,
  117(2), 126, 127,
  128, 130, 133, 152,
  158, 181, 188, 191
  James 161
  John 45, 58(2), 60(2),
  104, 105, 110, 117,
  118, 123, 129, 133,
  147(2), 153, 157,
  161, 170, 179, 194,
  197
  John Jr. 7(2), 58, 60,
  110
  Joseph 7, 8, 10, 53,
  62, 83, 87, 114,
  126, 127(2), 130,
  161, 179, 186, 205
  Mildred 110, 117
  Milla 45, 58
  Milly 117
  Samuel 7, 10(3), 11,

Caston cont.
  Samuel cont. 20, 45, 54,
  58, 60, 69, 77(2),
  83, 157, 165, 170,
  174, 185, 190, 192,
  207
  Seth 53, 58, 83, 126
  Susanna 190
  William 10, 53, 58, 83,
  86, 107, 117, 126,
  157, 189, 208
  Wilks 208(2)
Cato, Henry 1, 10(2), 11,
  54, 58, 82
  John 143, 144
  Jno. 3
  Needham 54, 77
  Starling 144
  Sterling 77, 82
  Susan 99
  Tabitha 1, 11, 54, 58,
  82
  Vinson 54
  William 99(2), 138(2),
  148, 165, 200, 211
Catoney, Elenore 3
Caudle, Stephen 78(2), 82
Caulkins, John 47
Cauthan, William 103
Cauthen, Thomas 89(2), 90
Cauthin, Thos. 209, 211
Cauthon, John 147, 186
  William 186
Cauthorn, James 88, 92, 93
  John 117, 167
  Thomas 75(2), 117, 147
  (2), 176, 193
  William 92, 112(2), 115,
  173, 192
Cauthran, Thos. 187
  Wm. 187
Cawthon, Thomas 193
  William 142
Cawthorn (Chewthorn), John
  162, 169
Cawthron, Thomas Jr. 166
Cay, Henry 64
Cayrey, James 30
Cearnes also see Carnes
Cearnes, Robert 71
Cerns, Frederick 190
Chaddock, Thomas 190
Chadwick, Thomas 27, 190
Chambers, John 202
  Maxwell 181
  Susanna 104
  Williams 87, 104, 114,
  164, 168, 186
Champion, Elinar 198
  Jacob 149, 198
  John 198
  John Lloyd 11
  Littleberry 156, 181
  Richard 3, 7, 8, 11,
  17(2), 18(2), 19,
  20(2), 24, 25, 39,
  69, 176
  Richard Lloyd 8, 20
  R. L. 153, 176
  Robert 149, 211
Chandler, Samuel 32
Chappel, Robert 105
Charlton, Dr. 29, 30
  Thomas 7, 30, 35, 59,
  175, 206
Chartten, Tho. 19(2)
Chassure, John 191
Chawthon, Thomas 65
Cherry, John 92
Chesher, John 69
Cheshire, John 12
Chestnut, Harriet 95
  James 26

Graham cont.
John cont. 83, 91, 93,
165, 177
Samuel 53, 56, 86, 113
William 25, 50, 53, 56,
70, 113, 132, 197
Winifred 14
Grann, William 142
Grave, James 150
Graves, Andrew 186
Elizh. 161
James 146, 154, 155
John 50, 107, 142, 167,
186, 204, 205
John Sr. 94
Jos. 143
Joseph 48, 104
Patrick 83, 107, 126,
132, 134, 135, 142,
146, 156, 159, 161,
166, 180, 182, 209
Jeremiah 142, 195
Richard 82, 127, 135,
174
William 104, 107(2),
130, 134, 186, 195,
202
Gray, Charles 3
Jacob 48, 84, 144
Jacob Sr. 84
John 14, 54
Mary 14
Samson 84
Shared 43, 84
Green, John 121, 181
William 99
Greer, James 55
John 151, 152, 180
Joseph 61, 72, 73
Nancy 72
Thos. 186
Greersow, George 15
Greeves, John Sr. 94
Gregory, Jno. 196
William 196
Gresham, Edmond 202
Gribble, Jas. 153
Grier, John 67(2)
Grierson, Jane 116
Griffen, Jonas 12, 72, 73
Griffith, David 26
William 203
Grimes, William 56
Grimkie, John F. 1
Grizle, Gale 9
Grizzle, Thomas 10
Guardner, Clemen 58
Guin, Jeptha(h) 147
Gunn, Jame 74
Guren(?), John 12
Guthrey, William 15
Guthrie, Elizabeth 26
James 12
Jane 12
Robert 12, 26, 92
William 12, 26, 83,
92, 99
Guy, James H. 195
Gynn, Jepthah 135

Hacket, James 95
Haddin, William 15
Haggan also see Haggin,
Hagin
Haggans, John 35, 134,
186, 208
Haggins, James 44, 49, 56,
62(2), 75
John 179
Martha 44
Samuel 62
William 35

Hagler, Abraham 36, 59,
107, 157, 181, 202
Boston 107
Jacob 107, 192
Paul 151
Hagon, John 179
Hague, Amasa 202
Hagwood, Isiah 157
Haig, Sarah 67
Hail, Benjamin 150, 189
Dudley 203
Ferguson 126, 128,
189, 190
George 135, 147
Joseph 162, 203
Thomas 154
Haile also see Hale, Hail
Haile, Benjamin 18, 28, 36
(2), 39, 44(2), 50
(3), 54, 58(3), 59,
61, 62(2), 64(3),
67, 72(4), 73, 74,
76, 78, 80, 82(3),
92, 93, 98, 99, 105,
106(2), 108(3), 109
(2), 110(2), 118,
119(2), 121, 127,
129, 132(2), 142,
143, 156
Benj. Jr. 64(2)
Benj. Sr. 72, 110
Catherine 72
Caty 110
Elizabeth 60
Dempsy 157, 165
Dudley 165
Dudly 197
Ferguson 67, 72, 98,
99, 106, 110, 119,
127, 130, 138, 156
George 203
Gustavis 194
Hardy 197
Joseph 50, 60, 82,
108, 197
Mary 121
Haings, James 148
Haize, James 63
Hale, Benjamin 199
Benjamin Jr. 24, 59
Ferguson 58
Hales, Sarah 30
Henry 30
Hall, James 13(2), 57, 70,
71(2), 178
James Jr. 71
John 48
Sarah 71(2)
Thomas 70
Thomas Lant 62, 66
William 165, 178
Hamilton, James 164
John 210
William 44, 98, 139
Hammet, William 87
Hammond, Leroy 82
Rawleigh 142
Samuel 63, 87, 88, 138
Hammons, Saml. 185
Hampton, Benjamin F. 194,
198
Henry 115
Wade 51, 115
Hancock, Clem 165, 166,
197, 203
Clement 197
Elizabeth 144
Francis 90
John 143, 144, 168,
177, 178, 186, 190
Jno. 188
Joseph J. 144
Josiah 132, 135, 136,

Hancock cont.
Josiah cont. 144, 149
Mary 90
Robert 48, 54, 65, 83,
106, 107, 134(2),
138, 139, 165, 197,
(2), 203
Sarah 83, 197, 203
Thomas 90
William 165, 173, 197
Hanks, Thos. 192
Hanna, W. J. 88
Hannah, Ben 193
Harenton, Sarah 175
Thomas 175
Harford, J. 162
John 169
Harker, John 18, 32
Harper, Andrew K. 207
Benjamin 13(2), 28(2),
59, 66, 68, 92, 93,
107, 120, 187, 195,
196, 201, 205, 208
Daniel 58, 207, 209,
210
Elizabeth 201
Gracey 154
Henry 83, 201, 205,
208, 211
James 123, 167, 184,
187, 201
John 154(2), 155, 171
John Linn 201
Martha 92
Margaret 201
Nancy 201
Nancy 201
Robert 12, 72(2), 92,
156, 187, 189, 201,
207, 209
Robert Jr. 72
Rosey 201
Sarah 53(2), 58, 75,
82, 101, 147, 187
William 13(2), 24, 27,
28, 46(2), 55, 68,
69, 71, 86, 93, 127,
130, 171, 176, 201,
207
William A. 132, 135,
207
William Sr. 48
Harmon, Robert 130(2), 133
Harrington, Elizabeth 13
Drury 13, 14(2), 20
Thomas 35, 175, 209
Harris, Francis 7
George 133, 192
James 3, 85
Little Berry 206
William 3, 26, 70, 77,
85, 116, 136, 148
Harrison, Berry 199
John 199
William 136, 148
Hart, Benjamin 123
Derrill 96
Jacob 65, 99
James 123
Susanna 99
Thomas 61
Thoas (Thomas) 124, 145
Harvis, James 31
Hase, James 121
Haslam, William T. 73
Hatfield, John 29
Havis, Jessie 123
Hawkins, James 149
Philip 113
Hay, William 71
Hayes, George 124, 166
James 154
Jesse 186

222

225

McMurray, John 56, 65, 75, 128
  John Jr. 109
  John Sr. 109
  Samuel 128, 136
McMurrey, John 149
  John Jr. 149
McMurry, Andrew 90
  John 124, 128, 136, 149
  Martha 149
  Samuel 148, 149
McNiel, Mary 75
McNutt, John 127
McOllough, James 8
McRa_____ 143
  Duncan 31, 33(2), 35, 40, 94(3), 95(2), 96(2), 146
  Mary 35
McRae, Duncan 146
McRee, Samuel 21
  William 20
McTeer, Francis 207
  James 124
McTier, Frances 65
  James 61
  John 65
McTyre, Robert 41
McVey, George 108
  James 99, 108, 172
  William 108
McWillie, Adam 122, 149, 189
  Dm. 196
  William 89

Mabry, Thomas 61
Macatire, James 139
MacCallum, Kenneth 70
MacCay, Benjamin 70
Mackey, Charles 97, 105, 147, 170
  Charles Jr. 60(3)
  James 140
  John 52, 97, 176, 207, 208
  Jonathan 47, 52
  Soloman 42(2), 55, 63
  Thomas 52, 179
Mackmanners, Charles 185
Maddocks, William 12, 45
Maddon, Samuel 177
Maddox, Benjamin 28, 46, 50, 53(3), 67, 82, 101(2), 140, 146, 151
  James 131
  Rose 28
  Rosemond 53
  Samuel 136, 177
  William 65, 83, 113
Madison, Rd. 5
Maffet, Elizabeth 9
  James 113
Magee, Myer 135
Mahaffy, Oliver 25
Makelvene, Samuel 145
Maler, George 167
Mallau, John 8
Mallet, Isaac 79, 108(3), 109(2)
  Jesse 78
  Providence 108
  Stephen 108
Malone, John 30
Maloy, Edward 38(2), 39
Manor, Hugh 60
Maples, Thomas 25
Marder, Samuel 135
Marion, William 66
Marlar, George 55, 167, 196

Marler, Elizabeth 140
  John 181
  William 140, 181, 182
Marlin, Benjamin 25
Marlow, George 87, 169, 178
  James 74
  William 83, 85, 174
  Wm. Jr. 8, 39
Marsh, Ann 7
Marshal, Mary 31
  John 142, 143
Marshall, John 143, 159
  Jno. R. 178
Marshel, Col. 17
  James 10, 16, 73
  John 6, 10(2), 12, 14, 15, 17, 18, 31, 35, 16(2), 37, 38, 48 (2), 72, 74(3), 81, 95, 106(2), 109,144
  Tabitha 144
Marshell, John 117, 118(3), 132
  Thomas 96
Martain, Samuel 125
Martin, Andrew 22(2)
  Benjamin 59
  Banun 26
  David 19
  J. G. 194
  Phebe 99
  Sam 84(2)
  Saml. 117, 136(2), 148, 158
Masho, Jesse 104
Mason, William 1
Massey, Arthur 85
  B. 183, 200, 204
  Drew 197
  Drewry 210
  Drury 210
  Elizabeth 85, 158
  George 11
  Henry 11, 36, 51, 52 (2), 62, 65(3), 66, 68, 71, 72, 75, 83, 92, 98(2), 99, 107, 108, 120, 129, 138, 158, 191, 199, 203, 211
  James 11, 51, 55, 68, 71(2), 80, 98, 152, 163
  James Jr. 203
  Joanna 108
  John 18, 36, 76, 87, 104
  Joseph 183, 200, 203
  Oliver 162
  William 2, 51, 53, 55 (2), 68, 87, 128, 134, 183
  William Jr. 51
Massy, James 183
Masters, John 157
Mathis, Daniel 19, 20
  Gov. 20
  Israel G. 208
  J. G. 197, 201, 204
  Philip 105
  Samuel 3, 18, 29, 32, 34, 61, 69(2), 96, 97, 125, 144
Mathison, Alexr. 117
Matthews, Daniel 20
Mattox, Benjamin 203
  Daniel 185
  James 185
  William 191
Mausmon, John 143
Maxfield, Alexd. 45
Maxwell, John 202

Maxwell cont.
  William 20
May, Benjamin 99
    211
  John 44, 48, 50, 86, 103(2), 121(2), 123, 132, 133, 134, 135, 136, 138, 140, 142, 150, 155, 166, 168, 180, 182, 198, 208 (3)
Mayerson, John 1
Mayhew, Ezekiel 209
Mayhank, William 24
Mays also see Maze
Mays, John 176
  William 7
Maze, William 51
Meacham, Mark 83, 134, 166
  Winnefred 166
  Winney 166
Meadors, John 193
Meados, John 193
Means, Hugh 139
Meassy, Oliver 189
Merriman, Ezra 209(2)
Merryman, Abraham 104, 110
  Joshua 104
  Mark 104, 110
Mesho, Charles 179
  Elizabeth 114, 144
  Jesse 87(2), 114, 135, 144, 155, 157, 179
Meyers, David 51
  William 61, 106
Mezle, Joseph 1
Mickes, Thomas 75
Mickie, James 94
Mickle, Jean 69
  Joseph 202
  Thomas 69
Middleton, John 10, 81
  Josiah 81
  Richard 74, 81
  Thos. 124, 192
  William 74, 81
Midwood, Samuel 29
Miers, Daniel 32
  David 117
  William 127
Milbank, John 32
Miles, Elizabeth 3
  John 3, 85
Milhany, Thomas 65(2)
Milhous, Abigail 8
  Henry 95
  John 7, 8(2), 20, 69, 94, 95
  Mary 95
  Samuel 95
Miller, Abm. 153
  Barbara 172(2)
  Brice 117, 134, 205
  Bryce 56, 57, 168, 202
  Charles 51, 53, 54, 55, 61, 75, 134, 149, 152, 160, 165, 191, 205, 211
  Charles Jr. 2, 72
  Charles Sr. 48, 52, 72
  Ebenezer 134
  Eliza 172(2)
  Elizabeth 172, 199
  George 14, 36, 81, 92, 133, 168, 199
  James 19(4), 25, 35, 97, 111, 134, 202, 203, 207
  James Jr. 25
  Jannet 26
  Jerome 39, 44
  Jerry 61
  Jesse 48, 49, 52(2)

Toland, James 3, 39
Tom, Alexander 153
Tombs, Alexander 168
  David 138
Tomlinson,_____ 33
  David 98
  Elizabeth 121
  Ferrby 45
  I___ 2
  John 2(2), 9, 27, 28,
    45, 65, 80, 83, 92,
    98, 99, 106, 112,
    121, 134, 138, 139,
    141, 160, 166, 203
  John Jr. 9
  Lucas 45
  Mary 112, 119
  Nathan 45, 106, 134,
    165, 195, 203(3)
  Nathaniel 2(4), 49,
    51, 54(2), 68, 99,
    112, 121, 127, 134,
    166
  Polly 165
  Rebecca 28, 45, 80, 121
  Rebekah 27
  Sarah 203
  Susannah 45, 65, 98
  Thomas 141
  William 9, 55, 99, 112,
    119, 121, 134, 160,
    165, 180
  Willm. Jr. 127
Tomlison, Cattey 180
Tommerlin, William 81
Tompson, Henry 74
  John 74
Touchstone, Frederick 75,
  115
Towland, Fea. 10
  James 6, 10
Trantham, James 56, 91
Trentham, Martin Jr. 36
Tribble, Benjamin 184
  James 36, 105(2), 160,
    194
  John 194
  Morris 194
  Wyly 194
Troup, John 17
Truesdal, John 148
Truesdell, John 89
Trusdal, Holis 147
Trusdale, Hollis 162
  Hollinsworth 130
Trusdel, James 163, 169
  Jno. 130
  Holinsworth 169
Tunston, John 141, 151
Tunstor, Henry 147
  John 147
  Sarah 147
  Saray 147
Turnball, Robert 32
Turner, Henry 122
  John 66
  Margery 66
  Molly Peggy 66
  Samuel 21
Turpin, William 134
Twadell, William 72
Twadle, William 73
Twety, Wynn 167
Twitty, John 11(2)
  Peter 87, 135, 148,
    197
  Thomas 89
  Winn 87, 112, 115
  Wynne 167
Tyler, Elias 121
Tynes, Samuel 16, 50, 56,
  73, 97, 111
Tyron, Gov. 32

Underwood, George 81
Upinger, John 36
Ushart, Daniel 48
  David 42, 48, 61
  John 172
  Margaret 42, 48
Usher also see Ushart
Usher, David 41, 42, 55
  (2), 106
  David Jr. 48
  John 41, 100, 172
  Margaret 41
Ussery, Cynthia 89
  Richard 113, 138, 153,
    200
  Saml. 89, 200
  Woodford 89

Vallandingham, Agnes 180
  Henry 92, 103, 142,
    149, 167, 180, 201
  William 92, 93, 160,
    161, 171, 184
Vanandingham, Henry 189
Vance, D. G. 199
Vanderhorst, Gov. Arnoldus
  114
Vanwinkel, Anne 179
  Jesse 146, 150, 153,
    160, 166, 179, 189,
    209
Vaughn, Benjamin 86
  Aven 208
  Benjamin 86
  Evan 208
  Francis P. 98
  Frederick 190
  Isaac 7
  Jane 203, 208
  Jenney 208
  Mary 7
  Thomas 7
  Wm. J. 90
Veason, John 34
Vermillion,_____ 131
  Samuel 130
Vernor,_____ 61
  Robert 55
Vick, James 145
  Jonas 148, 154, 155,
    171, 180, 187
Vickery, George 158
  George Sr. 170
Vickory, George 48, 92,
    107(2), 113
  Jacob 60, 171, 186
Videon, John 43
Viles, John Sr. 69
Vincent, Ann 173
  Edmund 173, 198, 200
  Henry 173, 187, 198,
    200
  Peter 173
  Peter P. 200
  Poley 200
  Rebecca 173
  Thos. 156, 166, 173,
    187, 189
  William 173
Vining, Ann 11
  Shadrack 11
Vinson, Drury 195, 196
Vites, Durantia 82
Vizant, John 14
Voel, William 120
Voile, John 61
Voyles, John 167

Wade, Daniel 40, 68, 83,
  99, 102, 105, 111,
  117, 122, 154, 159

Wade cont.
  Daniel cont. (3), 182
    (2)
  George 20, 63, 67, 75,
    122, 140, 146, 149,
    170, 182(2), 184,189
  Holden 141
  John 2, 74, 76, 190
  Joseph 190
  Jos. John 190
  Joseph J. 201
  Nathan C. 204
  Sarah 149
  Sally 149
  Thomas 1, 11(2), 21, 57,
    59(2), 60, 82, 105,
    129, 152
  Thomas Holden 154, 159
    (3), 182
  Thomas H. 127, 129, 136,
    144, 146, 152, 157
    (2), 164, 182, 184,
    185(2), 193, 204,207
  Thos. J. 122
Wadeson, Richd. 9, 94
Waggoner, Joseph 10
Wahop, Saml. 124
Waid, Thomas 84
Wailes, Thomas 56
Walker, Alexr. 94
  Andrew 107, 152, 158,
    188
  George 65
  James 6, 57, 65, 124,
    129, 187
  Jeremiah 172
  Joey 90
  John 43, 57, 69
  Joseph 6, 61
  Mary 6
  Philip 48, 57
  Rebekah 172(2)
  Robert 12
  Thomas 15, 45, 57, 180
  William 81, 90, 124,
    172(3), 173, 192
Wallace, Charity 157
  Guy 10, 51, 54, 106,
    134, 155, 156, 166
  John 21
  William 66
Waller, Mary 167
  William 167(2)
Walles, James 125
Wallis, Isabelle 27
Walls, James 1
Walnut, James 109
Walsh, Robt. 184
Walters, Catherine 96
  Joshua 143
  Matthew 96
  William 12, 21
Walteson, Richard 94
Ward, Elizabeth 47, 157
  Henry D. 129
  Mark 141
  Philip 58, 79, 133
  William 45, 47(5), 48,
    58, 62, 63, 66, 82,
    87(2), 89, 103, 110,
    117, 118, 120, 123,
    124, 131, 133(2),
    135, 136, 138, 141,
    142, 144, 153, 157,
    162, 191, 194
Ware, Agness 62
  Thomas 28, 62, 65, 80
    (3)
  William 156, 159
Warlor, George 196
Warters, William 136
  Washington D. 123
  Waters B. 96

Woods cont.
   John 161
   Joseph 35
   William 118, 119, 124,
     125, 139, 140, 141,
     142, 149, 156, 164,
     170, 171(2), 180,
     183
Woodson, David 181
Woodwin, John 80
Worter, Mathew 21
Wren, Alexander 166
   Allatha 134, 183
   George 134(2), 156,
     165, 166, 183, 197,
     203
   Jesse 205
   Mary 166
   Thos. Scot. 147
Wrenn, George 27, 37, 43,
     51, 54, 75, 112
   William 2(2), 27, 37,
     48
   Wineford 173
Wright, Abraham 42
   Alexander 90
   Anthony 94
   John 77, 194
   Mary 94
   Richard 12, 15, 77,183
   Thomas 51, 67(2), 152
Wyly, Dinah 32, 34, 38(4),
     39
   John 9, 38, 94(2), 139,
     153
   Robert 38
   Samuel 38, 101, 139,
     153
   William 18, 38(2), 58,
     139

Yancey, Abigail 88, 127,
     134
   James 71(2), 88, 114
   Richard 153
Yarborough, John 42
Yerby, Averet 78, 135
Yong, Jane 141, 160
Yongue, G. W. 47
   S. W. 105, 124
Young, Darcas 156
   Hugh 97
   James 57
   Jean 57
   Lovick 156
   Robert 57
   Samuel 35
   William 43, 57

Zin, Gronoman 21

www.ingramcontent.com/pod-product-compliance
Lightning Source LLC
Chambersburg PA
CBHW072103020426
42334CB00017B/1621